Worship, Gottesdienst, Cultus Dei

What the Lutheran Confessions Say about Worship

James L. Brauer

Concordia Publishing House · Saint Louis

ISBN 0-7586-0593-5
9 780758 605931
Historical Theology
53-1126

Published by Concordia Publishing House
3558 S. Jefferson Avenue
St. Louis, MO 63118-3968
1-800-325-3040 • www.cph.org

Manufactured in the United States of America

Library of Congress Cataloging-in-Publication Data

Brauer, James Leonard.
Worship, Gottesdienst, cultus Dei : what the Lutheran confessions say about worship / James L. Brauer.
p. cm.
Includes bibliographical references and index.
ISBN 0-7586-0593-5
1. Lutheran Church—Liturgy. 2. Lutheran Church—Creeds. I. Konkordienbuch. Polyglot. Selections. II. Title.
BX8067.A1B685 2005
264'.041—dc22 2005022382

---

1 2 3 4 5 6 7 8 9 10 14 13 12 11 10 09 08 07 06 05

Contents

Preface

Because the Lutheran Confessions are documents from the sixteenth century, some readers may ask how these writings are helpful in addressing issues that the church faces today. After all, the Confessions were written for other times and places; today's situation is vastly different. Some Lutherans suggest that to reach those who do not yet know Christ the church should put more stress on its missionary thrust and less on issues of doctrine. They observe the dramatic increase in interaction between church bodies, with the result that many Lutherans have become acquainted with or have begun to explore concepts and practices from other Christian traditions. In addition, many Christian groups around them are employing in their worship customs and preferences of people who have lived outside the Christian church. Lutheran defenders of this experimentation point out that the essence of worship as discussed in the Lutheran Confessions does not involve human tradition of any kind. Thus those interested primarily in evangelization feel they can justifiably ask, "What could we gain from examining historical questions on worship?"

Other Lutherans who are wary of change might ask, "How can these sixteenth-century writings be helpful in stemming the tide of change in worship among Lutherans in North America?" Indeed, they see that patterns and concepts from other Christian traditions have spilled into Lutheran worship without much debate or scrutiny. The result is worship practices never before seen in Lutheran congregations. Perhaps remembering the Chinese proverb "If an urn lacks the characteristics of an urn, how can we call it an urn?" these readers might ask, "If worship among Lutherans is so diluted by other traditions that it is no longer recognizable as Lutheran, how can it be called Lutheran?"

Although *The Book of Concord* was not designed as an all-encompassing prescription for future practice, the various documents were prepared to give witness to an evangelical Lutheran theology and practice that served the Gospel in a time of great religious and social upheaval. *The Book of Concord* presents an earnest search for the scriptural foundations of Christian worship, indeed, for measuring Christian worship by the Gospel. In this sense (1) the documents that comprise *The Book of Concord* reveal how the confessors pruned aberrations that were false worship; (2) the documents reveal how the reformers tried to be obedient to what Christ commanded; and (3) the documents provide examples of how the confessors discussed the selection of human traditions that would assist the true worship of God. Indeed, the issues *The Book of Concord* address identify the key questions for grasping the "content" of Lutheran worship. The documents testify to what is to be confessed in Christian worship, *Gottesdienst* (in the German), or *cultus dei* (in the Latin). Surely the Lutheran church today needs the same clear thinking about worship as it tries to speak in new languages and selects worship customs for new cultural territory. Similarly, evangelical Lutheran content is lost if it simply converges, is absorbed, and disappears into an ecumenically blended worship practice. In either case, if the content is lost, what purpose would there be in calling such worship "Lutheran"?

This collection of quotations from *The Book of Concord* seeks to present significant portions of the confessors' documents under a few central topics. After all, at the center of the sixteenth-century religious debate were important questions about worship. The following chapters treat the definition of worship/*Gottesdienst/cultus Dei*, the Word of God, the sacraments of Baptism and the Lord's Supper, Holy Absolution, prayer, praise, and matters of rite, ceremony, and order. Quotations are organized under overarching questions and numbered for easy reference. Those who already are well acquainted with the Lutheran Confessions could hardly expect to find anything new here, yet readers may find that this treatment helps clarify the issues. More important, this collection will help those who are exploring these topics for the first time and assist those who wish to gain an overview. Especially for these readers, there are summaries of the material within each chapter.

This book, then, is a tool for pastors and students of the Lutheran Confessions who wish to review and explore what was said, how it was said, and how the confessors argued their points. It is not a collection of one-liners to impress friends or silence opponents. These extended quotations allow the reader to observe the content of the argument and to sample the context in which a point is made.

Earlier generations of pastors were acquainted with the original German and Latin versions of the Lutheran Confessions and could more easily examine the precise wording and shades of meaning. Informed discussions of the confessional documents have always demanded attention to the vocabulary of the original texts. Too often a little knowledge is misleading. Because an English translation can only go so far, it rather easily imposes its own shadings of meaning. Indeed, having both a Latin and a German version of the same document does give later interpreters greater clues to the meaning. To aid those who are familiar with these original languages, the textual notes provide key phrases from the Latin and German texts. Perhaps having the German and Latin data so close at hand will invite the reader who has skills in such matters to make a deeper exploration.

The German and Latin texts included here are drawn from the 12th edition of *Die Bekenntnisschriften der evangelisch-lutherischen Kirche*. The English text used is that of the Kolb/Wengert edition of *The Book of Concord*, except when the Tappert edition is used to reflect the Latin of the quarto edition of the Apology of the Augsburg Confession, which one finds in the *Triglotta* and *Die Bekenntnisschriften*. For more information regarding the use of certain texts, please see the general textual notes on p. 41. At various points the reader will encounter textual notes designed to help explain features of the original text with respect to the English. These notes are meant to foster deeper levels of study and understanding.

It is hoped that the reader will discover how the insights and teachings of the confessors defined and defended a Lutheran understanding of worship. With such an understanding, the Lutheran church today can once more identify the content of the true worship of God and be reminded how the church, in any language or place, will carefully select "human traditions" to teach what the people need to know about Christ and to express that content in their worship.

James L. Brauer
St. Andrew, Apostle, 1999
St. Louis, Missouri

Introduction

At the start of the twenty-first century, the pressure for change in Lutheran worship comes from many directions. Two avenues seem dominant, namely, ecumenical exchange of traditions and cultural adjustments related to people groups.

Perhaps the greatest change in Christian worship in the twentieth century has been the reforms initiated at the Second Vatican Council (1962–1965) and promulgated in the Constitution on the Sacred Liturgy.[1] Roman Catholic practice has now altered worship in ways that the Protestant Reformation did in the sixteenth century. In particular, the Roman Catholic Church now uses the vernacular in the liturgy, features congregational participation in music, places greater emphasis on the Word, and has made adjustments in church architecture. Pressure for these changes had been growing for some time prior to Vatican II. The research of nineteenth-century scholars had made it possible to do comparative studies of liturgy from the earliest times, and the Liturgical Movement of the twentieth century had shaped new visions of worship.

Certainly, other Christians cannot ignore Roman Catholic work after Vatican II in teaching, revising, and testing liturgical change on a global scale. Indeed, among liturgical specialists in the United States, the exchange of information across denominational borders now flows rather freely. In the last quarter century, a whole new literature has developed based on new theological focuses and the examination of common traditions. The impact of all this is still unfolding and expanding. One result is that theological questions related to worship are being asked more often with an ecumenical scope and with a view to

1. The basic documents can be found in Austin Flannery, ed., *Vatican Council II, The Conciliar and Post Conciliar Documents*, new rev. ed. (Grand Rapids: Eerdmans, 1992).

the sweep of Christian history. This challenges Christians from every tradition to ask what borrowing various old or new traditions might mean to them. Lutherans, too, want to know how much of what is being exchanged, if any, might be useful in their worship.

Concurrent with the focus on liturgical issues in the Catholic church, there has developed a continuing exchange among Protestant denominations by those who search for techniques in global and local missionary work. In recent decades Lutheran missionaries have studied at Protestant graduate institutions of theological education. Perhaps an even greater influence can be attributed to Lutheran attendance at evangelism workshops sponsored by other Protestants and the appearance of non-Lutheran experts at Lutheran events. These presenters naturally offer ideas for worship from Reformed and Anabaptist traditions. This exchange across Protestant borders by local practitioners has grown significantly. In addition, there is a new body of literature filled with insights from sociology, demographic studies, and marketing. Lutherans who borrow concepts and practices from other Protestants defend their work, by claiming they are within Lutheran orthopraxy, yet their experimentation is regularly viewed with suspicion by others in the church. Experimenters argue that worship will be better if they borrow from other Protestant traditions or if they discover practices that seem more authentic to a new ethnic group.

Over time, these adjustments to Lutheran worship will be scrutinized and assessed by the church. In the ecumenical exchange by both liturgical scholars and by missionary practitioners, hard theological questions need to be asked. How do theology, mission work, and worship fit together? How much of what is shared between traditions can really be useful to Lutheran worship? What will erode the Gospel core of Lutheran worship? What will assist the delivery of the Gospel?

When one compares the study methods of these two arenas of ecumenical exchange, one notices that among specialists in worship the studies often involve examination of the theological presuppositions underlying the differing traditions. But among specialists in evangelism, particularly those presenting in workshop settings, the studies focus on finding techniques and methods, including elements of the worship service, that have immediate results. Seldom do those interested in evangelism examine theological presuppositions that may underlie different worship approaches. The desire to find something that works pushes aside questions of theology or, at best, in ecumenical settings simply asks individuals from various traditions to consider such theological matters on their own. Such presenters seldom give workshop attendees help in locating comparative studies of the theological implications or ramifications of worship practices—perhaps because their forum has no time for it, perhaps because it seems unimportant to the speakers, or perhaps because the speakers themselves are not informed about such differences.

But who would deny that a change in practice can alter the meaning of one's worship? After all, *lex orandi, lex credendi*, that is, "What is prayed is what is believed,"[2] can be said of any community. When a new idea, pattern, or resource is brought into a congregation's practice, how is its impact on the content of worship assessed? How does a pastor or a congregation measure these things? We know that if every medieval workman brought his own measuring rod to a building site, the lack of a standard would soon waste the resources and create an unusable structure. The key was a standard measure applied to all building steps. Thus the medieval master builder brought his own proper measuring rod (a standard yardstick), which each workman copied. In the same way, both worship specialists and mission specialists must continually ask, "What standard meaning is to be carried to the next generation or dialect or language or people?" For those who wish to be called Lutheran, would this standard not be found in the Confessions of the Lutheran Church?[3]

Before we identify what the Lutheran reformers confessed on topics that relate to worship, it is helpful to review worship traditions that surround and might be sources of influence on Lutherans in North America today. Although we could focus on one or two dominant traditions, it seems wiser to present a more complete spectrum of Christian worship through a series of thumbnail sketches. For our purposes, such sketches are only a starting point meant to identify the theological foundations and key practices of each worship tradition. These sketches also show relationships between and among the traditions.

2. Although the phrase *lex orandi, lex credendi* originated as a way to make the point that what is believed can be determined from what is prayed, it has also been used—at least by some in the twentieth century—to say the opposite, namely, that what is believed (the doctrinal substance) is what should be prayed and should form the community's faith. See Paul De Clerck, " 'Lex orandi, lex credendi': The Original Sense and Historical Avatars of an Equivocal Adage," *Studia Liturgica* 24/2 (1994): 178–200.

3. Obviously, such doctrine or meaning is related to the *sola scriptura* principle of the Reformation. This means that the *norma primiaria* for determining whether a doctrine is true or false is Scripture and that the *norma secondaria* for determining whether someone has clearly understood the doctrines in Scripture is the Lutheran Confessions.

TRADITIONS OF CHRISTIAN WORSHIP

The spectrum of Christian worship traditions is broad and complicated, spanning the whole of Christian history from the earliest patterns of New Testament congregations to the latest version of an historic form or last Sunday's invention. This spectrum, starting from the most ancient models and moving to the present day, can be thought of as going from East to West and from more conservative to more radical branches, namely, Eastern (Orthodox)—Roman Catholic—Lutheran—Anglican—Reformed—Anabaptist.[4] Following the Reformation era, the four Protestant branches generated five offshoots. In the eighteenth century the Reformed tradition gave rise to the Methodist tradition. The left-wing (Anabaptist) part of the spectrum saw the rise of the Revival tradition in the nineteenth century and the American Pentecostal tradition in the twentieth century. When the Quakers and Puritans of the seventeenth century are added to the scheme, nine "Protestant traditions" can be identified in the Western tradition.[5] The following ten sketches attempt to identify central aspects of liturgy and theology in each tradition and to highlight what is distinctive about each. The Lutheran tradition is not sketched here because it is dealt with in the main chapters of this book.

EASTERN

Eastern Orthodox liturgy has its roots in the traditions of Jerusalem and Antioch (the liturgy of St. James) and Alexandria (the liturgy of St. Mark). Its history is complex and has broad differences in practice.[6] Although the framework of Eastern Orthodox liturgy has the shape of the Western Mass, namely, Word and Lord's Supper, few Christians in the United States are familiar with it. Liturgical scholars can point to a breadth of accents. Eastern liturgy's perception of God can range from the distant "Other" to the incarnate God who dwelt among us. Participants in Eastern Orthodox liturgy are seen as not only free to participate in the heavenly mysteries but also as unworthy to approach the mystery. Generally, bread and wine are prepared before the liturgy and

4. The scheme for categories of Protestant worship was developed by James White, a Methodist historian of liturgy; see *Protestant Worship: Traditions in Transition* (Louisville: Westminster/John Knox, 1989), esp. 23.

5. See White, *Protestant Worship*.

6. See Peter Fink's description in "Traditions, Liturgical, in the East," in *The New Dictionary of Sacramental Worship*, ed. Peter Fink (Collegeville: Liturgical Press, 1990), 1255–72.

are considered to represent Christ from the start of the liturgy. In a few cases the liturgical order will contain no Words of Institution at all. Typically, the Word portion of the service is conducted away from the altar and the Lord's Supper portion at the altar. Typically, leavened bread is used, as opposed to unleavened. The distribution of the wine can range from intinction to spoon to chalice.

In the ancient Syro-Chaldean materials there is a strong doxological tone, giving glory and praise to God. Participants seek, through the heavenly mysteries now, to look forward to the *eschaton* (the last days). They see the *epiclesis* (calling the Holy Spirit on the elements) as signifying the resurrection of Christ from the tomb in what is now their enacting of the mystery. West Syrian materials often project a sense of anticipation and a confident hope in Christ's second coming, a yearning for the revelation of his glory. The West Syrians see the liturgy as a pledge of what is to come and as a tool for making citizens for heaven. The liturgy is, then, the *eschaton* unfolding in the lives of those who gather to pray.

By the thirteenth century, the Byzantine tradition, particularly the Divine Liturgy of St. John Chrysostom (ca. 347–407), had become dominant within Eastern Orthodoxy. Byzantine materials regard the liturgy as heaven brought down to earth. The Word portion is performed with the congregation, but the eucharistic portion is performed by clergy behind an iconostasis (icon screen). This decorative fence bridges between the two spheres, that of the nave (earthly) and that of the sanctuary (heavenly). It also gives worshipers a visual focus for contemplative prayer. The dominant theme in Eastern Orthodox liturgy is the presence of Christ in his incarnation and his heavenly ministry. Central acts of the liturgy are hidden from the assembly, which silently contemplates the experience of icon, incense, music, and movement. The assembly is "with Christ *to* the heavenly liturgy which is eternally enacted."[7] The liturgy is a mystery (heavenly realities made manifest in human form), "a spiritual process which unfolds in a higher sphere."[8]

Other parts of Eastern Orthodox tradition show contrasting accents. Armenian materials emphasize the notion of sacrifice, point to the majesty of God, and invoke the Holy Spirit. Alexandrian liturgical sources stress the majesty and otherness of God. They depend on the spiritual meaning of symbols and of the eternal realm. An example of this is seen early in the liturgy where much attention is given to bread

7. Fink, "Traditions, Liturgical, in the East," 1264.

8. Fink, "Traditions, Liturgical, in the East," 1264.

and wine. The altar, a place of sacrifice and the symbol of the one who is offered, is kissed on its four corners. Processions are made around it. Although Coptic materials are more austere, deriving from a monastic model, Ethiopian liturgies show more colorful, vibrant traditions.

In Eastern churches the mystery of the Lord's incarnation is enacted in the liturgy. His presence is symbolized by various actions around the bread and wine. In the service, Christ, the ruler of heaven, comes from heaven to earth and reaches out with his presence to those who come to contemplate and to pray. The poetic richness, artistic decoration, and unity of ritual celebration—a symbolic matrix—is, as one eighth-century liturgical commentator put it, "heaven on earth, where the God of heaven dwells and moves."[9] Alexander Schmemann, an important American interpreter of the Russian Orthodox tradition, gives this overview of what he labels a "fourth dimension," God's kingdom:

> The liturgy of the Eucharist is best understood as a journey or procession. It is the journey of the church into the dimension of the kingdom. . . . Our *entrance* into the presence of Christ is an entrance into a fourth dimension that allows us to see the ultimate reality of life. It is not an escape from the world, rather it is the arrival at a vantage point from where we can see more deeply into the reality of the world.
>
> The purpose of this "coming together" is not simply to add a religious dimension to the natural community, to make it "better"—more responsible, more Christian. The purpose is to *fulfill the Church*, and that means to make present the One in whom all things are at their *end*, and all things are at their *beginning*.[10]

From the Eastern Orthodox perspective the church fulfills its purpose by enacting its ancient liturgy handed down from the apostles and the earliest congregations. Through the liturgy, God comes into the world, drawing it into his heavenly kingdom. Participation in such sacramental life is a salvific union with the glorified Christ.

ROMAN CATHOLIC (WESTERN)

This ancient tradition has had many variants through the centuries. For our purposes, this sketch depicts the practice both at the time of

9. Robert F. Taft, *The Byzantine Rite: A Short History*, American Essays in Liturgy (Collegeville: Liturgical Press, 1992), 18.
10. Alexander Schmemann, *For the Life of the World: Sacraments and Orthodoxy*, 2d rev. ed. (Crestwood: St. Vladimir's Seminary Press, 1973), 26–27.

the Reformation and at the end of the twentieth century (after the Second Vatican Council).

The worship of the pre-Reformation Roman rite had become highly embellished with many variable elements ordered by the church year. Worship employed one language, Latin, and, when following its Roman characteristics, was brief and sober.[11] After the formal doctrine of transubstantiation was promulgated in 1215, worship became a mystery performed exclusively by clergy. This de-emphasized its corporate action (i.e., giving thanks to God) and made the climactic action of God the moment of consecration when the bread and wine became the body and blood of Christ. This ever-renewed sacrifice of the Mass acquired practices that allowed the celebration of the Mass to be done without communicants. With this practice came a tendency to adore Christ in bread and wine rather than receive the Sacrament. Communicants also saw the Mass form as a drama of Christ's life and Passion during which the faithful made their own devotions. At the time of the Reformation, people received only the bread, not the wine.

The dominant pattern was the private Mass, that is, a Mass in which worshipers had no obligation to participate directly and the priest and his assistants did everything at the altar. Also, because the Mass could be said on behalf of others (for the living and the dead), the number of Masses was increased. To accommodate this increase in Masses, churches added side altars. Because of the fact that the Roman practice focused on the epiphany of God in the reality of the eucharistic presence, because the action was a sacrifice offered to God for the benefit of the living and the dead, and because the Mass was considered a memorial of Christ's Passion (an allegorical interpretation of the whole economy of redemption) in which Christ's Passion was made present and actual, it was viewed primarily as a sacrifice or oblation, a propitiation having the power of atonement through the unbloody sacrifice of the Mass. By once again presenting to the Father a new offering, the fruits of Christ's bloody sacrifice on the cross were received. In this way the requirement that humans honor God was satisfied as the priest, at the bidding of the church and by the power of Christ, performed the Mass.[12]

During the Baroque era, the rites that had been standardized by the Council of Trent (1545–1563) were given artistic brilliance through

11. Bard Thompson, *Liturgies of the Western Church* (Cleveland: Meridian Books, 1961), 27ff.

12. Thompson, *Liturgies*, 48f.

elaborate music, procession, and architecture. Although the Enlightenment brought movement toward only one altar and theological debates concerning the validity of the sacraments, the rites were not changed. The Romantic period saw the revival of monasteries and the recovery of Gregorian chant. In the twentieth century, Vatican II and the Liturgical Movement brought about revisions of rites that demonstrated a cultural openness; a demand for "full, conscious, active participation"; an insistence on the vernacular and congregational song; a more elaborate (three-year) lectionary; and a requirement that preaching be a regular feature of the Mass.[13]

Alceste Catella has outlined a theological understanding of the liturgy and a concept of the church's worship that differs somewhat from the post-Tridentine period.[14] This theology of the liturgy wishes to speak of the experience of worship and its relation to faith and to practice. Catella explains that Christ has made obsolete all religious mediation and has created in the church his mystery of sacramental mediation. Worship is not a performance of a person for God but the place for God's communication to humans who are open to God "in the obedience of faith."[15] The churchly celebration has three dimensions: an intrinsic connection to salvation history, a community-based subject (people), and a mystery-based modality where the saving event makes its appearance. Its modality is that of "the ritual mystery that becomes celebrated where the believer/community, by opening itself to receive the salvific event, lives it in continual tension toward the eschaton."[16] Another Roman Catholic spokesman, Cipriano Vagaggni, has described liturgy as the way Christ (in time and space) communicates his divine life to the individual. Vagaggni also describes a theological study of liturgy as a "fundamental presupposition for being able to live it adequately on a spiritual level and to highlight its pastoral value concretely and usefully."[17] Such study, says Salvatore Marsili, is "a discourse on God in the light of the sacramentality that is the mode of being of the revelation both in its first historical existence and in its

13. White, *Protestant Worship*, 33f.
14. Alceste Catella, "Theology of the Liturgy," *Handbook for Liturgical Studies*, Vol. II: *Fundamental Liturgy*, ed. Anscar J. Chupungco (Collegeville: Liturgical Press, 1998), 3–28.
15. Catella, "Theology of the Liturgy," 5.
16. Catella, "Theology of the Liturgy," 5.
17. Catella, "Theology of the Liturgy," 9.

actuation in the liturgy."[18] It is through the sacramentality of liturgy that people are drawn into the mystery of Christ.

This makes liturgy the "summit and source" for Roman Catholics, part of Christ's work of salvation completed by him in the paschal mystery. The Roman liturgy circumscribes a holy people who are called to offer the sacrifice of Christ and to participate in his paschal banquet. The liturgical action is conducted through a system of symbolic ritual actions that are a realization of the mystery of Christ. In the words of Catella: "The liturgy is the action of the Church in which Christ becomes present, and this action assumes the features of ritual action similar to that described as well in anthropological sciences."[19]

According to Catella, liturgy is necessary because Jesus "must ritualize his gift and his testament in order to entrust it to his disciples."[20] It occurs through realities that are really and fully human. Ritual and symbol are "a modality of the presence and of the history of the mystery."[21] The liturgy is measured less by its content, as if it were some kind of container, and more by "the faith as it is celebrated."[22] This is the religious experience, an encounter between God and the believer, a believing appropriation of the gifts (mystery) of Jesus Christ. The liturgy expresses the salvation event and is part of salvation history by which people are brought into the kingdom. It is a grasping of the presence of salvation history in the liturgical celebrations. So the Constitution on the Sacred Liturgy I, 7 can say that the church offers worship to the eternal Father through Christ:

> The liturgy, then, is rightly seen as an exercise of the priestly office of Jesus Christ. It involves the presentation of man's sanctification under the guise of signs perceptible by the senses and its accomplishment in ways appropriate to each of these signs. In it full public worship is performed by the Mystical Body of Jesus Christ, that is, by the Head and his members.
>
> From this it follows that every liturgical celebration, because it is an action of Christ the Priest and of his body, which is the Church, is a sacred action surpassing all others. No other action of the Church can equal its efficacy by the same title and to the same degree.[23]

18. Catella, "Theology of the Liturgy," 11.
19. Catella, "Theology of the Liturgy," 15.
20. Catella, "Theology of the Liturgy," 16.
21. Catella, "Theology of the Liturgy," 18.
22. Catella, "Theology of the Liturgy," 19.
23. Flannery, *Vatican Council II*, 5.

Faith is then actually expressed through the encounter with the mystery of the Lord's passion. The celebration's fundamental purpose is revealed in the biblical text proclaimed and the gestures that engender celebrative action. This becomes a sustaining event for faith. It necessitates the response of faith. The liturgy is a communitarian action of those formally constituted in the church. It can be said that the church has a liturgical nature by its constitution. Liturgy is celebrated with one's whole being, using words, sounds (singing and music), silences, gestures, and movement. It occurs in time by a readiness for encounter with God and by grasping the meaning and value of days. It occurs in a space, an "environment," that helps tell of the mystery of Christ.

Today's Roman Catholic liturgy has moved the faithful from the prayerful "onlookers" of the pre-Reformation rite to full "participants" in the paschal mystery, which demands active and conscious involvement in the rite. Despite the many outward changes and the new accents in Rome's liturgical theology, it seems that the sacraments still drive the liturgy more than the Word of God. It is through the sacraments that sanctifying grace comes to those who are "open to God in the obedience of faith."[24]

ANGLICAN

The Anglican tradition began in the Protestant Reformation. Because of its many influences, both political and religious, Anglicanism has become a tradition able to absorb a broad span of worship patterns, both in theology and in practice. Its history reveals the tradition of compromise that characterizes the Anglican church and the "ambiguous" quality that results. Although it looks conservative, its theological origins are far more liberal than the Lutheran tradition.

Anglican unity is drawn from *The Book of Common Prayer*. Thus James White can call this tradition conservative because Anglicans remain constant in their use of common forms for the mass, morning prayer, and evening prayer. Although the primary architect of the first *Book of Common Prayer* (1549) was Thomas Cranmer, several editions followed almost immediately. The first North American edition was produced in 1789. The Anglican tradition carried the daily choral services into cathedrals and collegiate churches and employed London street language as spoken prose for the ear. It moved from seeing to hearing as the primary mode of participating, encouraging the voice of

24. White, *Protestant Worship*, 94ff.

the congregation in the Lord's Prayer, in penitential prayers, and, later, in the singing of the Psalms.

The nave and chancel were retained as essential worship spaces in the Anglican tradition, but a wooden table replaced the traditional altar—with the priest facing the people. Buildings were purged of images. Fonts were placed near the main entrance, and the pews that had been appearing in churches since the fourteenth century were kept. For nearly three centuries following the Reformation, the normal Sunday order was this: morning prayer, the litany, ante-Communion (the Mass without the Lord's Supper), and a sermon. The daily discipline consisted of morning and evening prayer without a sermon. This combination gave the pious Anglican a rich dose of Scripture.

The seventeenth century saw further reforms that strove to be acceptable to all English Protestants. In the period following the 1666 Great Fire of London, Christopher Wren designed 67 new buildings as Anglican worship spaces. These structures took on a distinctive spatial form that served the auditory needs of the worshiper: no chancel, altar table with a Communion rail at the east end, font near the door, few religious images, and a combination reading desk, clerk's desk, and pulpit. When Methodism arose in the eighteenth century, the general theological and liturgical direction was to minimize distinctions by downplaying the supernatural and viewing the Eucharist as purely in memory of Christ. Worship was to assist morality and social order. Medieval features (cross, vestments, incense, candles) were gone.

Beginning in 1833, a Catholic revival brought a strong change of direction. This revival was characterized by renewed interest in the past, turning from rationalism, high standards of taste, restoration of hymn singing, abolition of private pews, making the chief service on Sunday the Eucharist with emphasis on Christ's presence, and valuing of sacramental confession. There was a new desire to keep the liturgical year, to employ an architectural ideal drawn from the village Gothic church, to use lay choirs in the chancel, and to let choral music flower. The Catholic revival also sought to encourage daily family worship. In recent decades the Anglican tradition has given new prominence to sacraments, has shown a greater interest in the early church, especially the era of Hippolytus, and has more concern for cultural adaptability, including the incorporation of folk and pop music styles into the liturgy.

In general, the Anglican tradition seeks to hold the full Protestant spectrum under one heading and around one set of forms in its *Book of*

Common Prayer. Although it appears to be conservative, it wishes to be consciously ambiguous.

REFORMED

The reformation in Zurich and Geneva brought its own new direction in worship.[25] When Zwingli defined the word *is* as meaning "signifies," he redefined the Lord's Supper, making its focus what the community remembers—thus fulfilling the Lord's command, "Do this." When Zwingli removed the Canon of the Mass, his four replacement prayers referenced the story of salvation, invoked the Holy Spirit, and inculcated a new theology into the rite. The Lord's Supper occurred only on great festivals and patronal days in Zurich. The elements were carried to people in pews. By 1525 Zwingli had established a daily preaching service and a Sunday preaching service, based on the ancient Order of Prone, that had this shape: Lord's Prayer, Ave Maria (discontinued after 1563), sermon (usually on consecutive Bible lessons, frequently from the Old Testament), Lord's Prayer, Ave Maria, Apostles' Creed, Decalogue, and a confession and absolution. He eliminated all music from the service—singing was not restored until 1598, and no organs were permitted until 1874. What counted was not exterior elements but something that was honest and direct, even austere.

A second phase of the Geneva reforms occurred under John Calvin (1509–1564). Calvin carried Bucer's Strassburg German service into French and strove to make God's mercy clear through visible signs of God's love. Calvin's thought was to restore primitive, patristic worship. Saints days and festivals were eliminated. The service was verbose and could even be termed "a condensed course in theology and ethics."[26] In Calvin's order, the congregation sang the Ten Commandments and Psalms in French metrical verse. There were continuous readings from the Scriptures. Prayer had a tendency to be didactic. The service was led mostly from the pulpit. Although Calvin desired greater frequency, there was only a quarterly celebration of the Lord's Supper, preceded by self-examination and introspection. The emphasis was more on a being forgiven so one could receive the Sacrament than on being forgiven through receiving it. There were no organized daily services, but people were encouraged to have them at home. When John Knox (1505–1572) carried this French piety to Scotland, he emphasized didacticism even more than did Geneva.

---

25. White, *Protestant Worship*, 58–78.

26. White, *Protestant Worship*, 65.

The Reformed tradition transplanted in Scotland from Geneva carried a fixed Reformed liturgy and was preserved in John Knox's *The Forme of Prayers* (1564). In Scotland and North America the set structure with detailed models for prayers was kept, but ministers were free to improvise their wording. When the "new" radicals at the beginning of the seventeenth century proved to be biblicists, not pragmatists, they abolished the previous service books and insisted that everything had to have a biblical basis. Their 1645 *Directory for Public Worship* became normative for Presbyterians. Those who came to North America brought with them this biblicist version of the Reformed tradition. Only in recent decades, influenced by ecumenical exchange after Vatican II, have some of the early Reformed practices been revived.

The Reformed tradition stemming from Calvin did not seek to organize liturgy around practices of the inherited Western tradition; instead, it sought to serve discipline and promote instruction from early patristic times—to cultivate a penitential piety and to put preaching at the center. Its Biblicist version in the United States, described below, eventually developed a liturgy that was a tool for creating commitment to Christ and to moral behavior.

ANABAPTIST

In the 1520s and 1530s the Anabaptist movement arose when some Protestants disagreed concerning baptism of infants, claiming that it was unscriptural and unreasonable.[27] This provoked Luther to a vigorous defense of infant baptism, which drove the followers of Zwingli in Zurich to drive from town those who practiced infant baptism. It led to a radical break with medieval worship and the development of the "free church" tradition, as manifested today in the Mennonite, Amish, and Hutterian Brethren. The Amish especially have kept their tradition relatively intact by avoiding the surrounding culture and maintaining a self-disciplining community. Their reform of worship flowed from a desire to recover the pure worship of apostolic times. To this end the exclusive basis of worship was Scripture, and each community was free to determine the order of its own worship. For Anabaptists, the goal was "to model all worship on the revealed word of God in every possible detail."[28] A published liturgy was superfluous and idolatrous.

This liturgical congregationalism brought new practices. Theologians were frequently self-taught. Although preaching was a major part

27. White, *Protestant Worship*, 79–92.

28. White, *Protestant Worship*, 81.

of the worship and done by a pastor who was a scholar of Scripture, there was lay leadership of the worship, often with shared roles. And both men and women held leadership roles. Children were "dedicated" because Baptism was for believers only. Only after Baptism was a person permitted to join in the intercessory prayer with and for the community. The Lord's Supper was largely a commemoration but also a communal event for the pure and undefiled of the congregation. To keep the church pure, those who could not live up to the creedal or moral standards were shunned, but there was a provision for reconciliation through a laying on of hands. In the Anabaptist tradition, every practice had to be like that of the early church and drawn from Scripture.

SEPARATIST AND PURITAN

During the seventeenth century, Separatists in England wished to remain a part of the national church, yet they desired to be guided by a rigorous biblicism. They tried to distance themselves from late-medieval worship, at least the part that had been carried into the Anglican tradition.[29] Although Calvin had discarded elements that were antiscriptural, he still used things from outside Scripture that could fit with decency, order, and edification. However, Separatists demanded that the Scriptures be the "supreme liturgical criterion."[30] Human inventions had no place and could not be tolerated. The church could use only what Scripture prescribed, and such decisions were to be made at the level of the smallest unit, the congregation. In this way Separatists would ensure that worship would be more immediately "relevant" than any "fixed form" of the church. Prayers had to be extemporaneous. No sermon could be read from a published source. The relevancy criterion was almost as important as biblical authority. In addition, Separatists wanted a "pure" congregation in which the Lord's Supper could have worthy communicants, those who had clearly separated themselves from the wicked.

Similarly, the Puritans tried to build a national church—after the best of the Reformed churches, for example, Geneva—and to rid themselves of the human inventions of late-medieval worship. To a great extent this movement arose from liturgical controversy over such questions as the ceremonial, vestments, using wafer bread, kneeling, the sign of the cross, observing Lent, and retaining collects and litanies. In

29. White, *Protestant Worship*, 117–34.

30. White, *Protestant Worship*, 118.

the Puritan tradition, holy days were to be strictly kept: no work, no recreation. Prayers were to be for concrete, local circumstances. No humanly composed hymns were permitted, only Psalms. The Puritan concept of an ordained minister was that he should be primarily a biblical scholar and able to preach the details of the text, applying them vividly to life.

In the 1700s many Separatist and Puritan adherents came to North America. Their form of biblicism suggests that they be grouped with the Anabaptists, though the Anabaptists stem from Protestant (Geneva) roots. By the nineteenth century, the Reformed idea of four sacramental seasons a year gave rise to a penitential piety, camp meetings, and eventually to systematized revivals. Gradually the Reformed principles upon which Separatist and Puritan theology and practice had been based weakened. By the second half of the nineteenth century, they began to use hymnody alongside the singing of Psalms. The insistence on drawing everything liturgical from Scripture gave way to a desire to be relevant by placing liturgical decisions at the local, congregational level. This allowed considerable freedom in forms of worship and laid the groundwork for the revivalism of the American frontier. In the twentieth century the descendants of Separatists and Puritans have taken a direction that appeals more to the mind than to emotions through preaching that is cerebral and worship that is aesthetically pleasing.

Quaker and Shaker

The most radical departure from the medieval tradition of worship was one that occurred a century after the Reformation.[31] Quakerism, founded by George Fox (1624–1691), was perhaps the most ascetic in rejection of medieval worship and relied the most on inward resources alone. In its classic form, Quakerism had no clergy, no service books, no sacraments, no preaching, no singing or organ music, and almost no ceremonies. The central belief that "the inner light is accessible to all and the purpose of worship is common waiting upon God in stillness and quietness,"[32] was a rejection of Calvin's understanding that humans need visible signs. Quakers believe that "[v]isible sacraments are simply not necessary when one can experience the Spirit directly in community."[33] Among the Quakers no one could speak except as the Spirit

31. White, *Protestant Worship*, 135–43, 147–49.
32. White, *Protestant Worship*, 137.
33. White, *Protestant Worship*, 141.

prompted. Typically their gatherings were a kind of prayer act (meditative, silent, not directed by leaders).

The Shakers also made an extreme break with the past. Organized by Mother Ann Lee (ca. 1736–1784), the Shakers fostered a corporate mysticism, gave it free expression, and avoided clergy and sacraments entirely.[34] The priorities of a Shaker community were celibacy, a life of confession and shared goods, millennial orientation, and a worship unfettered by any Christian tradition. Typical daily gatherings in meetinghouses called for active participation of body and mind, accompanied by singing of hymns with ecstatic utterances permitted (nonsense syllables, barking, laughing) and with dancing—either a slow shuffle or vigorous whirling. Their tradition never thrived but is remembered today for its simple aesthetic that lives on in tunes and household furnishings.

METHODIST

The Methodist tradition arose in England during the eighteenth century during a time of general indifference to religion.[35] Founded by brothers John (1703–1791) and Charles (1707–1788) Wesley, Methodism drew from several traditions: the Puritans (avoiding their emphasis on predestination), John Calvin (particularly his view of the Eucharist), and Pietism. Primarily, the Wesleys drew their new Method from the Anglican tradition.

Distanced from Reformation controversies, Methodism restored some late-medieval piety ("the eucharist as it implies sacrifice, frequent celebrations of the eucharist, vigils, and fasting"[36]). Because of the Wesleys's methodical emphasis on sacraments (weekly) and daily prayer, they were called "Methodists" or "sacramentarians." Preaching and hymn singing were strong elements in their "pragmatic traditionalism" and were meant to reach the unchurched, especially the poor. Charles Wesley himself wrote some 6,000 hymns. Preaching services were regarded as supplemental to regular worship. Vigorous and loud participation was not discouraged. "Preaching houses" were built for indoor preaching. The Wesleys took the church year seriously, adding a Covenant Renewal Service on New Year's Day. Although prayer was a third means of grace, a balance was maintained between free and fixed forms of prayer. And though the Wesleys kept and defended

34. White, *Protestant Worship*, 144–47.

35. White, *Protestant Worship*, 150–70.

36. White, *Protestant Worship*, 151.

infant baptism, the crucial event for a Christian was the "conscious experience of conversion."[37]

In the United States, Francis Asbury (1745–1816) shaped the expansion of Methodism in the nineteenth century, emphasizing less of Wesley's traditionalism (sacraments and fixed forms of prayer) and more of his pragmatism (preaching and disciplined life). On the frontier this approach enabled Methodism to adapt to unchurched folk through simple songs, spontaneity, and an altar call. By the end of the century, "worship tended to be treated as a means to an end—making converts—rather than an end in itself."[38] In the early twentieth century in more affluent and educated communities there developed a more artistic (aesthetic) worship. The use of choral anthems and professional musicians to enrich the worship began to replace the previous emotional and spontaneous elements. There was also a greater emphasis placed on peace, social justice, and the solving of moral dilemmas. Recent decades have moved Methodist worship toward more exegetical preaching on lectionary texts and toward liturgical revisions drawn more from early Christian worship than from medieval practices.

In the spectrum of Protestant worship, the Methodist tradition clearly tries to draw on the ancient traditions while being pragmatic—sometimes simple and emotionally direct and sometimes more aesthetic and consciously traditional. In many ways it is a warmer, more personal version of the Anglicanism from which it grew.

REVIVAL

Especially important to the American story is the "frontier revival tradition," a tradition that acquired its distinctive characteristics on the frontier. The revival has been influential in the traditions of the American Baptists and Southern Baptists, Disciples of Christ and Churches of Christ, and is presently reshaping other traditions.[39] In a sense this Revival tradition is "a tradition of no tradition" (pragmatism uninhibited by service books) and "a form of worship for the unchurched."[40] It is a tradition built from Anabaptist and Reformed concepts and practices. From the Separatists and Puritans it got its biblicism (today this is largely superceded by pragmatism) and local autonomy. From the Reformed tradition, Revival took the camp meet-

37. White, *Protestant Worship*, 156.
38. White, *Protestant Worship*, 165.
39. White, *Protestant Worship*, 171–75.
40. White, *Protestant Worship*, 171.

ing and leadership of individuals (not clergy). From the Methodists it received a passion for making converts through evangelistic preaching, an emphasis on congregational song, and a link to the Great Awakening. According to White, the Revival tradition developed as an answer to the question of how to minister to a largely unchurched population scattered in thinly settled territory.

The camp meeting pattern developed out of the Presbyterian "sacramental seasons" three or four times a year. For several days people gathered for intense self-examination and preparation, followed by the celebration of the Lord's Supper. The first "camp meeting" (outdoor communion season) occurred in 1800. Then, in 1801 at Cane Ridge, Kentucky, more than 10,000 gathered for preaching, Baptism of converts, and the Eucharist. Typically this kind of event (usually four days long, ending with the Eucharist on Sunday) was ecumenically sponsored with sharing between the worship traditions and races. It employed music that was easy to learn (repetitive texts and tunes) and used clear steps toward conversion. The primary notion in this Revival tradition was that "worship" could build up the body of Christ by bringing in fresh converts. The converts, who were baptized at the camp meeting, were later received, after a period of scrutiny, by a congregation. The Revival tradition held to no fixed liturgical texts for Eucharist (only freely improvised thanksgivings by a layman who led songs), used a clergyman as preacher, employed no creeds (because these were written after the New Testament), and had Baptism for believers only (repentance often followed Baptism).

Eventually a version of the Revival tradition for established churches was developed in the "new measures" of Charles Finney (1792–1875).[41] He retained the pattern of several days of meetings and of the anxious bench for those to be converted. Finney also rejected the authority of tradition and instead employed pure pragmatism that looked for decency, order, and what was effective. The primary test was this: Does it produce converts from the unchurched? According to Finney, "[a] revival was the result of the *right* use of the appropriate means."[42] From this developed a typical Revival order of service that was to lead to immediate results: preliminary events (a praise service to warm up the heart), the sermon (an invitation to accept the Lord), and the harvest (the converted came forward during a hymn). The main function of this service was conversion. The pulpit was the focus of the

41. White, *Protestant Worship*, 176ff.

42. Cited in White, *Protestant Worship*, 191 (*original emphasis*).

auditorium, and the chief item was the sermon with its call to repentance and conversion—it was always necessary to call the converted forward.

There was no church year but a national calendar of holidays. Set forms of prayer were suspect. Instead, prayer was typically monopolized through a pastoral prayer that had confession, praise, thanksgiving, offering, intercession, and petition. In this movement "the gradualism of Christian nurture was foreign to its ethos."[43] There was an expectation of Bible reading and of developing knowledge of the Bible, even memorization. Sacraments had little emphasis. Baptism identified the converted. The Eucharist was moralized or used as a visual aid to the sermon.

Because music was a powerful emotional stimulant and could create a sense of expectancy, it was used to invite the congregation and to create common feelings and hopes. The musical repertoire tended to feature spirituals, gospel hymns, and texts that were personal, introspective, and gave the story of a soul. The music usually had a "music leader."

From the Revival tradition grew newly formed religions such as the Mormons, the Seventh Day Adventists, and Christian Science. In its most recent forms, the Revivalist tradition is marked by a concerted effort to show concern for the unchurched, to capture a religious market, and to project the personality of its minister. It is in this tradition that worship became a tool for reaching the unconverted.

AMERICAN PENTECOSTAL

The Pentecostal tradition is another movement that grew up in the United States.[44] It is a twentieth-century phenomenon and part of the radical break with the common Christian tradition of worship in place before the Reformation. Pentecostalism is an approach that is unstructured (no set worship forms), expecting the Holy Spirit to prompt both the contents and the sequence. It permits speaking in tongues, interpretation, prophecy, and ecstatic singing (even dancing). There are diverse denominational expressions of this tradition that move in the direction of both the Revival tradition featuring autonomy on order, preaching, and hymnody on one hand, and the Methodist tradition accenting holiness (the Christian life lived with perfection as its goal) on the other. Typically, the main distinction of Pentecostalism is that

43. White, *Protestant Worship*, 180.

44. White, *Protestant Worship*, 192–208.

after conversion a distinct experience with the Holy Spirit's gifts is required.

Pentecostalism in the United States has several characteristics. It baptizes believers only, often by immersion. In its early versions it appealed primarily to the disinherited in society and, after 1960, to a greater part of the entry level of U. S. society and to the upwardly mobile. In worship the minister must be able and willing to follow the Spirit—not dominate but be sensitive to the flow of events to invite the highest degree of active participation. For Pentecostals the Spirit's gifts are a sign of the immanent reign of Christ, so worship is a foretaste of the feast to come and a means to advance Christ's coming (deriving from a millennial hope). The Bible is used but for reading only short selections and for preaching often esoteric texts. The preaching ranges from a careful exegetical style to a highly emotional style with chantlike repetitions to illicit participatory interactions.

The highest gift is the baptism of the Spirit, which is present in worship in tongues (a unique experience of grace) and in the healing of individuals (Baptism and Lord's Supper are of less importance.) The Lord's Supper may occur one to four times each year. Except for the Lord's Prayer, Pentecostal prayer is oral, not written, often with one or both arms raised. It may be in ordinary speech or glossolalia. Sometimes all worshipers speak their petitions at once. There is a communal sense of piety, because all gifts are for the benefit of all to build up the body of Christ and to include everyone in a full expression of those gifts. Testimonies are valued because they narrate the acts of God in people's lives. According to White, "[a]ll Pentecostal worship is sacramental in manifesting visibly and audibly within the gathered community the action and presence of the Holy Spirit."[45] What distinguishes this movement from others, perhaps, is not its emphasis on Scripture but on the immediacy of the Spirit. It asks, "Is the Spirit present on the people?" The printed page offers little help in this quest for immediacy.

WHAT TRADITIONS FOR LUTHERANS?

The traditions of Christian worship are many, as the brief descriptions presented in this chapter have demonstrated. Particular attention was given to the Protestant patterns that have come to the United States as James White has identified their origins and characteristics. Lutherans

45. White, *Protestant Worship*, 200.

who become aware of and interact with these traditions may ask: "What, if anything, might be useful for our worship?"

Indeed, Christian worship is central to the life of the church. At the time of the Reformation, Lutherans chose ways of worship that were drawn from the Scriptures and were based on the commands that Christ gave his church. Some inherited practices were rejected and some were retained. As the Lutheran reformers sorted through these worship matters, they continually asked key questions: What fits with the teachings of Christ and the apostles as revealed in the Word of God (*sola scriptura*)? What fits with the gracious love of God in Christ Jesus that we are saved by grace alone without the deeds of the law (Ephesians 2:8–9; *sola gratia*)? What fits with God's declaration that "a man is justified by faith without the deeds of the law" (Romans 3:28; *sola fide*)?

Centuries later, the descendants of the early Lutherans look at the range of traditions in Christianity and pose the same questions. They want to know what makes Christian worship today godly and right in the eyes of God: Is worship some kind of heavenly fourth dimension? Is it valued for its ability to generate a Christian life? Is it a priestly offering of the church to God? Is it measured by how many converts it produces? Is it judged by how much the Holy Spirit seems to move people?

When any ecumenical exchange of traditions is considered or when mission work with new groups of people exposes differing traditions and forms of worship, the church does best when it returns to the primary questions around *sola scriptura*, *sola gratia*, and *sola fide* as she assesses what may be useful for worship. These *solas*, these governing principles, direct the church to once again listen to the Lutheran Confessions, listen for how they are obedient to Christ, how they avoid false worship, and how they select human traditions that serve the true worship of God. From the Confessions comes insight for the issues of our day, issues that revolve around worship, the Word of God, the sacraments of Baptism and Lord's Supper, Holy Absolution, prayer, praise, and matters of rite and order. As we listen to the confessors, we can learn to measure worship and select from the traditions that Christians invent. Only when worship follows God's commands and suits his way of creating faith and producing fruits of faith can it be true spiritual worship—*Gottesdienst*—*cultus Dei*.

Textual Overview and Table of Cross-References

The following table serves a number of functions. First, it lists the texts cited in this book in the same order as they occur in *The Book of Concord.* Thus this table provides the reader with an overview of this book and its contents. Passages are shown as they relate to one another and, implicitly, with the larger *Book of Concord*, which serves as a starting point for further study.

The table also lists the text numbers, not the page numbers, that correspond with each citation. Each text receives a number according to its chapter (100, 200, etc.) and its ordering within that chapter (1, 2, etc.), resulting in numbers that begin as 101, 102, etc. This informs the reader about the same or similar texts that can have multiple applications because they are repeated in different sections or chapters. An asterisk by a text number further indicates where the noted original language texts differ among a group of similar citations.

	Citation	Text Number
Nicene Creed		307
Athanasian Creed	3	101, 606, 702
Athanasian Creed	28	102
Augsburg Confession	V, 1–4	128, 802*
Augsburg Confession	VII, 1–3	152
Augsburg Confession	VII, 1–4	835
Augsburg Confession	IX, 1–2	313
Augsburg Confession	IX, 1–3	309
Augsburg Confession	X, 1–2	401

	Citation	Text Number
Augsburg Confession	XII, 1–10	521
Augsburg Confession	XIV, 1	224
Augsburg Confession	XV, 1–4	824
Augsburg Confession	XX, 27–31	723
Augsburg Confession	XXI, 1–4	609
Augsburg Confession	XXII, 8–12	141
Augsburg Confession	XXIV, 1–4	827
Augsburg Confession	XXIV, 10–13	143
Augsburg Confession	XXIV, 21–23	123
Augsburg Confession	XXIV, 30–34	429
Augsburg Confession	XXV, 1–3	520
Augsburg Confession	XXV, 3–6	515
Augsburg Confession	XXVI, 1–2	144
Augsburg Confession	XXVI, 1–3	809
Augsburg Confession	XXVI, 4	843
Augsburg Confession	XXVI, 8–11	150, 818
Augsburg Confession	XXVI, 12	819
Augsburg Confession	XXVI, 21	820
Augsburg Confession	XXVI, 33–39	803
Augsburg Confession	XXVI, 40–42	154
Augsburg Confession	XXVI, 40–45	838
Augsburg Confession	XXVII, 11–14	145
Augsburg Confession	XXVII, 38–40	119
Augsburg Confession	XXVII, 48–50	112
Augsburg Confession	XXVII, 49–50	603
Augsburg Confession	XXVIII, 5–7	514
Augsburg Confession	XXVIII, 35–39	146
Augsburg Confession	XXVIII, 47–52	140
Augsburg Confession	XXVIII, 53–60	826
Augsburg Confession	XXVIII, 55–60	153
Augsburg Confession	XXVIII, 61–64	808
Augsburg Confession	XXVIII, 69	142
Apology	I, 1–2	134
Apology	II, 35–38, 45	319
Apology	IV, 8	621
Apology	IV, 9–11	118, 813*
Apology	IV, 27	616
Apology	IV, 27–28	713
Apology	IV, 33–35	712, 807*
Apology	IV, 34–35	132, 219*

	Citation	Text Number
Apology	IV, 49	104
Apology	IV, 51–57	722
Apology	IV, 57	116
Apology	IV, 67–69	214
Apology	IV, 79	725
Apology	IV, 83	117
Apology	IV, 123–126	719
Apology	IV, 125	611
Apology	IV, 132	720
Apology	IV, 132–134	155
Apology	IV, 140–141	721
Apology	IV, 154–158	106
Apology	IV, 168	634
Apology	IV, 168–171	114
Apology	IV, 307–310	105
Apology	IV, 309–310	109, 703
Apology	IV, 310	223*
Apology	VII–VIII, 5–6	801
Apology	VII–VIII, 12–16	810
Apology	VII–VIII, 18–19	229
Apology	VII–VIII, 27–28	231
Apology	VII–VIII, 30–40	804
Apology	VII–VIII, 34	148
Apology	VII–VIII, 35–36	108
Apology	VII–VIII, 47–48	230
Apology	IX, 1–3	314
Apology	IX, 3	311
Apology	X, 4	405
Apology	XI, 2	504
Apology	XI, 6–7	508
Apology	XII, 8–9	525
Apology	XII, 13–16	528
Apology	XII, 39–41	530
Apology	XII, 41–43	532
Apology	XII, 61–62	526
Apology	XII, 72	213
Apology	XII, 95–96	527
Apology	XII, 99	502
Apology	XII, 100–105	516
Apology	XII, 107	529

	Citation	Text Number
Apology	XXIV, 38–40	424
Apology	XXIV, 49–51	425
Apology	XXIV, 50–51	832
Apology	XXIV, 51	127
Apology	XXIV, 58–60	426
Apology	XXIV, 59	122
Apology	XXIV, 69–73	427
Apology	XXIV, 74–75	740
Apology	XXIV, 78–83	159
Apology	XXIV, 87	741
Apology	XXIV, 89	124
Apology	XXIV, 97–98	428
Apology	XXVII, 27	814
Apology	XXVII, 51–56	815
Apology	XXVII, 69	823
Apology	XXVIII, 8–11	821
Smalcald Articles	III, III, 4	235
Smalcald Articles	III, III, 12–14	121
Smalcald Articles	III, III, 19–20	509
Smalcald Articles	III, III, 36–39	524
Smalcald Articles	III, V, 1–4	302
Smalcald Articles	III, VI, 1–4	415
Smalcald Articles	III, VI, 5	406
Smalcald Articles	III, VII, 1–3	505
Smalcald Articles	III, VIII, 1	501
Smalcald Articles	III, VIII, 2	511
Smalcald Articles	III, VIII, 3	130
Smalcald Articles	III, XII, 1–3	805
Smalcald Articles	III, XIV, 1–3	120
Treatise	44–46	507
Treatise	48	113, 816*
Small Catechism	I, 3–4	716
Small Catechism	I, 4	601
Small Catechism	II, 2	724
Small Catechism	III, 1–2	602
Small Catechism	III, 12–13	726
Small Catechism	IV, 1–4	301
Small Catechism	IV, 4	305, 312
Small Catechism	IV, 9–10	317

	Citation	Text Number
Large Catechism	III, 24	604
Large Catechism	III, 24–26	630
Large Catechism	III, 27–28	631
Large Catechism	III, 33	628
Large Catechism	III, 38–39	729
Large Catechism	III, 40–41	227
Large Catechism	III, 45	730
Large Catechism	III, 46–48	728
Large Catechism	III, 47–48	636, 717*
Large Catechism	III, 53–54	201
Large Catechism	III, 71–72	632
Large Catechism	III, 76–78	633
Large Catechism	III, 82–83	618
Large Catechism	III, 92	615
Large Catechism	III, 97	624
Large Catechism	III, 97–98	605
Large Catechism	III, 104	204
Large Catechism	III, 109–111	635
Large Catechism	III, 119–120	617
Large Catechism	III, 121–123	625
Large Catechism	IV, 2	306
Large Catechism	IV, 6–8	310
Large Catechism	IV, 17–18	209
Large Catechism	IV, 23–29	318
Large Catechism	IV, 31	316
Large Catechism	IV, 35–37	303
Large Catechism	IV, 41–42	324
Large Catechism	IV, 44–45	320
Large Catechism	IV, 65–67	326
Large Catechism	IV, 71–73	325
Large Catechism	IV, 74–79	323
Large Catechism	IV, 84–85	322
Large Catechism	V, 8–9	402
Large Catechism	V, 10–11	210
Large Catechism	V, 15–18	412
Large Catechism	V, 28–32	417
Large Catechism	V, 33–36	418
Large Catechism	V, 45–47	414
Large Catechism	V, 69–72	419
Large Catechism	Brief Exhort., 8–9	522

Abbreviations and General Textual Notes

The following are general notes that apply to the original languages of the documents that comprise the Lutheran Confessions.

- The use of two capitals in *HErr*, *JEsus*, and *CHristus* may occur in German.
- The German style of quotation marks is employed in quotations from the Lutheran Confessions. The style employs either ‚single' or „double" commas, one on the baseline and one inverted. The ends of the commas point away from the word. Similar to usage in the United Kingdom, the punctuation follows the quotation marks.
- A note regarding the quarto and octavo editions of the Apology of the Augsburg Confession: The quarto edition appeared either at the end of April or the beginning of May 1531. The octavo edition appeared in September of that year. Although an earlier German translation of the quarto edition existed, the translation/paraphrase of Justus Jonas was incorporated into the 1580 German *Book of Concord*. The Jonas translation was aware of both the quarto and the octavo editions. Although the later editions of the time favored the octavo edition, the 1584 Latin *Book of Concord* favored the quarto, which is also cited by the Formula of Concord. See pages 107–9 in Kolb/Wengert and pages XXII–XXIII in *BSLK*. It is not the intent of this book to favor any specific editorial positions in either *BSLK* or Kolb/Wengert. Where necessary, however, texts from the quarto edition of the Apology that were heavily edited or cut from the octavo will be cited from the Tappert edition.
- Boldface emphasis within quotations from the original languages of the Lutheran Confessions indicates the use of *Sperrdruck* in *BSLK*, a German typographical method of indicating emphasis

whereby a word's letterspacing (whitespace between letters) is increased. This method remains generally unused in English. Because it primarily occurs in the Formula of Concord, its use will be reflected with the use of boldface in citations from that document.

BSLK	*Die Bekenntnisschriften der evangelisch-lutherischen Kirche*. 12th ed. Göttingen: Vandehoeck & Ruprecht, 1992.
Kolb-Wengert	Kolb, Robert, and Timothy J. Wengert, eds. *The Book of Concord*. Translated by Charles Arand et al. Minneapolis: Fortress, 2000.
Tappert	Tappert, Theodore G., ed. *The Book of Concord*. Philadelphia: Fortress, 1959.
AC	Augsburg Confession
Ap	Apology of the Augsburg Confession
Ep	Epitome of the Formula of Concord
FC	Formula of Concord
LC	Large Catechism
SA	Smalcald Articles
SC	Small Catechism
SD	Solid Declaration of the Formula of Concord
Tr	Treatise on the Power and Primacy of the Pope

I

Worship

What is Christian worship?

101 This, however, is the catholic faith: that we worship[1] one God in trinity and the Trinity in unity, neither confusing the persons nor dividing the substance.

[1]L: *Fides autem catholica haec est, ut unum Deum in trinitate et trinitatem in unitate veneremur*; G: *Dies ist aber der rechte christliche Glaube, daß wir ein einigen Gott in drei Personen und drei Personen in einigen Gottheit ehren.*

Athanasian Creed, 3

102 Therefore it is the true faith that we believe and confess that our Lord Jesus Christ, the Son of God, is at once God and a human being.[1]

[1]L: *Est ergo fides recta, ut credamus et confiteamur, quia Dominus noster Jesus Christus Dei filius, et Deus pariter et homo est*; G: *So ist nu dies der rechte Glaube, so wir gleuben und bekennen, daß unser HErr Jesus Christus Gottes Sohn, Gott und Mensch ist.*

The rendering of Christ becoming *homo* and *Mensch* as becoming a "human being" is consistent with the texts and language of the creeds, the Augsburg Confession, and the Smalcald Articles, among other documents in *The Book of Concord*. Yet because the creeds and the Augsburg Confession also locate *filius* and *Sohn* with *homo* and *Mensch* in the person of Christ, one comprehends "human being" in the context of Christ being a man, the Son of his heavenly Father, who won salvation for all humans through his God-manhood

(Philippians 2; see also Romans 5:12–21; 1 Corinthians 14:34–35; Ephesians 4:4–6; 5:22–33).

Athanasian Creed, 28

103 And Christ says in John 4[:23–24], "[T]rue worshipers will worship the Father in spirit and truth,[1] for the Father seeks such as these to worship him.[2] God is spirit, and those who worship him must worship in spirit and truth."[3] This passage clearly condemns the notions about sacrifices that imagine they avail *ex opere operato*,[4] and teaches that one should "worship in spirit," that is, with the deepest activity of the heart and faith.[5]

[1]L: *Veri adoratores adorabunt Patrem in spiritu et veritate*; G: *„Die rechten Anbeter werden den Vater anbeten im Geist und in der Wahrheit"*, *das ist mit Herzen, mit herzlicher Furcht und herzlichem Glauben.*

[2]L: *Nam et Pater tales quaerit, qui adorent eum.*

The German translation omits this and the following noted parts of the verse given in the Latin original text.

[3]L: *Deus est spiritus, et eos, qui adorant eum, in spiritu et veritate oportet adorare.*

[4]L: *Haec sententia clare damnat opiniones de sacrificiis, quae fingunt ex opere operato valere*; G: *Darum ists eitel teufelisch, pharisäisch und antichristliche Lehre und Gottesdienst, daß unser Widersacher lehren, ihr Meß verdiene Vergebung Schuld und Pein ex opere operato.*

[5]L: *et* [*haec sententia*] *docet, quod oporteat spiritu, id est, motibus cordis et fide adorare.*

See also note 1 above, where the German paraphrase of the Latin does not expand this point in the manner of the Latin text but states: *das ist mit Herzen, mit herzlicher Furcht und herzlichem Glauben*. To understand the German use of *Furcht* (*fear*) in light of Latin *motibus*, see the definition of *motus* in Richard A. Muller, *Dictionary of Latin and Greek Theological Terms* (Grand Rapids: Baker, 1985).

Apology XXIV, 27

104 It is easy to determine the difference between this faith and the righteousness of the law. Faith is that worship[1] which receives the benefits that God offers; the righteousness of the law is that worship[2] which offers God our own merits. God wants to be honored by faith[3] so that we receive from him those things that he promises and offers.

[1]L: uses the Greek word λατρεία; G: *ein solcher Gottesdienst und latria.*

[2]L: uses the Greek λατρεία; G: *ein solcher Gottesdienst.*

[3]L: *Fide sic vult coli Deus*; G: *So will Gott nu durch den Glauben also geehret sein.*

Apology IV, 49

105 Because the righteousness of Christ is given to us through faith, therefore faith is righteousness in us by imputation. That is, by it we are made acceptable to God because of God's imputation and ordinances, as Paul says (Rom. 4:5), "Faith is reckoned as righteousness."

We must speak technically because of certain carping critics: faith is truly righteousness because it is obedience to the Gospel. Obedience to the edict of a superior is obviously a kind of distributive righteousness. Our good works or obedience to the law can be pleasing to God only because this obedience to the Gospel takes hold of Christ, the propitiator, and is reckoned for righteousness. We do not satisfy the law, but for Christ's sake this is forgiven us, as Paul says (Rom. 8:1), "There is now no condemnation for those who are in Christ Jesus." This faith gives honor to God,[1] gives him what is properly his; it obeys him by accepting his promises. As Paul says (Rom. 4:20), "No distrust made him waver concerning the promise of God, but he grew strong in his faith as he gave glory to God." Thus the service and worship of the Gospel is to receive good things from God,[2] while the worship of the law is to offer and present our goods to God.[3] We cannot offer anything to God unless we have first been reconciled and reborn. The greatest possible comfort comes from this doctrine that the highest worship in the Gospel is the desire to receive forgiveness of sins, grace, and righteousness.[4] About this worship Christ speaks in John 6:40, "This is the will of my Father, that everyone who sees the Son and believes in him should have eternal life." And the Father says (Matt. 17:5), "This is my beloved Son, with whom I am well pleased; listen to him."

[1]L: *Haec fides reddit Deo honorem.*

[2]L: *cultus et λατρεία evangelii est accipere bona a Deo.*

[3]L: *cultus legis est bona nostra Deo offerre et exhibere.*

[4]L: *cultus in evangelio praecipuus est a Deo velle accipere remissionem peccatorum, gratiam et iustitiam.*

Apology IV, 307–310
The Latin is from the quarto edition.
The English is from Tappert.

106 And the story [of the sinful woman desiring forgiveness in Luke 7:36–50] itself shows what he calls "love." The woman came with this conviction about Christ: that she should seek the forgiveness of sins from him. This is the highest way to worship Christ.[1] Nothing greater could she ascribe to Christ.[2] By seeking the forgiveness of sins from him, she truly acknowledged him as the Messiah. Now to think about Christ in this way, to worship and take hold of him in this way, is truly to believe.[3] Moreover, Christ used the word "love" not with respect to the woman but against the Pharisee, because he was contrasting the entire worship of the Pharisee with the entire worship of the woman.[4] He reprimands the Pharisee for not acknowledging that Christ was the Messiah, even though he showed Christ the outward courtesies due to a guest who is a great and holy man.[5] He points to the poor woman and praises her worship, her anointing, and her tears, etc., all of which were signs of faith and a kind of confession, namely, that she sought the forgiveness of sins from Christ.[6] It was not without reason that this truly powerful example moved Christ to reprimand the Pharisee, who was a wise and honorable man, but an unbelieving man. He charges him with ungodliness and admonishes him with the example of the poor woman. He shows that it is a disgrace to the Pharisee that an unlearned woman believes in God while he, a very teacher of the law, does not believe, does not acknowledge the Messiah, and does not seek the forgiveness of sins or salvation from him.

Therefore he praises her entire act of worship in this way—as often happens in Scripture—so that we may understand many things under this one phrase.[7] Later we shall take up at greater length similar passages, such as, "So give for alms those things that are within. . . . everything will be clean for you" [Luke 11:41]. He requires not only alms but also the righteousness of faith. In the same way he says here [Luke 7:47], "Her sins, which were many, have been forgiven; because she has shown great love," that is, because she truly worshiped me with faith and with the acts and signs of faith.[8] He includes the entire act of worship but teaches that it is faith, strictly speaking, that receives the forgiveness of sins even though love, confession, and other good fruits ought to follow.[9] Therefore by this he does not imply that these fruits are the payment or the sacrifice that earns the forgiveness of sins, that reconciles us to God.

We are debating about an important matter, namely, about the honor of Christ and the source from which the faithful might seek a sure and certain consolation—whether we should place our confidence in Christ or in our own works. But if we put it in our works, Christ will be robbed of his honor as our mediator and propitiator.[10] And, faced with God's judgment, we will discover that such confidence was futile, and consciences will then plunge into despair. For if the forgiveness of sins and reconciliation take place not freely on account of Christ but on account of our love, then no one will have the forgiveness of sins until he or she has kept the entire law, because the law does not justify as long as it can accuse us. Thus it is clear that, since justification is reconciliation on account of Christ, we are justified by faith, because it is most certain that the forgiveness of sins is received by faith alone.

[1]L: *Mulier venit hanc afferens de Christo opinionem, quod apud ipsum quaerenda esset remissio peccatorum. Hic cultus est summus cultus Christi*; G: *Die Frau kommt in der Zuversicht zu Christo, daß sie wolle Vergebung der Sünde bei ihm erlangen, das heißt recht Christum erkennen und ehren.*

[2]L: *Nihil potuit maius tribuere Christo*; G: *Denn größer Ehre kann man Christo nicht tun.*

[3]L: *Hoc erat vere Messiam agnoscere, quaerere apud eum remissionem peccatorem. Porro sic de Christo sentire, sic colere, sic complecti Christum est vere credere*; G: *Denn das heißt Messiam oder Christum wahrlich erkennen, bei ihm suchen Vergebung der Sunde. Dasselbige vom Christo halten, also Christum erkennen und annehmen, das heißt recht an Christum gläuben.*

[4]L: *quia totum cultum pharisaei cum toto cultu mulieris comparabat*; G: *Christus hältet gegenander die ganze Ehre, die ihm der Pharisäer getan hat, mit dem Erbieten und Werken, so die Frau ihm erzeiget hat.*

[5]L: *etsi haec externa officia ipsi praestaret, ut hospiti, viro magno et sancto*; G: *wiewohl er ihn äußerlich geehret als einen Gast und frommen heiligen Mann.*

[6]L: *Ostendit mulierculam et praedicat huius cultum, unguenta, lacrimas etc., quae omnia erant signa fidei et confessio quaedam, quod videlicet apud Christum quaereret remissionem peccatorem*; G: *Aber den Gottesdienst der Frauen, daß sie ihre Sunde erkennet und bei Christo Vergebung der Sunde suchet, diesen Dienst lobt Christus.*

[7]L: *Sic igitur totum cultum laudat, ut saepe fit in scripturis, ut uno verbo multa complectamur*; G: *Darum lobet er da nicht allein die Liebe, sondern den ganzen cultum oder Gottesdienst, den Glauben mit den Früchten, und nennet doch für den Pharisäo die Frucht.*

[8]L: *id est, quia me vere coluit fide et exercitiis et signis fidei. Totum cultum comprehendit.*

The German translation does not explicitly engage Luke 7:47 and the point made here; rather, it makes a general comment on works not being the treasure but the fruits of faith.

[9]L: *Interim tamen hoc docet, quod proprie accipiatur fide remissio peccatorum, etsi dilectio, confessio et alii boni fructus sequi debeant*; G: *Denn man kann den Glauben im Herzen andern nicht weisen und anzeigen, denn durch die Früchte, die beweisen für den Menschen den Glauben im Herzen.*

[10]L: *Quodsi in opera nostra collocanda erit, detrahitur Christo honos mediatoris et propitiatoris*; G: *Denn so wir auf unsere Werke vertrauen, so wird Christo sein Ehre genommen, so ist Christus nicht der Versühner noch der Mittler.*

Apology IV, 154–158

107 In summary, the worship of the New Testament is spiritual, that is, it is the righteousness of faith in the heart and the fruits of faith.[1]

[1]L: *cultus novi testamenti est spiritualis, hoc est, est iustitia fidei in corde et fructus fidei*; G: *im neuen Testament gilt kein Opfer ex opere operato sine bono motu utentis, das ist, das Werk ohn ein guten Gedanken im Herzen.*

Apology XXIV, 27

108 Paul clearly teaches this in Colossians [2:16–17] when he says, "Therefore do not let anyone condemn you in matters of food and drink or of observing festivals, new moons, or sabbaths. These are only a shadow of what is to come, but the substance belongs to Christ." Again [vv. 20–23], "If with Christ you died to the elemental spirits of the universe, why do you live as if you still belonged to the world? Why do you submit to regulations, 'Do not handle, Do not taste, Do not touch'? All these regulations refer to things that perish with use; they are simply human commands and teachings. These have indeed an appearance of wisdom in promoting self-imposed piety,[1] humility, and severe treatment of the body, but they are of no value in checking self-indulgence." Paul's meaning is this. The righteousness of the heart is a spiritual thing that enlivens the heart. It is evident that human traditions do not enliven the heart and are neither results of the Holy Spirit's working (as is love of neighbor, chastity, etc.) nor instruments through which God moves hearts to believe (as are the given Word and divinely instituted sacraments).[2] Instead, they are usages in that sphere of matters which do not pertain at all to the heart but which "perish with use."[3] It must not be thought that they are necessary for righteousness before God. In the same sense he says in Romans 14[:17], "The kingdom of God is not food and drink but righteousness and peace and joy in the Holy Spirit."

[1]The Latin cites the Vulgate of Colossians 2:23. The Vulgate translates Greek "in self-made religion" as *in superstitione*. The German text is more literal to the Greek: *durch selbst erwählet Geistlichkeit.*The usual German term for superstition is *Aberglaube*, and the terms for idolatry are *Götzendienst* and *Abgötterei*.

[2]L: *quod traditiones humanae non vivificent corda, nec sint effectus spiritus sancti, sicut dilectio proximi, castitas etc., nec sint instrumenta, per quae Deus movet corda ad credendum, sicut verbum et sacramenta divinitus tradita*; G: *Die Menschensatzungen aber sind nicht ein solch lebendig Licht und Kraft des heiligen Geistes im Herzen, sind nichts Ewiges, darum machen sie nicht ewig Leben.*

[3]L: *sed sint usus rerum nihil ad cor pertinentium, quae usu pereant*; G: *sondern sind äußerlich leibliche Übung, die das Herz nicht ändern.*

Apology VII–VIII, 35–36

SUMMARY

- Christians worship the Trinity—the Father, the Son, and the Holy Spirit—believing that Jesus is the Redeemer of the world. The spiritual worship that the Father seeks is this faith in Jesus Christ.
- Faith, desiring to receive the gracious forgiveness that Jesus has won, is the spiritual obedience (λατρεία) that God seeks. To believe is the highest spiritual act. This faith results from the work of the Holy Spirit in the believer's heart through the Word of God and the Sacraments (the Gospel), not through human traditions. A sacrament does not confer God's grace "by the act itself" apart from faith. Through the same means, the Holy Spirit moves hearts to fruits of faith.
- Outward acts of worship apart from such faith are not what God seeks, for they are not fruits of faith. Those who imagine that

such works gain God's favor or lead to righteousness reject the work of Christ. Their efforts only dishonor Christ and God. Furthermore, acts of worship that humans invent, even traditions found among people who confess Christ, are not necessary for salvation.

- The worship of God (*cultus Dei*, *Gottesdienst*) is not some outward act that contributes any merit before God. Instead, worship is a spiritual act that is a trusting in God, namely, to wish to receive remission of sins, grace, and righteousness (as detailed in text 105 above) from God through faith in Christ and the fruits of faith that flow from a believing heart.

How does faith truly honor and obey God?

109 This faith gives honor to God,[1] gives him what is properly his; it obeys him by accepting his promises. . . . The greatest possible comfort comes from this doctrine that the highest worship in the Gospel[2] is the desire to receive forgiveness of sins, grace, and righteousness. About this worship[3] Christ speaks in John 6:40, "This is the will of my Father, that everyone who sees the Son and believes in him should have eternal life." And the Father says (Matt. 17:5), "This is my beloved Son, with whom I am well pleased; listen to him."

[1]L: *Haec fides reddit Deo honorem.*

[2]L: *cultus in evangelio praecipuus.*

[3]L: *De hoc cultu.*

Apology IV, 309–310
The Latin is from the quarto edition.
The English is from Tappert.

110 For they deprive Christ of his honor when they teach that we are not freely justified on account of Christ through faith but through such rites,[1] and especially when they teach that such rites are not only useful for justification but even necessary.[2] In the article on the church above they also condemned us because we said that it is not necessary for the true unity of the church that rites instituted by human beings be everywhere alike.[3] Daniel 11[:38] indicates that new religious rites will be the very form and constitution of the kingdom of the Antichrist.[4] For there he says, "He shall honor the god of fortresses instead of these; a god whom his ancestors did not know he shall honor with gold and silver, with precious stones and costly gifts." Here he is describing the invention of new religious rites,[5] for he says that a god such as the Fathers did not know will be worshiped.[6]

[1]L: *Detrahitur enim honos Christo, cum docent, quod non propter Christum gratis iustificemur per fidem, sed per tales cultus*; G: *Denn da wird Christo seine Ehre genommen, wenn sie lehren, daß wir nicht durch Christum, ohne Verdienst gerecht werden durch den Glauben, sondern durch solche Gottesdienst.*

[2]L: *maximeque cum docent tales cultus non solum utiles esse ad iustificationem, sed necessarios etiam*; G: *sonderlich wenn sie lehren, daß solch selbsterwählt Gottesdienst nicht allein nütz sei, sondern auch nötig.*

[3]L: *quod non sit necessarium ad veram unitatem ecclesiae ubique similes esse ritus ab hominibus institutos*; G: *zu rechter Einigkeit der Kirche sei nicht not, daß allenthalben gleichförmige Menschensatzungen sein.*

[4]L: *novos cultus humanos ipsam formam et πολιτεíαν regni antichristi fore*; G: *daß solche neue Gottesdienst von Menschen erfunden, werde die Politia und das rechte Wesen des antichristischen Reichs sein.*

[5]L: *Hic describit novos cultus*; G: *Da beschreibet er solche neu Gottesdienst.*

[6]L: *quia inquit talem Deum coli, qualem patres ignoraverint.*

The German paraphrase here speaks of another "god" than that known by the church fathers, semantically connecting the knowledge of God with worship.

Apology XV, 18–20

111 Look, here you have the true honor and worship that please God,[1] which God also commands under penalty of eternal wrath, namely, that the heart should know no other consolation or confidence than in him, nor let itself be torn from him, but for his sake should risk everything and disregard everything else on earth. On the other hand, you will easily see and judge how the world practices nothing but false worship and idolatry.[2] There has never been a nation so wicked that it did not establish and maintain some sort of worship.[3] All people have set up their own god, to whom they looked for blessings, help, and comfort.

[1]G: *Siehe, da hast Du nu, was die rechte Ehre und Gottesdienst ist*; L: *Ecce jam tenes, quinam verus Dei cultus sit.*

In the catechisms, Luther writes in the manner of a personal communication between a mentor and a student; he uses the capitalized *Du* of direct address.

[2]G: *Dagegen wirst Du leichtlich sehen und urteilen, wie die Welt eitel falschen Gottesdienst und Abgötterei treibt*; L: *Et hoc facile jam videbis aut judicabis, quomodo mundus nihil aliud quam falsum Dei cultum passim constituerit atque exerceat.*

[3]G: *Denn es ist nie kein Volk . . . das nicht einen Gottesdienst aufgerichtet und gehalten habe*; L: . . . *hominun natio, quae non aliquem Dei cultum constituerit et servaverit.*

Large Catechism I, 16–17

112 **[German text]** Now it is no small offense in the Christian church to present to the people a service of God, which human beings have contrived without God's command,[1] teaching that such service of God makes people innocent and righteous before God.[2] For righteousness of faith, which ought to be emphasized most, is obscured when people are bedazzled with this strange angelic spirituality and false pretense of poverty, humility, and chastity.[3]

In addition, the commands of God and proper, true service of God are obscured when people hear that only monks must be in the state of perfection.[4] For Christian perfection is to fear God earnestly with the whole heart and yet also to have a sincere confidence, faith, and trust that we have a gracious, merciful God because of Christ; that we may and should pray for and request from God whatever we need and confidently expect help from him in all affliction, according to each person's vocation and walk of life; and that meanwhile we should diligently do external good works and attend to our calling. This is true perfection and true service of God—not being a mendicant or wearing a black or gray cowl, etc.[5]

[Latin text] It is no minor scandal in the church to propose to the people a certain act of worship invented by human beings without a command of God[1] and to teach that such worship justifies human beings.[2] For the righteousness of faith, which ought to be taught in the church most of all, is obscured when these astonishing angelic observances and this pretense of poverty, humility, and celibacy are blinding people.[3]

Furthermore, the precepts of God and true worship of God are obscured when people hear that only monks are in a state of perfection.[4] For Christian perfection means earnestly to fear God and, at the same time, to have great faith and to trust that we have a gracious God on account of Christ; to ask for and to expect with certainty help from

God in all things that are to be borne in connection with our calling; and, in the meantime, diligently to do good works for others and to serve in our calling. True perfection and true worship of God consist in all these things, not in celibacy, mendicancy, or shabby clothing.[5]

[1]G: *daß man dem Volke einen solchen Gottesdienst furträgt, den die Menschen ohn Gottes Gebot erdicht haben*; L: *populo proponere certum cultum ab hominibus excogitatum sine mandato Dei.*

The reader will note that here and elsewhere in the Augsburg Confession the translation of the German *Gottesdienst*, generally rendered in modern dictionaries as "divine service" or "public worship," is usually given in the Kolb/Wengert edition as "service of God." At various points in AC XXVI and in XXVIII, among other places, it is also given as "service to God." The translation of Latin *cultus* is given as "worship" or "act of worship" and that of *cultus Dei* as "worship of God." Any implied distinction between the German term and its Latin counterparts, of which the latter speak in the broadest ecumenical usage of the Western tradition, may well be less than the English translation suggests.

[2]G: *und lehren, daß ein solcher Gottesdienst die Menschen vor Gott fromb und gerecht mache*; L: *et docere, quod talis cultus iustificet homines.*

[3]G: *Dann Gerechtigkeit des Glaubens . . . wird verdunkelt, wann den Leuten die Augen aufgesperret werden mit dieser seltsamen Engelgeistlichkeit*; L: *Quia iustitia fidei . . . obscuratur, cum illae mirificae religiones angelorum . . . offunduntur oculis hominum.*

Note the subtle reference to Galatians 1:8 via the term "angel-spirituality."

[4]G: *Uber das werden auch die Gebote Gotts und der recht und wahre Gottsdienst dadurch verdunkelt*; L: *Praeterea obscurantur praecepta Dei et verus cultus Dei.*

[5]G: *Darin stehet die rechte Vollkommenheit und der rechte Gottsdienst, nicht in Betteln oder in einer schwarzen oder grauen Kappen etc.*; L: *In his rebus est vera perfectio et verus cultus Dei; non est in caelibatu aut mendicitate aut sordida veste.*

Augsburg Confession XXVII, 48–50

113 How many shameful acts have arisen from the tradition of celibacy? With what darkness has the teaching about vows eclipsed the gospel! They have pretended that a vow constitutes righteousness before God and merits forgiveness of sins. Thus they have transferred the benefit of Christ to human traditions and have completely destroyed the doctrine of faith. Utterly worthless traditions they have passed off as worship of God and the way of perfection[1] and given them preference over the work of the vocations that God does require and has ordained. These errors are not to be taken lightly. Truly they do harm to the glory of Christ[2] and bring souls to ruin. They cannot be ignored.

[1]L: *Finxerunt nugacissimas traditiones esse cultus Dei et perfectionem*; G: *und haben ihre närrichte und leichtfertige Satzungen fur den rechten Gottesdienst und Vollkummenheit geruhmet.*

[2]L: *Laedunt enim gloriam Christi*; G: *dann sie nehmen Christo seine Ehre.*

Treatise on the Power and Primacy of the Pope, 48

114 Therefore Paul says (Rom. 7:19), "I do not do the good I want, but the evil I do not want is what I do." Again (Rom. 7:25), "I of myself serve the law of God with my mind, but with my flesh I serve the law of sin." Here he openly says that he serves the law of sin. And David says (Ps. 143:2), "Enter not into judgment with thy servant; for no man living is righteous before thee." Even this servant of God prays God to avert his judgment. Again (Ps. 32:2), "Blessed is the man to whom the Lord imputes no iniquity." Therefore in our present weakness there is always sin that could be imputed to us; about this he says a little later, "Therefore let every one who is godly offer prayer to thee" (Ps. 32:6). Here he shows that even the godly must pray for the forgiveness of sins.

More than blind are those who do not believe that evil desires in the flesh are sins, about which Paul says (Gal. 5:17), "The desires of the flesh are against the Spirit, and the desires of the Spirit are against the flesh." The flesh distrusts God and trusts in temporal things; in trouble it looks to men for help; it even defies God's will and runs away from afflictions that it ought to bear because of God's command; and it doubts God's mercy. The Holy Spirit in our hearts battles against such feelings in order to suppress and destroy them and to give us new spiritual impulses. But later we shall assemble more testimonies on this subject, though they are obvious throughout not only the Scriptures but also the holy Fathers.

Apology IV, 168–171

The text is from Tappert, following the quarto edition.

115 And yet the chief worship of God is to preach the gospel.[1] And when the opponents do preach, they talk about human traditions, about the devotion to the saints and similar trifles.[2] This the people rightly loathe, and so they walk out on them immediately after the reading of the gospel.

[1]L: *Atqui praecipuus cultus Dei est docere evangelium.* G: *Denn der allergrößte, heiligste, nötigste, höchste Gottesdienst, welchen Gott im ersten und andern Gebot als das Größte hat gefordert, ist Gottes Wort predigen; denn das Predigtamt ist das höchste Amt in der Kirchen.*

[2]L: *Et cum concionantur adversarii, dicunt de traditionibus humanis, de cultu sanctorum et similibus nugis*; G: *Darum, wenn sie gleich in der Fasten oder sonst ander Zeit predigen, lehren sie nichts denn von solchen Menschensatzungen, von Anrufen der Heiligen, vom Weihwasser und von solchen Narrenwerken.*

Apology XV, 42

116 This worship, this *latreia*, is especially praised throughout the Prophets and Psalms.[1] Although the law does not appear to teach about the free forgiveness of sins, the patriarchs knew about the promise concerning Christ, that God intended to forgive sins on account of Christ. Therefore, since they understood that Christ would be the payment for our sins, they also knew that our works could not make so high a payment. Thus they received the free mercy and forgiveness of sins by faith, just like the saints in the New Testament.

[1]L: *Et hic cultus, haec λατρεία in prophetis et psalmis passim praecipue laudatur*; G: *Und solcher Glaub und Vertrauen auf Gottes Barmherzigkeit wird als der größte, heiligste Gottesdienst gepreiset, sonderlich in Propheten und Psalmen.*

Apology IV, 57

117 Third, in Acts 10[:43] Peter says: “All the prophets testify about him that everyone who believes in him receives forgiveness of sins through his name.” How could he say it more clearly? We receive the forgiveness of sins, he says, through his name, that is, on account of him, and therefore not on account of our merits and not on account of our contrition, attrition, love, acts of worship, or works.[1] And he adds: “When we believe in him.” He therefore requires faith. For we cannot take hold of the name of Christ in any other way than by faith.

[1]L: *ergo non propter nostra merita, non propter nostram contritionem, attritionem, dilectionem, cultus, opera*; G: *nicht durch unser Verdienst,*

nucht durch unser Reu oder Attrition, nicht durch unser Liebe, nicht durch einigen Gottesdienst, nicht durch einige Menschensatzung oder Werke.

Apology IV, 83

Summary

- Faith obeys God and gives God the honor, looking to him for blessing, help, comfort, and to receive the remission of sins that he offers through Jesus Christ.
- Those who would require other service or worship of God take the honor away from Christ and his saving work. They substitute false worship and idolatry with vows of poverty, humility, and celibacy, as if such worship of God or service to God were good works to make one righteous before God. However, what God wants is not a man-made recipe for perfection but a perfection that comes from trusting that for Christ's sake God is reconciled and that he will aid believers as they serve him in their everyday lives.
- Although the flesh distrusts God and doubts his mercy, the Holy Spirit by the teaching and preaching of the Gospel contends against this distrust and creates a reliance on God's mercy. Such faith the prophets and psalms praise as true worship.
- To trust in Christ, then, is to truly honor and obey God.

What are examples of false worship?

118 Here the scholastics in line with the philosophers teach only the righteousness of reason, namely, civil works. In addition, they fabricate the idea that reason, without the Holy Spirit, can love God above all things. Now as long as the human mind is undisturbed and does not feel God's wrath or judgment, it can imagine that it wants to love God and that it wants to do good for God's sake. In this way the scholastics teach that people merit the forgiveness of sins by "doing what is within them," that is, whenever reason, while grieving over sin, elicits an act of love for God or does good for God's sake. Because this opinion naturally flatters people, it has brought forth and multiplied many kinds of worship in the church, like monastic vows and abuses of the Mass.[1] On the basis of this opinion some devised some types, others other types of devotional acts or observances.[2] And in order to nourish and increase trust in such works, the scholastics have asserted that God necessarily gives grace to those who do these things, by a necessity not of coercion but of unchanging order.

[1]L: *Et haec opinio, quia naturaliter blanditur hominibus, peperit et auxit multos cultus in ecclesia, vota monastica, abusus missae*; G: *Und diese Meinung und irrige Lehre, dieweil die Leute natürlich dazu geneigt sind, . . . hat unzählig viel mißbräuchliche Gottesdienst in der Kirche angericht und geursacht, als sind die Klostergelübde, Mißbräuche der Messen.*

[2]L: *et subinde alii alios cultus atque observationes hac opinione excogitaverunt*; G: *wie dann solchs unzählig, immer ein Gottesdienst über den andern aus diesem Irrtum erdacht ist.*

Apology IV, 9–11

119 **[German text]** Now it is quite evident the monks have taught and preached that their contrived spiritual status makes satisfaction for sin and obtains God's grace and righteousness. What is this but to diminish the glory and praise of the grace of Christ and to deny the righteousness of faith? It follows from this that the customary vows have been improper and false services of God.[1] That is why they are also not binding. For a godless vow, made contrary to God's command, is null and void, just as the canons also teach that an oath should not bind a person to sin.

[Latin text] However, very clearly the monks have taught that their humanly invented observances make satisfaction for sins and merit grace and justification. What is this but to detract from the glory of Christ and to obscure and deny the righteousness of faith? It follows, therefore, that such customary vows were ungodly acts of worship and are invalid for that reason.[1] For an ungodly vow made contrary to God's command is invalid. For no vow ought to be a bond of iniquity, as the canon says.

[1]G: *Darum folget aus dem, daß solche gewohnliche Gelubd unrechte, falsche Gottesdienste gewesen*; L: *Sequitur igitur ista vota usitata impios cultus fuisse.*

Augsburg Confession XXVII, 38–40

120 Because monastic vows are in direct conflict with the first and chief article, they should simply be done away with. It is about these that Christ spoke in Matthew 24[:5] (" 'I am Christ . . .' "). For those who vow to live a monastic life believe that they lead a better life than the ordinary Christian, and through their works they intend to help not only themselves but others get to heaven. This is known as denying Christ, etc. They boast, on the basis of their St. Thomas, that monastic vows are equal to baptism. This is blasphemy against God.

Smalcald Articles III, XIV, 1–3

121 They divide such penance into three parts—contrition, confession, and satisfaction—with this comfort and pledge: that the person who is truly contrite, goes to confession, and makes satisfaction by these actions merits forgiveness and pays for sins before God. In this way, they directed the people who come to penance to place confidence in their own works. From this came the phrase that was spoken from the pulpit when they recited the general confession on behalf of the people: "Spare my life, Lord God, until I do penance and improve my life." Here there was no Christ. Nothing was mentioned about faith, but instead people hoped to overcome and blot out sin before God with their own works. We also became priests and monks with this intention: we wanted to set ourselves against sin.

Smalcald Articles III, III, 12–14

122 Again, because the priesthood of the New Testament is a ministry of the Spirit,[1] as Paul teaches in 2 Corinthians 3[:6], it has but the one sacrifice of Christ which makes satisfaction for and is applied to the sins of others. It has no sacrifices like the Levitical, which could be applied *ex opere operato* to others; instead, it presents the gospel and sacraments to others so that they may thereby receive faith and the Holy Spirit, be put to death and be made alive. For the ministry of the Spirit conflicts with the application of an *opus operatum*.[2] Through the ministry of the Spirit, the Holy Spirit works in our hearts.[3] Therefore his ministry benefits others when he works in them and gives them new birth and life.[4] This does not happen by applying, *ex opere operato*, one person's work to another.

[1]L: *Deinde quia sacerdotium novi testamenti est ministerium spiritus*; G: *Und dieweil das Priestertum des neuen Testaments ein Amt ist, dadurch der heilige Geist wirkt.*

[2]L: *quia ministerium spiritus pugnat cum applicatione operis operati.*

The German text elides much of the Latin text here and in the following notes into the sentence *Und dieweil das Priestertum das neuen Testaments ein Amt ist, dadurch der heilige Geist wirkt, kann kein Opfer sein, das ex opere operato andern helfe.*

[3]L: *Est enim ministerium spiritus, per quod spiritus sanctus efficax est in cordibus.*

[4]L: *quare habet tale ministerium, quod ita prodest aliis, cum in eis efficax est, cum regenerat et vivificat eos.*

Apology XXIV, 59

123 **[German text]** At the same time, an abominable error was also rebuked, namely, the teaching that our Lord Jesus Christ had made satisfaction by his death only for original sin and had instituted the Mass as a sacrifice for other sins.[1] Thus, the Mass was made into a sacrifice for the living and the dead for the purpose of taking away sin and appeasing God. Thereupon followed a debate as to whether one Mass celebrated for many people merited as much as a special Mass celebrated for an individual. This resulted in the countless multiplication of Masses, and with this work people wanted to obtain from God everything they needed. Meanwhile, faith in Christ and true worship of God were forgotten.[2]

[Latin text] The following view increased private Masses without end: Christ had by his passion made satisfaction for original sin and had instituted the Mass in which an offering might be made for daily sins,[1] mortal and venial. From this came the common opinion that the Mass is a work which *ex opere operato* blots out the sins of the living and the dead. Here began a debate on whether one Mass said for many is worth as much as special Masses for individuals. That debate produced this endless multitude of Masses.[2]

[1]G: *und die Messe eingesetzt zu einem Opfer fur die anderen Sunde*; L: *et instituerit missam, in qua fieret oblatio pro cotidianis dilectis, mortalibus et venialibus.*

[2]G: *und ist darneben des Glaubens an Christum und rechten Gottesdiensts vergessen worden.*

The Latin version does not include this sentence.

Augsburg Confession XXIV, 21–23

124 Our opponents in fact defend the application of the ceremony for freeing the souls of the dead[1] from which they receive unlimited revenue. Yet they have no testimonies and no command from Scripture for this. It is no small sin to establish such acts of worship in the church without the command of God and without the example of Scripture,[2] and to transfer the Lord's Supper, instituted for commemoration and preaching among the living, to the dead. This abuses the name of God contrary to the Second Commandment.

For one thing, it shows contempt for the gospel to hold that a ceremony without faith is a sacrifice that reconciles God and makes satisfaction for sins *ex opere operato*.[3] It is a horrible teaching to attribute as much to the work of the priest as to the death of Christ. For another thing, faith in Christ alone can conquer sin and death, as Paul teaches [Rom. 5:1], "[H]aving been justified by faith we have peace." Therefore, it is not possible to overcome the punishments of purgatory by the application of someone else's work.

[1]L: *ceremoniae pro liberandis animabus defunctorum*; G: *die Messe den Toten*.

[2]L: *Neque vero est leve peccatum, tales cultus sine mandato Dei, sine exemplo scripturae in ecclesia instituere*; G: *Nu ist es je ein unsäglicher großer Greuel und nicht ein kleine Sunde, daß sie dürfen ohn Gottes Wort, ohne alle Schrift ein Gottesdienst in der Kirchen anrichten*.

[3]L: *Primum enim contumelia est evangelii sentire, quod ceremonia ex opere operato sine fide sit sacrificium reconcilians Deum et satisfaciens pro peccatis*; G: *Denn erstlich ist das die höchste Schmach und Lästerung des Evangelii und Christi, daß das schlechte Werk der Messen ex opere operato ein Opfer sei, daß Gott versühne und für die Sunde gnug tue*.

Apology XXIV, 89

125 There is, moreover, another false worship. This is the greatest idolatry[1] that we have practiced up until now, and it is still rampant in the world. All the religious orders are founded upon it. It involves only that conscience that seeks help, comfort, and salvation in its own works and presumes to wrest heaven from God. It keeps track of how often it has made endowments, fasted, celebrated Mass, etc.[2] It relies on such things and boasts of them, unwilling to receive anything as a gift of God, but desiring to earn everything by itself or to merit everything by works of supererogation, just as if God were in our service or debt and we were his liege lords. What is this but to have made God into an idol—indeed, an "apple-god"[3]—and to have set ourselves up as God? But this reasoning is a little too subtle and is not suitable for young pupils.

[1]G: *Darüber ist auch ein falscher Gottesdienst und die hohiste Abgötterei*; L: *Praeter haec alius adhuc superest falsus et errorneus Dei cultus summam in sese complectens idololatriam*.

[2]G: *und rechnet, wieviel es gestiftet, gefastet, Messe gehalten hat etc.*; L: *quarum fundationum autor exstiterit, quantum jejunaverit, quot missarum myriadas lectitaverit etc.*

[3]Regarding the analysis of "apple-god," one might consider the use of the vulgar *Pferdapfel* ("horse-apple") to signify manure. The addition of *Apfel* to *König*, *Bischof*, or *Gott* would thus create a satirical, scatalogical caricature appropriate for the Shrove Tuesday carnival in the manner of *Simplicius Simplicissimus* ("Greatest of Fools") and *Das Narrenschiff* ("Ship of Fools").

Large Catechism I, 22–23

126 For this reason, too, believers require the teaching of the law: so that they do not fall back on their own holiness and piety[1] and under the appearance of God's Spirit establish their own service to God on the basis of their own choice, without God's Word or command.[2] As it is written in Deuteronomy 12[:8, 28, 32], "You shall not act . . . all of us according to our own desires," but "listen to the commands and laws which I command you," and "you shall not add to them nor take anything from them."

[1]G: *auf daß sie nicht auf eigene Heiligkeit und Andacht fallen*; L: *ne propria quadam sanctimonia religiosum vitae genus de suo ingenio excogitent.*

[2]G: *unter dem Schein des Geistes Gottes eigen erwählten Gottesdienst ohn Gottes Wort und Befehl anrichten*; L: *sub praetextu spiritus Dei electicios cultus sine verbo et mandato Dei instituant.*

Formula of Concord, Solid Declaration VI, 20

127 The true adornment of the churches is godly, useful, and clear doctrine, the devout use of the sacraments, ardent prayer, and the like.[1] Candles, golden vessels, and similar adornments are appropriate, but they are not the distinctive adornment of the church. Now if the opponents make such things the center of worship rather than the proclamation of the gospel, faith, and its struggles,[2] they should be numbered among those whom Daniel describes as worshiping their god with gold and silver [Dan. 11:38].[3]

[1]L: *Et verus ornatus est ecclesiarum doctrina pia, utilis et perspicua, usus pius sacramentorum, oratio ardens et similia*; G: *Denn der rechte äußerliche Kirchenschmuck ist auch rechte Predigt, rechter Brauch der Sakrament, und daß das Volk mit Ernst dazu gewöhnet sei und mit Fleiß und züchtig zusammen komme, lerne und bete.*

[2]L: *Candelae, vasa aurea et similes ornatus decent, sed non sunt proprius ornatus ecclesiae. Quodsi adversarii in talibus rebus collocant cultus, non in praedicatione evangelii, in fide, in certaminibus fidei*; G: *Über das, wo unser Widersacher ihre Kerzen, Altartücher, Bilder und dergleichen Zier für nötige Stück und damit Gottesdienst anrichten, sind sie des Antichrists Gesinde*.

[3]L: *sunt in istis numerandi, quos Daniel describit colere Deum suum auro et argento*; G: *davon Daniel sagt, daß sie ihren Gott ehren mit Silber, Gold und dergleichen Schmuck*.

Apology XXIV, 51

128 **[German text]** To obtain such faith God instituted the office of preaching, giving the gospel and the sacraments.[1] Through these, as through means, he gives the Holy Spirit who produces faith, where and when he wills, in those who hear the gospel.[2] It teaches that we have a gracious God, not through our merit but through Christ's merit, when we so believe.

Condemned are the Anabaptists and others who teach that we obtain the Holy Spirit without the external word of the gospel through our own preparation, thoughts, and works.[3]

[Latin text] So that we may obtain this faith, the ministry of teaching the gospel and administering the sacraments was instituted.[1] For through the Word and the sacraments as through instruments the Holy Spirit is given, who effects faith where and when it pleases God in those who hear the gospel,[2] that is to say, in those who hear that God, not on account of our own merits but on account of Christ, justifies those who believe that they are received into grace on account of Christ. Galatians 3[:14b]: "So that we might receive the promise of the Spirit through faith."

They condemn the Anabaptists and others who think that the Holy Spirit comes to human beings without the external Word through their own preparations and works.[3]

[1]G: *Solchen Glauben zu erlangen, hat Gott das Predigamt eingesetzt, Evangelium und Sakrament geben*; L: *Ut hanc fidem consequamur, institutum est ministerium docendi evangelii et porrigendi sacramenta*.

[2]G: *dadurch er als durch Mittel den heiligen Geist gibt, welcher den Glauben, wo und wenn er will, in denen, so das Evangelium hören, wirket*; L: *Nam per verbum et sacramenta tamquam per instrumenta*

donatur spiritus sanctus, qui fidem efficit, ubi et quando visum est Deo, in his, qui audiunt evangelium.

[3]G: *Und werden verdammt die Wiedertaufer und andere, so lehren, daß wir ohn das leiblich Wort des Evangelii den heiligen Geist durch eigene Bereitung, Gedanken und Werk erlangen*; L: *Damnant Anabaptistas et alios, qui sentiunt spiritum sanctum contingere hominibus sine verbo externo per ipsorum praeparationes et opera.*

Augsburg Confession V, 1–4

129 For the church has the mandate to appoint ministers,[1] which ought to please us greatly because we know that God approves this ministry and is present in it.[2] Indeed, it is worthwhile to extol the ministry of the Word with every possible kind of praise[3] against fanatics who imagine that the Holy Spirit is not given through the Word but is given on account of certain preparations of their own,[4] for example, if they sit idle and silent in dark places while waiting for illumination[5]—as the "Enthusiasts" formerly taught and the Anabaptists now teach.

[1]L: *Habet enim ecclesia mandatum de constituendis ministris*; G: *Denn die Kirche hat Gottes Befehl, daß sie soll Prediger und Diakonos bestellen.*

[2]L: *quod scimus Deum approbare ministerium illud et adesse in ministerio*; G: *so wir wissen, daß Gott durch Menschen und diejenigen, so von Menschen gewählet sind, predigen und wirken will.*

[3]L: *Ac prodest, quantum fieri potest, ornare ministerium verbi omni genere laudis*; G: *so ist gut, daß man solche Wahl hoch rühme und ehre.*

The term *Wahl* in the German paraphrase denotes the election and call of preachers and deacons (*Prediger und Diakonos*) mentioned in the German text. It correlates with the constitution of ministers of the Word (*ministerium verbi*) in the Latin text.

[4]L: *adversus fanaticos homines, qui somniant spiritum sanctum dari non per verbum, sed propter suas quasdam praeparationes.*

[5]L: *expectantes illuminationem.*

Apology XIII, 12–13

130 *In these matters, which concern the spoken, external Word,*[1] *it must be firmly maintained that God gives no one his Spirit or grace apart from the external Word which goes before.*[2] *We say this to protect ourselves from the enthusiasts, that is, the "spirits," who boast that they have the Spirit apart from and before contact with the Word.*[3] *On this basis, they judge, interpret, and twist the Scripture or oral Word according to their pleasure.*

[1]G: *Und in diesen Stücken, so das mündlich, äußerlich Wort betreffen*; L: *Et in his, quae vocale et externum verbum concernunt.*

[2]G: *ist fest darauf zu bleiben, daß Gott niemand seinen Geist oder Gnade gibt ohn durch oder mit dem vorgehend äußerlichem Wort*; L: *constanter tenendum est Deum nemini spiritum vel gratiam suam largiri nisi per verbum et cum verbo externo et praecedente.*

[3]G: *damit wir uns bewahren fur den Enthusiasten, das ist Geistern, so sich rühmen, ohn und vor dem Wort den Geist zu haben*; L: *ut ita praemuniamus nos adversum enthusiastas, id est spiritus, qui jacitant se ante verbum et sine verbo spiritum habere.*

Smalcald Articles III, VIII, 3
Italics from Kolb/Wengert reflect the 1538 additions.

131 Likewise, we also reject and condemn the error of the Enthusiasts, who contrive the idea that God draws people to himself, enlightens them, makes them righteous, and saves them without means, without the hearing of God's Word, even without the use of the holy sacraments.[1]

[1]G: *daß Gott ohne Mittel, ohne Gehör Gottes Worts, auch ohne Gebrauch der heiligen Sakramenten die Menschen zu sich ziehe, erleuchte, gerecht und selig mache*; L: *qui fingunt Deum immediate, absque verbi Dei auditu et sine sacramentorum usu, homines ad se trahere, illuminare, iustificare et salvare.*

A marginal note in the Epitome (see Kolb/Wengert, 493n22) defines "Enthusiasts [who] are those who await heavenly enlightenment of the Spirit without the preaching of God's Word." The German and Latin texts of that note read: G: *Enthusiasten heißen, die ohne die Predigt Gottes Worts uf himmlische Erleuchtung des Geistes warten*; L: *Enthusiastae vocantur, qui neglecta praedicatione verbi divini coelestes revelationes spiritus exspectant.*

Formula of Concord, Epitome II, 13

SUMMARY

The examples of false worship of God fall into two broad categories:

1. The first category replaces the righteousness of faith in Christ, offered through the means of grace, with a teaching that one can earn salvation by his or her own works or the works of others:

(a) that God necessarily gives grace to those who outwardly do good works,

(b) that services to God such as vows of poverty can make satisfaction for sin,

(c) that one can earn heaven by his or her own works,

(d) that in teaching repentance no mention is made of Christ or faith in his redemption,

(e) that the good works of another can make one godly or save one from God's wrath,

(f) that the Mass, by the outward act, can take away the sins of the living or the dead,

(g) that without God's word or command a self-chosen worship as a way of holiness can be established, and

(h) that worship consists of using candles, vessels, or images.

2. The second category divorces the Holy Spirit from the means of grace and thereby sets aside the ministry of the Gospel that Jesus instituted. It teaches that the Holy Spirit comes through an inner experience, by one's own preparation and works, and apart from the Word of God and the Sacraments.

It can be said of both categories of false worship that they have erred by not rightly teaching the Word of God and by not administering the Sacraments in the way that Christ gave them. Thus, their worship of God is a false worship, unacceptable to God.

In contrast, the true worship of God (*cultus Dei, Gottesdienst*) consists of "godly, useful, and clear doctrine, the devout use of the sacraments, ardent prayer, and the like" (Ap XXIV, 51).

DO THOSE WHO HAVE NO FAITH IN CHRIST REALLY WORSHIP WHEN THEY PERFORM AN ACT THAT SEEMS TO BE GODLY?

132 But without the Holy Spirit the human heart either despises the judgment of God in its complacency or in the face of punishment flees and hates God who judges them. Thus it does not obey the first table. Therefore since these things (contempt for God, doubt about the Word of God and about its threats and promises) cling to human nature, people truly sin even when they do respectable works without the Holy Spirit, because they do them with a godless heart, according to the text [Rom. 14:23], "Whatever does not proceed from faith is sin." Such people perform their works with contempt for God, just as when Epicurus did not think that God cared for him, paid attention to him, or heard his prayer. This contempt for God corrupts works that appear to be honorable, because God judges the heart.

Apology IV, 34–35

133 These three articles of the Creed, therefore, separate and distinguish us Christians from all other people on earth. All who are outside this Christian people, whether heathen, Turks, Jews, or false Christians and hypocrites—even though they believe in and worship only the one, true God[1]—nevertheless do not know what his attitude is toward them. They cannot be confident of his love and blessing, and therefore they remain in eternal wrath and condemnation. For they do not have the LORD Christ, and, besides, they are not illuminated and blessed by the gifts of the Holy Spirit.

[1]G: *Denn was außer der Christenheit ist, es seien Heiden, Türken, Jüden oder falsche Christen und Heuchler, ob sie gleich nur einen wahrhaftigen Gott gläuben und anbeten*; L: *Quicumque enim extra christianitatem sunt, sive gentiles, sive Turcae, sive Judaei aut falsi etiam christiani et hypocritae, quamquam unum tantum et verum Deum esse credant et invocent.*

Luther uses the indefinite article *einen* with a subject that should otherwise have the definite article *den*: "a one true god." The Latin text uses the subjunctive forms for "believe in and worship," indicating somone else's claim without admitting that it is true. Because the Latin uses the subjunctive, it is likely that the German uses the subjunctive of indirect discourse, which looks like the indicative in the third person plural. The larger argument and use of grammar suggest that Luther does not claim that those outside Christianity worship *the one true God* but a god *that they call* "*one and true*." Neither the Jacobs edition nor *Concordia Triglotta* translates *einen*. Tappert and Kolb/Wengert translate *einen* as "the."

Large Catechism II, 66

134 [W]e believe and teach that there is one divine essence, undivided, etc., and that there are nevertheless three distinct and coeternal persons of the same divine essence, Father, Son, and Holy Spirit. We have always taught and defended this article, maintaining that its testimonies in the Holy Scriptures are solid, firm, and cannot be overthrown. And we constantly affirm that those who believe otherwise stand outside the church of Christ,[1] are idolaters, and regard God with contempt.

[1]L: *Et constanter affirmamus, aliter sentientes extra ecclesiam Christi . . . esse*; G: *Darumb schließen wir frei, daß alle diejenigen . . . außerhalb der Kirchen Christi sein, die da anders halten oder lehren.*

Apology I, 1–2

135 For example, the pagans, who put their trust in power and dominion, exalted Jupiter as their supreme god. Others, who strove for riches, happiness, pleasure, and the good life, venerated Hercules, Mercury, Venus, or others, while pregnant women worshiped Diana or Lucina, and so forth. They all made a god out of what their heart most desired. Even in the mind of all the pagan, therefore, to have a god means to trust and believe. The trouble is that their trust is false and wrong, for it is not placed in the one God, apart from whom there truly is no god in heaven or on earth. Accordingly the pagans actually fashion their own fancies and dreams about God into an idol and rely on an empty nothing. So it is with all idolatry. Idolatry does not consist merely of erecting an image and praying to it, but it is primarily a matter of the heart,[1] which fixes its gaze upon other things and seeks help and consolation from creatures, saints, or devils. It neither cares for God nor expects good things from him sufficiently to trust that he wants to help, nor does it believe that whatever good it encounters comes from God.

[1]G: *denn sie stehet nicht allein darin, daß man ein Bild aufrichtet und anbetet, sondern fürnemlich im Herzen*; L: *Neque enim in hoc solo consistit, ut simulacrum aliquod erectum adoretur, sed in corde latet.*

Large Catechism I, 18–21

136 The human will possesses freedom regarding works and matters that reason can comprehend by itself. It can to some extent produce civil righteousness or the righteousness of works. It can talk about God and offer God acts of worship with external works; it can obey rulers and parents. By choosing an external work it can keep back the hand from murder, adultery, and theft. Because human nature still retains reason and judgment concerning things subject to the senses, it also retains the ability to choose in such matters, as well as the freedom and ability to achieve civil righteousness. For Scripture calls this the righteousness of the flesh, which carnal nature (that is, reason) produces by itself apart from the Holy Spirit. . . .

However, it is false to say that people do not sin when they do the works prescribed by the law outside of grace. Furthermore, they also add that the forgiveness of sins and justification *are necessarily due for such works*. For apart from the Holy Spirit human hearts lack the fear of God and trust in God.[1] They do not believe that God hears their prayers, forgives them, or helps and preserves them. Therefore they are ungodly; for a bad tree cannot bear good fruit [Matt. 7:18], and "without faith it is impossible to please God" [Heb. 11:6].

Therefore, even though we concede to free will the freedom and power to perform external works of the law, nevertheless we do not ascribe to free will those spiritual capacities, namely, true fear of God, true faith in God, the conviction and knowledge that God cares for us, hears us, and forgives us, etc.[2] These are the real works of the first table, which the human heart cannot produce without the Holy Spirit, just as Paul says [1 Cor. 2:14]: "Those who are natural," that is, those who use only their natural powers, "do not perceive the things which are of God."

[1]L: *sine timore Dei, sine fiducia erga Deum*; G: *ohne Gottes Furcht, ohne Glauben*.

[2]L: *tamen illa spiritualia non tribuimus libero arbitrio, scilicet vere timere Deum, vere credere Deo, vere statuere ac sentire, quod Deus nos respiciat, exaudiat, ignoscat nobis etc.*; G: *so sagen wir doch, daß der freie Wille und Vernunft in geistlichen Sachen nichts vermag, nämlich Gott wahrlich gläuben, gewiß sich zu verlassen, daß Gott bei uns sei, uns erhöre, unsere Sunde vergebe &c.*

Apology XVIII, 4, 6–7

137 Now the rest are eucharistic sacrifices,[1] which are called "sacrifices of praise," namely, the preaching of the gospel, faith, prayer, thanksgiving, confession, the afflictions of the saints, and indeed, all the good works of the saints. These sacrifices are not satisfactions for those who offer them, nor can they be applied to others so as to merit the forgiveness of sins or reconciliation for others *ex opere operato*. They are performed by those who are already reconciled.

These are the sacrifices of the New Testament,[2] as Peter teaches [1 Peter 2:5], "a holy priesthood, to offer spiritual sacrifices."[3] Spiritual sacrifices,[4] however, are contrasted not only with animal sacrifices but also with human works offered *ex opere operato*, because "spiritual" refers to the work of the Holy Spirit within us. Paul teaches the same thing in Romans 12[:1]: "[P]resent your bodies as a living sacrifice, holy and acceptable to God, which is your spiritual worship."[5] "Spiritual worship" refers to worship where God is recognized[6] and is grasped by the mind, as happens when it fears and trusts God. Therefore, it is contrasted not only to Levitical worship,[7] in which animals were slain, but with any worship in which people imagine that they are offering God a work *ex opere operato*.[8] The Epistle to the Hebrews, chapter 13[:15], teaches the same thing, "Through him, then, let us continually offer a sacrifice of praise to God,"[9] and it adds an interpretation, "that is, the fruit of lips that confess his name."[10] He commands us to offer praises,[11] that is, prayer, thanksgiving, confession, and the like.[12] These avail not *ex opere operato* but on account of faith. This is stressed by the phrase, "through him let us offer," that is, by faith in Christ.

In summary, the worship of the New Testament is spiritual,[13] that is, it is the righteousness of faith in the heart and the fruits of faith. Accordingly, it abrogates the Levitical worship.[14]

[1]L: *Nunc reliqua sunt sacrificia εὐχαριστικά*; G: . . . *die sind alle nur Dankopfer*.

[2]L: *Et talia sunt sacrificia novi testamenti*; G: *Und solch Opfer sind unser Opfer im neuen Testament*.

[3]L: *hostias spirituales*; G: *geistliche Opfer*.

[4]L: *hostiae spirituales*.

The last six sentences of this paragraph are not included in the German translation.

[5]L: *Exhibete corpora vestra hostiam viventem, sanctam, cultum rationalem*.

[6]L: *Significat autem cultus rationalis cultum, in quo Deus intelligitur*.

[7]L: *cultui levitico*.

[8]L: *sed etiam cultui, in quo fingitur opus ex opere operato offerri*.

[9]L: *hostiam laudis semper Deo*.

[10]L:.*fructum labiorum confitentium nomini eius*.

[11]L: *Iubet offerre laudes*.

[12]L: *invocationem, gratiarum actionem, confessionem et similia*.

[13]L: *cultus novi testamenti est spiritualis*; G: *Und im neuen Testament gilt kein Opfer ex opere operato sine bono motu utentis*.

[14]L: *leviticos cultus*.

Apology XXIV, 25–27

138 Accordingly, with the abrogation of Levitical worship,[1] the New Testament teaches that new and pure sacrifices will be made,[2] namely, faith, prayer, thanksgiving, confession, the preaching of the gospel, suffering on account of the gospel, and similar things.[3]

[1]L: *cultibus leviticis*; G: *die Opfer des Gesetzes Mosi.*

[2]L: *ut nova et munda sacrificia fiant*; G: *sein eitel reine Opfer ohne Makel.*

[3]L: *fides, invocatio, gratiarum actio, confessio et praedicatio evangelii, afflictiones propter evangelium et similia*; G: *der Glauben gegen Gott, Danksagung, Gottes Lob, Predigt des Evangelii, Kreuz und Leiden der Heiligen und dergleichen.*

Apology XXIV, 30

Summary

- A person who has no faith in Jesus Christ may be able to render civil righteousness or utter words that honor God. However, this is not a spiritual act acceptable to God, for it is rendered without the Holy Spirit. It does not rest on what God promises and does not rely on his Christ. The outward act is done without the fear of God in the heart; "without faith it is impossible to please God" (Hebrews 11:6). It is not worship of God.
- The New Testament teaches that a believer's "sacrifice of praise" (faith, prayer, thanksgiving, confession, etc.) is made on account of faith in Christ and the fear and trust of God that the Holy Spirit works in the heart.

Sections 139–154 on human traditions and 155–159 on rites and ceremonies are explored further in chapter 8.

Where do human traditions fit in the worship of God?

139 In the Old Testament, God set apart the seventh day, appointed it for rest, and commanded it to be kept holy above all other days. As far as outward observance is concerned,[1] the commandment was given to the Jews alone. They were to refrain from hard work and to rest, so that both human beings and animals might be refreshed and not be exhausted by constant labor. In time, however, the Jews interpreted this commandment too narrowly and grossly misused it. They slandered Christ and would not permit him to do the very same things they themselves did on that day, as we read in the gospel—as if the commandment could be fulfilled by refraining from work of any kind. This was not its intention, but rather, as we shall hear, it meant that we should sanctify the holy day or day of rest.

Therefore, according to its outward meaning, this commandment does not concern us Christians. It is an entirely external matter, like the other regulations of the Old Testament associated with particular customs, persons, times, and places, from all of which we are now set free through Christ.[2] . . . Second and most important, we observe them so that people will have time and opportunity on such days of rest, which otherwise would not be available, to attend worship services,[3] that is, so that they may assemble to hear and discuss God's Word and then to offer praise, song, and prayer to God.

[1]G: *dieser äußerlichen Feier nach*; L: *Ejus . . . externae.*

[2]G: *an sonderliche Weise, Person, Zeit und Stätte gebunden*; L: *certis quibusdam ritibus, personis, temporibus et locis destinatae.*

[3]G: *an solchem Rugetage . . . Raum und Zeit nehme, Gottesdiensts zu warten*; L: *die sabbati . . . otium et tempus sumatur cultui divino serviendi ita.*

Large Catechism I, 80–82, 84

140 **[German text]** In Matthew 15[:14] Christ himself also speaks of those who drive the people to human commandments: "Let them alone; they are blind guides of the blind." And he rejects such service of God,[1] saying [Matt. 15:13]: "Every plant that my heavenly Father has not planted will be uprooted."

If, then, bishops have the power to burden the churches with innumerable ordinances and to ensnare consciences, why does divine Scripture so frequently prohibit the making and keeping of human ordinances? Why does it call them teachings of the devil? Could the Holy Spirit possibly have warned against all this in vain?

Inasmuch as it is contrary to the gospel to establish such regulations as necessary[2] to appease God and earn grace, it is not at all proper for the bishops to compel observation of such services of God.[3] For in Christendom the teaching of Christian freedom must be preserved, namely, that bondage to the law is not necessary for justification, as Paul writes in Galatians 5[:1]: "For freedom Christ has set us free. Stand firm, therefore, and do not submit again to the yoke of slavery." For the chief article of the gospel must be maintained, that we obtain the grace of God through faith in Christ without our merit and do not earn it through service of God instituted by human beings.[4]

[Latin text] Christ says in Matthew 15[:14], concerning those who require traditions: "Let them alone; they are blind guides of the blind." And he rejects such acts of worship[1] [Matt. 15:13]: "Every plant that my heavenly Father has not planted will be uprooted."

If bishops have the right to burden consciences with such traditions, why does Scripture so often prohibit the establishment of traditions? Why does it call them teachings of demons? Did the Holy Spirit warn against them in vain?

Therefore, it follows that it is not lawful for bishops to institute such acts of worship or require them as necessary,[2] because ordinances[3] that are instituted as necessary or with the intention of meriting justification conflict with the gospel. For it is necessary to retain the teaching concerning Christian freedom in the churches, that bondage to the law is not necessary for justification, as it is written in Galatians [5:1]: "Do not submit again to a yoke of slavery." It is necessary to retain the chief article of the gospel: that we obtain grace through faith in Christ, not through certain observances or through acts of worship instituted by human beings.[4]

[1]G: *verwirft solche Gottesdienst*; L: *improbat tales cultus*.

[2]G: *solche Ordnung als notig aufgericht*; L: *cum ordinationes, institutae tamquam necessariae*.

[3]G: *solche Gottesdienste*; L: *tales cultus*.

[4]G: *nicht durch Gottsdienst, von Menschen eingesetzt, verdienen*; L: *non . . . per cultus ab hominibus institutos*.

Augsburg Confession XXVIII, 47–52

141 **[German text]** Not a single canon with the order to receive only one kind can be found.[1] Nobody knows when or through whom this custom of receiving only one kind was introduced, although Cardinal Cusanus mentions when this custom was formally approved. Now it is obvious that this custom, introduced contrary to God's command and to the ancient canons, is not right. Accordingly, it was not proper to burden the consciences of those who desired to use the sacrament according to Christ's institution and to compel them to act contrary to the order of our Lord Christ. Furthermore, because dividing the sacrament contradicts Christ's institution,[2] the customary procession with the sacrament has also been discontinued.

[Latin text] Only a quite recent custom holds otherwise. However, it is evident that a custom, introduced contrary to the commands of God, must not be approved,[1] as the canons testify (dist. 8, chap., "Concerning the Truth," and the subsequent chapters). In fact, this custom has been accepted not only in defiance of Scripture but also in opposition to the ancient canons and the example of the church. Accordingly, if persons preferred to use both kinds in the sacrament, they should not have been compelled with offense to their conscience to do otherwise. Because dividing the sacrament does not agree with the institution of Christ,[2] the procession, which has been customary up to now, is also omitted among us.

[1]G: *Man findet auch nindert keinen Canon, der do gebiete, allein ein Gestalt zu nehmen*; L: *quod consuetudo contra mandata Dei introducta non sit probanda.*

[2]G: *Und dieweil die Teilung des Sakraments der Einsetzung Christi zuentgegen ist*; L: *quia divisio sacramenti non convenit cum institutione Christi.*

Augsburg Confession XXII, 8–12

142 **[German text]** Bishops could easily foster obedience if they did not insist on the observance of ordinances that cannot be observed without sin.

[Latin text] However, the bishops could easily retain lawful obedience if they did not insist on keeping traditions that cannot be observed with a good conscience.

Augsburg Confession XXVIII, 69

143 **[German text]** Now, because previously the Mass was misused in many ways (as has come to light) by turning it into a fair, by buying and selling it, and, for the most part, by celebrating it in all churches for money, such misuse was repeatedly rebuked by learned and upright people—even before our time. Now the preachers among us preached about this, and the priests were reminded of the terrible responsibility, which should properly concern every Christian, that whoever uses the sacrament unworthily is "answerable for the body and blood" of Christ [1 Cor. 11:27]. Consequently, such mercenary

Masses and private Masses, which had up to now been celebrated under compulsion for the sake of money and stipends, were discontinued in our churches.[1]

[Latin text] However, for a long time there has been a serious public outcry by good people that Masses were being shamefully profaned and devoted to profit. It is public knowledge how widely this abuse extends in all places of worship, what kind of people celebrate Masses only for a revenue or stipend, and how many celebrate contrary to the canons' prohibitions. But Paul severely threatens those who treat the Eucharist unworthily, when he says [1 Cor. 11:27], "Whoever, therefore, eats the bread or drinks the cup of the Lord in an unworthy manner will be answerable for the body and blood of the Lord." Accordingly, when the priests among us were instructed concerning this sin, private Masses were discontinued among us, since there were hardly any private Masses held except for the sake of profit.[1]

[1]G: *darauf seind solche Kaufmeß und Winkelmeß, welche bis anher aus Zwang und Geldes und der Präbenden willen gehalten worden, in unseren Kirchen gefallen*; L: *Itaque cum apud nos admonerentur sacerdotes de hoc peccato, desierunt apud nos privatae missae, cum fere nullae privatae missae nisi quaestus causa fierent.*

Augsburg Confession XXIV, 10–13

144 **[German text]** In former times it was taught, preached, and written that distinction among foods[1] and similar traditions instituted by human beings serve to earn grace and make satisfaction for sin. For this reason, new fasts, new ceremonies, new monastic orders, and the like were invented daily. They were fervently and strictly promoted, as if such things were a necessary service of God whereby people earned grace[2] if they observed them or committed a great sin if they did not. Many harmful errors in the church have resulted from this.

[Latin text] It has been a general conviction, not only of the people but also of those who teach in the churches, that distinction of foods[1] and similar human traditions are useful works for meriting grace and making satisfaction for sins. That the world thought so is evident from the fact that daily new ceremonies, new ordinances, new holy days, and new fasts were instituted and that the teachers in places of worship exacted these works as necessary worship for meriting grace[2] and viciously terrified consciences if people omitted any of them. Much misfortune has ensued in the church from this conviction concerning traditions.

[1]G: *Unterschied der Speise*; L: *discrimina ciborum.*

[2]G: *als seien solche Dinge notige Gottesdienst, dardurch man Gnad vordien*; L: *haec opera tamquam necessarium cultum ad promerendam gratiam.*

Augsburg Confession XXVI, 1–2

145 **[German text]** It was pretended that monastic vows would be equal to baptism, and that through monastic life one could earn forgiveness of sin and justification before God. Indeed, they added that one earns through monastic life not only righteousness and innocence, but also that through it one keeps the commands and counsels written in the gospel. In this way monastic vows were praised more highly than baptism. It was also said that one could obtain more merit through the monastic life than through all other walks of life, which had been ordered by God, such as the office of pastor or preacher, the office of ruler, prince, lord, and the like. (These all serve in their vocations according to God's command, Word, and mandate without any contrived spiritual status.)[1] None of these things can be denied, for one can find them in their own books.

[Latin text] People said that vows were equal to baptism, and they taught that vows merited forgiveness of sins and justification before God through this kind of life. Indeed, they added that monastic life merited not only righteousness before God but even more: that it kept not only precepts but also the Evangelical counsels. In this way they were convinced that the monastic profession was far better than baptism and that the monastic life was more meritorious than the life of magistrates, pastors, and the like, who are subject to God's commands in their callings without artificial religious observance.[1] None of these things can be denied, for they appear in their books.

[1]G: *die alle nach Gottes Gebot, Wort und Befehl ihrem Beruf ohn erdichte Geistlichkeit dienen*; L: *qui sine facticiis religionibus in mandatis Dei suae vocationi serviunt.*

Augsburg Confession XXVII, 11–14

146 **[German text]** Now it is patently contrary to God's command and Word to make laws out of opinions or to require that by observing them a person makes satisfaction for sin and obtains grace. For the honor of Christ's merit is slandered when we take it upon ourselves to earn grace through such ordinances. It is also obvious that, because of this notion, human ordinances have multiplied beyond calculation while the teaching concerning faith and the righteousness of faith have been almost completely suppressed. Daily new festivals and new fasts have been commanded; new ceremonies and new venerations of the saints have been instituted[1] in order that by such works grace and everything good might be earned from God.

Moreover, those who institute human ordinances also act contrary to God's command when they attach sin to food, days, and similar things and burden Christendom with bondage to the law, as if in order to earn God's grace there had to be such service of God among Christians like the Levitical service,[2] which God supposedly commanded the apostles and bishops to establish, as some have written.

[Latin text] Furthermore, it is contrary to Scripture to establish traditions in order that, by observing them, we may make satisfaction for sins and merit justification. For the glory of Christ's merit is violated when we think that we are justified by such observances. However, it is evident that because of this notion countless traditions have arisen in the church, while the teaching concerning faith and the righteousness of faith has been suppressed. For repeatedly more holy days were created, fasts were announced, and new ceremonies and orders were instituted,[1] because the authors of these things imagined that they merited grace through such works. So the penitential canons increased in former times, and we can still see traces of them in the satisfactions.

Again, the authors of traditions act contrary to the command of God when they attach sin to food, days, and similar things and burden the church with the bondage of the law, as if, in order to merit justification, there had to be acts of worship among Christians similar to the Levitical ones,[2] and as if God had commissioned the apostles and bishops to institute them.

[1]G: *Man hat täglich neue Feiertag, neue Fasten geboten, neue Ceremonien und neue Ehrerbietung der Heiligen eingefaßt*; L: *quia subinde plures feriae factae sunt, ieiunia indicta, caerimoniae novae, ordines novi instituti.*

[2]G: *eben als mußte bei den Christen ein solcher Gottesdienst sein, Gotts Gnad zu verdienen, der gleich wäre dem levitischen Gottsdienst*; L: *quasi oporteat apud chistianos ad promerendam iustificationem cultum esse similem levitico.*

Augsburg Confession XXVIII, 35–39

147 [W]e unanimously believe, teach, and confess that ceremonies or ecclesiastical practices[1] that are neither commanded nor forbidden in God's Word, but have been established only for good order and decorum, are in and of themselves neither worship ordained by God nor a part of such worship.[2] "In vain do they worship me" with human precepts (Matt. 15[:9]).

[1]G: *die Ceremonien oder Kirchengebräuch*; L: *ceremoniae sive ritus ecclesiastici.*

[2]G: *an ihnen und für sich selbst kein Gottesdienst, auch kein Teil desselben seien*; L: *per se cultus divinus aut aliqua saltem pars cultus divini.*

Formula of Concord, Epitome X, 3

148 The question is whether or not the observances of human traditions are religious worship[1] necessary for righteousness before God. This is the point at issue in this controversy. Once it has been decided, it will be possible to decide whether for the true unity of the church it is necessary to have similar human traditions everywhere. For if human traditions are not acts of worship[2] necessary for righteousness before God, it follows that it is possible to be righteous and children of God even if a person does not observe the traditions that have been maintained elsewhere. Analogously, if the style of German clothing is not an act of devotion to God necessary[3] for righteousness before God, it follows that it is possible to be righteous and children of God and the church of Christ even if they wear not German, but French clothing.

[1]L: *cultus*; G: *Gottesdienst.*

[2]L: *cultus*; G: *Gottesdienst.*

[3]L: *cultus Dei necessarius*; G: *ein nötiger Gottesdienst.*

Apology VII–VIII, 34

149 For in such a case it is no longer a matter of external adiaphora,[1] which in their nature and essence are and remain in and of themselves free, which accordingly are not subject to either a command or a prohibition regarding their use or discontinuance. Instead, here it is above all a matter of the chief article of our Christian faith, as the Apostle testifies, "so that the truth of the gospel might always remain" [Gal. 2:5]. Such coercion and command obscure and pervert the truth of the gospel, because either these opponents will publicly demand such indifferent things as a confirmation of false teaching, superstition, and idolatry and for the purpose of suppressing pure teaching and Christian freedom, or they will misuse them and as a result falsely reinstitute them.

At the same time, this also concerns the article on Christian freedom. With deep concern the Holy Spirit, through the mouth of the holy Apostle, has commanded his church to maintain this freedom [Gal. 5:1, 13; 2:4], as we have just heard. For weakening this article and forcing human commands upon the church as necessary—as if their omission were wrong and sinful—already paves the way to idolatry. Through it human commands will ultimately increase and will be regarded as service to God[2] equal to that which God has commanded; even worse, they will even be given precedence over what he has commanded.

Thus, submission and compromise in external things[3] where Christian agreement in doctrine has not already been achieved strengthens idolaters in their idolatry. On the other hand, this grieves and offends faithful believers and weakens their faith. Christians are bound to avoid both for the welfare and salvation of their souls, as it is written, "Woe to the world because of stumbling blocks" [Matt. 18:7], and, "If any of you put a stumbling block before one of these little ones who believe in me, it would be better for you if a great millstone were fastened around your neck and you were drowned in the depth of the sea" [Matt. 18:6].

[1]G: *umb die äusserlichen Mitteldinge zu tun*; L: *de externis adiaphoris agitur*.

[2]G: *für ein Gottesdienst*; L: *pro cultu divino*.

[3]G: *durch solch Nachgeben und Vorgleichen in äusserlichen Dingen*; L: *eiusmodi intempestiva cessione in externis illis rebus adiaphoris*.

Formula of Concord, Solid Declaration X, 14–16

150 **[German text]** In the second place, such traditions have also obscured God's commands. For these traditions are placed far above God's commands.[1] This alone was considered the Christian life: whoever observed festivals this way, prayed in this way, fasted in this way, and was dressed in this way was said to live a spiritual, Christian life.[2] On the other hand, other necessary good works were considered secular, unspiritual ways of life: that each person is obliged to act according to his or her calling—for example, that the father of a family works to support his wife and children and raises them in the fear of God; that the mother of a family bears children and looks after them; that a prince or rulers govern a country; etc. Such works, commanded by

God, had to be a "secular and imperfect" way of life, while the traditions had to have impressive names, so that only they were called "holy and perfect" works.[3] That is why there was no end or limit in the making of such traditions.[4]

[Latin text] In the second place, these traditions obscured the precepts of God because traditions were preferred far more than the precepts of God.[1] All Christianity was thought to consist of the observance of certain holy days, rites, fasts, and vestments.[2] These observances possessed the most distinguished titles because they were the "spiritual life" and the "perfect life."[3] Meanwhile the commands of God pertaining to one's calling were not praised: that the head of the household should rear the children, that a mother should bear them, that a prince should govern his country. These were considered as "worldly" and "imperfect" works, far inferior to those splendid observances. This error greatly tormented pious consciences. They grieved that they were bound to an imperfect kind of life: in marriage, in government, or in other civil functions. They admired the monks and others like them and falsely imagined that the observances[4] of such people were more pleasing to God.

[1]G: *dann man setzt diese Traditiones weit über Gottes Gebot*; L: *quia traditiones longe praeferebantur praeceptis.*

[2]G: *Dies hielt man allein fur christlich Leben: wer die Feier also hielte, also betet, also fastet, also gekleidet wäre, das nennete man geistlich, christlich leben*; L: *Christianismus totus putabatur esse observatio certarum feriarum, rituum, ieiuniorum, vestitus.*

[3]G: *daß sie allein heilige, vollkommene Werke hießen*; L: *vita spiritualis et vita perfecta.*

[4]G: *Traditiones*; L: *observationes.*

Augsburg Confession XXVI, 8–11

151 We believe, teach, and confess that in a time of persecution, when an unequivocal confession of the faith is demanded of us, we dare not yield to the opponents in such indifferent matters. As the Apostle wrote, "Stand firm in the freedom for which Christ has set us free, and do not submit again to a yoke of slavery" [Gal. 5:1]. And: "Do not put on the yoke of the others; what partnership is there between light and darkness?" [2 Cor. 6:14]. "So that the truth of the gospel might always remain with you, we did not submit to them even for a moment" [Gal. 2:5]. For in such a situation it is no longer indifferent matters that are at stake. The truth of the gospel and Christian freedom are at stake. The confirmation of open idolatry,[1] as well as the protection of the weak in faith from offense, is at stake. In such matters we can make no concessions but must offer an unequivocal confession and suffer whatever God sends and permits the enemies of his Word to inflict on us.

[1]G: *sondern umb die Wahrheit des Evangelii, umb die christliche Freiheit und umb die Bestätigung öffentlicher Abgötterei*; L: *de veritate evangelii et de libertate Christiana sarta tectaque conservanda et quomodo cavendum sit, ne manifeste idololatria confirmetur.*

Formula of Concord, Epitome X, 6

152 **[German text]** It is also taught that at all times there must be and remain one holy, Christian church. It is the assembly of all believers among whom the gospel is purely preached and the holy sacraments are administered according to the gospel.

For this is enough for the true unity of the Christian church that there the gospel is preached harmoniously according to a pure understanding and the sacraments are administered in conformity with the divine Word. It is not necessary for the true unity of the Christian church that uniform ceremonies, instituted by human beings, be observed everywhere.[1] As Paul says in Ephesians 4[:4–5]: "There is one body and one Spirit, just as you were called to the one hope of your calling, one Lord, one faith, one baptism."

[Latin text] Likewise, they teach that one holy church will remain forever. The church is the assembly of saints in which the gospel is taught purely and the sacraments are administered rightly. And it is enough for the true unity of the church to agree concerning the teaching of the gospel and the administration of the sacraments. It is not necessary that human traditions, rites, or ceremonies instituted by human beings be alike everywhere.[1] As Paul says [Eph. 4:5, 6]: "One faith, one baptism, one God and Father of all . . ."

[1]G: *Und ist nicht not zur wahren Einigkeit der christlichen Kirche, daß allenthalben gleichformige Ceremonien, von den Menschen eingesetzt, gehalten werden*; L: *Nec necesse est ubique similes esse traditiones humanas seu ritus aut cerimonias ab hominibus institutas.*

Augsburg Confession VII, 1–3

153 **[German text]** Such regulation belongs rightfully in the Christian assembly for the sake of love and peace,[1] to be obedient to bishops and pastors in such cases, and to keep such order to the extent that no one offends another—so that there may not be disorder or unruly conduct in the church. However, consciences should not be burdened by holding that such things are necessary for salvation or by considering it a sin when they are violated without giving offense to others; just as no one would say that a woman commits a sin if, without offending people, she leaves the house with her head uncovered.

The same applies to the regulation of Sunday, Easter, Pentecost, or similar festivals and customs.[2] For those who think that the sabbath had to be replaced by Sunday are very much mistaken. For Holy Scripture did away with the sabbath, and it teaches that after the revelation of the gospel all ceremonies of the old law may be given up. Nevertheless, the Christian church instituted Sunday because it became necessary to set apart a specific day so that the people might know when to assemble; and the church was all the more pleased and inclined to do this so that the people might have an example of Christian freedom and so that everyone would know that neither the keeping of the sabbath nor any other day is necessary.

[Latin text] It is fitting for the churches to comply with such ordinances for the sake of love and tranquillity and to keep them[1] insofar as they do not offend others. Thus, everything may be done in an orderly fashion in the churches without confusion, but in such a way that consciences are not burdened by thinking such things are necessary for salvation or that they sin when violating them without offense. Just as no one would say that a woman commits a sin by leaving the house with her head uncovered in an inoffensive way.

Such is the case with the observance of Sunday, Easter, Pentecost, and similar festivals and rites.[2] For those who judge that the necessary observance of Sunday in place of the sabbath was instituted by the church's authority are mistaken. Scripture, not the church, abrogated the sabbath. For after the revelation of the gospel all Mosaic ceremonies can be omitted. Yet, since it was necessary to establish a certain day so that the people would know when they should assemble, it appears that the church designated Sunday for this purpose. Apparently, this was even more pleasing because people would have an example of Christian freedom and would know that it was not necessary to keep either the sabbath or any other day.

[1]G: *Solch Ordnung gebuhrt der christlichen Versamblung umb der Lieb und Friedes willen zu halten*; L: *Talibus ordinationibus convenit ecclesias propter caritatem et tranquillitatem obtemperare easque servare eatenus.*

[2]G: *Also ist die Ordnung vom Sonntag, von der Osterfeier, von den Pfingsten und dergleichen Feier und Weise*; L: *Talis est observatio diei dominici, paschatis, pentecostes et similium feriarum et rituum.*

Augsburg Confession XXVIII, 55–60

154 **[German text]** Our side also retains many ceremonies and traditions, such as the order of the Mass and other singing, festivals, and the like, which serve to preserve order in the church.[1] At the same time, however, the people are taught that such external worship of God does not make them righteous before God and that it is to be observed without burdening consciences, that is, no one sins by omitting it without causing offense. The ancient Fathers also maintained such liberty with respect to external ceremonies.[2]

[Latin text] Nevertheless, many traditions are kept among us, such as the order of readings in the Mass, holy days, etc., which are conducive to maintaining good order in the church.[1] But at the same time, people are warned that such acts of worship do not justify before God and that no punishable sin is committed if they are omitted without offense. Such freedom in human rites[2] was not unknown to the Fathers.

[1]G: *Auch werden dieses Teils viel Ceremonien und Tradition gehalten, als Ordnung der Messe und andere Gesäng, Feste etc., welche darzu dienen, daß in der Kirchen Ordnung gehalten werde.* L: *Servantur tamen apud nos pleraeque traditiones, ut ordo lectionum in missa, feriae etc., quae conducunt ad hoc, ut res ordine geratur in ecclesia.*

[2]G: *Diese Freiheit in äußerlichen Ceremonien*; L: *Haec libertas in ritibus humanis.*

Augsburg Confession XXVI, 40–42

SUMMARY

- Christ has freed New Testament believers from the Old Testament system of worship given through Moses.
- It is against Scripture to compel Christians to observe humanly designed ordinances that become a bondage of the Law or require anything that is contrary to the command of Christ or the Gospel

(such as distributing only the bread at Holy Communion or making processions with it or the practice of private Masses for fees). A humanly invented tradition cannot merit grace, cannot be more beneficial than what God commands, and must not suppress, obscure, or pervert faith and the righteousness of faith. It does not justify before God. It is no "divine worship"; it is not an act of worship that is required nor is it necessary for the true unity of the church.

- However, Christians do have the freedom to observe human traditions such as Sunday, Easter, Pentecost, and other holy days and rites when they are used in love, contribute to order and tranquility, do not offend, and can be used without confusion.
- Furthermore, in times of persecution, when a clear confession of faith is needed, Christians dare not—so as to preserve the Gospel and prevent offending the weak—yield on indifferent things (adiaphora), though they are human inventions.

HOW DO RITES AND CEREMONIES CONTRIBUTE TO CHRISTIAN WORSHIP?

155 But Christ was given for this very purpose: that on account of him the forgiveness of sins and the Holy Spirit, who produces in us a new and eternal life and also eternal righteousness, may be given to us. *First, the Spirit reveals Christ, just as it is written in John 16[:14], "He will glorify me, because he will take what is mine and declare it to you." Then he also brings the other gifts: love, prayer, thanksgiving, chastity, endurance, etc.*

Therefore we cannot truly keep the law until we have received the Holy Spirit through faith [John 16:15]. Therefore Paul states that the law is established, not abolished, through faith, because the law can be kept only when the Holy Spirit is given. And Paul teaches in 2 Corinthians 3[:15] that the veil, by which the face of Moses was covered, cannot be removed except by faith in Christ, by which the Holy Spirit is received. For this is what he says, "Indeed, to this very day whenever Moses is read, a veil lies over their minds; but when one turns to the Lord, the veil is removed. Now the Lord is the Spirit, and where the Spirit of the Lord is, there is freedom" [3:15–17]. Paul understands the "veil" to be human opinion about the entire law (the Decalogue and ceremonial laws), as when hypocrites suppose that external and civil works satisfy the law of God and that sacrifices and rituals justify before God *ex opere operato*.[1]

[1]L: *et sacrificia et cultus ex opere operato iustificare coram Deo*; G: *und als machen die Opfer, item allerlei Gottesdienst ex opere operato jemands gerecht für Gott.*

Apology IV, 132–134
Italicized text was added in the octavo edition.

156 Now if someone wants to institute certain works for the purpose of meriting the forgiveness of sins or righteousness, how will that person know that these works please God without the testimony of God's Word? How will they make others certain about God's will without God's command and Word? Does not God throughout the prophets prohibit people from instituting peculiar rites of worship[1] without his command? In Ezekiel 20[:18–19], it is written, "Do not follow the statutes of your parents, nor observe their ordinances, nor defile yourselves with their idols. I the Lord am your God; follow my statutes, and be careful to observe my ordinances." If people are allowed to establish acts of worship[2] and to merit grace through such acts of worship,[3] then the religious rites of all nations[4] will have to be approved—even the acts of worship[5] instituted by Jeroboam [1 Kings 12:26f.] and by others apart from the law. For what is the difference? If we are allowed to establish religious rites[6] that are useful for meriting grace or righteousness, why were the Gentiles and Israelites not allowed to do the same? In fact, the religious rites[7] of the Gentiles and Israelites were condemned because they believed that they merited the forgiveness of sins and righteousness through them, and because they were ignorant of the righteousness of faith.

[1]L: *peculiares cultus*; G: *sonderliche Gottesdienst.*

[2]L: *cultus*; G: *Gottesdienst.*

[3]L: *cultus.*

[4]L: *omnium gentium cultus*; G: *aller Heiden Gottesdienst.*

[5]L: *cultus*; G: *alle Abgötterei.*

[6]L: *cultus utiles*; G: *Gottesdienst.*

[7]L: *cultus improbati*; G: *Dienste.*

Apology XV, 14–16

157 Second and most important, we observe them so that people will have time and opportunity on such days of rest, which otherwise would not be available, to attend worship services,[1] that is, so that they may assemble to hear and discuss God's Word and then to offer praise, song, and prayer to God.

But this, I say, is not restricted, as it was among the Jews, to a particular time so that it must be precisely this day or that, for in itself no one day is better than another. Actually, worship ought to take place daily. However, because this is more than the common people can do, at least one day a week ought to be set apart for it. Because Sunday has been appointed for this purpose from ancient times, it should not be changed, so that things may be done in an orderly fashion and no one create disorder by unnecessary innovation.

[1]G: *Gottesdienst*; L: *cultui divino*.

Large Catechism I, 84–85

158 Furthermore, we gladly keep the ancient traditions[1] set up in the church because they are useful and promote tranquillity, and we interpret them in the best possible way, by excluding the opinion that they justify. But our enemies falsely charge that we abolish good ordinances and church discipline.[2] We can claim that the public liturgy in the church is more dignified among us[3] than among the opponents. If anyone would look at it in the right way, we keep the ancient canons better[4] than the opponents.

[1]L: *Ceterum traditiones veteres factas in ecclesiae . . . servamus*; G: *die ältesten Satzungen aber in der Kirchen . . . halten wir gerne*.

[2]L: *quod bonas ordinationes, quod disciplinam ecclesiae aboleamus*; G: *daß wir alle gute Ceremonien, alle Ordnung in der Kirchen abbringen und niederlegen*.

[3]L: *publicam formam ecclesiarum apud nos honestiorem esse*; G: *daß es christlicher, ehrlicher in unsern Kirchen mit rechten Gottesdiensten gehalten wird*.

[4]L: *verius servamus canones*; G: *so halten wir die alten Canones und mentem legis mehr, reiner und fleissiger*.

Apology XV, 38–39

159 It does not follow from the fact that the Mass is called a sacrifice[1] that it confers grace *ex opere operato* or that when it is transferred to others it merits for them the forgiveness of sins, etc. The word "liturgy" [*leitourgia*] in Greek means sacrifice,[2] they say, and the Greek church calls the Mass the liturgy.[3] Why do they omit here the old term

"Communion," which shows that the Mass was formerly the Communion of many? But let us speak about the term "liturgy."[4] This word does not properly mean a sacrifice[5] but rather public service.[6] Thus, it agrees quite well with our position, namely, that the one minister[7] who consecrates gives the body and blood of the Lord to the rest of the people, just as a minister[8] who preaches sets forth the gospel to the people, as Paul says [1 Cor. 4:1], "Think of us in this way, as servants of Christ[9] and stewards of God's mysteries," that is, of the gospel and the sacraments. And 2 Corinthians 5:20, "So we are ambassadors for Christ, since God is making his appeal through us; we entreat you on behalf of Christ, be reconciled to God. . . ." Thus the term "liturgy" fits well with the ministry.[10] It is an old word, ordinarily used in public civil law. To the Greeks it meant "public responsibilities," like taxes collected for the equipping of a fleet or similar things. As Demosthenes' oration *Leptines* shows, it is completely taken up with public responsibilities and exemptions: "He will say that some unworthy people have found an exemption to avoid public duties [*leitourgia*]." They also used it this way during Roman times, as the rescript of Pertinax, concerning the law of immunity, shows. "Even though the number of children does not excuse parents from all public duties [*leitourgia*] . . ." A commentary on Demosthenes states that "liturgy" is a kind of tax to pay for the expense of the games, the equipping of naval vessels, the care of the school, and similar public responsibilities.

Paul uses the same word for the collection in 2 Corinthians 9[:12]. Taking of the collection not only supplied what the saints needed but also led them to give thanks to God more abundantly, etc. And in Philippians 2[:25], he calls Epaphroditus a *leitourgos*, a "minister to my need,"[11] where Paul certainly does not mean a sacrificer.[12] But there is no need for more testimonies. Anyone who reads the Greek authors can find examples everywhere of how *leitourgia* meant public duties or services.[13] Moreover, because of the diphthong, philologists do not derive it from the *lite*, which means prayers, but from *leita*, which means public goods; thus the verb *leitourgeo* means, "I attend to or I administer public goods."

[1]L: *sacrificium.*

[2]L: *sacrificium.*

[3]L: *liturgiam.*

[4]L: *liturgia.*

[5]L: *sacrificium.*

[6]L: *publicum ministerium.*

[7]L: *minister.*

[8]L: *minister.*

[9]L: *ministros Christi.*

[10]L: *ministerium.*

[11]L: *ministrum necessitatis suae.*

[12]L: *sacrificulus.*

[13]L: *pro publicis oneribus civilibus seu ministeriis.*

Apology XXIV, 78–83

SUMMARY

- Rites and ceremonies are not used as works to satisfy the Law of God. That is what God prohibits. On the contrary, the highest service of God (*cultus Dei, Gottesdienst*) is the righteousness of faith.
- When humanly invented customs, such as gathering on the Lord's Day for Divine Service (to hear God's Word, to receive the Lord's Supper, to praise God, and to pray), are useful innovations for assisting people toward faith and a life of service to God, they should be continued and be interpreted in a Gospel manner.
- A service such as the Mass does not confer God's grace *ex opere operato* or merit remission of sins as some kind of sacrifice to God. It is rather a "liturgy," that is, a public ministry offering the forgiveness of sins, won by Christ, which is conveyed through the means of grace and received by faith.

SYNOPSIS

The Lutheran Confessions address central questions about worship (*cultus Dei, Gottesdienst*), teaching what worship is, what it is not, and how human traditions can be used in the worship of God.

The Confessions teach that worship is a spiritual act, not an outward act. It is a trusting in God and a desiring of the forgiveness, grace, and righteousness of God. The righteousness of faith truly honors and obeys God, for through the Gospel (Word and Sacrament) the Holy Spirit overcomes distrust and creates faith. The Spirit does not come directly, through an inner experience, or by one's own efforts, but he comes through this ministry of the Gospel in teaching the Word of

God and rightly administering the sacraments. Reliance on one's own works as a way of making peace with God has no place in this kind of faith; Christ has earned salvation for us, and God freely and graciously gives it to us. Without faith there can be no worship nor can there be any fruits of faith.

Human traditions are not divine worship, yet when they contribute to order and tranquility and are used in love, without offense or confusion, they may be profitably used. Human traditions are not necessary to salvation; they are not essential to the unity of the church. However, it may be that in times of persecution, for the sake of confessing Christ, it is necessary not to give them up. When used properly, rites and ceremonies contribute to the public ministry of conveying forgiveness of sins that is received by faith. This faith also bears fruit, thanking and serving God.

2

Word

What purpose does the Word of God have?

201 "The coming of God's kingdom to us" takes place in two ways: first, it comes here, in time, through the Word and faith,[1] and second, in eternity, it comes through the final revelation. Now, we ask for both of these things: that it may come to those who are not yet in it and that, by daily growth here and in eternal life hereafter, it may come to us who have attained it. All this is nothing more than to say: "Dear Father, we ask you first to give us your Word,[2] so that the gospel may be properly preached throughout the world and then that it may also be received in faith and may work and dwell in us, so that your kingdom may pervade among us through the Word and the power of the Holy Spirit[3] and the devil's kingdom may be destroyed so that he may have no right or power over us until finally his kingdom is utterly eradicated and sin, death, and hell wiped out, that we may live forever in perfect righteousness and blessedness."

[1]G: *durch das Wort und den Glauben*; L: *per verbum et fidem.*

[2]G: *Lieber Vater . . . gib uns erstlich Dein Wort*; L: *Coelestis ac omnipotens pater, precamur te, ut nobis sub initium tuum verbum impertire digneris.*

[3]G: *durch das Wort und Kraft des heiligen Geists*; L: *per verbum ac virtutem spiritus sancti.*

Large Catechism III, 53–54

202 The reasons for our position against the sacramentarians on this matter are those which Dr. Luther set forth in his *Great Confession*: . . . "The third, that the Word of God is not false or deceitful. . . ."[1]

[1]G: *daß Gottes Wort nicht falsch ist oder lüge*; L: *quod verbum Dei non est falsum aut mendax.*

Formula of Concord, Epitome VII, 10, 13

203 We must carefully distinguish between what is specifically revealed in God's Word concerning this article and what is not.[1] For, beyond what has been said to this point (all of which is revealed in Christ), God has maintained silence and has hidden a great deal related to this mystery, reserving it for his wisdom and knowledge alone. We may not inquire into this or follow our own thoughts in this matter. We may not form conclusions or brood about this but must cling to the revealed Word.[2] This reminder is most necessary.

For our impertinence always desires to concern itself much more with those things we cannot make sense of than with what God has revealed to us in his Word.[3] Moreover, we have no command from God to do so.

[1]G: *Es muß aber mit sonderm Fleiß Unterschied gehalten werden zwischen dem, was in Gottes Wort ausdrücklich hiervon offenbaret oder nicht geoffenbaret ist*; L: *Accurate autem discrimen observandum et retinendum est inter id, quod de hoc negotio expresse in sacris litteris revelatum est, et inter ea, quae non sunt revelata.*

[2]G: *sondern uns an das geoffenbarte Wort halten sollen*; L: *sed toti a verbo Dei revelato, quod ipse nobis proponit, pendere debemus.*

[3]G: *das Gott uns in seinem Wort darvon geoffenbaret hat*; L: *quae de hoc negotio Deus in verbo suo nobis revelavit.*

Formula of Concord, Solid Declaration XI, 52–53

204 Then comes the devil, who baits and badgers us on all sides, but especially exerts himself where the conscience and spiritual matters are concerned. His purpose is to make us scorn and despise both the Word and the works of God,[1] to tear us away from faith, hope, and love, to draw us into unbelief, false security, and stubbornness, or, on the contrary, to drive us into despair, denial of God, blasphemy, and countless other abominable sins. These are snares and nets; indeed, they are the real "flaming darts" that are venomously shot into our hearts, not by flesh and blood but by the devil.

[1]G: *nämlich daß man beide Gottes Wort und Werk in Wind schlage und verachte*; L: *nimirum ut ex aequo et verbum et opera Dei ventis discerpenda tradamus et contemnamus.*

Large Catechism III, 104

205 Wherever there are upright preachers and Christians,[1] they must endure having the world call them heretics, apostates, even seditious and desperate scoundrels. Moreover, the Word of God[2] must undergo the most shameful and spiteful persecution and blasphemy; it is contradicted, perverted, misused, and misinterpreted. But let this pass; it is the blind world's nature to condemn and persecute the truth and the children of God and yet consider this no sin.

[1]G: *Denn wo fromme Prediger und Christen sind*; L: *Ubicunque enim gentium probi agunt christiani et praedicatores.*

[2]G: *Gottes Wort*; L: *Dei . . . verbum.*

Large Catechism I, 262

206 It is correct and true when it is said, "No one comes to Christ unless drawn by the Father" [John 6:44]. But the Father does not intend to draw us apart from means. Instead, he has preordained his Word and sacraments as the regular means and instruments[1] for drawing people to himself. It is not the will of either the Father or the Son that people not hear the proclamation of his Word[2] or have contempt for it, nor should they expect to be drawn by the Father apart from Word and sacrament.[3] According to his normal arrangement, the Father draws people by the power of his Holy Spirit through the hearing of his holy, divine Word,[4] as with a net, through which the elect are snatched out of the jaws of the devil. For this reason every poor sinner should act in such a way as to hear the Word diligently and not doubt that the Father is drawing people to himself. For the Holy Spirit wills to be present with his power in the Word and to work through it.[5] This is the drawing of the Father.

[1]G: *Aber der Vater will das nicht tun ohne Mittel, sondern hat darzu sein Wort und Sakrament als ordentliche Mittel und Werkzeug verordnet*; L: *Pater autem neminem trahere vult absque mediis; sed utitur tanquam ordinariis mediis et instrumentis verbo suo et sacramentis.*

[2]G: *die Predigt seines Worts*; L: *praedicationem verbi.*

[3]G: *ohn Wort und Sakrament*; L: *absque verbo et sacramento.*

[4]G: *durch das Gehör seines H[eiligen] göttlichen Worts*; L: *per auditionem verbi sui divini.*

[5]G: *denn der H[eilige] Geist will mit seiner Kraft bei dem Worte sein und dardurch wirken*; L: *Spiritus enim sanctus virtute sua ministerio adesse et per illud ad hominum salutem vult operari.*

Formula of Concord, Solid Declaration XI, 76–77

207 It is not God's will that any are damned but that all turn to him and be saved. Ezekiel 33[:11]: "As I live, says the Lord God, I have no pleasure in the death of the wicked, but that the wicked turn back from their ways and live." "For God so loved the world that he gave his only Son, so that everyone who believes in him may not perish but may have eternal life" [John 3:16].

Therefore, in his immeasurable goodness and mercy God provides for the public proclamation[1] of his divine, eternal law and of the wondrous counsel of our redemption, the holy gospel of his eternal Son, our only Savior Jesus Christ, which alone can save. By means of this proclamation he gathers an everlasting church from humankind,[2] and he effects in human hearts true repentance and knowledge of sin and true faith in the Son of God, Jesus Christ. God wants to call human beings to eternal salvation, to draw them to himself, to convert them, to give them new birth, and to sanctify them through these means, and in no other way than through his holy Word (which people hear proclaimed or read)[3] and through the sacraments (which they use according to his Word).[4]

[1]G: *öffentlich predigen*; L: *publice annuntientur*.

[2]G: *dadurch er ihme ein ewige Kirche aus dem menschlichen Geschlecht sammlet*; L: *Ea praedicatione aeternam ecclesiam sibi e genere humano colligit*.

[3]G: *und will Gott durch dieses Mittel, und nicht anders, nämlich durch sein heiliges Wort, so man dasselbige predigen höret oder lieset*; L: *Et visum est Deo per hoc medium, et non alio modo, nimirum per sanctum verbum suum, cum id vel praedicari auditur vel legitur*.

[4]G: *und die Sacramenta nach seinem Wort gebrauchet*; L: *et per sacramentorum legitimum usum*.

Formula of Concord, Solid Declaration II, 49–50

208 Likewise, we also reject and condemn the error of the Enthusiasts, who contrive the idea that God draws people to himself, enlightens them, makes them righteous, and saves them without means, without the hearing of God's Word, even without the use of the holy sacraments.[1]

[1]G: *welche dichten, daß Gott ohne Mittel, ohne Gehör Gottes Worts, auch ohne Gebrauch der heiligen Sakramenten*; L: *qui fingunt Deum immediate, absque verbi Dei auditu et sine sacramentorum usu*.

A marginal note in the Formula of Concord gives this definition: "Enthusiasts [who] are those who await heavenly enlightenment of the Spirit without the preaching of God's Word" (Kolb/Wengert, 493n22). The German reads, in part: *ohne die Predigt Gottes Worts uf himmlische Erleuchtung des Geistes warten*; the Latin: *qui neglecta praedicatione verbi divini coelestes revelationes spiritus exspectant.*

Formula of Concord, Epitome II, 13

209 Note the distinction, then: Baptism is a very different thing from all other water, not by virtue of the natural substance but because here something nobler is added, for God himself stakes his honor, his power, and his might on it. Therefore it is not simply a natural water, but a divine, heavenly, holy, and blessed water—praise it in any other terms you can—all by virtue of the Word, which is a heavenly, holy Word[1] that no one can sufficiently extol, for it contains and conveys all that is God's. This, too, is where it derives its nature so that it is called a sacrament, as St. Augustine taught, "Accedat verbum[2] ad elementum et fit sacramentum," which means that "when the Word[3] is added to the element or the natural substance, it becomes a sacrament," that is, a holy, divine thing and sign.

[1]G: *alles ümb des Worts willen, welches ist ein himmlisch, heilig Wort*; L: *non nisi verbi gratia, quod coeleste ac sanctum verbum est.*

[2]G/L: *verbum.*

[3]G: *das Wort.*

The Latin text does not repeat or interpret the citation from St. Augustine.

Large Catechism IV, 17–18

210 It is the Word,[1] I say, that makes this a sacrament and distinguishes it from ordinary bread and wine, so that it is called and truly is Christ's body and blood. For it is said, "Accedat verbum[2] ad elementum et fit sacramentum," that is, "When the Word[3] is joined to the external element, it becomes a sacrament." This saying of St. Augustine is so appropriate and well put that he could hardly have said anything better. The Word[4] must make the element a sacrament; otherwise, it remains an ordinary element. Now, this is not the word and ordinance[5] of a prince or emperor, but of the divine Majesty at whose feet all creatures should kneel and confess that it is as he says, and they should accept it with all reverence, fear, and humility.

[1]G: *Das Wort*; L: *Verbum.*

[2]G/L: *verbum.*

[3]G: *das Wort.*

The Latin text does not repeat or interpret the prior citation.

[4]G: *Das Wort*; L: *Virtute verbi.*

[5]G: *Wort und Ordnung*; L: *verbum et institutio.*

Large Catechism V, 10–11

211 Let me tell you this. Even though you know the Word perfectly and have already mastered everything, you are daily under the dominion of the devil, and he does not rest day or night in seeking to take you unawares and to kindle in your heart unbelief and wicked thoughts against these three and all the other commandments. Therefore you must constantly keep God's Word in your heart, on your lips, and in your ears.[1] For where the heart stands idle and the Word is not heard,[2] the devil breaks in and does his damage before we realize it. On the other hand, when we seriously ponder the Word, hear it, and put it to use, such is its power[3] that it never departs without fruit. It always awakens new understanding, pleasure, and devotion, and it constantly creates clean hearts and minds. For this Word is not idle or dead, but effective and living.[4]

[1]G: *Darümb muß Du immerdar Gottes Wort im Herzen, Mund und fur den Ohren haben*; L: *Quare omnibus modis necessarium est, ut verbum Dei in promptu habeas et, quod dici solet, in numerato, hoc est in corde, in ore, in auribus.*

[2]G: *Wo . . . das Wort nicht klinget*; L: *Quiescente . . . nec verbo Dei.*

[3]G: *Wiederümb hat es die Kraft*; L: *Contra ea vis et virtus verbi est.*

[4]G: *Denn es sind nicht faule noch tote, sondern schäftige, lebendige Wort*; L: *Neque enim verba sunt putrida aut emortua succo et vigore carentia, sed plane viva et efficacia.*

Large Catechism I, 100–101

212 *Why should I waste words? If I were to tell all the benefits and advantages that God's Word accomplishes,*[1] *where would I find enough paper and time? The devil is called a master of a thousand arts. What then can we call God's Word that routs and destroys such a master of a thousand arts along with all his cunning and power?*[2] *Indeed, it must be master of more than* *a hundred thousand arts. And should we so flippantly despise such might, benefits, power, and fruit—especially we who want to be pastors and preachers?*[3] *If so, we deserve not only to be given no food to eat, but also to have the dogs set upon us and to be pelted with horse manure. For not only do we daily need God's Word just as we do our daily bread; we also must have it every day in order to stand against the daily and incessant attacks and ambushes of the devil with his thousand arts.*

[1]G: *so Gottes Wort wirkt*; L: *quam verbum Dei operatur.*

[2]G: *wie will man aber Gottes Wort heißen, das solchen Tausendkünstiger mit aller seiner Kunst und Macht verjagt und zunichte macht?* L: *At ipsum Dei sermonem, qui non solum variam ac multiplicem potestatem habet, verum etiam illum ipsum mille artium artificem cum omni potentia et arte sua opprimit et ad nihilum redigit?*

[3]G: *Pfarrherr und Prediger*; L: *parochi et concionatores.*

Large Catechism, Luther's Preface, 12–13
Italics indicate a different textual ordering in the 1580 *Book of Concord.*

213 Therefore let pious consciences know that God commands[1] them to believe that they are forgiven freely on account of Christ and not on account of our works. Let them sustain themselves with this command of God against despair and against the terrors of sin and death.

[1]L: *hoc esse mandatum Dei*; G: *daß dieses Gottes Wort und Gebot ist.*

Apology XII, 72

214 However, God cannot be dealt with and cannot be grasped in any other way than through the Word. Accordingly, justification takes place through the Word,[1] just as St. Paul notes [Rom. 1:16]: the gospel "is the power of God for salvation to everyone who has faith." Likewise [Rom. 10:17], "Faith comes from what is heard." At this point we could even take up the argument that faith justifies, because if justification takes place only through the Word and the Word is grasped only by faith, it follows that faith justifies.[2] But there are other and more important arguments. We have discussed these things so far in order to show how regeneration takes place and in order that it might be understood what kind of faith we are talking about.

Now we shall show that faith justifies. First of all, we would remind the readers that just as it is necessary to uphold the proposition that Christ is the mediator, so it is necessary to maintain that faith justifies.

[1]L: *At cum Deo non potest agi, Deus non potest apprehendi nisi per verbum. Ideo iustificatio fit per verbum*; G: *Nu kann man mit Gott doch je nicht handeln; so lässt sich Gott nicht erkennen, suchen noch fassen, denn allein im Wort und durchs Wort.*

[2]L: *si tantum fit iustificatio per verbum et verbum tantum fide apprehenditur, sequitur, quod fides iustificet*; G: *Denn so wir allein durchs Wort Gottes zu Gott kommen und gerecht werden, und das Wort kann niemands fassen, denn durch den Glauben, so folget, daß der Glaub gerecht macht.*

Apology IV, 67–69

Summary

- The Word of God is the revelation of God. It is not false nor does it deceive. Above all, it reveals the Gospel of Jesus Christ, which is received in faith and which makes one righteous before God. The devil would separate believers from the Word of God, have it despised, and cause doubt, but God sends preachers of his holy, divine Word to draw all to himself and to deliver the salvation that Christ has won. Through the Gospel, God's holy Word, and his holy sacraments, God enlightens, justifies, and saves all who believe. To imagine that God comes to us apart from these means is to despise and reject God's Word. Even the sacraments of Baptism and the Lord's Supper are no sacraments except that they are joined to the Word.
- Believers must always have the Word of God in their hearts, on their lips, and in their ears, for wherever it is contemplated, heard, and used, it produces fruit that awakens understanding, pleasure, and a devout life. The Word's power and strength foil the devil, who sows doubt, disbelief, and despair.
- Thus because God cannot be apprehended except through the Word, the Word of God is the "power of God for salvation" to those who believe it (Romans 1:16).

What power does the Word of God have in worship?

215 However, God the Holy Spirit does not effect conversion without means,[1] but he uses the preaching and the hearing of God's Word[2] to accomplish it, as it is written (Rom. 1[:16]), the gospel is a "power of God" to save. Likewise, faith comes from hearing God's Word (Rom. 10[:17]). And it is God's will that people hear his Word and not plug their ears.[3] In this Word the Holy Spirit is present[4] and opens hearts that they may, like Lydia in Acts 16[:14], listen to it and thus be converted, solely through the grace and power of the Holy Spirit, who alone accomplishes the conversion of the human being. For apart from his grace our "willing and exerting," our planting, sowing, and watering, amount to nothing "if he does not give the growth" [Rom. 9:16; 1 Cor. 3:7]. As Christ says, "Apart from me, you can do nothing" [John 15:5]. With these brief words he denies the free will its powers and ascribes everything to God's grace, so that no one has grounds for boasting before God (1 Cor. [9:16]).

[1]G: *nicht ohne Mittel*; L: *non sine mediis*.

[2]G: *die Predigt und das Gehör Gottes Worts*; L: *praedicatione et auscultatione verbi Dei*.

[3]G: *Der Glaub kompt aus dem Gehöre Gottes Worts. Ro. 10. Und ist Gottes Wille, daß man sein Wort hören und nicht die Ohren vorstopfen solle*. L: *Fides est ex auditu verbi Dei. Et sane vult Dominus, ut ipsius verbum audiatur neque ad illius praedicationem aures obturentur*.

[4]G: *Bei solchem Wort ist der Heilige Geist gegenwärtig*; L: *Huic verbo adest praesens spiritus sanctus*.

Formula of Concord, Epitome II, 4–6

216 This comfort would be taken away from us completely if we could not conclude from his call, which takes place through Word and sacraments,[1] what God's will toward us is.

Such a view would also destroy and deprive us of the foundation, namely, that the Holy Spirit most certainly wills to be present, effective, and active through the Word as it is preached, heard, and considered.[2] Therefore, there is no basis at all for the opinion described above, that those who have contempt for the Word of God,[3] push it away, slander it, or persecute it can be considered to be the elect (Matt. 22[:5, 6]; Acts 15 [= 13:40–41, 45]), or those who harden their hearts when they hear the Word (Heb. 4[:2, 7]), or those who resist the Holy Spirit (Acts 7[:51]), or those who persist in sin without repentance (Luke 14[:18, 24]), or those who do not truly believe in Christ (Mark 16[:16]), or those who present only an external appearance of being believers (Matt. 7[:15] and 22[:12]), or those who seek another way to righteousness and salvation apart from Christ (Rom. 9[:31]). On the contrary, as God preordained in his counsel that the Holy Spirit would call, enlighten, and convert the elect through the Word[4] and that he would justify and save all those who accept Christ through true faith, so also he concluded in his counsel that he would harden, reject, and condemn all those whom he called through the Word when they spurn the Word and resist and persist in resisting the Holy Spirit,[5] who wants to exercise his power in them and be efficacious through the Word.[6] This is why "many are called and few are chosen" [Matt. 22:14].

For few accept the Word and follow it.[7] Most have contempt for the Word[8] and do not want to come to the wedding [Matt. 22:1–6; Luke 14:18–20]. God's foreknowledge is not the cause of such contempt for the Word;[9] the cause is instead the perverted human will, which rejects or perverts the means and instruments of the Holy Spirit[10] that God presents to the will when he calls: it then resists the Holy Spirit, who wants to exercise his power and be efficacious through the Word,[11] as Christ said, "How often have I desired to gather you, and you were not willing" (Matt. 23[:37]).

[1]G: *durchs Wort und durch die Sakrament*; L: *per verbum et sacramenta.*

[2]G: *daß der H[eilige] Geist bei dem gepredigten, gehörten, betrachten Worte gewißlich gegenwärtig und dardurch kräftig sein und wirken wölle*; L: *quod credimus spiritum sanctum cum verbo praedicato, audito et diligenter considerato praesentem atque efficacem esse et operari velle.*

[3]G: *sie gleich das Wort Gottes verachten*; L: *qui verbum Dei contemnunt.*

[4]G: *durchs Wort*; L: *per verbum.*

[5]G: *daß er diejenigen, so durch Wort berufen werden, wann sie das Wort von sich stoßen und dem Heiligen Geist . . . widerstreben und darin vorharren*; L: *quod eos, qui per verbum vocati illud repudiant et spiritui sancto . . . resistunt et obstinati in ea contumacia perseverant.*

[6]G: *durchs Wort kräftig sein und wirken will*; L: *per verbum efficaciter operari et efficax esse vult.*

[7]G: *Dann wenig nehmen das Wort an und folgen ihme*; L: *Pauci enim verbum Dei serio recipiunt eique sincere obtemperant.*

[8]G: *der größeste Haufe verachtet das Wort*; L: *maior pars contemnit verbum.*

[9]G: *Solcher Verachtung des Worts*; L: *Huius contemptus verbi.*

[10]G: *der das Mittel und Werkzeug des H[eiligen] Geistes . . . von sich stößet oder verkehret*; L: *quae medium illud et instrumentum spiritus sancti . . . reiicit aut depravat.*

[11]G: *der durchs Wort kräftig sein will und wirket*; L: *qui per verbum efficaciter operari cupit.*

Formula of Concord, Solid Declaration XI, 38–41

217 In the same vein, Holy Scripture[1] also testifies that God, who has called us, is so faithful that when he has "begun a good work in us," he will also continue it to the end and complete it, if we do not turn away from him, but "remain steadfast to the end in that which he has begun." For this purpose he has promised his grace (1 Cor. 1[:8]; Phil. 1[:6]; 2[:16]; 2 Peter 3[:9]; Heb. 3[:6, 14]).

We should concern ourselves with this revealed will of God, follow it, and devote our attention to it, because the Holy Spirit bestows grace, power, and ability through the Word,[2] through which he calls us. We should therefore not attempt to fathom the abyss of God's hidden foreknowledge, as it is written in Luke 13[:23, 24]. When someone asked, "Lord, do you think that only a few will be saved?" Christ answered, "Strive to enter through the narrow door." Thus, Luther says, "Follow the order of the Epistle to the Romans. Worry first about Christ and the gospel, that you may recognize your sin and his grace, and then fight your sin, as Paul teaches from the first to the eighth chapters. Then, when you come under the cross and suffering in the eighth chapter, this will teach you of foreknowledge in chapters 9, 10, and 11, and how comforting it is."

[1]G: *So zeuget auch die Heilige Schrift*; L: *Praeteria scriptura testatur.*

[2]G: *durchs Wort*; L: *per verbum.*

Formula of Concord, Solid Declaration XI, 32–33

218 A person who has not yet been converted to God and been reborn can hear and read this Word externally,[1] for in such external matters, as stated above, people have a free will to a certain extent even after the fall, so that they may go to church and listen or not listen to the sermon.

Through these means (the preaching and hearing of his Word),[2] God goes about his work and breaks our hearts and draws people, so that they recognize their sins and God's wrath through the preaching of the law[3] and feel real terror, regret, and sorrow in their hearts. Through the preaching of the holy gospel of the gracious forgiveness of sins in Christ and through meditating upon it,[4] a spark of faith is ignited in them, and they accept the forgiveness of sins for Christ's sake and receive the comfort of the promise of the gospel. In this way the Holy Spirit, who effects all of this, is sent into their hearts.

It is indeed true that both the planting and watering of the preacher[5] and the activity and desire of the hearer would be in vain, and no conversion would result from these efforts, if the power and action of the Holy Spirit were not added to them. For the Spirit enlightens and converts hearts through the Word that is proclaimed and heard, so that people believe the Word and say yes to it.[6]

Therefore, neither the preacher nor the hearer should doubt this grace and activity of the Holy Spirit,[7] but they should be certain that when the Word of God is preached purely and clearly according to God's command and will[8] and people listen to it seriously and diligently and meditate upon it, God will certainly be present with his grace and give, as has been said, what human beings otherwise could neither receive nor take on the basis of their own powers. For the presence, effectiveness, and gift of the Holy Spirit should not and cannot always be assessed *ex sensu*, as a person feels it in the heart. Instead, because the Holy Spirit's activity is often hidden under the cover of great weakness, we should be certain, on the basis of and according to the promise, that the Word of God, when preached and heard, is a function and work of the Holy Spirit,[9] through which he is certainly present in our hearts and exercises his power there (2 Corinthians 2 [1 Cor. 2:11ff. or 2 Cor. 3:5–6]).

However, if people do not want to hear or read the proclamation of God's Word, but disdain it and the congregation of God's people[10] and then die and perish in their sins, they can neither find comfort in God's eternal election nor obtain mercy. For Christ, in whom we are chosen, offers his grace to all people in the Word and in the holy sacraments,[11] and he earnestly desires that people should hear it. He has promised that where "two or three are gathered" in his name and are occupied with his holy Word,[12] he will be "there among them" [Matt. 18:20].

If such people disdain the tools of the Holy Spirit and do not want to hear,[13] no injustice is done to them if the Holy Spirit does not enlighten them but lets them remain and perish in the darkness of unbelief, as it is written, "How often have I desired to gather your children together as a hen gathers her brood under her wings, and you were not willing!" [Matt. 23:37].

[1]G: *Dieses Wort kann der Mensch . . . äußerlich hören und lesen*; L: *Hoc Dei verbum homo . . . externis auribus audire aut legere potest.*

[2]G: *Durch dieses Mittel, nämblich die Predigt und Gehör seines Worts*; L: *Per hoc medium seu instrumentum, praedicationem nimirum et auditionem verbi.*

[3]G: *durch die Predigt des Gesetzs*; L: *ex concionibus legis.*

[4]G: *durch die Predigt und Betrachtung des heiligen Evangelii von der gnadenreichen Vorgebung der Sünden in Christo*; L: *per annuntiationem ac meditationem evangelii de gratuita et clementissima peccatorum remissione in Christo.*

[5]G: *des Predigers Pflanzen und Begiessen*; L: *concionatoris plantare et rigare.*

[6]G: *daß die Menschen solchem Wort gläuben und das Jawort darzu geben*; L: *ut homines Verbo credere et assentire possint.*

[7]G: *So soll doch weder Prediger noch Zuhörer an dieser Gnade und Wirkung des Heiligen Geistes zweifeln*; L: *tamen neque concionator neque auditor de hac spiritus sancti gratia et operatione dubitare debent.*

[8]G: *sondern gewiß sein, wenn das Wort Gottes nach dem Befehl und Willen Gottes rein und lauter geprediget*; L: *Quin potius uterque certo sciat, si verbum Dei iuxta mandatum et voluntatem Dei pure et sincere praedicatum fuerit.*

[9]G: *daß das gepredigte, gehörte Wort Gottes sei ein Ambt und Werk des Heiligen Geists*; L: *quod verbum Dei praedicatum et auditum revera sit ministerium et organon spiritus sancti.*

Note that in the original languages the Latin *ministerium* (ministry, office, and work) is linked with the Latin *organum*. That is a transliteration having the same meaning as the Greek word ὄργανον ("means, tool"). The German *Ampt*, denoting the duty of an officeholder, the official position itself, and its jurisdiction, is linked with *Werk* ("work"). Thus the translation "function" ("action of performing") may not fully convey the sense of performing the action as a member of an office instituted by God, which is implied by the words *ministerium* ("office") and *Ampt* ("office"). See also Ap XXIV, 58–60.

[10]G: *Da aber ein Mensch die Predigt nicht hören noch Gottes Wort lesen will, sondern das Wort und die Gemeine Gottes verachtet*; L: *At si homo quispiam neque verbum Dei audire neque legere velit, sed potius ministerium verbi et ecclesiam Dei contemnat.*

In this text *Gemeine* does not mean something that is *vulgar* but something that is *in common*, that is, having a common fellowship: a congregation or *Gemeinde*. See text 840, note 3. Note also that

Kolb/Wengert's use of the word *people* offers a plural, gender neutral quality not in the original singular words *Mensch* and *homo*.

[11]G: *dann Christus . . . allen Menschen seine Gnade im Wort und heiligen Sakramenten anbeut*; L: *Christus enim . . . omnibus hominibus clementiam suam in verbo et sacramentis offert.*

[12]G: *und mit seinem heiligen Wort umbgehen*; L: *et verbum eius pie tractaverint.*

[13]G: *Da aber ein solch Mensch verachtet des Heiligen Geistes Werkzeug und will nich hören*; L: *Quare cum homo profanus instrumenta seu media spiritus sancti contemnit neque verbum Dei audire vult.*

Formula of Concord, Solid Declaration II, 53–58

219 The opponents consider only the commandments of the second table, which entail the civil righteousness that reason understands. Being content with this they suppose that they satisfy the law of God. Meanwhile they fail to notice the first table, which instructs us to love God, to conclude that God is angry with sin, truly to fear God, truly to conclude that God hears our prayers. But without the Holy Spirit the human heart either despises the judgment of God in its complacency or in the face of punishment flees and hates God who judges them. Thus it does not obey the first table. Therefore since these things (contempt for God, doubt about the Word of God and about its threats and promises)[1] cling to human nature, people truly sin even when they do respectable works without the Holy Spirit, because they do them with a godless heart, according to the text [Rom. 14:23], "Whatever does not proceed from faith is sin." Such people perform their works with contempt for God, just as when Epicurus did not think that God cared for him, paid attention to him, or heard his prayer. This contempt for God corrupts works that appear to be honorable, because God judges the heart.

[1]L: *contemptus Dei, dubitatio de verbo Dei, de minis et promissionibus*; G: *daß wir alle von Art Gott verachten, sein Wort, seine Verheißung und Dräuen in Zweifel setzen.*

Apology IV, 34–35

220 To explain this conflict in a Christian fashion according to the guidance of God's Word[1] and to settle it by his grace, we submit the following as our teaching, faith, and confession:

That in spiritual and divine matters, the mind, heart, and will of the unreborn human being can in absolutely no way, on the basis of its own natural powers, understand, believe, accept, consider, will, begin, accomplish, do, effect, or cooperate. Instead, it is completely dead to the good—completely corrupted. This means that in this human nature, after the fall and before rebirth, there is not a spark of spiritual power left or present with which human beings can prepare themselves for the grace of God or accept grace as it is offered. Nor are they capable of acting in their own behalf or of applying this grace to themselves or to prepare themselves for it. Nor do they have the ability, on the basis of their own powers, to help, act, effect, or cooperate—completely, halfway, or in the slightest, most insignificant way—in their own conversion; they cannot bring it about or cooperate in it "of ourselves, as coming from us" [2 Cor. 3:5]. Rather they are "the slave of sin" (John 8[:34]) and prisoners of the devil, by whom they are driven (Eph. 2[:2]; 2 Tim. 2[:26]). Therefore, according to its own perverted character and nature, the natural free will has only the power and ability to do whatever is displeasing and hostile to God.

The following arguments from the Word of God[2] confirm and corroborate this explanation and basic answer to the basic questions and *status controversiae* as set forth in the introduction of this article. Although these answers are contrary to reason and philosophy in all their arrogance, nonetheless, we know that "the wisdom of this 'perverted' world is only foolishness in God's sight" [cf. 1 Cor. 3:19] and that only on the basis of God's Word can judgments on articles of faith be made.[3]

[1]G: *nach Anleitung Gottes Worts*; L: *iuxta verbi Dei analogiam*.

[2]G: *folgende Gründe des göttlichen Worts*; L: *e verbo Dei desumpta argumenta*.

[3]G: *alleine aus Gottes Wort*; L: *tantummodo ex verbo Dei*.

Formula of Concord, Solid Declaration II, 6–8

221 Conversely, any conduct or work apart from God's Word is unholy in the sight of God,[1] no matter how splendid and brilliant it may appear, or even if it is altogether covered with holy relics, as are the so-called spiritual walks of life, which do not know God's Word[2] but seek holiness in their own works.

Note, then, that the power and force of this commandment consists not in the resting but in the hallowing, so that this day may have its special holy function. Other work and business are really not designated holy activities unless the person doing them is first holy. In this case, however, a work must take place through which a person becomes holy. This work, as we have heard, takes place through God's Word.[3] Places, times, persons, and the entire outward order of worship have therefore been instituted and appointed in order that God's Word may exert its power publicly.

Because so much depends on God's Word that no holy day is sanctified without it,[4] we must realize that God wants this commandment to be kept strictly and will punish all who despise his Word[5] and refuse to hear and learn it, especially at the times appointed. Therefore this commandment is violated not only by those who grossly misuse and desecrate the holy day, like those who in their greed or frivolity neglect the hearing of God's Word or lie around in taverns dead drunk like swine. It is also violated by that other crowd who listen to God's Word as they would to any other entertainment, who only from force of habit go to hear the sermon and leave again with as little knowledge at the end of the year as at the beginning. It used to be thought that Sunday had been properly observed if one went to Mass or listened to the Gospel being read; however, no one asked about God's Word,[6] and no one taught it either. Now that we have God's Word, we still fail to eliminate this abuse, for we permit ourselves to be preached to and admonished,[7] but we listen without serious concern.

Remember, then, that you must be concerned not only about hearing the Word, but also about learning it and retaining it. Do not think that it is up to your discretion or that it is an unimportant matter. It is the commandment of God, who will require of you an accounting of how you have heard, learned, and honored his Word.[8]

[1]G: *was fur Wesen und Werk außer Gottes Wort gehet, das ist fur Gott unheilig*; L: *quaecunque res aut opera extra Dei verbum feruntur et instituuntur, haec coram Deo profana sunt et immunda.*

[2]G: *als da sind die erdichte geistliche Stände, die Gottes Wort nicht wissen*; L: *Cujus generis sunt ficti atque excogitati religiosorum ordines verbum Dei iuxta cum Turcis prorsus ignorantes.*

[3]G: *welchs alleine (wie gehört) durch Gottes Wort geschicht*; L: *id quod solum, ut dixi, verbo Dei fieri potest.*

[4]G: *Weil nu soviel an Gottes Wort gelegen ist, daß ohn dasselbige kein Feiertag geheiligt wird*; L: *Cum itaque tanti momenti sit verbum Dei, ut citra hujus tractationem nullas ferias sanctas esse.*

[5]G: *sollen wir wissen, daß Gott dies Gepot strenge will gehalten haben und strafen alle, die sein Wort verachten*; L: *scire debamus Deum hoc praeceptum severe atque adeo serio conservari velle suppliciumque de his omnibus esse sumpturum quotquot verbum ejus proterve contemnunt.*

[6]G: *wenn man des Sonntags eine Messe oder das Evangelium hätte hören lesen, aber nach Gottes Wort hat niemand gefragt*; L: *si die Dominico missa ac evangelium audiretur. Ceterum verbum Dei nemo admodum requisivit.*

[7]G: *wir . . . lassen uns immer predigen und vermahnen*; L: *sinimus quidem nobis multa predicari ac nos moneri sedulo.*

[8]G: *wie Du sein Wort gehört, gelernet und geehret habst*; L: *a te verbi sui rationem tecum initurus est, quinam illud didiceris aut quam reverenter habueris.*

Large Catechism I, 93–98

222 For the Word of God is the true holy object above all holy objects. Indeed, it is the only one we Christians know and have.[1] Even if we had the bones of all the saints or all the holy and consecrated vestments gathered together in one pile, they would not help us in the least, for they are all dead things that cannot make anyone holy. But God's Word is the treasure that makes everything holy.[2] By it all the saints have themselves been made holy. At whatever time God's Word is taught, preached, heard, read, or pondered, there the person, the day, and the work is hallowed,[3] not on account of the external work but on account of the Word that makes us all saints. Accordingly, I constantly repeat that all our life and work must be based on God's Word[4] if they are to be God-pleasing or holy. Where that happens the commandment is in force and is fulfilled.

[1]G: *Denn das Wort Gottes ist das Heiligtumb über alle Heiligtumb, ja das einige, das wir Christen wissen und haben*; L: *Siquidem Dei verbum unicum illud sacrum est, quod omnes res sacras longe lateque sanctitate praecellit et exsuperat, imo potius unicum illud mysterium, quod nos christiani et scimus et habemus.*

[2]G: *Aber Gottes Wort ist der Schatz, der alle Ding heilig machet*; L: *Verum enim vero Dei verbum thesaurus ille et gaza est pertiosissima, quae omnia sanctificat.*

[3]G: *Welche Stund man nu Gottes Wort handlet, prediget, höret, lieset oder bedenket, so wird dadurch Person, Tag und Werk geheiligt*; L: *Jam quacunque hora verbum Dei docetur, praedicatur, auditur, legitur aut*

repetitur memoria, ea hujus tractatione audientis persona dies et opus sanctificatur.

[4]G: *daß alle unser Leben und Werk in dem Wort Gottes gehen müssen*; L: *omnem vitam et opera nostra verbi Dei ductu et auspicio gubernari debere atque institui.*

Large Catechism I, 91–92

223 Thus the service and worship of the Gospel[1] is to receive good things from God, while the worship of the law is to offer and present our goods to God. . . . The greatest possible comfort comes from this doctrine that the highest worship in the Gospel[2] is the desire to receive forgiveness of sins, grace, and righteousness. About this worship[3] Christ speaks in John 6:40, "This is the will of my Father, that everyone who sees the Son and believes in him should have eternal life." And the Father says (Matt. 17:5), "This is my beloved Son, with whom I am well pleased; listen to him."

[1]L: *cultus et λατρεία evangelii.*

[2]L: *cultus in evangelio praecipuus.*

[3]L: *De hoc cultu.*

Apology IV, 310
The Latin is from the quarto edition.
The English is from Tappert.

SUMMARY

- The Gospel is the power of God unto salvation. It is the means that the Holy Spirit uses to open hearts, convert, and console. Where the Word and Sacraments are, there is the Holy Spirit. He works repentance in all who by true faith receive Christ.
- Because the Holy Spirit works through the Word that is externally heard and read, to despise the Word of God is to reject God. In the Word of God, the Law shows sin and the preaching of the Gospel offers the forgiveness of sins for Christ's sake. One cannot always judge the presence and working of the Spirit in the heart, for this is hidden from human sight. The Word of God preached and heard is an office and work of the Holy Spirit.
- Without the Holy Spirit, the unregenerate are unable by their own powers to understand, believe, accept, or do anything that is pleasing to God. There is nothing the unregenerate can do that is

holy. The Spirit makes holy what is holy—whether person, place, time, or order of worship. Where the Word of God, the great treasure, is taught, preached, heard, read, or meditated upon, there the person, day, and work are sanctified. The Spirit makes holy saints when faith receives God's gifts of forgiveness, grace, and righteousness, offered through the Word.

HOW IS THE WORD OF GOD DELIVERED?

224 **[German text]** Concerning church government it is taught that no one should publicly teach, preach,[1] or administer the sacraments without a proper [public] call.[2]

[Latin text] Concerning church order they teach that no one should teach publicly[1] in the church or administer the sacraments unless properly called.[2]

[1]G: *niemand in der Kirchen offentlich lehren oder predigen*; L: *nemo debeat in ecclesia publice docere*.

[2]G: *ohn ordentlichen Beruf*; L: *nisi rite vocatus*.

A comment on the phrase "properly called" may be helpful. The Latin word *rite* existed from antiquity, attested by Cicero, Livy, Vergil, and others as meaning "with due observances" or "rules, according to religious usage." Cicero used *rite* in connection with the proper observance of rituals used in worshiping the gods (*deos colere*). Another use in which *rite* refers to worship occurs in the first paragraph of AC XV. There was also a juridical sense of *rite* as having the proper legal form. In a wider sense, it also meant "duly, rightly, fully, justly, according to custom, fortunately, successfully." Medieval usage did not depart in any significant way from this. The German *ordentlich* in Luther's adverbial usage means "instituted and determined according to divine or human ordering, proper, formal."

Augsburg Confession XIV, 1

225 For the ministry of the Word has the command of God[1] and has magnificent promises like Romans 1[:16]: the gospel "is the power of God for salvation to everyone who has faith." Likewise, Isaiah 55[:11], ". . . so shall my word be that goes out from my mouth;[2] it shall not return to me empty, but it shall accomplish that which I purpose. . . ." If ordination is understood in this way, we will not object to calling the laying on of hands a sacrament. For the church has the mandate to appoint ministers,[3] which ought to please us greatly because we know that God approves this ministry and is present in it.[4] Indeed, it is worthwhile to extol the ministry of the Word[5] with every possible kind of praise against fanatics who imagine that the Holy Spirit is not given through the Word but is given on account of certain preparations of their own,[6] for example, if they sit idle and silent in dark places while waiting for illumination—as the "Enthusiasts" formerly taught and the Anabaptists now teach.

[1]L: *ministerium verbi habet mandatum Dei*; G: *das Predigtamt hat Gott eingesetzt und geboten*.

[2]L: *Verbum meum, quod egredietur de ore meo*; G: *Das Wort, daß aus meinem Mund gehet*.

[3]L: *Habet enim ecclesia mandatum de constituendis ministris*; G: *Denn die Kirche hat Gottes Befehl, daß sie soll Prediger und Diakonos bestellen*.

[4]L: *quod scimus Deum approbare ministerium illud et adesse in ministerio*; G: *so wir wissen, daß Gott durch Menschen und diejenigen, so von Menschen gewählet sind, predigen und wirken will*.

[5]L: *ministerium verbi*; G: *solche Wahl*.

[6]L: *qui somniant spiritum sanctum dari non per verbum, sed propter suas quasdam praeparationes*; G: *welche solche Wahl samt dem Predigtamt und leiblichen Wort verachten und lästern*.

Apology XIII, 11–13

226 Article fourteen, in which we say that no one should be allowed to administer the Word and the sacraments unless they are duly called,[1] they accept with the proviso that we use canonical ordination. Concerning this subject we have frequently testified in the assembly that it is our greatest desire to retain the order of the church and the various ranks in the church—even though they were established by human authority. We know that church discipline in the manner described by the ancient canons was instituted by the Fathers for a good and useful purpose.

. . . We know that the church exists among those who rightly teach the Word of God and rightly administer the sacraments;[2] it does not exist among those who not only try to destroy the Word of God with their edicts, but who also butcher those who teach what is right and true.

[1]L: *in quo dicimus nemini nisi rite vocato concedendam esse administrationem sacramentorum et verbi in ecclesia*; G: *da wir sagen, daß man nie-*

mands gestatte zu predigen oder die Sakrament zu reichen in der Kirchen, „denn allein denjenigen, so recht gebührlich berufen sein“.

[3]L: *Et ecclesiam esse, scimus apud hos, qui verbum Dei recte docent et recte administrant sacramenta*; G: *daß die christliche Kirche da ist, da Gottes Wort recht gelehret wird.*

Apology XIV, 1, 4

227 Now, the name of God is profaned by us either in words or deeds. (For everything we do on earth may be classified as word or deed, speech or act.) In the first place, then, it is profaned when people preach, teach, and speak in the name of God[1] anything that is false and deceptive, using his name to dress up their lies and make them acceptable; this is the worst desecration and dishonor of the divine name.

[1]G: *wenn man predigt, lehret und redet unter Gottes Namen, daß doch falsch und verführisch ist*; L: *quando sub divini nominis praetextu id praedicatur, docetur ac dicitur, quod falsum est atque erroneum et quo seducuntur homines.*

Large Catechism III, 40–41

228 If you are asked, "What does the Second Commandment mean?" or, "What does it mean to take the name of God in vain or to misuse it?" you should answer briefly: "It is a misuse of God's name if we call upon the LORD God in any way whatsoever to support falsehood or wrong of any kind." What this commandment forbids, therefore, is appealing to God's name falsely or taking his name upon our lips when our heart knows or should know that the facts are otherwise—for example, when taking oaths in court and one party lies about the other. God's name cannot be abused more flagrantly than when it is used to lie and deceive.

. . . The greatest abuse, however, is in spiritual matters, which affect the conscience, when false preachers arise and present their lying nonsense as God's Word.[1]

See, all of this is an attempt to deck yourself out with God's name or to put up a good front and justify yourself with his name, whether in ordinary worldly affairs or in sophisticated and difficult matters of faith and doctrine. Also to be numbered among the liars are the blasphemers, not only the very crass ones who are known to everyone and disgrace God's name flagrantly—they should take lessons from the hangman, not from us—but also those who publicly slander the truth and God's Word and consign it to the devil.[2] There is no need to say anything more about this now.

[1]G: *wenn falsche Prediger aufstehen und ihren Lügentand fur Gottes Wort dargeben*; L: *quae pertingunt conscientiam falsis doctoribus emergentibus suaque mandacia divini verbi loco venditantibus.*

[2]G: *sondern auch, die die Wahrheit und Gottes Wort offentlich lästern und dem Teufel geben*; L: *verum etiam illi, qui veritatem et verbum Dei propalam contumeliose lacerant ac diaboli verbum impudenter et impie esse confirmant.*

Large Catechism I, 51, 55

229 Just because the revelation has not yet taken place does not make the ungodly the church. For the kingdom of Christ is always that which he makes alive by his Spirit, whether it has been revealed or is hidden under the cross, just as Christ is the same, whether now glorified or previously afflicted. Christ's parables agree with this. He clearly teaches in Matthew 13[:38] that "the good seed are the children of the kingdom; the weeds are the children of the evil one." "The field," he says, "is the world," not the church. So also John [Matt. 3:12] speaks about the whole Jewish nation and says that it will come to pass that the true church will be separated from it. Thus, this passage is more against the opponents than for them because it shows that the true and spiritual people will be separated from the physical people. Christ also speaks about the outward appearance of the church when he says, "The kingdom of heaven is like a net" [Matt. 13:47], or like "ten bridesmaids" [Matt. 25:1]. Thus he teaches that the church has been hidden under a crowd of wicked people in order that this stumbling block may not offend the faithful, and so that we might know that the Word and sacrament are efficacious even when they are administered by wicked people.[1] Meanwhile, he teaches that although the ungodly possess certain outward signs in common, they are, nevertheless, not the true kingdom of Christ and members of Christ. For they are members of the devil's kingdom.

[1]L: *ut sciamus verbum et sacramenta efficacia esse, etsi tractentur a malis*; G: *daß wir wissen sollen, daß das Wort und die Sakrament darum nicht ohne Kraft sein, obgleich Gottlose predigen oder die Sakrament reichen.*

Apology VII–VIII, 18–19

230 They approved the entire eighth article. In it, we confess that hypocrites and evil people are mixed together in the church and that the sacraments are efficacious even though they may be dispensed by evil ministers,[1] because the ministers act in the place of Christ and so do not represent their own person.[2] This accords with that passage [Luke 10:16], "Whoever listens to you listens to me." The ungodly teachers must be avoided because they no longer act in the person of Christ but are Antichrists.[3] Christ says [Matt. 7:15], "Beware of false prophets," and Paul says [Gal. 1:9], "If anyone proclaims to you a gospel contrary to what you received, let that one be accursed!"

[1]L: *et quod sacramenta sint efficacia, etiamsi per malos ministros tractentur*; G: *und daß die Sakramente nicht darum ohne Kraft sein, ob sie durch Heuchler gereicht werden.*

[2]L: *quia ministri funguntur vice Christi, non repraesentant suam personam*; G: *denn sie reichens an Christus statt und nicht für ihre Person.*

[3]L: *Impii doctores deserendi sunt, quia hi iam non funguntur persona Christi, sed sunt antichristi*; G: *Doch soll man falsche Lehrer nicht annehmen oder hören; denn dieselbigen sind nicht mehr an Christus statt sondern sind Widerchristi.*

Apology VII–VIII, 47–48

231 Many even publicly ridicule all religions, or if they approve anything, they approve only those things that agree with human reason.[1] They regard the rest as fabulous tales, similar to the tragedies of the poets.

Therefore in accordance with the Scriptures we maintain that the church is, properly speaking, the assembly of saints who truly believe the gospel of Christ and have the Holy Spirit.[2] Nevertheless, we admit that in this life many hypocrites and wicked people, who are mixed in with these, participate in the outward signs. They are members of the church according to their participation in the outward signs and even hold office in the church.[3] Nor does this detract from the efficacy of the sacraments when they are distributed by the unworthy,[4] because they represent the person of Christ on account of the call of the church and do not represent their own persons,[5] as Christ himself testifies [Luke 10:16], "Whoever listens to you listens to me." When they offer the Word of Christ or the sacraments, they offer them in the stead and place of Christ.[6] The words of Christ teach us this[7] so that we are not offended by the unworthiness of ministers.

[1]L: *aut si quid probant, probant illa, quae humanae rationi consentanea sunt*; G: *Und lassen sie ihnen etwas gefallen, so lassen sie ihnen das gefallen, das menschlicher Vernunft gemäß.*

[2]L: *Quare nos iuxta scripturas sentimus ecclesiam proprie dictam esse congregationem sanctorum, qui vere credunt evangelio Christi et habent spiritum sanctum*; G: *Darum sagen und schließen wir nach der heiligen Schrift, daß die rechte christliche Kirche sei der Haufe hin und wieder in der Welt derjenigen, die da wahrlich gläuben dem Evangelio Christi und den heiligen Geist haben.*

[3]L: *qui sunt membra ecclesiae secundum societatem externorum signorum ideoque gerunt officia in ecclesia*; G: *welche auch Glieder sind der Kirchen, sofern äußerliche Zeichen betrifft. Denn sie haben Aemter in der Kirchen, predigen, reichen Sakrament, und tragen den Titel und Namen der Christen.*

[4]L: *Nec adimit sacramentis efficaciam, quod per indignos tractantur*; G: *Und die Sakramente, Taufe &c. sind darum nicht ohne Wirkung oder Kraft, daß sie durch Unwirdige und Gottlose gereicht werden.*

[5]L: *quia repraesentant Christi personam propter vocationem ecclesiae, non repraesentant proprias personas*; G: *Denn um des Berufs willen der Kirchen sind solche da, nicht für ihre eigen Person, sondern als Christus.*

[6]L: *Cum verbum Christi, cum sacramenta porrigunt, Christi vice et loco porrigunt*; G: *Wenn nu gleich Gottlose predigen und die Sakrament reichen, so reichen sie dieselbigen an Christus statt.*

[7]L: *Id docet nos illa vox Christi*; G: *Und das lehret uns das Wort Christi.*

Apology VII–VIII, 27–28

232 Many other kinds of spirits are mentioned in Scripture, such as the human spirit, heavenly spirits, and the evil spirit. But God's Spirit alone is called a Holy Spirit, that is, the one who has made us holy and still makes us holy. As the Father is called a Creator and the Son is called a Redeemer, so on account of his work the Holy Spirit must be called a Sanctifier, or one who makes us holy. How does such sanctifying take place? Answer: Just as the Son obtains dominion by purchasing us through his birth, death, and resurrection, etc., so the Holy Spirit effects our being made holy through the following: the community of saints or Christian church, the forgiveness of sins, the resurrection of the body, and the life everlasting. That is, he first leads us into his holy community, placing us in the church's lap, where he preaches to us and brings us to Christ.

Neither you nor I could ever know anything about Christ, or believe in him and receive him as Lord, unless these were offered to us and bestowed on our hearts through the preaching of the gospel by the Holy Spirit.[1] The work is finished and completed; Christ has acquired and won the treasure for us by his sufferings, death, and resurrection, etc. But if the work remained hidden so that no one knew of it, it would have been all in vain, all lost. In order that this treasure might not remain buried but be put to use and enjoyed, God has caused the Word to be published and proclaimed,[2] in which he has given the Holy Spirit to offer and apply to us this treasure, this redemption. Therefore being made holy is nothing else than bringing us to the Lord Christ to receive this blessing, to which we could not have come by ourselves.

[1]G: *durch die Predigt des Evangelii*; L: *per evangelii praedicationem*.

[2]G: *hat Gott das Wort ausgehen und verkünden lassen*; L: *Deus verbum suum emisit praedicandum et invulgandum omnibus*.

Large Catechism II, 36–39

233 *Indeed, among the nobility there are also some louts and skinflints who declare that they can do without pastors and preachers*[1] *now because we now have everything in books and can learn it all by ourselves. So they blithely let parishes fall into decay and brazenly allow both pastors and preachers*[2] *to suffer distress and hunger. This is what one can expect of crazy Germans. We Germans have such disgraceful people among us and have to put up with them.*

[1]G: *wider Pfarrherr noch Prediger*; L: *sive parochis sive concionatoribus*.

[2]G: *beide Pfarrherr und Prediger*; L: *parochos autem et concionatores*.

Large Catechism, Luther's Preface, 6
Italics indicate a different textual ordering in the 1580 *Book of Concord*.

234 On the contrary, in our churches all the sermons[1] deal with topics like these: repentance, fear of God, faith in Christ, the righteousness of faith, consolation of consciences through faith, the exercise of faith, prayer (what it should be like and that everyone may be completely certain that it is efficacious and is heard), the cross, respect for the magistrates and all civil orders, the distinction between the kingdom of Christ (the spiritual kingdom) and political affairs, marriage, the education and instruction of children, chastity, and all the works of love.

[1]L: *omnes conciones*; G: *werden von Predigern . . . gelehret*.

Apology XV, 43

235 We now want to return to the gospel, which gives guidance and help against sin in more than one way, because God is extravagantly rich in his grace: first, through the spoken word,[1] in which the forgiveness of sins is preached to the whole world[2] (which is the proper function of the gospel);[3] second, through baptism; third, through the holy Sacrament of the Altar; fourth, through the power of the keys and also through the mutual conversation and consolation of brothers[4] and sisters. Matthew 18[:20]: "Where two or three are gathered . . ."

[1]G: *durchs mundlich Wort*; L: *per verbum vocale*.

[2]G: *darin gepredigt wird Vergebung der Sunde in alle Welt*; L: *quo jubet praedicari remissionem peccatorum in universo mundo*.

[3]G: *das eigentliche Ampt des Evangelii*; L: *proprium officium evangelii*.

The English translation "function of the Gospel," as mentioned in text 218 footnote 9, does not fully convey the sense of performing the action as a member of a divinely called office that the German *Ampt* and the Latin *officium* seem to carry. See also Ap XXIV, 58–60.

[4]G/L: *per mutuum colloquium et consolationem fratrum*.

Both versions use Latin at this point. The English translation "brothers and sisters" adds a gender inclusive aspect not in the Latin *fratrum* ("of the brothers"). We see a similar use of the Latin *frater* coupled with *minister* to denote the German *Beichtiger*, "confessor," as given in the Latin translation of SC V, 24–25. See also *BSLK* XXIX–XXXI regarding the Latin text of the Small Catechism.

Smalcald Articles III, 4

236 *For this reason alone you should gladly read, recite, ponder, and practice the catechism, even if the only advantage and benefit you obtain from it is to drive away the devil and evil thoughts. For he cannot bear to hear God's Word.*[1] *And God's Word is not like some idle tale,*[2] *such as about Dietrich of Bern, but, as St. Paul says in Romans 1[:16], it is "the power of God," indeed, the power of God*[3] *that burns the devil's house down and gives us immeasurable strength, comfort, and help.*

[1]G: *denn er kann Gottes Wort nicht hören noch leiden*; L: *Non enim potest nec ferre nec audire verbum Dei Satan*.

[2]G: *Und Gottes Wort ist nicht wie ein ander lose Geschwätz*; L: *Et ipsum verbum non est tale, quales sunt aniles fabulae aut carmina lyricorum*.

[3]G: *eine Kraft Gottes*; L: *potentia Dei.*

Large Catechism, Luther's Preface, 11
Italics indicate a different textual ordering in the 1580 *Book of Concord.*

237 *Nothing is so powerfully effective against the devil, the world, the flesh, and all evil thoughts as to occupy one's self with God's Word, to speak about it and meditate upon it,*[1] *in the way that Psalm 1[:2] calls those blessed who "meditate on God's law day and night." Without doubt, you will offer up no more powerful incense or savor against the devil than to occupy yourself with God's commandments and words and to speak, sing, or think about them.*[2] *Indeed, this is the true holy water and sign that drives away the devil and puts him to flight.*

[1]G: *so man mit Gottes Wort ümbgehet, davon redet und tichtet*; L: *quam si sedulo tractetur verbum Dei, de eo sit sermo et meditatio nostra.*

[2]G: *denn so Du mit Gottes Geboten und Worten ümbgehest, davon redest, singest oder denkest*; L: *quam si verbum et praecepta Dei multo usu tractes, de iis familiares misceas sermones, illa canas ac mediteris.*

Large Catechism, Luther's Preface, 10
Italics indicate a different textual ordering in the 1580 *Book of Concord.*

SUMMARY

- God has established the ministry of the Word, the office of preaching and teaching, to which men are called. Where the Word of God is rightly taught and the sacraments are rightly administered there is the Lord's church. Those who teach falsehood not only dishonor God's name but also do not act in place of Christ. However, as comfort to those who suffer godless or wicked ministers of the Word and Sacraments, it is clear that these means of God's grace are still efficacious. The ministers do not represent themselves but act in place of Christ, whose ministry it really is.
- Through this ministry, God causes his Word to be proclaimed. Sermons of God's preachers take up the spiritual topics revealed in the Word of God. This spoken Word delivers the forgiveness of sins, as God has commanded.
- The Word of God also drives the devil and evil thoughts away because it is the power of God. Thus Christians continually occupy themselves with the Word, that is, hear it, speak it, and meditate on it both when they gather in Christ's name and when they go about their daily lives.

SYNOPSIS

The Word of God is the power of God unto salvation. It reveals God's truth. Above all, it reveals that in Christ God has reconciled the world to himself and makes righteous those who receive this Word in faith. To accomplish this, God sends preachers to proclaim his Word and by it draws all people, enlightens, justifies, and saves. The Holy Spirit uses this external Word so by the preaching of the Law, sin is revealed, and by the preaching of the Gospel, forgiveness in Christ is offered. By the Word, the Holy Spirit makes holy the person, a time, a place, or an action. So his Word might be delivered, God has established the office of the ministry of the Word to faithfully proclaim that Word. Through this office, the work of the Holy Spirit is accomplished and believers are made holy. Indeed, without such proclamation, we could not know God or the one whom the Father has sent, Christ, who now sends his ministers of the Word.

3

Baptism

What is Baptism?

301 What is baptism? Answer:

Baptism is not simply plain water.[1] Instead it is water enclosed in God's command and connected with God's Word.

What then is this Word of God? Answer:

Where our Lord Christ says in Matthew 28[:19], "Go into all the world, teach all nations, and baptize them in the name of the Father and of the Son and of the Holy Spirit."

[1]G: *Die Taufe ist nicht allein schlecht Wasser*; L: *Baptismus non est simpliciter aqua.*

Small Catechism IV, 1–4

302 Baptism is nothing other than God's Word in the water, commanded by God's institution,[1] or, as Paul says, "washing by the Word." Moreover, Augustine says, "Let the Word be added to the element, and a sacrament results." Therefore we do not agree with Thomas and the Dominicans who forget the Word (God's institution)[2] and say that God has placed a spiritual power in the water which, through the water, washes away sin. We also disagree with Scotus and the Franciscans, who teach that baptism washes away sin through the assistance of the divine will, that is, that this washing takes place only through God's will[3] and not at all through the Word and the water.

We maintain that we should baptize children because they also belong to the promised redemption that was brought about by Christ. The church ought to extend it to them.

[1]G: *Gottes Wort im Wasser, durch seine Einsetzung befohlen*; L: *verbum Dei cum mersione in aquam secundum ipsius institutionem et mandatum.*

[2]G: *die des Worts (Gottes Einsetzung) vergessen*; L: *qui verbi et institutionis Dei obliti.*

[3]G: *geschicht allein durch Gottes Willen*; L: *ex assistentia divinae voluntatis.*

Smalcald Articles III, V, 1–4

303 Baptism, however, is not our work, but God's work[1] (for, as was said, you must distinguish Christ's baptism quite clearly from a bath-keeper's baptism). God's works are salutary and necessary for salvation, and they do not exclude but rather demand faith, for without faith one cannot grasp them. Just by allowing the water to be poured over you, you do not receive or retain baptism in such a manner that it does you any good. But it becomes beneficial to you if you accept it as God's command and ordinance,[2] so that, baptized in God's name, you may receive in the water the promised salvation. Neither the hand nor the body can do this, but rather the heart must believe it.[3]

Thus you see plainly that baptism is not a work that we do but that it is a treasure that God gives us and faith grasps,[4] just as the LORD Christ upon the cross is not a work but a treasure placed in the setting of the Word and offered to us in the Word and received by faith.[5] Therefore, those who cry out against us as if we were preaching against faith do commit violence against us. Actually, we insist on faith alone as so necessary that without it nothing can be received or enjoyed.

[1]G: *die Taufe aber ist nicht unser, sondern Gottes Werk*; L: *baptismus non nostrum, sed Dei opus est.*

[2]G: *Gottes Befehl und Ordnung*; L: *Dei mandato et institutioni.*

[3]G: *sondern das Herz muß es gläuben*; L: *sed corde credendum est.*

[4]G: *ein Schatz, den . . . der Glaube ergreifet*; L: *verum thesaurum . . . sola fides apprehendit.*

[5]G: *ein Schatz im Wort gefasset und uns furgetragen und durch den Glauben empfangen*; L: *thesaurus verbo comprehensus et nobis oblatus, quem sola fides apprehendit et consequitur.*

Large Catechism IV, 35–37

304 As a matter of course, theologians rightly distinguish between a sacrament and a sacrifice.[1] Therefore, the genus that includes both of these could be either a "ceremony" or a "sacred work."[2] A sacrament is a ceremony or work in which God presents to us what the promise joined to the ceremony offers.[3] Thus baptism is not a work that we offer to God, but one in which God, through a minister who functions in his place,[4] baptizes us, and offers and presents the forgiveness of sins, etc., according to the promise [Mark 16:16], "The one who believes and is baptized will be saved." By contrast, a sacrifice is a ceremony or work that we render to God in order to give him honor.[5]

[1]L: *sacramentum et sacrificium*; G: *sacrificium und sacramentum, Opfer und Sakrament.*

[2]L: *vel ceremonia vel opus sacrum*; G: *ceremonia oder heilig Werk.*

[3]L: *Sacramentum est ceremonia vel opus in quo Deus nobis exhibet hoc, quod offert annexa ceremoniae promissio*; G: *Sacramentum ist ein ceremonia oder äusserlich Zeichen oder ein Werk, dadurch uns Gott gibt dasjenige, so die göttliche Verheißung, welche derselbigen Ceremonien angehest ist, anbeutet.*

[4]L: *sed in quo Deus nos baptizat, videlicet minister vice Dei*; G: *sondern in welchen uns Gott . . . täuft oder der Diener an Gottes Statt.*

[5]L: *Econtra sacrificium est ceremonia vel opus, quod nos Deo reddimus, ut eum honore afficiamus*; G: *Wiederum sacrificium oder Opfer ist ein ceremonia oder ein Werk, daß wir Gott geben, damit wir ihnen ehren.*

Apology XXIV, 17–18

WHY BAPTIZE?

305 [O]ur LORD Christ says in Matthew 28[:19], "Go into all the world, teach all nations, and baptize them in the name of the Father and of the Son and of the Holy Spirit."

Small Catechism IV, 4

306 First we shall take up baptism, through which we are initially received into the Christian community.[1]

[1]G: *dadurch wir erstlich in die Christenheit genommen werden*; L: *per quem primitus in christianorum communionem cooptamur.*

Large Catechism IV, 2

307 We acknowledge one baptism for the forgiveness of sins;[1]

[1]L: *Confiteor unum baptisma in remissionem peccatorum*; G: *Ich bekenne ein einige Taufe zur Vergebung der Sünden.*

The Latin and German texts derive from the medieval Roman Mass. The Kolb/Wengert text reflects more of the original Greek from the Council of Chalcedon, thus resulting in a plural "we" instead of the singular.

Nicene Creed

308 However, if the baptized act against their conscience, permit sin to reign in them, and thus grieve the Holy Spirit in themselves and lose him,[1] then, although they may not be rebaptized, they must be converted again, as has been sufficiently demonstrated above.

[1]G: *Da aber die Getauften wider das Gewissen gehandelt, die Sünde in ihnen herrschen lassen und also den Heiligen Geist in ihnen selbst betrübet und verloren*; L: *Cum vero homines baptizati contra conscientiam aliquid patrarint et peccato in mortali suo corpore dominium concesserint atque ita spiritum sanctum in se ipsis contristarint et amiserint.*

Formula of Concord, Solid Declaration II, 69

309 **[German text]** Concerning baptism it is taught that it is necessary,[1] that grace is offered through it,[2] and that one should also baptize children, who through such baptism are entrusted to God and become pleasing to him.

Rejected, therefore, are the Anabaptists who teach that the baptism of children is not right.

[Latin text] Concerning baptism they teach that it is necessary for salvation,[1] that the grace of God is offered through baptism,[2] and that children should be baptized. They are received into the grace of God when they are offered to God through baptism.

They condemn the Anabaptists who disapprove of the baptism of children and assert that children are saved without baptism.

[1]G: *Von der Tauf wird gelehret, daß sie notig sei*; L: *De baptismo docent, quod sit necessarius ad salutem.*

[2]G: *daß dadurch Gnad angeboten werde*; L: *per baptismum offeratur gratia Dei.*

Augsburg Confession IX, 1–3

310 Observe, first, that these words contain God's commandment and institution,[1] so that no one may doubt that baptism is of divine origin, not something devised or invented by human beings.[2] As truly as I can say that the Ten Commandments, the Creed, and the Lord's Prayer were not spun out of anyone's imagination but are revealed and given by God himself, so I can boast that baptism is no human plaything but is instituted by God himself.[3] Moreover, it is solemnly and strictly commanded that we must be baptized or we shall not be saved, so that we are not to regard it as an indifferent matter, like putting on a new red coat. It is of the greatest importance that we regard baptism as excellent, glorious, and exalted. It is the chief cause of our contentions and battles because the world is now full of sects who scream that baptism is an external thing and that external things are of no use. But no matter how external it may be, here stand God's Word and command that have instituted, established, and confirmed baptism.[4] What God institutes and commands cannot be useless.[5] Rather, it is a most precious thing, even though to all appearances it may not be worth a straw.

[1]G: *hie stehet Gottes Gebot und Einsetzung*; L: *hic stare Dei mandatum et institutionem.*

[2]G: *des man nicht zweifele, die Taufe sei ein göttlich Ding, nicht von Menschen erdacht noch erfunden*; L: *ne in dubium veniamus baptismum rem divinam esse, non ab hominibus excogitatam aut inventam.*

[3]G: *daß die Taufe kein Menschentand sei, sondern von Gott selbs eingesetzt*; L: *baptismum non esse humanae rationis commentum, sed ab ipso Deo institutum.*

[4]G: *da stehet aber Gottes Wort und Gebot, so die Taufe einsetzet, gründet und bestätigt*; L: *hic autem stat Dei praeceptum et verbum, quibus baptismus institutus et confirmatus est.*

[5]G: *Was aber Gott einsetzet und gebeut, muß nicht vergeblich . . . sein*; L: *Ceterum quicquid Deus instituerit et faciendum praeceperit, certum est non esse rem nihili.*

Large Catechism IV, 6–8

311 That God approves the baptism of little children is shown by the fact that God gives the Holy Spirit to those so baptized.[1]

[1]L: *Deus dat spiritum sanctum sic baptizatis*; G: *daß er vielen, so in der Kindheit getauft sein, den heiligen Geist hat gegeben.*

Apology IX, 3

WHO IS TO BE BAPTIZED?

312 [O]ur LORD Christ says in Matthew 28[:19], "Go into all the world, teach all nations, and baptize them in the name of the Father and of the Son and of the Holy Spirit."

Small Catechism IV, 4

313 (see **309**) **[German text]** Concerning baptism it is taught that it is necessary, that grace is offered through it, and that one should also baptize children, who through such baptism are entrusted to God and become pleasing to him.

[Latin text] Concerning baptism they teach that it is necessary for salvation, that the grace of God is offered through baptism, and that children should be baptized. They are received into the grace of God when they are offered to God through baptism.

Augsburg Confession IX, 1–2

314 They approve the ninth article, in which we confess that baptism is necessary for salvation,[1] that children are to be baptized, and that the baptism of children is not ineffective but is necessary and efficacious for salvation.[2] Since the gospel is purely and carefully taught among us, we have received, by God's favor, this additional fruit from it: that no Anabaptists have arisen in our churches, because the people have been fortified by God's Word against the ungodly and seditious faction of these crooks. Among the many other errors of the Anabaptists we also condemn their assertion that the baptism of little children is useless. For it is most certain that the promise of salvation also pertains to little children.[3] But it does not pertain to those who are outside the church of Christ, where there is neither Word nor sacrament, because Christ regenerates through Word and sacrament.[4] Therefore it is necessary to baptize little children in order that the promise of salvation might be applied to them according to Christ's mandate [Matt. 28:19], "Baptize all nations." Just as salvation is offered to all in that passage, so baptism is also offered to all—men, women, children, and infants. Therefore it clearly follows that infants are to be baptized because salvation is offered with baptism.

Second, it is evident that God approves the baptism of little children. The Anabaptists who condemn the baptism of little children teach wickedly. That God approves the baptism of little children is shown by the fact that God gives the Holy Spirit to those so baptized.[5] For if this baptism had been ineffectual, the Holy Spirit would have been given to no one, none would have been saved, and ultimately there would be no church.

[1]L: *quod baptismus sit necessarius ad salutem*; G: *daß die Taufe zur Seligkeit vonnöten sei.*

[2]L: *quod baptismus puerorum non sit irritus, sed necessarius et efficax ad salutem*; G: *daß die Taufe der jungen Kinder nicht vergeblich sei, sondern nötig und seliglich.*

[3]L: *Certissimum est enim, quod promissio salutis pertinet etiam ad parvulos*; G: *Denn es ist ganz gewiß, daß die Göttlichen Verheißungen der Gnaden des heiligen Geistes nicht allein die Alten, sondern auch die Kinder belangen.*

[4]L: *Neque vero pertinet ad illos, qui sunt extra ecclesiam Christi, ubi nec verbum nec sacramenta sunt, quia Christus regenerat per verbum et sacramenta*; G: *Nu gehen die Verheißungen diejenigen nicht an, so ausserhalb der Kirchen Christi sein, da weder Evangelium noch Sakramente ist. Denn das Reich Christi ist nirgend, denn wo das Wort Gottes und die Sakramente sind.*

[5]L: *hoc ostendit, quod Deus dat spiritum sanctum sic baptizatis*; G: *daß er vielen, so in der Kindheit getauft sein, den heiligen Geist hat gegeben.*

Apology IX, 1–3

315 First, we reject and condemn the Anabaptists' erroneous, heretical teaching, which is not to be tolerated or permitted in the church, or in public affairs, or in domestic life. For they teach:

1. That our righteousness before God does not only depend upon the sole obedience and merit of Christ, but also upon our renewal and on the godliness of our own way of life before God. They base this for the most part on their own special regulations and "self-imposed spirituality" [Col. 2:23] as if on a new monasticism.[1]

2. That unbaptized children are not sinners in God's sight but instead are righteous and innocent and therefore in their innocence are saved without baptism, which they do not need. They thus deny and reject the entire teaching of original sin and everything connected with it.

3. That children should not be baptized until they attain the use of their reason and can confess their faith themselves.

4. That the children of Christians, because they are born to Christian and believing parents, are holy and God's children without and before

baptism. Therefore they do not regard infant baptism as very important nor do they advocate it, against the expressed words of God's promise, which only extends to those who keep his covenant and do not despise it (Gen. 17[:4–8, 19–21]). . . .

Likewise, we reject and condemn it when the Schwenckfelders teach: . . .

3. That the water of baptism is not a means through which the Lord God seals the adoption of his children and effects new birth.[2]

[1]G: *sondern in der Erneuerung und unser eigenen Frombkeit stehe in welcher wir für Gott wandeln; welche sie das mehrer Teil auf eigene, sonderliche Satzunge und selbsterwählete Geistligkeit wie auf eine naue Muncherei setzen*; L: *ut plurimum in peculiaribus observationibus et sua quadam electicia sanctimonia, quasi in quodam novo monachatu, collocant.*

[2]G: *ein Mittel, dardurch Gott der Herr die Kindschaft vorsiegele und die Wiedergeburt wirke*; L: *medium aut instrumentum, quo Dominus adoptionem filiorum Dei obsignet et homines regeneret.*

Formula of Concord, Solid Declaration XII, 9–13, 28, 31

316 We have here the words, "The one who believes and is baptized will be saved." To what do they refer if not to baptism, that is, the water placed in the setting of God's ordinance? Hence it follows that whoever rejects baptism rejects God's Word, faith, and Christ,[1] who directs and binds us to baptism.

[1]G: *wer die Taufe verwirft, der verwirft Gottes Wort, den Glauben und Christum*; L: *qui baptismum contemnit et rejicit, verbum Dei, fidem et Christum quoque rejiciat.*

Large Catechism IV, 31

SUMMARY

- Baptism is water connected to the Word of God. As the Word is brought and taught to all nations, they also are baptized in the name of the Father and of the Son and of the Holy Spirit. It is a ceremony in which God offers us the content of his promise. This is God's work through the minister in the place of God. The power is not in the water but in God's Word; faith comprehends the Word and receives the promise.
- Baptism is done at Christ's command and is necessary for salvation. It is done only once. By it the believer receives the forgiveness of sins and the Holy Spirit. The believer also is received into

the Christian church. Children, also infants, are baptized because the promise pertains to them too. To reject Baptism is to reject the Word of God and Christ.

WHAT ARE THE BENEFITS OF BAPTISM?

317 How can water do such great things? Answer:

Clearly the water does not do it, but the Word of God, which is with and alongside the water, and faith, which trusts this Word of God in the water.[1] For without the Word of God the water is plain water and not a baptism, but with the Word of God it is a baptism, that is, a grace-filled water of life and a "bath of the new birth in the Holy Spirit," as St. Paul says to Titus in chapter 3[:5–8], "through the bath of rebirth and renewal of the Holy Spirit, which he richly poured out over us through Jesus Christ our Savior, so that through that very grace we may be *righteous and* heirs in hope of eternal life. This is *surely* most certainly true."

[1]G: *Wasser tut's freilich nicht, sondern das Wort Gottes, so mit und bei dem Wasser ist, und der Glaube, so solchem Wort Gottes im Wasser trauet*; L: *Aqua procul dubio non efficit, sed verbum Dei juxta aquam et una cum aqua et fides, quae tali verbo Dei in aqua credit.*

Small Catechism IV, 9–10

318 In the second place, because we now know what baptism is and how it is to be regarded, we must also learn why and for what purpose it has been instituted, that is, what benefits, gifts, and effects it brings. Nor can we better understand this than from the words of Christ quoted above, "The one who believes and is baptized will be saved." This is the simplest way to put it: the power, effect, benefit, fruit, and purpose of baptism is that it saves.[1] For no one is baptized in order to become a prince, but, as the words say, "to be saved." To be saved, as everyone well knows, is nothing else than to be delivered from sin, death, and the devil, to enter into Christ's kingdom, and to live with him forever.

Here again you see how baptism is to be regarded as precious and important, for in it we obtain such an inexpressible treasure. This indicates that it cannot be simple, ordinary water, for ordinary water could not have such an effect. But the Word does it, and this shows also, as we said above, that God's name is in it. And where God's name is, there must also be life and salvation. Thus it is well described as a divine, blessed, fruitful, and gracious water, for it is through the Word that it receives the power to become the "washing of regeneration," as St. Paul calls it in Titus 3[:5].

Our know-it-alls, the new spirits, claim that faith alone saves and that works and external things add nothing to it. We answer: It is true, nothing that is in us does it but faith, as we shall hear later on. But these leaders of the blind are unwilling to see that faith must have something to believe—something to which it may cling and upon which it may stand.[2] Thus faith clings to the water and believes it to be baptism, in which there is sheer salvation and life, not through the water, as we have sufficiently stated, but through its incorporation with God's Word and ordinance and the joining of his name to it. When I believe this, what else is it but believing in God as the one who has bestowed and implanted his Word in baptism and has offered us this external thing within which we can grasp this treasure?

[1]G: *daß dies der Taufe Kraft, Werk, Nutz, Frucht und Ende ist, daß sie selig mache*; L: *hanc videlicet baptismi virtutem, opus, fructum et finem esse denique homines salvos facere.*

[2]G: *daß er glaube, das ist, daran er sich halte und darauf stehe und fuße*; L: *quod credat, hoc est, cui innitatur et qua re suffulta persistat.*

Large Catechism IV, 23–29

319 Here the opponents lash out at Luther, who wrote that "original sin remains after baptism." They add that this article was rightly condemned by Leo X. But His Imperial Majesty will detect an obvious slander here. For the opponents know in what sense Luther intended the statement that original sin remains after baptism. He has always written that baptism removes the guilt of original sin,[1] even if the "material element" of sin, as they call it, remains, namely, concupiscence. He even added about the material element that when the Holy Spirit is given through baptism he begins to put concupiscence to death and to create new impulses in the human creature.[2] Augustine also says the same thing when he states, "In baptism sin is forgiven, not that it no longer exists, but that it is not accounted [as sin]." Here he clearly confesses that sin remains, even if it is not accounted [as sin]. This position so pleased subsequent generations that it was cited in the decretals. And in *Against Julian*, Augustine says, "That law, which is in the members, is forgiven by the regeneration of the spirit, but it remains in mortal flesh. It is forgiven because the guilt is absolved in the sacrament by which the faithful are reborn. But it remains because it produces desires against which the faithful struggle."

The opponents know that this is what Luther thinks and teaches. But since they cannot refute the principle, they twist the words in order to crush an innocent man by their fabrication.

They contend that concupiscence is punishment, not sin. Luther maintains that it is sin. But earlier it was shown that Augustine defined original sin in terms of concupiscence.

. . . Therefore, when Luther wanted to expose the magnitude of original sin and human weakness, he taught that the remnants of original sin in the human being are not in their essence neutral, but need both the grace of Christ, so that they might not be held [against us], and also the Holy Spirit, so that they might be put to death.[3]

[1]L: *quod baptismus tollat reatum peccati originalis*; G: *daß die heilige Taufe die ganze Schuld und Erbpflicht der Erbsunde wegnimmt und austilget.*

[2]L: *incipit mortificare concupiscentiam et novos motus creat in homine*; G: *anfähet inwendig die übrige böse Lüste täglich zu töten und zu löschen, und brengt ins Herz ein neu Licht, ein neuen Sinn und Mut.*

[3]L: *sed indigere gratia Christi, ne imputentur, item spiritu sancto, ut mortificentur*; G: *sondern bedarf des Mittlers Christi, daß sie uns Gott nicht zurechne, und ohne Unterlaß des Lichts und Wirkung des heiligen Geistes, durch welchen sie ausgefeget und getödtet werde.*

Apology II, 35–38, 45

320 Thus, we must regard baptism and put it to use in such a way that we may draw strength and comfort from it when our sins or conscience oppress us, and say: "But I am baptized![1] And if I have been baptized, I have the promise that I shall be saved and have eternal life, both in soul and body." This is the reason why these two things are done in baptism; the body has water poured over it, because all it can receive is the water, and in addition the Word is spoken so that the soul may receive it.[2]

[1]G: *Ich bin dennoch getauft*; L: *Ego tamen baptizatus sum.*

[2]G: *weil er mit der Seele vereinigt ist und die Taufe auch ergreifet, wie er's ergreifen kann*; L: *quoniam animae unitum est et baptismum quoque apprehendit, qua ratione potest apprehendere.*

Large Catechism IV, 44–45

How is Baptism used?

321 What then is the significance of such a baptism with water? Answer:

It signifies that the old creature in us with all sins and evil desires is to be drowned and die through daily contrition and repentance,[1] and on the other hand that daily a new person is to come forth and rise up to live before God in righteousness and purity forever.[2]

[1]G: *durch täglich Reu und Buße*; L: *per mortificationem ac poenitentiam.*

[2]Note that the English translation "old creature" provides a gender inclusivity where the German has *der alte Adam* and the Latin has *vetus Adam* ("the old Adam"). Likewise, the English translation employs "a new person" where the original languages of Luther's Small Catechism have *ein neuer Mensch* and *novus homo* ("a new man"). In both cases Luther simply uses the language of passages such as the original Greek of Romans 5:12–19.

Small Catechism IV, 11–12

322 Therefore let all Christians[1] regard their baptism as the daily garment that they are to wear all the time. Every day they should be found in faith and with its fruits,[2] suppressing the old creature[3] and growing up in the new. If we want to be Christians, we must practice the work that makes us Christians,[4] and let those who fall away return to it.

[1]G: *ein iglicher*; L: *Eam.*

[2]G: *daß er sich allezeit in dem Glauben und seinen Fruchten finden lasse*; L: *quo indutus semper debet incedere, ut nunquam non in fide ejusque fructibus inveniatur.*

[3]G: *den alten Menschen*; L: *veteris hominis.*

[4]G: *so müssen wir das Werk treiben, davon wir Christen sind*; L: *baptismi opus sedulo nobis exercendum est, unde christiani appellationem promeremur.*

Large Catechism IV, 84–85

323 Here you see that baptism, both by its power and by its signification, comprehends also the third sacrament, formerly called penance, which is really nothing else than baptism.[1] What is repentance but an earnest attack on the old creature[2] and an entering into a new life? If you live in repentance, therefore, you are walking in baptism,[3] which not only announces this new life but also produces, begins, and exercises it. In baptism we are given the grace, Spirit, and strength to suppress the old creature so that the new may come forth and grow strong.

Therefore baptism remains forever. Even though someone falls from it and sins, we always have access to it so that we may again subdue the old creature. But we need not have the water poured over us again. Even if we were immersed in water a hundred times, it would nevertheless not be more than one baptism, and the effect and significance would continue and remain. Repentance, therefore, is nothing else than a return and approach to baptism,[4] to resume and practice what has earlier been begun but abandoned.

[1]G: *als die eigentlich nicht anders ist denn die Taufe*; L: *quae proprie nihil aliud est quam baptismus aut ejus exercitium.*

[2]G: *den alten Menschen*; L: *veterem hominem.*

[3]G: *Darümb wenn Du in der Buße lebst, so gehest Du in der Taufe*; L: *Quare vivens in poenitentia in baptismo versaris.*

[4]G: *Also ist die Buße nicht anders denn ein Wiedergang und Zutreten zur Taufe*; L: *Ita resipiscentia aut poenitentia nihil aliud est quam regressus quidam et reditus ad baptismum.*

Large Catechism IV, 74–79

324 In baptism, therefore, every Christian has enough to study and practice all his or her life. Christians always have enough to do to believe firmly what baptism promises and brings—victory over death and the devil, forgiveness of sin, God's grace, the entire Christ, and the Holy Spirit with his gifts. In short, the blessings of baptism are so boundless[1] that if our timid nature considers them, it may well doubt whether they could all be true.

[1]G: *es ist so überschwänglich*; L: *ista omnia . . . omnem humanam cogitationem exsuperant.*

Large Catechism IV, 41–42

325 The old creature[1] therefore follows unchecked the inclinations of its nature if not restrained and suppressed by the power of baptism. On the other hand, when we become Christians, the old creature daily decreases[2] until finally destroyed. This is what it means truly to plunge into baptism and daily to come forth again. So the external sign has been appointed not only so that it may work powerfully on us but also so that it may point to something.[3] Where faith is present with its fruits, there baptism is no empty symbol, but the effect accompanies it; but where faith is lacking, it remains a mere unfruitful sign.[4]

[1]G: *der alte Mensch in seiner Natur*; L: *vetus homo naturam suam.*

[2]G: *nimmpt er täglich abe*; L: *decrescit quotidie.*

[3]G: *sondern auch etwas deuten*; L: *ut aliquid significet.*

[4]G: *Wo aber der Glaube nicht ist, da bleibt es ein bloß unfruchtbar Zeichen*; L: *Porro autem absente fide nudum et inefficax signum tantummodo permanet.*

Large Catechism IV, 71–73

326 This act or ceremony[1] consists of being dipped into the water, which covers us completely, and being drawn out again. These two parts, being dipped under the water and emerging from it, point to the power and effect of baptism, which is nothing else than the slaying of the old Adam and the resurrection of the new creature,[2] both of which must continue in us our whole life long. Thus a Christian life is nothing else than a daily baptism,[3] begun once and continuing ever after. For we must keep at it without ceasing, always purging whatever pertains to the old Adam, so that whatever belongs to the new creature may come forth.[4] What is the old creature? It is what is born in us from Adam,[5] irascible, spiteful, envious, unchaste, greedy, lazy, proud—yes—and unbelieving; it is beset with all vices and by nature has nothing good in it. Now, when we enter Christ's kingdom, this corruption must daily decrease so that the longer we live the more gentle, patient, and meek we become, and the more we break away from greed, hatred, envy, and pride.

This is the right use of baptism among Christians, signified by baptizing with water.

[1]G: *Das Werk aber oder Gebärde ist das*; L: *Opus vero aut gestus est.*

[2]Here the translation provides "old/new creature" for *alter/neuer Mensch* yet retains "old Adam" for *alter Adam.*

[3]G: *daß ein christlich Leben nichts anders ist denn eine täglich Taufe*; L: *christiani vita nihil aliud sit quam quotidianus quidam baptismus.*

[4]G: *Denn es muß ohn Unterlaß also getan sein, daß man immer ausfege, was des alten Adams ist, und erfürkomme, was zum neuen gehöret*; L: *Ita enim fieri necesse est, ut subinde veteris Adami sordes repurgentur atque eluantur, ut novi hominis nitor et forma prodeat.*

[5]G: *Was ist denn der alte Mensch? Das ist er, so uns angeboren ist von Adam*; L: *Quid autem est vetus homo? Hoc nimirum est, quod ab Adamo, patre nostro, nobis successione quadam haereditaria innatum est.*

Large Catechism IV, 65–67

SUMMARY

- Baptism saves, for it brings washing from sin and new birth in the Holy Spirit. Faith comprehends the Word and receives the gifts of God. By Baptism the guilt of original sin is removed.
- After Baptism the old Adam needs to be suppressed daily and faith renewed so the new man in Christ (Romans 5:12–21), the renewed person, bears the fruits of faith. Walking in Baptism is a life of repentance, believing firmly what the Gospel and Baptism brings, namely, "victory over death and the devil, forgiveness of sin, God's grace, the entire Christ, and the Holy Spirit with his gifts" (LC IV, 41–42).
- By water and Word, the old Adam dies and by it the new man comes forth. From the moment of Baptism forward, "life is nothing else than a daily baptism," ("*eine täglich Taufe*; *quotidianus quidam baptismus*") (LC IV, 65).

SYNOPSIS

Baptism is commanded by Christ. It is a ceremony in which God offers us the content of his promise. Baptism saves. It is water connected to the Word of God. Faith receives the gift of life, salvation, and the Holy Spirit that comes from God.

To walk in Baptism is to live in repentance, that is, returning to God with sins that need forgiveness, trusting in Christ, and eager to receive the gift again. Baptism occurs only once. It is the Holy Spirit who calls and regenerates. Yet where the means of grace (the Word of God and the sacraments that Christ instituted) are, there is the Holy Spirit, renewing, strengthening, and bringing forth fruits of faith. The Christian lives by a daily Baptism of repentance.

4
The Lord's Supper

What is the Lord's Supper?

401 **[German text]** Concerning the Lord's Supper it is taught that the true body and blood of Christ are truly present under the form of bread and wine in the Lord's Supper and are distributed[1] and received there. Rejected, therefore, is also the contrary teaching.

[Latin text] Concerning the Lord's Supper they teach that the body and blood of Christ are truly present and are distributed[1] to those who eat the Lord's Supper. They disapprove of those who teach otherwise.

[1]G: *daß wahrer Leib und Blut Christi wahrhaftiglich unter der Gestalt des Brots und Weins im Abendmahl gegenwärtig sei*; L: *quod corpus et sanguis Christi vere adsint et distribuantur vescentibus in coena Domini.*

Augsburg Confession X, 1–2

402 Now, what is the Sacrament of the Altar? Answer: It is the true body and blood of the Lord Christ, in and under the bread and wine, which we Christians are commanded by Christ's word to eat and drink. And just as we said of baptism that it is not mere water, so we say here, too, that the sacrament is bread and wine, but not mere bread and wine such as is served at the table. Rather, it is bread and wine set within God's Word and bound to it.[1]

[1]G: *das Sakrament ist . . . nicht schlecht Brot noch Wein, so man sonst zu Tisch trägt, sondern Brot und Wein, in Gottes Wort gefasset und daran gebunden*; L: *sed non simpliciter panem et vinum esse, quae proponuntur discumbentibus, sed panem et vinum Dei verbo inclusa et huic alligata.*

Large Catechism V, 8–9

403 This reliable, almighty Lord, our creator and redeemer Jesus Christ, spoke these words, which established and instituted the Supper, concerning the bread that he had consecrated and distributed, "Take and eat, this is my body which is given for you," and concerning the chalice or wine, "This is my blood of the New Testament, which is poured out for you for the forgiveness of sins" [Matt. 26:26–28; Mark 14:24; Luke 22:19–20]. He spoke these words deliberately and carefully at his Last Supper, as he began his bitter suffering and death for our sins, in that last, sad hour. Thereby he instituted this most holy sacrament, which is to be used until the end of the world with great reverence and in all obedience.[1] It is to be a continual memorial of his bitter suffering and death and of all his benefits,[2] a seal of the New Testament,[3] a comfort for all troubled hearts,[4] and a continual bond and union of Christ's people with Christ their head and among themselves.[5]

Because of all these things, we are bound to interpret and construe these words of the eternal, reliable, and almighty Son of God, our Lord, creator, and redeemer Jesus Christ, not as embellished, figurative, exotic expressions, as would appear in line with our reason. Instead, we should accept the words as they stand, in their proper, clear sense, with simple faith and appropriate obedience and not permit ourselves to be drawn away from this position by any objection or human counterargument spun out of human reason, no matter how attractive it may appear to our reason.

[1]G: *welchs bis ans Ende der Welt mit großer Reverenz und Gehorsamb gebraucht worden*; L: *quod usque ad finem mundi magna cum reverentia, obedientia et humilitate sumendum.*

[2]G: *ein stetes Gedächtnus seins bittern Leidens und Sterbens und aller seiner Guttaten*; L: *perpetuum acerbissimae passionis et mortis et omnium beneficiorum eius monumentum futurum.*

[3]G: *eine Versieglung des neuen Testaments*; L: *obsignatio et confirmatio novi testamenti.*

[4]G: *ein Trost aller betrübten Herzen*; L: *solatium omnium perturbatarum conscientiarum.*

[5]G: *stetes Band und Vereinigung der Christen mit ihrem Häupt Christo und unter sich selbst sein sollte*; L: *firmum vinculum societatis Christianae et cum capite suo Christo et inter se invicem coniunctio arctissima.*

Formula of Concord, Solid Declaration VII, 44–45

404 All the circumstances of the institution of this Supper testify that these words of our Lord and Savior Jesus Christ, which are in themselves so simple, clear, plain, firm, and beyond doubting, can and should be understood in no other way than in their usual, proper, commonly accepted meaning. For since Christ gave this command at the table during supper, there is no doubt that he was speaking about real, natural bread and natural wine and also about oral eating and drinking.[1] There can be no *metaphora* (that is, a change in the meaning) of the word "bread," as if the body of Christ were a spiritual bread or a spiritual meal for the soul.[2] Christ himself also gives the assurance that this is no *metonymia* (that is, in a similar manner, no change of meaning) of the word "body"—he was not speaking of a sign of his body, or of a symbol, or of a figurative body, or of the power of his body and its benefits, which he won with the sacrifice of his body. On the contrary, he was speaking of his true, essential body, which he gave into death for us, and of his true, essential blood, which was poured out for us on the tree of the cross for the forgiveness of sins.

Now there is no more faithful and more reliable interpreter of the words of Jesus Christ than the Lord Christ himself. He understands his own words and his heart and intention best. Given his wisdom and intelligence, he best understands how they are to be explained. Here, in the institution of his last will and testament and this enduring covenant and agreement,[3] he did not use flowery language but rather the most appropriate, simple, unambiguous, and plain words.[4] He also did so in all articles of faith and in every other institution of the signs of his covenant and grace, or sacraments, such as circumcision, the various sacrifices in the Old Testament, and Holy Baptism. Moreover, so that there can be absolutely no misunderstanding, he explained this more clearly with the words, "given for you, poured out for you." He lets his disciples retain the simple, proper understanding of the words, and he commands them to teach all nations and to hold to everything that he commanded them, the apostles.

[1]G: *daß er von rechtem, natürlichen Brot und von natürlichen Wein, auch von mündlichen Essen und Trinken redet*; L: *quin de vero naturali pane et de vero naturali vino atque de manducatione, quae ore fit, loquatur.*

[2]G: *als daß der Leib Christi ein geistlich Brot oder ein geistliche Speise der Seelen sei*; L: *quasi Christi corpus spiritualem panem aut spiritualem cibum animae dicere voluerit.*

[3]G: *welcher allhie als in Stiftung seins letzten Willens und Testaments und stets währender Bündnus und Vereinigung*; L: *Hic in declaratione inprimis ultimae suae voluntatis, testamenti et perpetui foederis atque coniunctionis.*

[4]G: *nicht verblümte, sondern ganz eigentliche, einfältige, unzweifelhaftige und klare Wort gebraucht*; L: *non verbis obscuris, figuratis aut amgibuis uti solitus est.*

Formula of Concord, Solid Declaration VII, 48–51

IS CHRIST TRULY PRESENT IN THE SACRAMENT OF THE LORD'S SUPPER?

405 We have cited this entire testimony here not in order to begin an argument on this subject here (for His Imperial Majesty does not disapprove of this article) but in order that whoever reads this might perceive more clearly that we defend the position received in the entire church—that in the Lord's Supper the body and blood of Christ are truly and substantially present[1] and are truly offered with those things that are seen, bread and wine.[2] Moreover, we are talking about the presence of the living Christ, for we know that death no longer has dominion over him [Rom. 6:9].

[1]L: *quod in coena Domini vere et substantialiter adsint corpus et sanguis Christi.*

[2]L: *et vere exhibeantur cum his rebus, quae videntur, pane et vino.*

In both of these texts, the German translation does not speak at this point.

Apology X, 4

406 Concerning transubstantiation,[1] we have absolutely no regard for the subtle sophistry of those who teach that bread and wine surrender or lose their natural substances[2] and that only the form and color of the bread remain, but it is no longer real bread.[3] For it is in closest agreement with Scripture to say that bread is and remains there, as St. Paul himself indicates [1 Cor. 10:16; 11:28]: "The bread that we break . . ." and "Eat of the bread."

[1]G: *Transsubstantiatio*; L: *transsubstantiatione.*

[2]G: *ihr naturlich Wesen*; L: *naturalem suam substantiam.*

[3]G: *und bleibe allein Gestalt und Farbe des Brots und nicht recht Brot*; L: *et tantum formam et colorem panis et non verum panem remanere.*

Smalcald Articles III, VI, 5

407 In the Holy Supper are the true body and blood of our Lord Jesus Christ truly and essentially present, distributed with the bread and wine, and received by mouth by all those who avail themselves of the sacrament[1]—whether they are worthy or unworthy, godly or ungodly, believers or unbelievers—to bring believers comfort and life and to bring judgment upon unbelievers?

The sacramentarians say no; we say yes.

To explain this controversy, it must first of all be noted that there are two kinds of sacramentarians. There are the crude sacramentarians, who state in plain language what they believe in their hearts: that in the Holy Supper there is nothing more than bread and wine present, nothing more distributed and received with the mouth.[2] Then there are the cunning sacramentarians, the most dangerous kind, who in part appear to use our language and who pretend that they also believe in a true presence of the true, essential, living body and blood of Christ in the Holy Supper, but that this takes place spiritually, through faith.[3] Yet, under the guise of such plausible words, they retain the former, crude opinion, that nothing more than bread and wine is present in the Holy Supper and received there by mouth.[4]

For "spiritually" means to them nothing other than "the spirit of Christ" that is present, or "the power of the absent body of Christ and his merit."[5] The body of Christ, according to this opinion, is, however, in no way or form present, but it is only up there in the highest heaven; to this body we lift ourselves into heaven through the thoughts of our faith. There we should seek his body and blood, but never in the bread and wine of the Supper.

[1]G: *mit Brot und Wein ausgeteilet und mit dem Mund empfangen werde*; L: *cum pane et vino distribuantur et ore sumantur.*

[2]G: *daß im heiligen Abendmahl mehr nicht denn Brot und Wein gegenwärtig sei, ausgeteilet und mit dem Munde empfangen werde*; L: *quod videlicet in coena Domini nihil amplius quam panis et vinum sint praesentia ibique distribuantur et ore percipiantur.*

[3]G: *doch solches [Abendmahl] geschehe geistlich, durch den Glauben*; L: *praesentiam et manducationem . . . esse spiritualem, quae fiat fide.*

Here the German *solches* refers back to *Abendmahl* at the beginning of the text that encapsulates the sacramental action connected with the presence to coincide with the Latin *praesentiam et manducationem*.

[4]G: *daß nämblich nichts denn Brot und Wein im heiligen Abendmahl gegenwärtig sei und mit dem Mund empfangen werde*; L: *quod videlicet praeter panem et vinum nihil amplius in coena Domini sit praesens et ore sumatur*.

[5]G: *Dann geistlich heißet ihnen anders nichts denn den Geist Christi, welcher gegenwärtig sei, oder die Kraft des abwesenden Leibs Christi und sein Verdienst*; L: *Vocabulum enim* ***spiritualiter*** *nihil aliud ipsis significat, quam spiritum Christi seu virtutem absentis corporis Christi eiusque meritum, quod praesens sit*.

Formula of Concord, Epitome VII, 2–5

408 Some sacramentarians make every effort to speak using words that are very close to the terminology and formulations of the Augsburg Confession and of its churches and to confess that in the Holy Supper the body of Christ is truly received by believers. Nevertheless, if pressed to set forth their essential position in all candor and clarity, they all with one voice declare that the true, essential body and blood of Christ are absent in the Supper, as far away from the consecrated bread and wine as the highest heaven is from the earth.[1] For according to their own words, "We say that the body and blood of Christ are so far from and distant from the signs as the earth is from the very highest heaven." Therefore, they understand the presence of Christ's body not as a presence on earth, but only *respectu fidei* [with respect to faith]. This latter phrase means that, reminded and awakened through visible signs in the same manner as through the preached Word, our faith rises up and ascends above all the heavens, where it truly and essentially, but still only spiritually, receives and enjoys the body of Christ which is present in heaven—indeed, Christ himself together with all his benefits. For, just as the bread and wine are here on earth and not in heaven, so the body of Christ is now in heaven and not on earth; therefore, in the Supper, they say, nothing else is received orally than bread and wine.

In the beginning they alleged that the Lord's Supper is only an outward sign[2] through which Christians can be identified and in which nothing other than mere bread and wine (which are the bare signs of the absent body of Christ) are distributed. When this just did not hold water, they then confessed that the Lord Christ is truly present in his Supper, but *per communicationem idiomatum*, that is, only according to his divine nature but not with his body and blood.

Later on, when they were constrained by Christ's own words to confess that the body of Christ is present in the Supper, they understood this and explained this as meaning nothing other than a spiritual presence.[3] That meant that he is present with his power, his activity, his benefits, to be enjoyed through faith, because through the Spirit of Christ, which is omnipresent, our bodies, in which the Spirit of Christ dwells here on earth, are united with Christ's body, which is in heaven.

In this way many important people were deceived through these magnificent, alluring words. For they pretended and boasted that they held no other opinion than that the Lord Christ is present in his Supper in a true, essential, and living way. However, they understood that presence only as a presence according to his divine nature, not the presence of his body and blood, which are now supposedly in heaven and nowhere else. In the Supper, with the bread and wine, he gives us his true body and blood to eat (but to be enjoyed in a spiritual manner through faith, not orally through the mouth).[4]

[1]G: *daß der wahre wesentliche Leib und Blut Christi vom gesegneten Brot und Wein im Abendmahl ja so weit als der höchste Himmel von der Erden abwesend sei*; L: *quod credant verum et substantiale Christi corpus eiusque sanguinem a benedicto pane et vino in coena sacra tanto locorum intervallo abesse, quanto summum coelum ab infima terra distet.*

[2]G: *nur ein äußerlich Zeichen*; L: *tantum externum signum.*

[3]G: *haben sie es doch nicht anders verstanden und erklärt als geistlich*; L: *id tamen aliter non intellexerunt et declararunt, quam quod spiritualem tantum praesentiam crederent.*

[4]G: *und gibt uns mit Brot und Wein seinen wahren Leib und Blut zu essen (geistlich durch den Glauben, aber nicht leiblich mit dem Munde zu genießen)*; L: *ideoque Christum nobis cum pane et vino verum corpus et verum sanguinem manducandum et bibendum dare, spiritualiter per fidem, sed non corporaliter ore sumendum.*

Formula of Concord, Solid Declaration VII, 2–6

409 For they understand the words of the Supper, "Take, eat, this is my body," not in a real sense, literally, but as figurative speech. They interpret the words as though eating the body of Christ means nothing other than faith, and as though body means nothing other than *sym-*

bolum (that is, a sign or figure) of Christ's body,[1] which is not in the Supper on earth but is only in heaven. They interpret the word "is" as follows: the body of Christ is united with the bread sacramentally or in a figurative manner, so that no one will imagine that the reality is joined to the symbols in such a way that Christ's body is even now present on earth in some invisible and incomprehensible way. That is, the body of Christ is sacramentally or symbolically united with the bread[2] in such a way that faithful, godly Christians enjoy Christ's body, which is above in heaven, spiritually through faith, as certainly as they eat the bread with their mouths. However, they continue to curse and condemn as a horrible blasphemy the teaching that Christ's body in the Supper is essentially present here on earth, although in an invisible and incomprehensible way, and is orally received with the consecrated bread also by hypocrites and counterfeit Christians.[3]

[1]G: *daß* ***Essen*** *den Leib Christi nicht anders heiße als* ***Glauben****, und* ***Leib*** *soviel als Symbolum, das ist, ein Zeichen oder Figur des Leibes Christi*; L: *ut* ***edere*** *corpus Christi nihil aliud ipsis significet quam* ***credere*** *in Christum. Et vocabulum corporis illis nil nisi symbolum, hoc est signum seu figuram corporis Christi denotet.*

[2]G: *das ist, der Leib Christi sei mit dem Brot sakramentlich oder bedeutlich voreiniget*; L: *Hoc nimirum volunt, corpus Christi cum pane sacramentaliter seu significative unitum esse.*

[3]G: *Aber daß der Leib Christi im Abendmahl allhier auf Erden wesentlich, wiewohl unsichtbarlich und unbegreiflich gegenwärtig und mit dem gesegneten Brot mündlich auch von Heuchlern oder Scheinchristen empfangen werde*; L: *Quod vero corpus Christi in sacra coena in his terris substantialiter (licet invisibili et incomprehensibili modo) praesens sit et una cum pane benedicto ore etiam ab hypocritis et nomine duntaxat Christianis sumatur.*

Formula of Concord, Solid Declaration VII, 7–8

410 3. Concerning the consecration, we believe, teach, and confess that neither human effort nor the recitation of the minister effect this presence of the body and blood of Christ in the Holy Supper,[1] but that it is to be attributed solely and alone to the almighty power of our Lord Jesus Christ.

4. In addition, we believe, teach, and hold with one accord that in the use of the Holy Supper the words of Christ's institution may under no circumstances be omitted but must be spoken publicly,[2] as it is written,

"The cup of blessing that we bless . . ." (1 Cor. 11 [10:16]). This blessing takes place through the pronouncement of the words of Christ.[3]

[1]G: *daß solliche Gegenwärtigkeit des Leibs und Bluts Christi im H[eiligen] Abendmahl nicht schaffe einiches Menschen Werk, oder Sprechen des Dieners*; L: *quod nullum opus humanum neque ulla ministri ecclesiae pronuntiatio praesentiae corporis et sanguinis Christi in coena causa sit.*

[2]G: *daß im Gebrauch des H[eiligen] Abendmahls die Wort der Einsatzung Christi keineswegs zu unterlassen, sunder öffentlich gesprochen werden sollen*; L: *in usu coenae dominicae verba institutionis Christi nequaquam omittenda, sed publice recitanda esse.*

[3]G: *Wölchs Segnen durch das Sprechen der Wort Christi geschicht*; L: *Illa autem benedictio fit per recitationem verborum Christi.*

Formula of Concord, Epitome VII, 8–9

411 For Paul expressly teaches in 1 Corinthians 11[:27] that "whoever eats the bread or drinks the cup of the Lord in an unworthy manner" is sinning not only against bread and wine and not only against a sign or symbol or figure of the body and blood. Such a person is "guilty of the body and blood of the Lord" Jesus Christ and dishonors, misuses, and desecrates Christ, who is present there, just as those Jews did who in fact really seized the body of Christ and put him to death. The ancient Christian Fathers and teachers of the church unanimously understood and explained this passage in this way. Paul means that not only the pious, godly, and faithful Christians but also the unworthy, godless hypocrites, such as Judas and his kind, who participate in no spiritual sharing with Christ[1] and who go to the table of the Lord without true repentance and conversion to God, also receive the true body and blood of Christ orally in the sacrament.[2] Thus, they sin grievously by eating and drinking the body and blood of Christ unworthily.

So there is a twofold eating of Christ's flesh. First, there is a spiritual kind of eating, which Christ treats above all in John 6[:35–58]. This occurs in no other way than with the Spirit and faith in the proclamation of and meditation on the gospel, as well as in the Supper.[3] It is in and of itself useful, salutary, and necessary for all Christians at all times for their salvation. Without this spiritual reception even the sacramental or oral eating in the Supper is not only not salutary but also harmful and damning.[4]

This spiritual eating, however, is nothing other than faith—namely, hearkening to, accepting with faith, and applying to ourselves God's

Word, which presents Christ to us as true God and a true human being along with all his benefits (God's grace, forgiveness of sins, righteousness, and eternal life). These he won for us with his flesh, which he gave into death for us, and with his blood, which he poured out for us. Moreover, this faith means relying firmly upon this comfort (that we have a gracious God and eternal salvation for the sake of the Lord Jesus Christ) with unshakable assurance and trust, holding on to this assurance in every difficulty and tribulation.[5]

[1]G: *so keine geistliche Gemeinschaft mit Christo haben*; L: *qui nullam prorsus spiritualem cum Christo communicationem habent.*

[2]G: *und sich mit ihrem unwirdigen Essen und Trinken am Leib und Blut Christi schwerlich versündigen*; L: *et grande scelus indigne edendo et bibendo in corpus et sanguinem Christi admittant.*

[3]G: *welches nicht anders als mit dem Geist und Glauben in der Predigt und Betrachtung des Evangelii ebensowohl als im Abendmahl geschicht*; L: *quae non alio modo, quam spiritu et fide in praedicatione et meditatione evangelii fit, non minus quam cum coena Domini digne et in fide sumitur.*

[4]G: *ohne welche geistliche Nießung auch das sakramentliche oder mündliche Essen im Abendmahl nicht allein unheilsamb, sondern auch schädlich und verdammlich ist*; L: *sine qua spirituali participatione sacramentalis illa, aut quae ore duntaxat fit, manducatio in coena non modo accipientibus non salutaris, sed noxia etiam et damnationis causa esse solet.*

[5]G: *Solches geistlich Essen aber ist nichts anders als der Glaube, nämblich Gottes Wort . . . hören, mit Glauben annehmen und ihme selbs zueignen und uf diesen Trost, daß wir einen gnädigen Gott und ewige Seligkeit umb des Herrn Jesu Christi willen haben, uns mit gewisser Zuversicht und Vertrauen festiglich verlassen und in aller Not und Anfechtung halten*; L: *Spiritualiter igitur manducare nihil aliud est, quam* ***credere*** *praedicato verbo Dei. . . . Haec qui ex verbo Dei commemorari audit, fide accipit sibique applicat, et hac consolatione totus nititur (quod Deum placatum et vitam aeternam propter mediatorem Iesum Christum habeamus), qui, inquam, vera fiducia in verbo evangelii firmiter in omnibus tribulationibus et tentationibus acquiescit, hic spiritualiter corpus Christi edit et sanguinem eius bibit.*

Paragraph 62 is one sentence in the German with much subordination of clauses. The long list of modifiers regarding God's Word was elided for simplicity; they denote the content of that Word, which the Latin identifies with *evangelium*. The Kolb/Wengert edition does an excellent job of rendering this text into good English.

Regarding the rendering of Christ becoming a "human being," see the note with text 102.

Formula of Concord, Solid Declaration VII, 60–62

412 Hence it is easy to answer all kinds of questions that now trouble people—for example, whether even a wicked priest can administer the sacrament, and similar questions. Our conclusion is: Even though a scoundrel receives or administers the sacrament, it is the true sacrament (that is, Christ's body and blood), just as truly as when one uses it most worthily.[1] For it is not founded on human holiness but on the Word of God. As no saint on earth, yes, no angel in heaven can make bread and wine into Christ's body and blood, so likewise can no one change or alter the sacrament, even through misuse. For the Word by which it was constituted a sacrament is not rendered false because of an individual's unworthiness or unbelief.[2] Christ does not say, "If you believe or if you are worthy, you have my body and blood," but rather, "Take, eat and drink, this is my body and blood." Likewise, when he says, "Do this" (namely, what I now do, what I institute, what I give you and bid you take), this is as much as to say, "No matter whether you are worthy or unworthy, you have here his body and blood by the power of these words that are connected to the bread and wine."[3] Mark this and remember it well. For upon these words rest our whole argument, our protection and defense against all errors and deceptions that have ever arisen or may yet arise.

[1]G: *Obgleich ein Bube das Sakrament nimmpt oder gibt, so nimmpt er das rechte Sakrament, das ist Christus' Leib und Blut, ebensowohl als der es aufs allerwirdigst handlet*; L: *Quamquam nebulo perditissimus sacramentum aliis ministret aut ipse sumat, verum sacramentum illum sumere, hoc est Christi corpus et sanguinem non secus atque eum, qui omnium reverentissime et dignissime sumpserit aut tractaverit.*

[2]G: *Denn ümb der Person oder Unglaubens willen wird das Wort nicht falsch, dadurch es ein Sakrament worden und eingesetzt ist*; L: *Quippe propter personae indignitatem aut incredulitatem verbum non fit falsum aut irritum, per quod sacramentum factum et institutum est.*

[3]G: *Du seist unwirdig oder wirdig, so hast Du hie sein Leib und Blut aus Kraft dieser Wort, so zu dem Brot und Wein kommen*; L: *Sive dignus, sive indignus fueris, hic corpus et sanguinem meum habes horum verborum virtute, quae pani ac vino adjecta sunt.*

Large Catechism V, 15–18

WHO IS TO RECEIVE THE LORD'S SUPPER, AND HOW IS IT TO BE RECEIVED?

413 Who, then, receives this sacrament worthily? Answer:

Fasting and bodily preparation are in fact a fine external discipline, but a person who has faith in these words, "given for you" and "shed for you for the forgiveness of sins," is really worthy and well prepared.[1] However, a person who does not believe these words or doubts them is unworthy and unprepared,[2] because the words "for you" require truly believing hearts.

[1]G: *recht wirdig und wohl geschickt*; L: *vere dignus ac probe paratus.*

[2]G: *unwirdig und ungeschickt*; L: *indignus ac imparatus.*

Small Catechism VI, 9–10

414 In the first place, we have a clear text in the very words of Christ, "DO THIS in remembrance of me." These are words that instruct and command us, urging all those who want to be Christians to partake of the sacrament. Therefore, whoever wants to be a disciple of Christ—it is those to whom he is speaking here—must faithfully hold to this sacrament, not from compulsion, forced by humans, but to obey and please the Lord Christ.[1] However, you may say, "But the words are added, 'as often as you do it'; so he compels no one, but leaves it to our free choice."[2] Answer: That is true, but it does not say that we should never partake of it. Indeed, precisely his words, "as often as you do it," imply that we should do it frequently.[3] And they are added because he wishes the sacrament to be free, not bound to a special time like the Passover, which the Jews were obligated to eat only once a year, precisely on the evening of the fourteenth day of the first full moon, without variation of a single day. He means to say: "I am instituting a Passover or Supper for you, which you shall enjoy not just on this one evening of the year, but frequently, whenever and wherever you will, according to everyone's opportunity and need, being bound to no special place or time."[4]

[1]G: *nicht aus Zwang, als von Menschen gedrungen, sondern dem Herrn Christo zu Gehorsam und Gefallen*; L: *non quidem coactu velut impulso ab hominibus, verum ut Christo Jesu placeat et obsequatur.*

[2]G: *sondern lässet's in freier Willköre*; L: *sed relinquit sacramenti usum in cujusque arbitratu liberum.*

[3]G: *daß man's oft tuen soll*; L: *ut saepe sacramenti communionem iteremus.*

[4]G: *sondern oft sollet genießen, wann und wo Ihr wöllet nach eines iglichen Gelegenheit und Notdurft, an keinen Ort oder bestimmpte Zeit angebunden*; L: *sed ea saepe fruamini, quando et quotiescumque libitum fuerit, prout cuique integrum erit et necessarium nulli loco aut tempori alligatum.*

Large Catechism V, 45–47

415 We maintain that the bread and the wine in the Supper are the true body and blood of Christ and that they are not only offered to and received by upright Christians but also by evil ones.

And we maintain that no one should distribute only one kind in the sacrament.[1] Nor do we need the lofty learning[2] which teaches us that there is as much under one kind as under both. This is how the sophists and the Council of Constance teach. Even if it were true that there is as much under one kind as under both, one kind is still not the complete order and institution as established and commanded by Christ.[3] Especially do we condemn and curse in God's name those who not only allow distribution of both kinds to be omitted but also dictatorially prohibit, condemn, and slander the distribution of both kinds as heresy. Thereby they set themselves against and above Christ, our Lord and God, etc.

[1]G: *daß man nicht soll einerlei Gestalt allein geben*; L: *non tantum unam speciem esse dandam.*

[2]G: *der hohen Kunst*; L: *doxosophia.*

[3]G: *so ist doch die eine Gestalt nicht die ganze Ordnung und Einsetzung, durch Christum gestift und befohlen*; L: *tamen una species non est tota ordinatio et institutio per Christum facta, tradita et mandata.*

Smalcald Articles III, VI, 1–4

WHAT ARE THE BENEFITS OF THE LORD'S SUPPER?

416 What is the benefit of such eating and drinking? Answer:

The words "given for you" and "shed for you for the forgiveness of sins" show us that forgiveness of sin, life, and salvation are given to us in the sacrament through these words, because where there is forgiveness of sin, there is also life and salvation.[1]

How can bodily eating and drinking do such a great thing? Answer:

Eating and drinking certainly do not do it, but rather the words that are recorded: "given for you" and "shed for you for the forgiveness of sins." These words, when accompanied by the physical eating and drinking, are the essential thing in the sacrament, and whoever believes these very words has what they declare and state, namely, "forgiveness of sins."[2]

[1]G: *denn wo Vergebung der Sunde ist, da ist auch Leben und Seligkeit*; L: *Ubi enim remissio peccatorum est, ibi est et vita et justitia.*

[2]G: *Und wer denselbigen Worten gläubt, der hat, was sie sagen und wie sie lauten, nämlich, „Vergebung der Sunden"*; L: *Et qui fidit his verbis, ille habet, quod dicunt ac sonant, nempe 'remissionem peccatorum'.*

Small Catechism VI, 5–8

417 Here again our clever spirits contort themselves with their great learning and wisdom; they rant and rave, "How can bread and wine forgive sins or strengthen faith?" Yet they have heard and know that we do not claim this of bread and wine—for in itself bread is bread—but of that bread and wine that are Christ's body and blood and that are accompanied by the Word. These and no other, we say, are the treasure through which such forgiveness is obtained. This treasure is conveyed and communicated to us in no other way than through the words "given and shed for you."[1] Here you have both—that it is Christ's body and blood and that they are yours as a treasure and gift. Christ's body cannot be an unfruitful, useless thing that does nothing and helps no one. Yet, however great the treasure may be in itself, it must be set within the Word and offered to us through the Word, otherwise we could never know of it or seek it.[2]

Therefore it is absurd for them to say that Christ's body and blood are not given and poured out for us in the Lord's Supper and hence that we cannot have forgiveness of sins in the sacrament. Although the work took place on the cross and forgiveness of sins has been acquired, yet it cannot come to us in any other way than through the Word.[3] How should we know that this took place or was to be given to us if it were not proclaimed by preaching, by the oral Word?[4] From what source do they know of forgiveness, and how can they grasp and appropriate it, except by steadfastly believing the Scriptures and the gospel? Now, the whole gospel and the article of the Creed, "I believe in one holy Christian church . . . the forgiveness of sins," are embodied in this sacrament and offered to us through the Word. Why, then, should we allow such a treasure to be torn out of the sacrament? They must still confess that these are the very words that we hear everywhere in the gospel. They can no more say that these words in the sacrament are of no value than they can dare to say that the whole gospel or Word of God apart from the sacrament is of no value.

[1]G: *Nu wird es uns ja nicht anders denn in den Worten „Fur Euch gegeben und vergossen" gebracht und zugeeignet*; L: *Jam ille non aliter quam per verba ('pro vobis traditur et effunditur') nobis offertur et donatur.*

[2]G: *Doch wie groß der Schatz fur sich selbs ist, so muß er in das Wort gefasset und uns gereicht werden, sonst würden wir's nicht können wissen noch suchen*; L: *Veruntamen quamlibet magnus per se thesaurus exsistat, verbo includendus eoque nobis ministrandus est, alioqui eundem neque scire neque quaerere possumus.*

[3]G: *so kann sie doch nicht anders denn durchs Wort zu uns kommen*; L: *neque tamen alia ratione quam per verbum ad nos pervenire aut perferri potest.*

[4]G: *Denn was wußten wir sonst davon, daß solchs geschehen wäre oder uns geschenkt sein sollte, wenn man's nicht durch die Predigt oder mündlich Wort furtrüge?* L: *Quid enim hac de re nos comperti haberemus haec facta esse aut nobis condonata, nisi haec praedicatione aut corporali verbo nobis annuntiarentur?*

Large Catechism V, 28–32

418 So far we have treated the whole sacrament from the standpoint both of what it is in itself and of what it brings and benefits. Now we must also consider who the person is who receives such power and benefit. Briefly, as we said above about baptism and in many other places, the answer is: It is the one who believes what the words say and what they give,[1] for they are not spoken or preached to stone and wood but to those who hear them, those to whom he says, "Take and eat," etc. And because he offers and promises forgiveness of sins, it can be received in no other way than by faith.[2] This faith he himself demands in the Word when he says, "given FOR YOU" and "shed FOR YOU," as if he said, "This is why I give it and bid you eat and drink, that you may take it as your own and enjoy it." All those who let these words be addressed to them and believe that they are true have what the words declare. But those who do not believe have nothing,[3] for they let this gracious blessing be offered to them in vain and refuse to enjoy it. The treasure is opened and placed at everyone's door, yes, upon the table, but it is also your responsibility to take it and confidently believe that it is just as the words tell you.[4]

Now this is the sum total of a Christian's preparation to receive this sacrament worthily. Because this treasure is fully offered in the words, it can be grasped and appropriated only by the heart.[5] Such a gift and eternal treasure cannot be seized with the hand.

[1]G: *Wer da solchs gläubt, wie die Wort lauten und was sie bringen*; L: *Quicumque ea crediderit, quae verba loquuntur et afferunt.*

[2]G: *kann es nicht anders denn durch den Glauben empfangen werden*; L: *non possunt haec aliter atque per fidem percipi.*

[3]G: *Wer aber nicht gläubt, der hat nichts*; L: *Ceterum hisce verbis diffidens minimo minus habet.*

[4]G: *daß Du Dich auch sein annehmest und gewißlich dafur haltest, wie Dir die Wort geben*; L: *huic manum extensam admoveas constanter credens, quemadmodum ipsa verba te docent.*

[5]G: *Denn weil solcher Schatz gar in den Worten furgelegt wird, kann man's nicht anders ergreifen und zu sich nehmen denn mit dem Herzen*; L: *Cum enim hic thesaurus in verbis prorsus nobis proponatur, non aliter quam corde apprehendi potest.*

Large Catechism V, 33–36

419 Of course, it is true that those who despise the sacrament and lead unchristian lives receive it to their harm and damnation.[1] To such people nothing can be good or wholesome, just as when a sick person willfully eats and drinks what is forbidden by the physician. But those who feel their weakness, who are anxious to be rid of it and desire help, should regard and use the sacrament as a precious antidote against the poison in their systems. For here in the sacrament you are to receive from Christ's lips the forgiveness of sins, which contains and brings with it God's grace and Spirit with all his gifts, protection, defense, and power against death, the devil, and every trouble.[2]

Thus you have on God's part both the commandment and the promise of the Lord Christ. Meanwhile, on your part, you ought to be induced by your own need, which hangs around your neck and which is the very reason for this command, invitation, and promise. For he himself says [Matt. 9:12], "Those who are well have no need of a physician, but those who are sick," that is, those who labor and are burdened with sin, fear of death, and the attacks of the flesh and the devil. If you are burdened and feel your weakness, go joyfully to the sacrament and let yourself be refreshed, comforted, and strengthened.[3]

[1]G: *nehmen's ihn zu Schaden und Verdammnis*; L: *tantum in perniciem et damnationem sibi sumere.*

[2]G: *Denn hie sollt Du im Sakrament empfahen aus Christus' Mund Vergebung der Sunde, welche bei sich hat und mit sich bringet Gottes Gnade und Geist mit alle seinen Gaben, Schutz, Schirm und Gewalt wider Tod und Teufel und alles Unglück*; L: *Hic enim ex ore Christi sumes peccatorum condonationem secum habentem unaque apportantem Dei gratiam et spiritum una cum omnibus suis donis, tutela, protectione et potestate contra mortem, diabolum atque omnia mala.*

[3]G: *Bist Du nu beladen und fühlest Dein Schwachheit, so gehe fröhlich hin und lasse Dich erquicken, trösten und stärken*; L: *Jam si peccatorum fasce gravatus es tuamque sentis infirmitatem, tum alacri accedas animo teque Christo refocillandum, levandum et corroborandum offeras.*

Large Catechism V, 69–72

SUMMARY

- The Lord's Supper is the true body and blood of Christ in and under the bread and wine that Christians are commanded by Christ to eat and drink. It is not mere bread and wine, as at an ordinary meal, for the words of Christ, "This is my body . . . This is my blood," are to be understood in a simple, clear, and plain sense, not in any allegorical or figurative sense. It is a memorial of his suffering and death and of a firm bond of believers with Christ, their Head, and with one another.
- The church always taught that the body and blood of Christ are truly received with the bread and wine. The bread and wine do not lose their natural substance but remain bread and wine. In the Sacrament Christ gives us his true body and blood not just in a spiritual sense, as if the bread and wine are only a sign or figure of Christ's body that has ascended to heaven. But as Christ says, his body and blood are received orally in the eating and drinking. Even unworthy persons, hypocrites, or unbelievers receive Christ's body and blood, not just those who believe his words.
- Those who have faith in Christ's words "Given and shed for you for the remission of sins" are truly worthy and well prepared to receive his body and blood in the Sacrament. One who doubts or does not believe these words is unworthy and unfit. Believers receive the Lord's Supper out of obedience, freely, without coer-

cion, and often. They are given not just one form but both body and blood (bread and wine), as Christ has commanded.

- In this sacramental eating and drinking, believers receive the forgiveness of sins, life, and salvation as the words "given and shed for you for the remission of sins" promise. Whoever believes it has what the words declare and bring. Those who despise or reject Christ's words receive the Sacrament to their hurt and damnation. Those who are heavy-laden with their sins, therefore, come to the Lord's Supper joyfully and there receive refreshment, comfort, and strength.
- The Sacrament comforts hearts with the knowledge of Christ and brings his merits, righteousness, and forgiveness to the believer who receives it.

IS IT POSSIBLE TO SPEAK OF THE SACRAMENT OF THE LORD'S SUPPER, THAT IS, THE CEREMONY OF THE MASS, AS A SACRIFICE?

420 For we have shown in our Confession that we hold that the Lord's Supper does not confer grace *ex opere operato*,[1] nor does it *ex opere operato* confer merit for others, living or dead, the forgiveness of sins, guilt or punishment.[2] And this is the clear and firm proof of this position: It is impossible to receive the forgiveness of sins *ex opere operato* on account of our works. Instead, faith must conquer the terrors of sin and death, when we comfort our hearts with the knowledge of Christ and realize that we are forgiven on account of Christ and are given the merits and righteousness of Christ. "Therefore, since we are justified by faith, we have peace" [Rom. 5:1]. These things are so certain and so firm that they can prevail against all the gates of hell [cf. Matt. 16:18].

[1]L: *quod coena Domini non conferat gratiam ex opere opearto*; G: *daß das Abendmahl oder die Messe niemand fromm mache ex opere operato.*

[2]L: *mereatur eis ex opere operato remissionem peccatorum, culpae aut poenae*; G: *ihnen nicht verdiene Vergebung der Sunde, Verlassung Pein und Schuld.*

Apology XXIV, 11–12

421 As a matter of course, theologians rightly distinguish between a sacrament and a sacrifice. Therefore, the genus that includes both of these could be either a "ceremony" or a "sacred work." A sacrament is a ceremony or work in which God presents to us what the promise joined to the ceremony offers.[1] Thus baptism is not a work that we offer to God, but one in which God, through a minister who functions in his place, baptizes us, and offers and presents the forgiveness of sins, etc., according to the promise [Mark 16:16], "The one who believes and is baptized will be saved." By contrast, a sacrifice is a ceremony or work that we render to God in order to give him honor.[2]

Now there are two, and no more than two, basic kinds of sacrifice. One is the atoning sacrifice, that is, a work of satisfaction for guilt and punishment[3] that reconciles God, conciliates the wrath of God, or merits the forgiveness of sins for others. The other kind is the eucharistic sacrifice. It does not merit the forgiveness of sins or reconciliation but is rendered by those who have already been reconciled as a way for us to give thanks or express gratitude for having received forgiveness of sins and other benefits.[4]

In this controversy and in other disputes, we must never lose sight of those two kinds of sacrifices, and we should take special care not to confuse them. If this type of book allowed it, we would include the reasons for making this distinction, for it has more than enough testimonies in the Letter to the Hebrews and elsewhere.

[1]L: *Sacramentum est ceremonia vel opus, in quo Deus nobis exhibet hoc, quod offert annexa ceremoniae promissio*; G: *Sacramentum ist ein ceremonia oder äußerlich Zeichen oder ein Werk, dadurch uns Gott gibt dasjenige, so die göttliche Verheißung, welche derselbigen Ceremonien angeheft ist, anbeutet.*

[2]L: *Econtra sacrificum est ceremonia vel opus, quod nos Deo reddimus, ut eum honore afficiamus*; G: *Wiederum sacrificium oder Opfer ist ein ceremonia oder ein Werk, das wir Gott geben, damit wir ihnen ehren.*

[3]L: *Quoddam est sacrificium propitiatorium, id est, opus satisfactorium pro culpa et poena*; G: *Für eins ist ein Versühnopfer, dadurch gnug getan wird für Pein und Schuld.*

[4]L: *Altera species est sacrificum εὐχαριστικόν, quod non meretur remissionem peccatorum aut reconciliationem, sed fit a reconciliatis, ut pro accepta remissione peccatorum et pro aliis beneficiis acceptis gratias agamus, seu gratiam referamus*; G: *Zum andern ist ein Dankopfer, dadurch nicht Vergebung der Sunde oder Versühnung erlangt wird, sondern geschiehet von denjenigen, welche schon versühnet sein, daß sie für die erlangte Vergebung der Sunde und andere Gnaden und Gaben Dank sagen.*

Apology XXIV, 17–20

422 In point of fact there has been only one atoning sacrifice in the world, namely, the death of Christ,[1] as the Letter to the Hebrews teaches when it says [10:4], "For it is impossible for the blood of bulls and goats to take away sins." A little later [v. 10] it says about the will of Christ, "And it is by God's will that we have been sanctified through the offering of the body of Jesus Christ once for all." Isaiah, too, interprets the law to mean that the death of Christ—not the ceremonies of the law—is a real satisfaction or expiation for our sins.[2] Thus he says [53:10], "When you make his life an offering for sin, he shall see his offspring, and shall prolong his days," etc. Now the word he uses here (*'asam*) refers to a victim sacrificed for transgression. In the Old Testament this meant that a certain Victim was to come in order to make satisfaction for our sins and reconcile us to God, so that people might know that God wants to be reconciled to us not on account of our righteousness but on account of another's merits, namely, Christ's. Paul interprets the same word (*'asam*) as sin in Romans 8[:3]: "through sin he condemned sin," that is, he punished sin through sin, that is, through a sacrificial victim for sin. We can understand the meaning of the word more easily if we look at the customs the pagans adopted from their misinterpretation of the patriarchal tradition. The Latins spoke of a sacrificial victim offered to conciliate the wrath of God in great calamities, when it seemed that God was unusually angry. Sometimes they offered human sacrifices, perhaps because they had heard that a human sacrifice was going to conciliate God for the entire human race. The Greeks at times called them "refuse" and at other times "offscouring." Isaiah and Paul understand that Christ was made a sacrificial victim, that is, an expiation,[3] and that by his merits and not ours, God would be reconciled. Therefore let this remain the case, that the death of Christ alone is truly an atoning sacrifice.[4] The Levitical sacrifices of atonement were so called only in order to point to a future expiation.[5] By some sort of analogy, therefore, they were satisfactions since they purchased a righteousness of the law and thereby prevented those persons who sinned from being excluded from the community. But they had to come to an end after the revelation of the gospel. Moreover, because they had to come to an end with the revelation of the gospel, they were not truly atoning sacrifices, since the gospel was promised for the very reason that it set forth the atoning sacrifice.

Now the rest are eucharistic sacrifices, which are called "sacrifices of praise,"[6] namely, the preaching of the gospel, faith, prayer, thanksgiving, confession, the afflictions of the saints, and indeed, all the good works of the saints. These sacrifices are not satisfactions for those who offer them,[7] nor can they be applied to others so as to merit the forgiveness of sins or reconciliation for others *ex opere operato*. They are performed by those who are already reconciled.

These are the sacrifices of the New Testament, as Peter teaches [1 Peter 2:5], "a holy priesthood, to offer spiritual sacrifices." Spiritual sacrifices,[8] however, are contrasted not only with animal sacrifices but also with human works offered *ex opere operato*, because "spiritual" refers to the work of the Holy Spirit within us. Paul teaches the same thing in Romans 12[:1]: "[P]resent your bodies as a living sacrifice, holy and acceptable to God, which is your spiritual worship." "Spiritual worship" refers to worship where God is recognized and is grasped by the mind, as happens when it fears and trusts God. Therefore, it is contrasted not only to Levitical worship, in which animals were slain, but with any worship in which people imagine that they are offering God a work *ex opere operato*. The Epistle to the Hebrews, chapter 13[:15], teaches the same thing, "Through him, then, let us continually offer a sacrifice of praise to God," and it adds an interpretation, "that is, the fruit of lips that confess his name." He commands us to offer praises, that is, prayer, thanksgiving, confession, and the like. These avail not *ex opere operato* but on account of faith. This is stressed by the phrase, "through him let us offer," that is, by faith in Christ.

[1]L: *Sed revera unicum tantum in mundo fuit sacrificium propitiatorium, videlicet mors Christi*; G: *aber es ist allein ein einiges, wahrhaftiges Sühneopfer, Opfer für Sunde, in der Welt gewesen, nämlich der Tod Christi*.

[2]L: *Esaias interpretatur legem, ut sciamus mortem Christi vere esse satisfactionem pro peccatis nostris seu expiationem, non ceremonias legis*; G: *Und Esaias der Prophet hat auch zuvor das Gesetz Mosi ausgelegt und zeigt an, daß der Tod Christi die Bezahlung für die Sunde ist, und nicht die Opfer im Gesetz*.

[3]L: *Intelligunt igitur Esaias et Paulus, Christum factum esse hostiam, hoc est piaculum*.

The German paraphrase speaks of a *Schuldopfer* but does not engage the Latin regarding the specific meaning of the vocabulary.

[4]L: *quod sola mors Christi est vere propitiatorium sacrificium*; G: *Darum bleibt dieses fest stehen, daß nur ein einig Opfer gewesen ist, nämlich der Tod Christi*.

[5]L: *ad significandum futurum piaculum*.

The German text does not cover this point.

[6]L: *sacrifica laudis*; G: *Dankopfer*.

[7]L: *Haec sacrificia non sunt satisfactiones pro facientibus*; G: *Dasselbige sind nicht solche Opfer, dadurch wir versühnet werden*.

[8]L: *hostiae spirituales*.

The German text's use of *geistliche Opfer* from 1 Peter 2 would apply to the Latin text here, though the German does not speak at this point.

Apology XXIV, 22–26

423 We readily concede that all who want to include the ceremony [of the Mass] here may do so as long as they do not interpret it as a mere ceremony or do not mean that by itself (*ex opere operato*) the ceremony is beneficial. For just as among the sacrifices of praise, that is, among the praises of God, we include the proclamation of the Word, so the reception of the Lord's Supper itself can be a praise or thanksgiving.[1] However, it does not justify *ex opere operato*, nor should it be applied to others as if it merited the forgiveness of sins. In a little while we shall show how even this ceremony is sacrifice.[2] But because Malachi is talking about all the acts of worship of the New Testament[3]—not only about the Lord's Supper—and because he does not favor the Pharisaical opinion about *ex opere operato*, he is not against our position. More than that, he supports it. For he requires the worship of the heart, by which the name of the Lord truly becomes great.[4]

They cite another passage from Malachi [3:3], "[A]nd he will purify the descendants of Levi and refine them like gold and silver, until they present offerings to the Lord in righteousness." This passage clearly requires the sacrifices of the righteous;[5] therefore it does not support the opinion concerning *ex opere operato*. For the sacrifices of the sons of Levi (that is, those in the New Testament who teach) are the preaching of the gospel and the good fruits of such a preaching, as Paul speaks in Romans 15[:16] of "the priestly service of the gospel of God, so that the offering of the Gentiles may be acceptable, sanctified by the Holy Spirit," that is, that the Gentiles might become offerings acceptable to God through faith, etc.[6] For the slaughter of animals in the Old Testament signified both the death of Christ and the preaching of the gospel, by which this old flesh should be killed, and the new and eternal life be begun in us.

But at every turn our opponents twist the word "sacrifice" until it only includes the mere ceremony.[7] They omit the proclamation of the gospel, faith, prayer, and the like, even though the ceremony has been established on account of these. The New Testament requires that sacrifices of the heart, not the ceremonial sacrifices for sin, must be offered according to the practice of the Levitical priesthood.[8]

They also refer to the "daily sacrifice." Just as in the Old Testament there was a daily sacrifice, so also the Mass ought to be the daily sacrifice of the New Testament. It will go well for opponents if we allow ourselves to be conquered by allegories. It is evident that allegories do not prove or establish anything. We are perfectly willing for the Mass to be understood as a daily sacrifice, provided that this includes the entire Mass, that is, the ceremony together with the proclamation of the gospel, faith, prayer, and thanksgiving.[9] For these things are joined together as a daily sacrifice in the New Testament; the ceremony was instituted for the sake of these things, and must not be separated from them. Accordingly, Paul says [1 Cor. 11:26], "For as often as you eat this bread and drink the cup, you proclaim the Lord's death until he comes." But it in no way follows from this Levitical analogy that a ceremony necessarily justifies *ex opere operato* or that it should be applied to others so as to merit the forgiveness of sins for them, etc.

[1]L: *Sicut enim inter sacrificia laudis, hoc est, inter laudes Dei complectimur praedicationem verbi: ita laus esse potest seu gratiarum actio ipsa sumptio coenae Domini*; G: *Denn wie wir die Predigt heissen ein Lobopfer, so mag die ceremonia des Abendmahls an ihm selbst ein Lobopfer sein.*

[2]L: *quomodo et ceremonia sacrificium sit*; G: *wie die ceremonia ein Opfer sei.*

[3]L: *Verum quia Malachias de omnibus cultibus novi testamenti*; G: *Dieweil aber Malachias redet von allen Gottesdiensten und Opfern des neuen Testaments.*

[4]L: *Requirit enim cultus cordis, per quos vere fit magnum nomen Domini*; G: *denn er fordert inwendig das Herz, Gott Dankopfer zu tun, durch welchs der Namen des Herren recht groß werde.*

[5]L: *sacrificia iustorum*; G: *Opfern der Gerechtigkeit.*

[6]L: *ut gentes fiant hostiae acceptae Deo per fidem etc.*; G: *auf daß die Heiden ein Opfer werden, Gott angenehm durch den Glauben.*

[7]L: *Sed adversarii ubique sacrificii nomen ad solam ceremoniam detorquent*; G: *Aber die Widersacher deuten allenthalben das Wort Opfer oder sacrificium allein auf die Ceremonien der Meß.*

[8]L: *et novum testamentum debeat habere sacrificia cordis, non ceremonialia pro peccatis facienda more levitici sacerdotii*; G: *so doch das neue Testament eitel geistliche Opfer hat inwendig des Herzens, und nicht solche Opfer wie das levitische Priestertum.*

[9]L: *modo ut tota missa intelligatur, hoc est, ceremonia cum praedicatione evangelii, fide, invocatione et gratiarum actione*; G: *wenn sie die ganze Messe, das ist, die Ceremonien mit der Danksagung, mit dem Glauben im Herzen, mit dem herzlichen Anrufen göttlicher Gnad iuge sacrificium nenneten.*

Apology XXIV, 33–35

424 Therefore, although the ceremony is a memorial of Christ's death,[1] nevertheless in itself it is not a daily sacrifice. Instead, the commemoration is the real daily sacrifice, that is, proclamation and faith that truly believes God is reconciled by the death of Christ.[2] A drink offering is required, namely, the effect of the proclamation, that through the gospel we are sanctified by the blood of Christ having been put to death and made alive. Offerings are also required, that is, thanksgiving, confession, and affliction.[3]

Now that we have overthrown the Pharisaical opinion about the *opus operatum*, let us understand that spiritual worship and the daily sacrifice of the heart are signified here,[4] because in the New Testament we must consider "the body" of good things [cf. Col. 2:17], that is, the Holy Spirit, being put to death, and being made alive. From these things it is quite clear that the type of a daily sacrifice does not refute us, instead it supports us because we require all the actions signified by the daily sacrifice.[5] Our opponents falsely imagine that the ceremony alone is signified and not the proclamation of the gospel, putting the heart to death, bringing it to life, etc.[6]

[1]L: *etiamsi ceremonia est memoriale mortis Christi*; G: *wiewohl die Messe oder Ceremonia im Abendmahl ein Gedächtnis ist des Tods Christi.*

[2]L: *sed ipsa memoria est iuge sacrificium, hoc est, praedicatio et fides, quae vere credit, Deum morte Christi reconciliatum esse*; G: *sondern das Gedächtnis des Tods Christi zusamt mit der Ceremonia ist das tägliche Opfer, das ist, die Predigt vom Glauben und Christo, welcher Glaube wahrlich gläubet, daß Gott durch den Tod Christi versühnet sei.*

[3]L: *Requiruntur et oblationes, hoc est, gratiarum actiones, confessiones, et afflictiones*. G: *Darnach sollen wir auch danken und Gott loben und den Glauben mit Leiden und guten Werken bekennen, das ist durch Mehl und Öle bedeutet.*

[4]L: *significari cultum spiritualem et iuge sacrificium cordis*; G: *daß durch das iuge sacrificium bedeut ist das geistliche Opfer und tägliche Opfer der Herzen.*

[5]L: *quia nos omnes partes significatas iugi sacrificio requirimus.* G: *daß alles, was zum täglichen Opfer im Gesetz Mosi gehöret hat, muß ein wahr herzlich Opfer, nicht opus operatum bedeuten.*

[6]L: *Adversarii falso somniant solam ceremoniam significari, non etiam praedicationem evangelii, mortificationem et vivificationem cordis etc.* G: *Der Widersacher Traum ist falsch, da sie wähnen wollen, es werde allein das schlechte äußerliche Werk und Ceremonia bedeut, so doch der Glaube im Herzen, das Predigen Bekennen, Danksagung und herzliches Anrufen die rechten täglichen Opfer sein und das Beste an der Messe, sie nennens gleich Opfer oder anders.*

Apology XXIV, 38–40

425 Now if the use of the sacrament were the daily sacrifice, we could lay more claim to observing it than our opponents, because among them the priests use the sacrament to make money. Among us it is used more frequently and more devoutly. For the people use it, but only after they have been instructed and examined.[1] They are taught about the proper use of the sacrament, that it was instituted as a seal and testimony of the gracious forgiveness of sins[2] and therefore as an encouragement to sensitive consciences in order that they may be completely convinced and believe that their sins are freely forgiven. Since, therefore, we retain the proclamation of the gospel and the proper use of the sacraments, a daily sacrifice remains among us.[3]

Moreover, if we must speak about outward appearances, attendance in our churches is greater than among the opponents'. Practical and clear sermons hold an audience.[4] But neither the people nor the theologians have ever understood the opponents' teaching. The true adornment of the churches is godly, useful, and clear doctrine, the devout use of the sacraments, ardent prayer, and the like.[5] Candles, golden vessels, and similar adornments are appropriate, but they are not the distinctive adornment of the church. Now if the opponents make such things the center of worship[6] rather than the proclamation of the gospel, faith, and its struggles, they should be numbered among those whom Daniel describes as worshiping their god with gold and silver [Dan. 11:38].

[1]L: *Nam populus utitur, sed prius institutus atque exploratus*; G: *Denn da wird niemand mit Geld dazu getrieben, sondern man lässet die Gewissen sich prüfen.*

[2]L: *ut sit sigillum et testimonium gratuitae remissionis peccatorum*; G: *daß es sei ein Siegel und gewiß Zeichen der Vergebung der Sunde.*

[3]L: *Cum igitur et praedicationem evangelii et legitimum usum sacramentorum retineamus, manet apud nos iuge sacrificium.* G: *So wir nu die Predigt des Evangelii und den rechten Brauch des Sakraments bei uns behalten, so haben wir ohne Zweifel das tägliche Opfer.*

[4]L: *Tenentur enim auditoria utilibus et perspicuis concionibus.*

The German text does a considerable amount of paraphrasing before arriving at: *Denn es ist kein Ding, das die Leute mehr bei der Kirchen behält, denn die gute Predigt.*

[5]L: *Et verus ornatus est ecclesiarum doctrina pia, utilis et perspicua, usus pius sacramentorum, oratio ardens et similia.* G: *Denn der rechte äußerliche Kirchenschmuck ist auch rechte Predigt, rechter Brauch der Sakrament und daß das Volk mit Ernst dazu gewöhnet sei und mit Fleiß und züchtig zusammen komme, lerne und bete.*

[6]L: *in talibus rebus collocant cultus*; G: *für nötige Stück und damit Gottesdienst anrichten.*

Apology XXIV, 49–51

426 Therefore, if anyone argues that the New Testament must have a priest who makes offerings for sins, this must be applied only to Christ. The entire Epistle to the Hebrews supports this interpretation. If we required some other satisfaction for application to the sins of others and reconciliation with God, we would simply be setting up another mediator besides Christ. Again, because the priesthood of the New Testament is a ministry of the Spirit,[1] as Paul teaches in 2 Corinthians 3[:6], it has but the one sacrifice of Christ which makes satisfaction for and is applied to the sins of others.[2] It has no sacrifices like the Levitical, which could be applied *ex opere operato* to others; instead, it presents the gospel and sacraments to others so that they may thereby receive faith and the Holy Spirit, be put to death and be made alive. For the ministry of the Spirit conflicts with the application of an *opus operatum*.[3] Through the ministry of the Spirit, the Holy Spirit works in our hearts. Therefore his ministry benefits others when he works in them and gives them new birth and life.[4] This does not happen by applying, *ex opere operato*, one person's work to another.[5]

We have shown why the Mass does not justify *ex opere operato* and why, when applied on behalf of others, it does not merit forgiveness for them: both conflict with the righteousness of faith.[6] For the forgiveness of sins cannot take place and the terrors of sin and death cannot be conquered by any work or anything else except by faith in Christ, as it says [Rom. 5:1]: "[S]ince we are justified by faith, we have peace."

[1]L: *sacerdotium novi testamenti est ministerium spiritus*; G: *das Priestertum des neuen Testaments ein Amt ist, dadurch der heilige Geist wirkt.*

[2]L: *ideo unicum habet sacrificium Christi satisfactorium et applicatum pro peccatis aliorum.*

The German text does not make this point nor the two that follow.

[3]L: *quia ministerium spiritus pugnat cum applicatione operis operati.*

[4]L: *Est enim ministerium spiritus, per quod spiritus sanctus efficax est in cordibus, quare habet tale ministerium, quod ita prodest aliis, cum in eis efficax est, cum regenerat et vivificat eos.*

[5]L: *Id non fit applicatione alieni operis pro aliis ex opere operato*; G: *Denn wo nicht eigner Glaube und Leben durch den heiligen Giest gewirkt wird, kann mich eines andern opus operatum nicht fromm und selig machen.*

[6]L: *quia utrumque pugnat cum iustitia fidei*; G: *denn beides ist stracks wider den Glauben und die Lehre von Christo.*

Apology XXIV, 58–60

427 Sacraments are signs of God's will toward us,[1] not simply signs of the people's will among themselves, and so it is right to define the New Testament sacraments as signs of grace. A sacrament consists of two parts, the sign and the Word.[2] In the New Testament the Word is the added promise of grace. The promise of the New Testament is the promise of the forgiveness of sins, just as this text says [cf. Luke 22:19 and Matt. 26:28], "This is my body, which is given for you. . . . [T]his is the cup of the New Testament in my blood, which is poured out for many for the forgiveness of sins." The Word, therefore, offers forgiveness of sins. The ceremony is like a picture of the Word or a "seal,"[3] as Paul calls it [Rom. 4:11], that shows forth the promise. Therefore, just as the promise is useless unless it is received by faith, so also the ceremony is useless unless faith, which really confirms that the forgiveness of sins is being offered here, is added. Such a faith encourages contrite minds. Just as the Word was given to awaken this faith, so also the sacrament was instituted in order that, as the outward form meets the eyes, it might move the heart to believe.[4] For the Holy Spirit works through the Word and the sacrament.[5]

Such use of the sacrament, in which faith gives life to terrified hearts, is the New Testament worship, because the New Testament involves spiritual impulses: being put to death and being made alive.[6] Christ instituted the sacrament for this use when he commanded [1 Cor. 11:24], "Do this in remembrance of me." For to remember Christ is not an empty celebration or a show[7] nor something instituted for the sake of an example, the way plays celebrate the memory of Hercules or Ulysses.[8] It is rather to remember Christ's benefits and to receive them by faith so that we are made alive through them.[9] Accordingly the psalm [111:4, 5] says, "He has gained renown by his wonderful deeds; the Lord is gracious and merciful. He provides food for those who fear him." This means that in the ceremony we should acknowledge the will and mercy of God.[10] Now faith that recognizes mercy makes alive. This is the principal use of the sacrament,[11] through which it becomes clear both that terrified consciences are the ones worthy of it and how they ought to use it.

[1]L: *Sacramenta sunt signa voluntatis Dei erga nos*; G: *Die Sakramente aber sind Zeichen des göttlichen Willens gegen uns.*

[2]L: *signum et verbum*; G: *das äußerliche Zeichen und das Wort.*

[3]L: *ceremonia est quasi pictura verbi seu sigillum*; G: *Das äußerliche Zeichen ist wie ein Siegel und Bekräftigung der Wort und Verheißung.*

[4]L: *ita sacramentum institutum est, ut illa species incurrens in oculos moveat corda ad credendum*; G: *also ist auch das äußerliche Zeichen daneben geben und für die Augen gestellet, daß es die Herzen zu gläuben bewege und den Glauben stärke.*

[5]L: *Per haec enim, videlicet per verbum et sacramentum, operatur spiritus sanctus.* G: *Denn durch die zwei, durchs Wort und äußerliche Zeichen, wirket der heilige Geist.*

[6]L: *Et talis usus sacramenti, cum fides vivificat perterrefacta corda, cultus est novi testamenti, quia novum testamentum habet motus spirituales, mortificationem et vivificationem.* G: *Und dies ist der rechte Brauch des heiligen Sakraments, wenn durch den Glauben an die göttlichen Verheißung die erschrockenen Gewissen werden wieder aufgericht. Und das ist der rechte Gottesdienst im neuen Testament; denn im neuen Testament gehet der höchste Gottesdienst inwendig im Herzen zu, daß wir nach dem alten Adam getötet werden, und durch den heiligen Geist neu geboren werden.*

[7]L: *Nam meminisse Christi non est otiosa spectaculi celebratio*; G: *Denn solchs zu Christi Gedächtnis tun, ist nicht ein solch Ding, das allein mit Geberden und Werken zugehet, allein zu einer Erinnerung.*

[8]L: *aut exempli causa instituta, sicut in tragoediis celebratur memoria Herculis aut Ulyssis*; G: *und zu einen Exempel, wie man in Historien Alexandri und dergleichen gedenkt, &c.*

[9]L: *sed est meminisse beneficia Christi, eaque fide accipere, ut per ea vivificemur*; G: *sondern heißt da Christum recht erkennen, Christi Wohltat suchen und begehren.*

[10]L: *Significat enim voluntatem et misericordiam Dei agnoscendam esse in illa ceremonia*; G: *Und der Glaube, der da erkennet solche Barmherzigkeit, der macht lebendig, und das ist der rechte Brauch des Sakraments.*

The German text provides a citation from Psalm 111:4 to make the illustration of *misericordias Dei* or *Barmherzigkeit Gottes*, then expounds on that. It completes the thought with the text that follows.

[11]L: *Et hic principalis usus est sacramenti*; G: *Und das ist der fürnehmste Brauch des Sakraments.*

Apology XXIV, 69–73

428 Among the godless in the Old Testament there was a similar opinion, that they merited the forgiveness of sins through sacrifices *ex opere operato and did not receive it* freely through faith. Thus they increased those acts of worship and sacrifices, introduced the worship of Baal in Israel, and in Judah even sacrificed in the groves.[1] Therefore when the prophets condemned those notions, they waged war not only against the worshipers of Baal but also against other priests who performed the sacrifices instituted by God with this wicked notion in mind.[2] But this notion, that acts of worship and sacrifices make atonement, clings to the world now and always will.[3] Carnal human beings cannot stand that this honor is ascribed only to the sacrifice of Christ or that he is the atoning sacrifice, because they do not understand the righteousness of faith. Instead, they ascribe equal honor to other services and sacrifices.[4] Therefore, just as a false opinion concerning sacrifices clung to the godless priests in Judah and just as in Israel services of Baal continued[5]—even though the church of God was there, which condemned the godless services—so Baal worship clings to the realm of the pope, namely, the abuse of the Mass,[6] which they direct in such a way that by it they might merit the remission of guilt and punishment for the unrighteous. It appears that this Baal worship will endure together with the reign of the pope until Christ comes for judgment[7] and by the glory of his coming destroys the kingdom of the Antichrist.

Meanwhile, everyone who truly believes the gospel should reject this ungodly worship,[8] which was invented contrary to the command of God in order to obscure the glory of Christ and the righteousness of faith.

[1]L: *Itaque augebant illos cultus et sacrificia, instituebant cultum Baal in Israel, in Iuda etiam sacrificabant in lucis*; G: *Denn wie in Israel ein falscher Gottesdienst ward angericht mit Baal.*

[2]L: *Quare prophetae damnata illa persuasione beligerantur non solum cultoribus Baal, sed etiam cum aliis sacerdotibus, qui sacrificia a Deo ordinata, cum illa opinione impia faciebant*. G: *auch unrechte Gottesdienst waren unterm Schein des Gottesdiensts, den Gott geordnet hat; also hat der Antichrist in der Kirchen auch ein falschen Gottesdienst aus dem Nachtmahl Christi gemacht.*

[3]L: *et haerebit semper, quod cultus et sacrificia sint propitiationes.*

In this section the German departs from the Latin.

[4]L: *sed parem honorem tribuunt reliquis cultibus et sacrificiis.*

[5]L: *Sicut igitur in Iuda haesit apud impios pontifices falsa persuasio de sacrificiis, sicut in Israel baalitici cultus duraverunt.*

Baalitic is an adjective formed from the Hebrew gentilic ending.

[6]L: *et tamen erat ibi ecclesia Dei, quae impios cultus improbabat: ita haeret in regno pontificio cultus baaliticus, hoc est, abusus missae*. G: *Und doch, wie Gott unter Israel und Juda dennoch seine Kirche, das ist, etliche Heiligen behalten hat, also hat Gott seine Kirche, das ist, etliche Heiligen unterm Pabsttum dennoch erhalten, daß die christliche Kirche nicht ganz untergangen ist.*

[7]L: *Et videtur hic baaliticus cultus una cum regno pontificio duraturus esse, donec veniet Christus ad iudicandum*; G: *der Antichrist mit seinem falschen Gottesdienst zum Teil bleiben wird, bis daß Christus der Herr öffentlich kommen und richten wird.*

[8]L: *Interim omnes, qui vere credunt evangelio, debent improbare illos impios cultus*. G: *so sollen doch alle Christen verwarnet sein, sich zu hüten vor solcher Abgötterei, und sollten lernen, wie man Gott recht dienen und Vergebung der Sunde durch den Glauben an Christum erlangen soll, daß sie Gott recht ehren und beständigen Trost wider die Sunde haben können.*

Apology XXIV, 97–98

429 **[German text]** In the third place, the holy sacrament[1] was not instituted to provide a sacrifice for sin—for the sacrifice has already occurred—but to awaken our faith and comfort our consciences. The sacrament makes them aware that they are promised grace and forgiveness of sin by Christ. That is why this sacrament requires faith and without faith is used in vain.

Now since the Mass is not a sacrifice for others, living or dead, to take away their sins but should be a Communion where the priest and others receive the sacrament for themselves, we celebrate it in this fashion. On holy days[2] and at other times when communicants are present, Mass is celebrated, and those who desire it receive the sacrament.

[Latin text] But Christ commands that it be done in memory of him. The Mass,[1] therefore, was instituted so that the faith of those who use the sacrament should recall what benefits are received through Christ and should encourage and console the anxious conscience. For to remember Christ is to remember his benefits and realize that they are truly offered to us. It is not enough to remember the history, because the Jews and the ungodly can also remember that. The Mass is to be used for the purpose of offering the sacrament to those who need consolation, just as Ambrose says: "Because I always sin, I ought always to take the medicine."

Since the Mass is such an imparting of the sacrament, among us one common Mass is held on every holy day,[2] and it is also administered on other days if there are those who desire it.

[1]G: *das heilige Sakrament*; L: *missa*.

[2]G: *an Feiertagen*; L: *feriis*.

Augsburg Confession XXIV, 30–34

SUMMARY

- Receiving the Lord's Supper does not earn or merit remission of sins. Its benefits cannot be transferred from one person to another. It does not confer grace *ex opere operato* (a teaching that the Sacrament brings about the desired result independent of the recipient's dispostion, e.g., somehow infusing a spiritual quality into a soul when the soul puts no obstacle in the way). Rather, it is God offering and presenting the remissions of sins. That is what a sacrament does, namely, presents to us that which the promise connected to it offers.
- The sacrament of the Lord's Supper cannot be made into the recipient's sacrifice, that is, into a propitiatory sacrifice—some-

thing rendered to God to reconcile or appease his wrath. Christ's death on the cross has already accomplished this reconciliation. He was made the victim (an expiation) and bore the punishment for the sins of the whole world. To imagine that receiving the Lord's Supper merits forgiveness and makes satisfaction for one's sins only dishonors and rejects the work of Christ. Indeed, in the Sacrament, Christ's reconciliation is offered and given to the recipient who believes Christ's words "for you for the forgiveness of sins."

- A eucharistic sacrifice, however, is a sacrifice of praise. By it a believer renders thanks for the forgiveness of sins. Because it is made by the one who has been reconciled, this thanksgiving flows from the work of the Holy Spirit within the believer. Among the sacrifices of praise are the preaching of the Word and the receiving of the Lord's Supper.
- A sacrifice of praise has nothing to do with meriting God's grace. Thus it is possible to call the entire Mass, that is, "the ceremony together with the proclamation of the gospel, faith, prayer, and thanksgiving" (Ap XXIV, 33–35), a daily sacrifice but not a propitiatory sacrifice. For the ceremony's true character remembers the reconciling death of Christ by which we are made holy, thus it is a spiritual worship, a daily sacrifice of the heart.
- When the Lord's Supper is thus taught and used, it is a seal and testimony of the free forgiveness of sins. This is the ministry of the Spirit, who by the power of the Word brings the righteousness of faith, regenerates, and quickens the believer who receives the Sacrament. Thus not a private Mass but a Mass "when communicants are present" (AC XXIV, 30–34) is observed on holy days and at other times. It is faith that apprehends the mercy of God, receives it, and thereby glorifies the work of Christ.

Synopsis

In the Lord's Supper the true body and blood of Christ in and under the bread and wine are received. Christ's presence in the Sacrament is not figurative or allegorical or spiritual. As he says, it is truly his body and blood that is received orally in the sacramental eating and drinking. Both forms are given and received. The Christian comes to the Supper freely, without coercion, and often. In this Sacrament the believer receives forgiveness, life, and salvation and from it obtains comfort, refreshment, and strength.

Participation in the Lord's Supper does not earn salvation or confer grace *ex opere operato*, thus it is not a propitiatory sacrifice. Christ has already accomplished our salvation. Because the Spirit works faith and strengthens faith through the means of grace, the Lord's Supper can be considered a spiritual worship and a daily sacrifice of the heart, in the sense that it is a sacrifice of praise that flows from the heart in which the Holy Spirit is working. The Lord's Supper is a seal and testimony of the remission of sins that the believer has in Christ.

5

Absolution

What is (private) Absolution?

501 Because absolution or the power of the keys[1] is also a comfort and help against sin and a bad conscience and was instituted by Christ in the gospel,[2] confession, or absolution,[3] should by no means be allowed to fall into disuse in the church—especially for the sake of weak consciences and for the wild young people, so that they may be examined and instructed in Christian teaching.

[1]G: *Absolutio oder Kraft des Schlussels*; L: *absolutio et virtus clavium.*

[2]G: *im Evangelio durch Christum gestift*; L: *in evangelio ab ipso Christo instituta.*

[3]G: *die Beicht oder Absolutio*; L: *confessio et absolutio.*

Smalcald Articles III, VIII, 1

502 For we also retain confession especially on account of absolution, which is the Word of God that the power of the keys proclaims to individuals by divine authority.[1] Therefore it would be unconscionable to remove private absolution from the church.[2]

[1]L: *Nam et nos confessionem retinemus praecipue propter absolutionem, quae est verbum Dei quod de singulis auctoritate divina pronuntiat potestas clavium*; G: *Denn die Beicht behalten wir auch um der Absolution willen, welche ist Gottes Wort, dadurch uns die Gewalt der Schlüssel los spricht von Sunden.*

[2]L: *Quare impium esset ex ecclesia privatam absolutionem tollere*; G: *Darum wäre es wider Gott die Absolution aus der Kirchen also abtun &c.*

Apology XII, 99–100

503 If we define the sacraments as rites, which have the command of God and to which the promise of grace has been added, it is easy to determine what the sacraments are, properly speaking.[1] For humanly instituted rites are not sacraments, properly speaking,[2] because human beings do not have the authority to promise grace. Therefore signs instituted without the command of God are not sure signs of grace,[3] even though they perhaps serve to teach or admonish the common folk. Therefore, the sacraments are actually baptism, the Lord's Supper, and absolution (the sacrament of repentance).[4] For these rites have the command of God and the promise of grace,[5] which is the essence of the New Testament. For surely our hearts ought to be certain that when we are baptized, when we eat the body of the Lord, and when we are absolved, God truly forgives us on account of Christ. And God moves our hearts through the word and the rite at the same time so that they believe and receive faith[6] just as Paul says [Rom. 10:17], "So faith comes from what is heard." For just as the Word enters through the ear in order to strike the heart, so also the rite enters through the eye in order to move the heart.[7] The word and the rite have the same effect.[8] Augustine put it well when he said that the sacrament is a "visible word," because the rite is received by the eyes and is, as it were, a picture of the Word, signifying the same thing as the Word.[9] Therefore both have the same effect.

[1]L: *Si sacramenta vocamus ritus, qui habent mandatum Dei et quibus addita est promissio gratiae, facile est iudicare, quae sint proprie sacramenta*; G: *So wir Sakrament nennen die äußerlichen Zeichen und Ceremonien, die da haben Gottes Befehl und haben ein angehefte göttliche Zusage der Gnaden, so kann man bald schließen, was Sakrament sein.*

[2]L: *Nam ritus ab hominibus instituti non erunt hoc modo proprie dicta sacramenta*; G: *Denn Ceremonien und andere äußerliche Ding, von Menschen eingesetzt, sein auf die Weise nicht Sakrament.*

[3]L: *Quare signa sine mandato Dei instituta non sunt certa signa gratiae*; G: *Darum Zeichen, so ohn Gottes Befehl sein eingesetzt, die sind nicht Zeichen der Gnade.*

[4]L: *Vere igitur sunt sacramenta baptismus, coena Domini, absolutio, quae est sacramentum poenitentiae*; G: *So sind nu rechte Sakrament die Taufe und das Nachtmahl des Herrn, die Absolutio.*

[5]L: *Nam hi ritus habent mandatum Dei et promissionem gratiae*; G: *Denn diese haben Gottes Befehl, haben auch Verheißung der Gnaden.*

[6]L: *Et corda simul per verbum et ritum movet Deus, ut credant et concipiant fidem*; G: *daß dadurch beweget werden die Herzen, nämlich durchs Wort und äußerliche Zeichen zugleich, daß sie gläuben.*

[7]L: *Sicut autem verbum incurrit in aures, ut feriat corda: ita ritus ipse incurrit in oculos, ut moveat corda*; G: *Wie aber das Wort in die Ohren gehet, also ist das äußerliche Zeichen für die Augen gestellet, also inwendig das Herz zu reizen und zu bewegen zum Glauben.*

[8]L: *Idem effectus est verbi et ritus*; G: *Denn das Wort und äußerliche Zeichen wirken einerlei im Herzen.*

[9]L: *sacramentum esse verbum visibile, quia ritus oculis accipitur et est quasi pictura verbi, idem significans, quod verbum*; G: *„Das Sakrament"*, *sagt er*, *„ist ein sichtlich Wort". Denn das äußerliche Zeichen ist wie ein Gemäle, dadurch dasselbige bedeutet wird, das durchs Wort gepredigt wird.*

Apology XIII, 3–5

504 It is well known that we have so explained and extolled the benefit of absolution and the power of the keys[1] that many troubled consciences have received consolation from our teaching. They have heard that it is a command of God—indeed, the very voice of the gospel[2]—so that we may believe the absolution and regard as certain that the forgiveness of sins is given to us freely on account of Christ[3] and that we should maintain that we are truly reconciled to God by this faith. This approach has encouraged many devout minds, and in the beginning it brought Luther the highest praise of all good people. For it discloses a certain and firm consolation for the conscience, whereas previously the entire power of absolution was smothered by teachings about works,[4] since the scholastics and monks taught nothing about faith and the gracious forgiveness of sins.

[1]L: *Constat nos beneficium absolutionis et potestatem clavium ita illustravisse et ornavisse*; G: *Es ist am Tage und es können die Widersacher nicht leugnen, daß die Unsern von der Absolution, von den Schlüsseln, also christlich, richtig, rein geprediget, geschrieben und gelehret haben.*

[2]L: *imo propriam evangelii vocem*; G: *der rechte Brauch des Evangelii.*

[3]L: *et certo statuamus nobis gratis donari remissionem peccatorum propter Christum*; G: *daß ohne unsern Verdienst uns Sünde vergeben werden durch Christum.*

[4]L: *quia antea tota vis absolutionis erat oppressa doctrinis operum*; G: *Denn zuvor was die ganze nötige Lehre von der Buß und Absolution unterdrückt.*

Apology XI, 2

505 The keys are an office and authority given to the church by Christ to bind and loose sins[1]—not only the crude and notorious sins but also the subtle, secret ones that only God knows. As it is written [Ps. 19:12], "But who can detect their errors?" And Paul himself complains in Romans 7[:23] that with his flesh he served the "law of sin." For it is not in our power but in God's alone to judge which, how great, and how many sins there are. As it is written [Ps. 143:2]: "Do not enter into judgment with your servant, for no one living is righteous before you." And Paul also says in 1 Corinthians 4[:4]: "I am not aware of anything against myself, but I am not thereby acquitted."

[1]G: *Die Schlussel sind ein Ampt und Gewalt, der Kirchen von Christo gegeben, zu binden und zu losen die Sunde*; L: *Claves sunt officium et potestas ecclesiae a Christo data ad ligandum et solvendum peccata.*

See also Apology XXIV, 58–60.

Smalcald Articles III, VII, 1–3

How does a Christian confess?

506 *Which sins is a person to confess?*

Before God one is to acknowledge the guilt for all sins, even those of which we are not aware, as we do in the Lord's Prayer. However, before the confessor we are to confess only those sins of which we have knowledge and which trouble us.

Which sins are these?

Here reflect on your walk of life in light of the Ten Commandments:[1] *whether you are father, mother, son, daughter, master, mistress, servant; whether you have been disobedient, unfaithful, lazy, whether you have harmed anyone by word or deed; whether you have stolen, neglected, wasted, or injured anything.*

[1]G: *Da siehe Deinen Stand an nach den zehen Geboten*; L: *Hic diligenter considera vitae genus, in quo es, et confer cum eo decem praecepta.*

Walk of life as *Stand* may be seen in the context of Ephesians 2:10.

Small Catechism V, 17–20
Italics in Kolb/Wengert reflect Luther's later changes.

507 Nowhere do they teach that sins are pardoned freely for Christ's sake and that by this faith we obtain the remission of sins. Thus they obscure the glory of Christ,[1] rob consciences of sure consolation, and destroy true worship, that is, the exercise of faith wrestling with despair.[2]

They have obscured the doctrine of sin and fashioned a tradition regarding the enumeration of transgressions[3] which has spawned many errors and much despair. To this they joined satisfactions, with which they also have obscured the benefit of Christ. From these came indulgences—unadulterated lies concocted for profit.

[1]L: *Ita gloriam Christi obscurant*; G: *Mit solcher Lehre nehmen sie Christo sein Ehr.*

[2]L: *et abolent veros cultus, scilicet exercitia fidei luctantis cum desperatione*; G: *und tun ab die rechten Gottesdienst, nämblich die Ubung des Glaubens, welcher mit dem Unglauben und Verzweifelung uber der Verheißung des Evangelii kämpfet.*

[3]L: *Obscuraverunt doctrinam de peccato et finxerunt traditionem de enumeratione delictorum*; G: *Dergleichen haben sie auch die Lehr verdunkelt von der Sunde und eigene Satzungen erdichtet, wie man alle Sund erzählen und beichten muesse.*

Treatise on the Power and Primacy of the Pope, 44–46

508 With regard to the enumeration of sins, our people are taught in such a way as not to ensnare their consciences. Even though it is beneficial to accustom the inexperienced to enumerate some things in order that they might be taught more easily, here we are discussing what is necessary by divine mandate. Therefore the opponents should not cite against us the regulation *Omnis utriusque*; we are aware of it. Instead they ought to demonstrate that the enumeration of sins is necessary for the reception of forgiveness on the basis of divine mandate.[1] The entire church throughout all of Europe knows what kind of snares this clause in the regulation requiring a confession of every sin has cast upon consciences.[2]

[1]L: *sed ex iure divino ostendere, quod enumeratio peccatorum sit necessaria ad consequendam remissionem*; G: *sondern aus der heiligen Schrift, aus Gottes Wort uns beweiset haben, daß solch Erzählen der Sunde von Gott geboten wäre.*

[2]L: *Tota ecclesia per universam Europam scit, quales laqueos iniecerit conscientiis illa particula constitutionis, quae iubet omnia peccata confiteri*; G: *Es ist leider allzu klar am Tage und rüchtig durch alle Kirchen in ganz Europa, wie dieses particula des Kapitels: Omnis utriusque sexus, da es gebeut, man solle schuldig sein, alle Sunde zu beichten, die Gewissen in Elend, Jammer und Verstrickung bracht hat.*

Apology XI, 6–7

509 Confession worked like this: Each person had to enumerate all of his or her sins (which is impossible). This was a great torment. Whatever the person had forgotten was forgiven only on the condition that when it was remembered it still had to be confessed.[1] Under these circumstances people could never know whether they had confessed perfectly enough or whether confession would ever end.[2] At the same time, people were directed to their works and told that the more perfectly they confessed and the more ashamed they were and the more they degraded themselves before the priest,[3] the sooner and better they would make satisfaction for their sin. For such humility would certainly earn the grace of God.

Here, too, there was neither faith nor Christ, and the power of the absolution was not explained to them.[4] Rather, their comfort was based on the enumeration of sins and humiliation. It is not possible to recount here what torments, rascality, and idolatry such confession has produced.

[1]G: *Welche er aber vergessen hatte, wurden ihm sofern vergeben, wenn sie ihm wurden einfallen, daß er sie noch mußt' beichten*; L: *Et si quis quorundam peccatorum oblitus esset, is eatenus absolvebatur, ut, si in memoriam illa recurrerent, ea postea confiteretur.*

[2]G: *Damit kunnte er nimmer wissen, wenn er rein gnug gebeicht oder wenn des Beichtens einmal ein Ende haben sollt*; L: *Nemo igitur scire potuit, num unquam sufficienter, pure et recte confessus esset et quando confessionis finis futurus esset.*

[3]G: *und je mehr er sich schämet und [solch] sich selbs also fur dem Priester schändet*; L: *pudore et ignominia coram sacerdote suffusa.*

The bracketed word is provided by the editors of the German text.

[4]G: *Hie war auch kein Glaube noch Christus, und die Kraft der Absolution ward ihm nicht gesagt*; L: *Nulla hic fides, nullus Christus erat. Et virtus absolutionis non explicabatur confitenti.*

Smalcald Articles III, III, 19–20

510 *We, on the contrary, do not say that a person should look to see how full of filthiness they are*[1] *or should reflect on their condition. Rather we give this advice: If you are poor and miserable, then go and make use of the healing medicine.*[2] *Those who feel their misery and need will no doubt develop such a desire for confession*[3] *that they will run to it with joy. But those who ignore it and do not come of their own accord, we let go their way. However, they ought to know that we do not regard them as Christians.*

[1]G: *wie voll Unflats Du seist*; L: *quantopere tu sordeas ac quantis immundicitiis repletus sis.*

[2]G: *der heilsamen Ärznei*; L: *hac medicina.*

[3]G: *wird wohl solch Verlangen darnach kriegen*; L: *is eo desiderio afficietur.*

Large Catechism, Brief Exhortation to Confession, 26–27
Italics according to Kolb/Wengert, noting omission
in the 1580 *Book of Concord.*

511 However, the enumeration of sins[1] ought to be a matter of choice for each individual: each person should be able to determine what and what not to enumerate.[2] As long as we are in the flesh we will not lie if we say, "I am a poor person, full of sin." Romans 7[:23] states: "I see in my members another law. . . ." Because private absolution is derived from the office of the keys,[3] we should not neglect it but value it highly, just as all the other offices of the Christian church.

[1]G: *Die Erzählung . . . der Sunden*; L: *Enumeratio . . . peccatorum.*

[2]G: *was er erzählen oder nicht erzählen will*; L: *quid enumerare aut non enumerare velit.*

[3]G: *denn dieweil die absolutio privata von dem Ampt herkommpt der Schlussel*; L: *Et cum absolutio privata ab officio clavium oriatur.*

Smalcald Articles III, VIII, 2

512 *However, if some individuals do not find themselves burdened by these or greater sins, they are not to worry, nor are they to search for or invent further sins and thereby turn confession into torture.*[1] *Instead mention one or two that you are aware of in the following way: "In particular I confess that I cursed once, likewise that one time I was inconsiderate in my speech, one time I neglected this or that, etc." Let that be enough.*

If you are aware of no sins at all (which is really quite unlikely), then do not mention any in particular, but instead receive forgiveness on the basis of the general confession,[2] *which you make to God in the presence of the confessor.*[3]

[1]G: *damit eine Marter aus der Beicht machen*; L: *ne ex confessione crucem sibi faciat.*

[2]G: *auf die gemeine Beicht*; L: *generali confessione.*

The phrase *gemeine Beicht* here and in SA III refers to a "general" confession *zur offenen Schuld*, meaning a public confession of sin made on behalf of the congregation by the priest ("*der Geistliche*") as an adjunct to the sermon. This German practice dates from the tenth century and does not appear in the oldest churchly formulas of Confession and Absolution. See *BSLK*, 439n3.

[3]G: *gegen dem Beichtiger*; L: *coram ministro aut fratre*.

This use of the Latin *frater* may inform the usage in SA III, III, 4 regarding the "mutual conversation and consolation of the brothers." See also text 235.

Small Catechism V, 24–25
Italics in Kolb/Wengert reflect Luther's later changes.

513 *For, as I have said, we teach this: Let those who do not go to confession willingly and for the sake of absolution just forget about it.*[1] *Yes, and let those who go there relying on the purity of their confession just stay away from it.*[2] *We urge you, however, to confess and express your needs, not for the purpose of performing a work but to hear what God wants to say to you.*[3] *The Word or absolution,*[4] *I say, is what you should concentrate on, magnifying and cherishing it as a great and wonderful treasure to be accepted with all praise and gratitude.*

[1]G: *Wer nicht willig und ümb der Absolution willen zur Beicht gehet, der lasse es nur anstehen*; L: *Qui non sponte ac propter absolutionem confessionem accedit, is plane supersedeat ab hoc labore ac intermittat.*

[2]G: *Ja, wer auch auf sein Werk hingehet, wie rein er seine Beicht getan habe, der bleibe nur davon*; L: *Imo vero, qui fiducia sui operis fretus accedit, quantumvis pure confessus sit, is etiam abstineat ab ea.*

[3]G: *Wir vermahnen aber, Du sollt beichten und Deine Not anzeigen nicht darümb, daß Du es fur ein Werk tuest, sondern hörest, was Dir Gott sagen lässet*; L: *Adhortamur vero et admonemus te, ut confitearis ac necessitatem tuam conqueraris non propterea, ut pro opere quodam reputes, sed ut audias et animadvertas, quidnam Deus ipse tibi loquatur.*

[4]G: *Das Wort . . . oder Absolutio*; L: *Verbum . . . aut absolutionem.*

Large Catechism, Brief Exhortation to Confession, 21–22
Italics according to Kolb/Wengert, noting omission
in the 1580 *Book of Concord*.

HOW IS THE SINNER ABSOLVED?

514 **[German text]** Our people teach as follows. According to the gospel the power of the keys or of the bishops is a power and command of God to preach the gospel, to forgive or retain sin, and to administer and distribute the sacraments.[1] For Christ sent out the apostles with this command (John 20[:21–23]): "As the Father has sent me, so I send you. . . . Receive the Holy Spirit. If you forgive the sins of any, they are forgiven them; if you retain the sins of any, they are retained."

[Latin text] However, they believe that, according to the gospel, the power of the keys or the power of the bishops is the power of God's mandate to preach the gospel, to forgive and retain sins, and to administer the sacraments.[1] For Christ sent out the apostles with this command [John 20:21–23]: "As the Father has sent me, so I send you. . . . Receive the Holy Spirit. If you forgive the sins of any, they are forgiven them; if you retain the sins of any, they are retained." And Mark 16[:15]: "Go . . . and proclaim the good news to the whole creation. . . ."

[1]G: *daß der Gewalt der Schlussel oder der Bischofen sei, lauts des Evangeliums, ein Gewalt und Befehl Gottes, das Evangelium zu predigen, die Sunde zu vergeben und zu behalten und die Sakrament zu reichen und handeln*; L: *potestatem clavium seu potestatem episcoporum iuxta evangelium potestatem esse seu mandatum Dei praedicandi evangelii, remitendi et retinendi peccata et administrandi sacramenta.*

Augsburg Confession XXVIII, 5–7

515 **[German text]** For [Absolution] is not the voice or word of the person speaking it, but it is the Word of God, who forgives sin. For it is spoken in God's stead and by God's command.[1] Great diligence is used to teach about this command and power of the keys, and how comforting and necessary it is for terrified consciences. It is also taught how God requires us to believe this absolution as much as if it were God's voice resounding from heaven and that we should joyfully find comfort in the absolution, knowing that through such faith we obtain forgiveness of sin.[2] In former times, the preachers, while teaching much about confession, never mentioned a single word about these necessary matters but instead only tormented consciences with long enumerations of sins, with satisfactions,[3] with indulgences, with pilgrimages, and the like. Moreover, many of our opponents themselves confess that our side has written about and dealt with true Christian repentance[4] more appropriately than had been done in a long time.

[Latin text] People are taught to make the most of absolution because it is the voice of God and is pronounced following the command of God.[1] The power of the keys is praised and remembered for bringing such great consolation to terrified consciences, both because God requires faith so that we believe such absolution as God's own voice resounding from heaven and because this faith truly obtains and receives the forgiveness of sins.[2] In former times, satisfactions[3] were immoderately extolled; nothing was mentioned about faith, the merits of Christ, or the righteousness of faith. On this point our churches can scarcely be faulted. For even our adversaries are compelled to grant us that the teaching concerning confession[4] has been most carefully treated and brought to light by our people.

[1]G: *Dann es sei nicht des gegenwärtigen Menschen Stimme oder Wort, sondern Gottes Wort, der die Sunde vergibt. Dann sie wird an Gottes Statt und aus Gottes Befehl gesprochen*; L: *Docentur homines, ut absolutionem plurimi faciant, quia sit vox Dei et mandato Dei pronuntietur.*

The German text makes the subtle equation that *das Wort = die Absolution.*

[2]G: *darzu, wie Gott forder, dieser Absolution zu glauben, nicht weniger, denn so Gottes Stimme vom Himmel erschulle, und uns der Absolution frohlich trosten und wissen, daß wir durch solchen Glauben Vergebung der Sunde erlangen*; L: *et quod requirat Deus fidem, ut illi absolutioni tamquam voci suae de coelo sonanti credamus, et quod illa fides vere consequatur et accipiat remissionem peccatorum.*

[3]G: *Genugtun*; L: *satisfactiones.*

[4]G: *von rechter christlicher Buß*; L: *doctrina de poenitentia.*

Augsburg Confession XXV, 3–6

516 It would therefore be wicked to remove private absolution from the church.[1] And those who despise private absolution understand neither the forgiveness of sins nor the power of the keys. As for the enumeration of sins in confession, we have said earlier that we do not believe that it is necessary by divine right. When someone objects that a judge must hear a case before pronouncing sentence, that is irrelevant because the ministry of absolution is in the area of blessing or grace, not of judgment or law. The ministers of the church therefore have the command to forgive sins; they do not have the command to investigate secret sins. In addition, they absolve us of those which we do not remember; therefore absolution, which is the voice of the Gospel forgiving sins and consoling consciences, does not need an investigation.[2]

[1]L: *Quare impium esset ex ecclesia privatam absolutionem tollere*; G: *Darum wäre es wider Gott die Absolution aus der Kirche also abtun &c.*

[2]L: *Itaque ministri in ecclesia habent mandatum remittendi peccata, non habent mandatum cognoscendi occulta peccata. Et quidem absolvunt ab his, quae non meminimus, quare absolutio, quae est vox evangelii remittens peccata et consolans conscientias, non requirit cognitionem*; G: *Denn die Absolution ist schlecht der Befehl los zu sprechen, und ist nicht ein neu Gerichtzwang, Sunde zu erforschen. Denn Gott ist der Richter, der hat den Aposteln nicht das Richteramt, sondern die Gnadenexecution befohlen, diejenigen loszusprechen, so es begehren, und sie entbinden auch und absolvieren von Sunden, die uns nicht einfallen. Darum ist die Absolution eine Stimme des Evangelii, dadurch wir Trost empfangen, und ist nicht ein Urteil oder Gesetz.*

Apology XII, 100–105
The Latin is from the quarto edition.
The English is from Tappert.

517 However, the keys only have the power to bind and loose on the earth[1] according to [Matt. 18:18], "Whatever you bind on earth will be bound in heaven, and whatever you loose on earth will be loosed in heaven." As we said earlier, the keys do not have the power to impose penalties or to institute rites of worship but only have the command to remit the sins of those who are converted and to convict and excommunicate those who refuse to be converted.[2] For just as "to loose" means to forgive sins, so also "to bind" means not to forgive sins.[3] For Christ is talking of a spiritual kingdom.[4] And God's mandate is that ministers of the gospel absolve those who are converted,[5] according to [2 Cor. 10:8], ". . . our authority, which the Lord gave for building you up." Now the reservation of cases is a secular matter, for it is the reservation of canonical punishments, not the reservation of guilt before God in the case of those who are truly converted. Therefore the opponents judge rightly when they confess that in the hour of death the reservation of cases should not prevent absolution.

[1]L: *At clavis non habet potestatem nisi super terram ligandi et solvendi*; G: *so doch die ganze Gewalt der Schlüssel in der Kirchen nicht weiter sich erstreckt, denn allein hie auf Erden.*

[2]L: *clavis potestatem habet non imponendi poenas aut cultus instituendi, sed tantum habet mandatum remittendi peccata his, qui convertuntur, et arguendi et excommunicandi istos, qui nolunt converti*; G: *So ist die Gewalt der Schlüssel nicht ein solch Gewalt, sonderliche eigene Strafe oder Gottesdienst aufzurichten, sondern allein Sunde zu vergeben denjenigen, so sich bekehren, und zu verbannen diejenigen, die sich nicht bekehren.*

[3]L: *Sicut enim solvere significat remittere peccata, ita ligare significat non remittere peccata*; G: *Denn auflösen an dem Ort heißt Sunde vergeben, binden heißt Sunde nicht vergeben.*

[4]L: *Loquitur enim Christus de regno spirituali*; G: *Denn Christus redet von einem geistlichen Reich.*

[5]L: *Et mandatum Dei est, ut ministri evangelii absolvant hos, qui convertuntur*; G: *und Gott hat befohlen, diejenigen, so sich bekehren, von Sunden zu entbinden.*

Apology XII, 176–177

518 Here and there this form of absolution[1] has come into use: "The passion of our Lord Jesus Christ and the merits of the most blessed Virgin Mary and all the saints be to you for the forgiveness of sins." Here an absolution is pronounced that declares that we are reconciled and accounted righteous not only by the merits of Christ but also by the merits of the other saints. Some of us have seen a case where a teacher of theology was dying and a certain monastic theologian was summoned to offer consolation. He could do no better than press upon the dying man this prayer, "Mother of grace, protect us from the enemy; receive us in the hour of death."

[1]L: *haec forma absolutionis*; G: *eine gemeine Form der Absolution.*

Apology XXI, 25–26

519 Therefore, as is stated in the Augsburg Confession article eleven, we retain private absolution and teach that it is God's command that we "believe this kind of absolution and regard it as certain, that we are truly reconciled with God when we believe the word of absolution, as if we had heard a voice from heaven," as the Apology also explains in this article [German translation: XI, 2]. This comfort would be taken away from us completely if we could not conclude from his call, which takes place through Word and sacraments, what God's will toward us is.

Such a view would also destroy and deprive us of the foundation, namely, that the Holy Spirit most certainly wills to be present, effective, and active through the Word as it is preached, heard, and considered.[1] Therefore, there is no basis at all for the opinion described above, that those who have contempt for the Word of God, push it away, slander it, or persecute it can be considered to be the elect (Matt. 22[:5, 6]; Acts 15 [= 13:40–41, 45]), or those who harden their hearts when they hear the Word (Heb. 4[:2, 7]), or those who resist the Holy Spirit (Acts 7[:51]), or those who persist in sin without repentance (Luke 14[:18, 24]), or those who do not truly believe in Christ (Mark 16[:16]), or those who present only an external appearance of being believers[2] (Matt. 7[:15] and 22[:12]), or those who seek another way to righteousness and salvation apart from Christ (Rom. 9[:31]). On the contrary, as God preordained in his counsel that the Holy Spirit would call, enlighten, and convert the elect through the Word and that he would justify and save all those who accept Christ through true faith, so also he concluded in his counsel that he would harden, reject, and condemn all those whom he called through the Word when they spurn the Word and resist and persist in resisting the Holy Spirit, who wants to exercise his power in them and be efficacious through the Word. This is why "many are called and few are chosen" [Matt. 22:14].[3]

[1]G: *Es würde uns auch der Grund umbgestoßen und genommen, daß der H. Geist bei dem gepredigten, gehörten, betrachten Worte gewißlich gegenwärtig und dardurch kräftig sein und wirken wölle*; L: *Quin etiam illud fundamentum religionis nostrae everteretur, quod credimus spiritum sanctum cum verbo praedicato, audito et diligenter considerato praesentem atque efficacem esse et operari velle.*

[2]G: *nur einen äußerlichen Schein führen*; L: *externa tantum specie pietatem prae se ferunt.*

[3]G: *Sondern wie Gott in seinem Rat verordnet hat, daß der Heilige Geist die Auserwähleten durchs Wort berufen, erleuchten und bekehren und daß er alle die, so durch recten Glauben Christum annehmen, gerecht und selig machen wölle: also hat er auch in seinem Rat beschlossen, daß er diejenigen so durch Wort berufen werden, wann sie das Wort von sich stoßen und dem Heiligen Geist, der in ihnen durchs Wort kräftig sein und wirken will, widerstreben und darin vorharren, sie vorstocken, verwerfen und verdammen wölle. Und also sind „viel berufen und wenig auserwählet"*. L: *Ut enim Deus in aeterno suo consilio ordinavit, ut spiritus sanctus electos per verbum vocet, illuminet atque convertat atque omnes illos, qui Christum vera fide amplectuntur, iustificet atque in eos aeternam salutem conferat: ita in eodem suo consilio decrevit, quod eos, qui per verbum vocati illud repudiant et spiritui sancto (qui in ipsis per verbum efficaciter operari et efficax esse vult) resistunt et obstinati in ea contumacia perseverant, indurare, reprobare et aeternae damnationi devovere velit. Et secundum has rationes intelligendum est, quod scriptura dicit: Multos vocatos, paucos vero electos esse.*

Formula of Concord, Solid Declaration XI, 38–40

520 **[German text]** Confession has not been abolished by the preachers on our side.[1] For the custom has been retained among us of not administering the sacrament to those who have not previously been examined and absolved.[2] At the same time, the people are diligently instructed how comforting the word of absolution is and how highly and dearly absolution is to be esteemed.[3] For it is not the voice or word of the person speaking it, but it is the Word of God, who forgives sin. For it is spoken in God's stead and by God's command.[4]

[Latin text] Confession has not been abolished in our churches.[1] For it is not customary to administer the body of Christ except to those who have been previously examined and absolved.[2] The people are also most diligently taught concerning faith in the word of absolution,[3] about which there was a great silence before now. People are taught to make the most of absolution because it is the voice of God and is pronounced following the command of God.[4]

[1]G: *Die Beicht ist durch die Prediger dieses Teils nicht abgetan*; L: *Confessio in ecclesiis apud nos non est abolita.*

[2]G: *Dann diese Gewohnheit wird bei uns gehalten, das Sakrament nicht zu reichen denen, so nicht zuvor verhort und absolviert seind*; L: *Non enim solet porrigi corpus Domini nisi antea exploratis et absolutis.*

[3]G: *Darbei wird das Volk fleißig unterricht, wie trostlich das Wort der Absolution sei, wie hoch und teuer die Absolution zu achten*; L: *Et docetur populus diligentissime de fide absolutionis.*

[4]G: *Dann es sei nicht des gegenwärtigen Menschen Stimme oder Wort, sondern Gottes Wort, der die Sunde vergibt. Dann sie wird an Gottes Statt und aus Gottes Befehl gesprochen*; L: *Docentur homines, ut absolutionem plurimi faciant, quia sit vox Dei et mandato Dei pronuntietur.*

Augsburg Confession XXV, 1–3

Summary

- The power of the Keys, also called private Absolution, was instituted by Christ. The rite was retained by the Lutheran reformers despite the abuses that had surrounded it; it was returned to what Christ had commanded. It served troubled consciences and helped overcome the power of sin. It was to be counted among the sacraments, a "visible word," the rite received by the eyes signifying the same thing as the Word (Ap XIII, 3–5).
- Sinners should confess what they know and feel in their hearts, recalling thoughts, words, and actions from their stations in life

that broke the commandments and that trouble their consciences. Not all sins have to be enumerated or elaborated; it is enough to admit, "I am a poor person, full of sin" (SA III, VIII, 2).

- The Absolution is the "voice of God" and pronounced at God's command. Faith believes the Absolution as God's "voice resounding from heaven" (AC XXV, 4). Such faith receives the forgiveness of sins. The minister who absolves has no command to investigate secret sins or to absolve in the name of anyone but Christ. It is unusual to give the Lord's Supper except to those who have confessed and been absolved.

WHAT IS TRUE REPENTANCE?

521 **[German text]** Concerning repentance it is taught that those who have sinned after baptism obtain forgiveness of sins whenever they come to repentance and that absolution should not be denied them by the church.[1] Now properly speaking, true repentance is nothing else than to have contrition and sorrow, or terror about sin,[2] and yet at the same time to believe in the gospel and absolution[3] that sin is forgiven and grace is obtained through Christ. Such faith, in turn, comforts the heart and puts it at peace. Then improvement should also follow, and a person should refrain from sins. For these should be the fruits of repentance,[4] as John says in Matthew 3[:8]: "Bear fruit worthy of repentance."

Rejected here are those who teach that whoever has once become righteous cannot fall again.

However, also condemned are the Novatians, who denied absolution to those who had sinned after baptism.

Also rejected are those who do not teach that a person obtains forgiveness of sin through faith but through our own satisfactions.[5]

[Latin text] Concerning repentance they teach that those who have fallen after baptism can receive forgiveness of sins whenever they are brought to repentance and that the church should impart absolution to those who return to repentance.[1] Now, properly speaking, repentance consists of two parts: one is contrition or the terrors that strike the conscience when sin is recognized;[2] the other is faith, which is brought to life by the gospel or absolution.[3] This faith believes that sins are forgiven on account of Christ, consoles the conscience, and liberates it from terrors. Thereupon good works, which are the fruit of repentance,[4] should follow.

They condemn both the Anabaptists, who deny that those who have once been justified can lose the Holy Spirit, and also those who contend that some may attain such perfection in this life that they cannot sin.

Also condemned are the Novatians who were unwilling to absolve those who had fallen and returned to repentance after baptism.

Also rejected are those who do not teach that forgiveness of sins comes through faith but command us to merit grace through our own satisfactions.[5]

[1]G: *und ihnen die Absolution von der Kirche nicht soll geweigert werden*; L: *et quod ecclesia talibus ad poenitentiam redeuntibus debeat absolutionem impartiri.*

[2]G: *Reue und Leid oder Schrecken haben über die Sünde*; L: *altera est contritio seu terrores incussi conscientiae agnito peccato.*

[3]G: *daneben glauben an das Evangelium und Absolution*; L: *altera est fides, quae concipitur ex evangelio seu absolutione.*

[4]G: *die Fruchte der Buß*; L: *fructus poenitentiae.*

[5]G: *durch unser Genugtun*; L: *per satisfactiones nostras.*

Augsburg Confession XII, 1–10

522 *To begin with, I have said that, in addition to the confession that we are discussing here, there are two other kinds, which have an even greater right to be called the common confession of Christians.*[1] *I refer to the practice of confessing to God alone or to our neighbor alone, asking for forgiveness. These two kinds are included in the Lord's Prayer when we say, "Forgive us our debts, as we forgive our debtors," etc. Indeed, the entire Lord's Prayer is nothing else than such a confession.*[2] *For what is our prayer but a confession that we neither have nor do what we ought and a plea for grace and a joyful conscience? This kind of confession should and must take place continuously as long as we live. For this is the essence of a genuinely Christian life, to acknowledge that we are sinners and to pray for grace.*[3]

[1]G: *die da mehr heißen mögen ein gemein Bekenntnis aller Christen*; L: *quas rectius communem christianorum confessionem dixeris.*

[2]G: *Ja das ganze Vaterunser ist nicht anders denn ein solche Beichte*; L: *Imo tota oratio Dominica nihil aliud est quam hujusmodi confessio.*

[3]G: *Denn darin stehet eigentlich ein christlich Wesen, daß wir uns fur Sunder erkennen und Gnade bitten*; L: *In hoc enim revera ac serio chris-*

tiana vita consistit, ut nos non gravate et peccatores agnoscamus et gratiam petamus.

Large Catechism, Brief Exhortation to Confession, 8–9
Italics according to Kolb/Wengert, noting omission
in the 1580 *Book of Concord.*

523 *Besides this public, daily, and necessary confession, there is also the secret confession that takes place privately before a single brother or sister.*[1] *This comes into play when some particular issue weighs on us or attacks us, eating away at us until we can have no peace nor find ourselves sufficiently strong in faith. Then we may at any time and as often as we wish lay our troubles before a brother or sister, seeking advice, comfort, and strength.*[2] *This type of confession is not included in the commandment like the other two but is left to all to use whenever they need it. Thus by divine ordinance Christ himself has placed absolution in the mouths of his Christian community and commanded us to absolve one another from sins.*[3] *So if there is a heart that feels its sin and desires comfort, it has here a sure refuge where it finds and hears God's Word because through a human being God looses and absolves from sin.*[4]

Note, then, as I have often said, that confession consists of two parts. The first is our work and act, when I lament my sin and desire comfort and restoration for my soul.[5] *The second is a work that God does, when he absolves me of my sins through the Word placed on the lips of another person.*[6] *This is the surpassingly grand and noble thing that makes confession so wonderful and comforting. . . .*

We should therefore take care to keep the two parts clearly separate. We should set little value on our work but exalt and magnify God's Word. We should not go to confession as if we wanted to perform a magnificent work to present to God, but simply to accept and receive something from him. You dare not come and say how upright or how wicked you are. If you are a Christian, I know this well enough anyway; if you are not, I know it even better. But you must do it for this reason: to lament your need and allow yourself to be helped so that you may attain a joyful heart and conscience.[7]

[1]G: *Über solche offentliche, tägliche und nötige Beichte ist nu diese heimliche Beichte, so zwischen einem Bruder allein geschiehet;* L: *Praeter hanc manifestam, quotidianam ac necessariam confessionem etiam occulta haec confessio fit coram uno aliquo fratre tantum.*

In light of the uses of *Bruder* informed by the original German of SA III, III, 4; SA III, VII, 1–3; and SC V, 24–25, the reader will note that the English translation introduces an element of gender inclusivity not in the original texts.

[2]G: *daß wir solchs einem Bruder klagen, Rat, Trost und Stärke zu holen, wenn und wie oft wir wollen*; L: *ut tunc coram fratre aliquo hoc ipsum conqueramur ac veluti in sinum ipsius deponamus consilium auxilium et consolationem ab eo accepturi, quando et quoties opus sit.*

See note above regarding gender inclusivity in the English.

[3]G: *daß Christus selbs die Absolutio seiner Christenheit in Mund gelegt und befohlen hat, uns von Sunden aufzulosen*; L: *quod Christus ipse absolutionem christianitati suae in os posuit ac commendavit, ut a peccatis absolveremur.*

[4]G: *daß ihn Gott durch ein Menschen von Sunden entbindet und losspricht*; L: *cum a Deo per hominem aliquem a peccatis absolvitur ac liber pronunciatur.*

See the notes on *Bruder* above regarding the context of *Mensch*.

[5]G: *Das erste ist unser Werk und Tuen*; L: *Prima est opus et factum nostrum.*

[6]G: *Das ander ist ein Werk, das Gott tuet*; L: *Altera est opus, quod Deus facit.*

[7]G: *daß Du Deine Not klagest und lassest Dir helfen und ein fröhlich Herz und Gewissen machen*; L: *ut necessitatem tuam aperias ac conqueraris et patiaris tibi consuli et opem ferri, ut cor laetum ac conscientiam tranquillam auferas.*

Large Catechism, Brief Exhortation to Confession, 13–15, 18
Italics according to Kolb/Wengert, noting omission
in the 1580 *Book of Concord.*

524 This repentance is not fragmentary or paltry[1]—like the kind that does penance for actual sins—nor is it uncertain like that kind. It does not debate over what is a sin or what is not a sin. Instead, it simply lumps everything together and says, "Everything is pure sin with us. What would we want to spend so much time investigating, dissecting, or distinguishing?" Therefore, here as well, contrition is not uncertain,[2] because there remains nothing that we might consider a "good" with which to pay for sin. Rather, there is plain, certain despair concerning all that we are, think, say, or do, etc.

Similarly, such confession also cannot be false, uncertain, or fragmentary.[3] All who confess that everything is pure sin with them embrace all sins, allow no exceptions, and do not forget a single one. Thus, satisfaction can never be uncertain either.[4] For it consists not in our uncertain, sinful works but rather in the suffering and blood of the innocent "Lamb of God, who takes away the sin of the world" [John 1:29].

About this repentance John preached and, after him, Christ in the Gospels, and we, too.[5] With this repentance, we topple the pope and everything that is built upon our good works, because it is all built upon a rotten, flimsy foundation: good works or law. In fact, there are no good works but exclusively evil works, and no one keeps the law (as Christ says in John 7[:19]), but all transgress it. Therefore the whole edifice is nothing but deceitful lies and hypocrisy, especially where it is at its holiest and most beautiful.

[1]G: *Diese Buße ist nicht stucklich und bettelisch*; L: *Haec poenitentia non est partialis et mutilata.*

[2]G: *Darumb so ist auch hie die Reu nicht ungewiß*; L: *Quamobrem etiam contritio hic non est dubia aut incerta.*

[3]G: *Desgleichen kann die Beicht auch nicht falsch, ungewiß oder stucklich sein*; L: *Similiter confessio quoque non potest esse falsa, incerta, manca aut mutila.*

[4]G: *Also kann die Gnugtuung auch nicht ungewiß sein*; L: *Sic et satisfactio non potest esse incerta.*

[5]G: *Von dieser Buße predigt Johannes und dernach Christus [auch] im Evangelio, und wir auch*; L: *De hac poenitentia concionatur Johannes, deinde Christus in evangelio et nos etiam.*

Smalcald Articles III, III, 36–39

525 They teach that by contrition we merit grace.[1] Why, then, someone might ask, did Saul, Judas, and others like them, who were dreadfully contrite, not receive grace?[2] Here it is necessary to say something about faith and the gospel, namely, that Judas did not believe and did not find strength through the gospel and the promise of Christ. In other words, faith made the difference between the contrition of Judas and Peter. The opponents reply instead from the law's perspective, namely, that Judas did not love God but feared punishment. However, when will a terrified conscience, especially in those serious, genuine, and great terrors that are described in the Psalms and the Prophets and certainly experienced by those who are truly converted, be able to determine whether it fears God on account of himself or in fear is fleeing eternal punishments?

[1]L: *Docent nos contritione mereri gratiam*; G: *sie lehren, man könne durch Reue Gnade verdienen.*

[2]L: *Ubi si quis interroget, quare Saul, Iudas et similes non consequantur gratiam, qui horribiliter contriti sunt*; G: *und wenn sie da gefragt werden, warum denn Saul und Judas und dergleichen nicht Gnade verdienet haben, in welchen gar ein schreckliche Contrition gewesen ist.*

Apology XII, 8–9

526 However, first we ask the opponents whether the reception of absolution is a part of repentance or not.[1] If they try to make a subtle distinction that separates absolution from confession, we fail to see what good confession is without absolution. If, however, they do not separate the reception of absolution from confession, then they must maintain that faith is part of repentance, because absolution is received in no other way than by faith.[2] That only faith receives absolution can be proved from Paul, who teaches in Romans 4[:16] that only faith is able to accept a promise. Now absolution is the promise of the forgiveness of sins. Therefore it necessarily requires faith.[3] We do not see how anyone could be said to receive absolution without assenting to it. And what else is the rejection of absolution than to accuse God of falsehood? If the heart doubts, it maintains that God's promises are uncertain and futile. So in 1 John 5[:10] it is written, "Those who do not believe in God have made him a liar by not believing in the testimony that God has given concerning his Son."

[1]L: *utrum absolutionem accipere pars sit poenitentiae nec ne*; G: *ob es auch ein Stück der Buß sei, die Absolution hören oder empfahen.*

[2]L: *quod fides sit pars poenitentiae, quia absolutio non accipitur nisi fide*; G: *daß der Glaub an das Wort Christi sei ein Stücke der Buß, so man die Absolution nicht empfahen kann, denn allein durch den Glauben.*

[3]L: *Absolutio autem est promissio remissionis peccatorum. Igitur necessario requirit fidem*; G: *Die Absolution aber ist nichts anders, denn das Evangelium, ein göttliche Zusage der Gnaden und Hulde Gottes &c. Darum kann man sie nicht haben noch erlangen, denn allein durch den Glauben.*

Apology XII, 61–62

527 Thus, it is necessary to know that this faith ought to hold that God freely forgives us on account of Christ and on account of his promise, and not on account of our works, contrition, confession, or satisfactions, *or love*.[1] For if faith relies on these works, it immediately becomes uncertain, because an anxious conscience sees that these works are not good enough. Accordingly, Ambrose speaks brilliantly about repentance:[2] "Therefore it is proper to believe both that we are to repent and that we are to be pardoned, but in such a way as to expect pardon from faith just as faith obtains it from the written agreement." Again, "It is faith that covers up our sins."

[1]L: *Atque hic sciendum est, quod haec fides debeat sentire, quod gratis nobis ignoscat Deus propter Christum, propter suam promissionem, non propter nostra opera, contritionem, confessionem aut satisfactiones*; G: *Und hie müssen wir wissen, daß der Glaub gewiß dafür halten soll, daß uns Gott aus Gnaden Sunde vergibt um Christus willen, nicht um unser Werk willen, um Beicht oder Gnugtun willen.*

[2]L: *de poenitentia*; G: *von der Buß.*

Apology XII, 95–96

528 There remains the third step, satisfactions.[1] Here their discussions become really confusing. They imagine that eternal penalties are commuted into punishments of purgatory, and of these, they teach that one part is remitted by the power of the keys and the other part must be redeemed by means of satisfactions.[2] They add further that satisfactions ought to be works of supererogation.[3] These consist of the most stupid observances, like pilgrimages, rosaries, and similar observations, none of which have the command of God. Then, just as they buy off purgatory with satisfactions, so they also devised a way to buy off satisfactions, which turned out to be very profitable. For they sell indulgences, which they interpret as the remission of satisfactions. They collect this revenue not only from the living but even more from the dead. They buy off the satisfactions for the dead not only with indulgences but also with the sacrifice of the Mass. In short, the subject of satisfactions is endless. Beneath these scandals and demonic teachings—too numerous to mention—the teaching of the righteousness by faith in Christ and Christ's benefits lies buried. All good people, therefore, will understand that for useful and godly reasons we must censure the teaching of the sophists and canonists about penance.

[1]L: *Restat tertius actus de satisfacionibus*; G: *Das dritte Stück von diesem Spiel ist die satisfactio oder Gnugtuung für die Sunde.*

[2]L: *partem docent redimendam esse satsifactionibus*; G: *für ein Teil aber müsse man gnugtun mit Werken.*

[3]L: *quod oporteat satisfactiones esse opera supererogationis*; G: *und nennen die Gnugtuung opera supererogationis.*

Apology XII, 13–16

529 At various places the Psalms mention confession, as in [Ps. 32:5], "Then I acknowledged my sin to you, and I did not hide my iniquity; I said, 'I will confess my transgressions to the Lord,' and you forgave the guilt of my sin." Such confession of sin, which is made to God, is itself contrition.[1] For when confession is made to God, it is of necessity made with the heart and not simply with the mouth, as is done by actors on the stage. Therefore such a confession is contrition.[2] In it, we, aware of God's wrath, confess that God is rightly angry and cannot be conciliated by our works and nevertheless we seek mercy on account of God's promise.

[1]L: *Talis confessio peccati, quae Deo fit, est ipsa contritio*; G: *Dasselbige Beichten und Bekennen, das Gott geschiehet, ist die Reue selbst.*

[2]L: *Est igitur talis confessio contritio*; G: *So ist dieselbig Beicht, die Gott geschiehet, ein Solche Reue im Herzen.*

Apology XII, 107

530 The power of the keys administers and offers the gospel through absolution, which is the true voice of the gospel.[1] Thus, we also include absolution when we talk about faith, because "faith comes from what is heard," as Paul says [Rom. 10:17]. For when the gospel is heard, when absolution is heard, the conscience is uplifted and receives consolation. Because God truly makes alive through the Word, the keys truly forgive sins before God[2] according to [Luke 10:16], "Whoever listens to you listens to me." Therefore we must believe the voice of the one absolving no less than we would believe a voice from heaven. Absolution can properly be called the sacrament of penance,[3] as even the more learned scholastic theologians say.

[1]L: *Porro potestas clavium administrat et exhibet evangelium per absolutionem, quae est vera vox evangelii*; G: *Die Gewalt nu der Schlüssel, die verkündiget uns durch die Absolution das Evangelium. Denn das Wort der Absolution verkündigt mir Friede und ist das Evangelium selbst.*

[2]L: *Et quia Deus vere per verbum vivificat, claves vere coram Deo remittunt peccata*; G: *Und dieweil Gott durch das Wort wahrlich neu Leben und Trost ins Herz gibt, so werden auch durch Gewalt der Schlüssel wahrhaftig hier auf Erden die Sunde los gezählet also, dass sie für Gott im Himmel los sein.*

[3]L: *Et absolutio proprie dici potest sacramentum poenitentiae*; G: *und die Absolution, das selige, tröstliche Wort, sollt billig das Sacrament der Buß heißen.*

Apology XII, 39–41

HOW IS REPENTANCE THE CHRISTIAN WAY OF LIFE, THE WAY OF FAITH?

531 *Therefore, when I exhort you to go to confession, I am doing nothing but exhorting you to be a Christian.*[1] *If I bring you to this point, I have also brought you to confession. For those who really want to be upright Christians and free from their sins, and who want to have a joyful conscience, truly hunger and thirst already. They snatch at the bread just like a hunted deer, burning with heat and thirst, as Psalm 42[:1] says, "As a deer longs for flowing streams, so my soul longs for you, O God." That is, as a deer trembles with eagerness for a fresh spring, so I yearn and tremble for God's Word or absolution and for the sacrament, etc.*[2] *In this way, you see, confession would be taught properly, and such a desire and love for it would be aroused that people would come running after us to get it, more than we would like. We shall let the papists torment and torture themselves and other people who ignore such a treasure and bar themselves from it. As for ourselves, however, let us lift our hands in praise and thanks to God that we have attained to this knowledge and grace.*

[1]G: *Darümb wenn ich zur Beichte vermahne, so tue ich nits anders, denn daß ich vermahne, ein Christen zu sein*; L: *Quare cum ad confessionem adhortor, non aliud ago, quam quod unumquemlibet adhortor, ut pergat christianus esse.*

[2]G: *das ist, wie wehe und bange einem solchen ist nach einem frischen Born, so angst und bange ist mir nach Gottes Wort oder Absolution und Sakrament etc.*; L: *In hunc modum recte de confessione doceretur atque hoc pacto amor et cupido ad illam in hominibus excitari possit.*

Large Catechism, Brief Exhortation to Confession, 32–35
Italics according to Kolb/Wengert, noting omission
in the 1580 *Book of Concord.*

532 Absolution can properly be called the sacrament of penance,[1] as even the more learned scholastic theologians say. At the same time, this faith is nourished in many ways in the midst of temptations through the proclamation of the gospel and the use of the sacraments. For these are signs of the New Testament, that is, signs of the forgiveness of sins. They offer, therefore, the forgiveness of sins,[2] as the words of the Lord's Supper clearly state [cf. Matt. 26:26, 28], "This is my body, which is given for you. . . . This cup . . . is the new covenant in my blood. . . ." Thus faith is formed and strengthened through absolution, through hearing the gospel, and through use of the sacraments,[3] so that it might not succumb in its struggle against the terrors of sin and death. This understanding of repentance is plain and clear. It increases the value of the sacraments and the power of the keys, illumines the benefits of Christ, and teaches us to make use of Christ as our mediator and propitiator.

[1]L: *Et absolutio proprie dici potest sacramentum poenitentiae*; G: *und die Absolution, das selige, tröstliche Wort, sollt billig das Sacrament der Buß heißen*.

[2]L: *Offerunt igitur remissionem peccatorum*; G: *Denn sie bieten an Vergebung der Sunde*.

[3]L: *Ita fides concipitur et confirmatur per absolutionem, per auditum evangelii, per usum sacramentorum*; G: *Also wird auch der Glaub gestärkt durch das Wort der Absolution, durch die Prediger des Evangelii, durch Entpfahen des Sakraments*.

Apology XII, 41–43

SUMMARY

- Repentance involves contrition and faith. Contrition is the conscience troubled by the knowledge of sin, lamenting that sin, and seeking comfort and restoration. It does not debate with God over what sin is. Faith believes that for Christ's sake sins are forgiven, which brings comfort to the conscience and delivers from terror over sin. Good works, the fruits of repentance, are bound to follow.
- Christians also confess to God alone in their prayers or to another Christian alone, as the Lord's Prayer expresses and is itself a confession when it says, "Forgive us our debts, as we forgive our debtors." Such is the essence of Christian life and the way to a happy heart.
- Sins are not forgiven "on account of our works, contrition, confession, or satisfactions" (Ap XII, 95–96). Any requirement for satisfaction—extra works after Absolution to prove true repentance or to contribute merit toward forgiveness—is outside the command of Christ and a distortion of the righteousness of faith in Christ.
- To go to confession is simply being a Christian, that is, truly hungering and thirsting for God's Word, absolution, sacrament, etc. Through these means, faith is strengthened and the benefits of Christ are received. Daily repentance is the essence of the Christian life.

SYNOPSIS

It is God who makes us spiritually alive through his Word and the work of the Holy Spirit in the heart. He does this through the Word and its visible signs in the sacraments. The Lutheran Confessions often number Absolution among the sacraments. Thus the "power of the keys administers and offers the gospel through absolution, which is the true voice of the gospel" (Ap XII, 39–41). Absolution has an important place in the Christian life of repentance.

6

PRAYER

WHAT IS CHRISTIAN PRAYER?

601 We are to fear and love God, so that we do not curse, swear, practice magic, lie, or deceive using God's name, but instead use that very name in every time of need to call on, pray to,[1] praise, and give thanks to God.

[1]G: *denselbigen in all Nöten anrufen, beten*; L: *in omni necessitate illud invocemus.*

Small Catechism I, 4

602 Our Father, you who are in heaven.

What is this? Answer:

With these words God wants to entice us, so that we come to believe he is truly our Father and we are truly his children, in order that we may ask him boldly and with complete confidence,[1] *just as loving children ask their loving father.*

[1]G: *mit aller Zuversicht ihn bitten sollen*; L: *ut eum confidentius pleni fiducia invocemus.*

The Latin version cited here comes from the 1584 *Book of Concord* that reflects the post-1531 editions. Another Latin version exists from 1543 as an addition to the 1529 Latin version. See *BSLK*, 512, textual apparatus for line 17. The German text for the Lord's Prayer follows the local custom in Wittenberg, not that of Luther's German Bible.

Small Catechism III, 1–2
Italics in Kolb/Wengert reflect Luther's later changes.

603 **[German text]** In addition, the commands of God and proper, true service of God[1] are obscured when people hear that only monks must be in the state of perfection. For Christian perfection is to fear God earnestly with the whole heart and yet also to have a sincere confidence, faith, and trust that we have a gracious, merciful God because of Christ; that we may and should pray for and request from God whatever we need and confidently expect help from him in all affliction, according to each person's vocation and walk of life;[2] and that meanwhile we should diligently do external good works and attend to our calling. This is true perfection and true service of God—not being a mendicant or wearing a black or gray cowl, etc.

[Latin text] Furthermore, the precepts of God and true worship of God[1] are obscured when people hear that only monks are in a state of perfection. For Christian perfection means earnestly to fear God and, at the same time, to have great faith and to trust that we have a gracious God on account of Christ; to ask for and to expect with certainty help from God in all things that are to be borne in connection with our calling;[2] and, in the meantime, diligently to do good works for others and to serve in our calling. True perfection and true worship of God consist in all these things, not in celibacy, mendicancy, or shabby clothing.

[1]G: *der recht und wahre Gottsdienst*; L: *verus cultus Dei*.

[2]G: *daß wir mugen und sollen von Gott bitten und begehren, was uns not ist, und Hilfe von ihm in allen Trubsalen gewißlich, nach eins jeden Beruf und Stand, gewarten*; L: *petere a Deo et certo exspectare auxilium in omnibus rebus gerendis iuxta vocationem*.

Augsburg Confession XXVII, 49–50

604 It has been prescribed for this reason also, that we should reflect on our need, which ought to drive and compel us to pray without ceasing.[1] A person who wants to make a request must present a petition, naming and describing something that he or she desires;[2] otherwise it cannot be called a prayer.[3]

[1]G: *ohn Unterlaß zu beten*; L: *qua ad indesinenter orandum*.

[2]G: *Denn wer da bitten will, der muß etwas bringen, furtragen und nennen, des er begehret*; L: *Etenim qui orare voluerit, necessum est, ut is aliquid apportet, exponat et nominatim perstringat, quod petierit*.

[3]G: *wo nicht, so kann es kein Gebete heißen*; L: *quod nisi fit, non potest dici precatio*.

Large Catechism III, 24

605 Therefore, this sign is attached to the petition[1] so that when we pray we may recall the promise and think,[2] "Dear Father, I come to you and pray that you will forgive me for this reason:[3] not because I can make satisfaction or deserve anything by my works, but because you have promised and have set this seal on it, making it as certain as if I had received an absolution pronounced by you yourself." For whatever baptism and the Lord's Supper, which are appointed to us as outward signs, can effect, this sign can as well, in order to strengthen and gladden our conscience. Moreover, above and beyond the other signs, it has been instituted precisely so that we can use and practice it every hour, keeping it with us at all times.[4]

[1]G: *Darümb ist nu solchs Zeichen bei diesem Gebete mit angeheftet*; L: *Proinde huic orationi tale signum annexum est.*

[2]G: *daß, wenn wir bitten, uns der Verheißung erinnern und also denken*; L: *ut nos orantes promissionis admoneat, ut ita cogitemus.*

[3]G: „*Lieber Vater, darümb komme und bitte ich, daß Du mir vergebest . . .*"; L: '*Optime pater, ideo ad te oratum venio, ut mihi ignoscas propitius . . .*'

[4]G: *Denn wieviel die Taufe und Sakrament, äußerlich zum Zeichen gestellet, schaffen, soviel vermag auch dies Zeichen, unser Gewissen zu stärken und fröhlich zu machen, und ist fur andern eben darumb gestellet, daß wir's alle Stunden künnden brauchen und uben, als daß wir allezeit bei uns haben*; L: *Quantum enim baptismus et sacramentum pro externo signo constitutum praestat, tantum etiam hoc signum conscientiam nostram corroborare atque exhilarare potest estque ideo institutum pro aliis, ut hoc omnibus horis uti atque exercere queamus ut re, quam semper nobiscum in parato habeamus.*

Large Catechism III, 97–98

TO WHOM SHOULD WE PRAY?

606 This, however, is the catholic faith: that we worship[1] one God in trinity and the Trinity in unity, neither confusing the persons nor dividing the substance.

[1]L: *Fides autem catholica haec est, ut unum Deum in trinitate et trinitatem in unitate veneremur*; G: *Dies ist aber der rechte christliche Glaube, daß wir ein einigen Gott in drei Personen und drei Personen in einiger Gottheit ehren.*

Athanasian Creed, 3

607 This much, however, should be said to the common people, so that they may mark well and remember the sense of this commandment: We are to trust in God alone, to look to him alone, and to expect him to give us only good things; for it is he who gives us body, life, food, drink, nourishment, health, protection, peace, and all necessary temporal and eternal blessings. In addition, God protects us from misfortune and rescues and delivers us when any evil befalls us. It is God alone (as I have repeated often enough) from whom we receive everything good and by whom we are delivered from all evil.

Large Catechism I, 24–25

608 They condemn article twenty-one completely, because we do not require the invocation of the saints.[1]

[1]L: *invocationem sanctorum*; G: *Anrufen der Heiligen*.

Apology XXI, 1

609 **[German text]** Concerning the cult of the saints[1] our people teach that the saints are to be remembered so that we may strengthen our faith when we see how they experienced grace and how they were helped by faith. Moreover, it is taught that each person, according to his or her calling, should take the saints' good works as an example. For instance, His Imperial Majesty, in a salutary and righteous fashion, may follow the example of David in waging war against the Turk. For both hold a royal office that demands defense and protection of their subjects. However, it cannot be demonstrated from Scripture that a person should call upon the saints or seek help from them.[2] "For there is only one single reconciler and mediator set up between God and humanity, Jesus Christ" (1 Tim. 2[:5]). He is the only savior, the only high priest, the mercy seat, and intercessor before God (Rom. 8[:34]). He alone has promised to hear our prayers.[3] According to Scripture, in all our needs and concerns it is the highest worship to seek and call upon this same Jesus Christ with our whole heart.[4] "But if anyone does sin, we have an advocate with the Father, Jesus Christ, the righteous . . ." [1 John 2:1].

[Latin text] Concerning the cult of the saints[1] they teach that saints may be remembered in order that we imitate their faith and good works, according to our calling. Thus, the emperor can imitate the example of David in waging war to drive the Turks from our native land. For both of them are kings. However, Scripture does not teach calling on the saints or pleading for help from them.[2] For it sets before us Christ alone as mediator, atoning sacrifice, high priest, and intercessor. He is to be called upon, and he has promised that our prayers will be heard.[3] Furthermore, he strongly approves this worship most of all, namely, that he be called upon in all afflictions.[4] 1 John 2[:1]: "But if anyone does sin, we have an advocate with the Father. . . ."

[1]G: *Vom Heiligendienst*; L: *De cultu sanctorum.*

[2]G: *Durch Schrift aber mag man aber nicht beweisen, daß man die Heiligen anrufen oder Hilf bei ihnen suchen soll*; L: *Sed scriptura non docet invocare sanctos seu petere auxilium a sanctis.*

[3]G: *Und der hat allein zugesagt, daß er unser Gebet erhoren welle*; L: *Hic invocandus est et promisit se exauditurum esse preces nostras.*

[4]G: *Das ist auch der hochste Gottesdienst nach der Schrift, daß man denselbigen Jesum Christum in allen Noten und Anliegen von Herzen suche und anrufe*; L: *et hunc cultum maxime probat, videlicet ut invocetur in omnibus afflictionibus.*

Augsburg Confession XXI, 1–4

610 Moreover, even supposing that the saints do pray for the church,[1] it still does not follow that they are to be invoked.[2] However, our Confession affirms only this much, that Scripture does not teach us to call upon the saints or to ask the saints for help.[3] Because neither a command, nor a promise, nor an example from Scripture about invoking saints can be brought forward,[4] it follows that the conscience can find no certainty about such invocation.[5]

[1]L: *Porro ut maxime pro ecclesia orent sancti*; G: *Weiter, ob die Heiligen gleich beten für die Kirchen.*

[2]L: *tamen non sequitur, quod sint invocandi*; G: *so folget doch daraus nicht, daß man die Heiligen solle anrufen.*

[3]L: *quod scriptura non doceat sanctorum invocationem seu petere a sanctis auxilium*; G: *in der Schrift stehet nichts von dem Anrufen der Heiligen oder daß man Hilf suchen solle bei den Heiligen.*

[4]L: *Cum autem neque praeceptum neque promissio neque exemplum ex scripturis de invocandis sanctis afferri possit*; G: *So man nu weder Gebot noch Zusage noch Exempel aus der Schrift mag fürbringen.*

[5]L: *sequitur conscientiam nihil posse certi de illa invocatione habere*; G: *so folget, daß kein Herz noch Gewissen darauf sich verlassen kann.*

Apology XXI, 10

WHO SHOULD PRAY?

611 Therefore, after we have been justified and reborn by faith, we begin to fear and love God, to pray for and expect help from him,[1] to thank and praise him, and to obey him in our afflictions. We also begin to love our neighbor because our hearts have spiritual and holy impulses.

[1]L: *petere et exspectare ab eo auxilium*; G: *von ihm alle Hilfe zu bitten und zu warten.*

Apology IV, 125

612 To be sure, we hold that repentance ought to produce good fruits on account of the glory and commandment of God and that good fruits, such as true fasting, true prayer,[1] true almsgiving, and the like, have God's command. However, nowhere in Holy Scripture do we find that only the punishment of purgatory or canonical satisfactions (that is, certain "nonobligatory works") can remit eternal punishments or that the power of the keys carries with it the command to commute penalties or to remit them in part.

[1]L: *verae orationes*; G: *Beten.*

Apology XII, 139

613 For All in the Community

"Love your neighbor as yourself. In this all the commandments are summarized." From Romans 13[:9]. "And entreat [God] with prayers for all people."[1] From 1 Timothy 2[:1].

[1]G: „*Und haltet an mit Beten fur alle Menschen*"; L: '*Et ante omnia fiant deprecationes, obsecrationes, interpellationes, gratiarum actiones pro omnibus hominibus.*'

Small Catechism, Table of Duties, 14

614 Neither Christ nor Paul praises virginity because it justifies but because it provides more time for praying, teaching, and serving and is less distracted by domestic activities.[1] Accordingly, Paul says [1 Cor. 7:32], "The unmarried man is anxious about the affairs of the Lord." Therefore, virginity is praised on account of meditation and study.

[1]L: *sed quia sit expeditior, et minus distrahatur domesticis occupationibus in orando, docendo, serviendo*; G: *desto freier, unverhindert mit Haushalten, Kinderziehen, &c., lesen, beten, schreiben, dienen können.*

Apology XXIII, 40

615 Thus this petition really means that God does not wish to regard our sins and punish us as we daily deserve but to deal graciously with us, to forgive as he has promised, and thus to grant us a joyful and cheerful conscience so that we may stand before him in prayer.[1] For where the heart is not right with God and cannot generate such confidence, it will never dare to pray.[2] But such a confident and joyful heart can never come except when one knows that his or her sins are forgiven.

[1]G: *also ein fröhlich und unverzagt Gewissen geben, fur ihm zu stehen und zu bitten*; L: *atque ita nobis laetam eac interritam largiatur conscientiam, qua animati coram eo et stare et precari queamus.*

[2]G: *so wird es nimmermehr sich türren unterstehen zu beten*; L: *numquam in perpetuum aliquid ab eo precari sustinebit.*

Large Catechism III, 92

616 And it is furthermore false that reason by its own powers is able to love God above all things and to fulfill God's law, namely, truly to fear God, truly to conclude that God hears prayer,[1] willingly to obey God in death and in other visitations of God, and not to covet things that belong to others, etc.—although reason can produce civil works.

[1]L: *vere timere Deum, vere statuere, quod Deus exaudiat*; G: *ihnen zu fürchten, gewiß darauf zu stehen, daß Gott das Gebet erhöre.*

Apology IV, 27

617 Thus God has laid before us very briefly all the afflictions that may ever beset us in order that we may never have an excuse for failing to pray.[1] But the efficacy of prayer consists in our learning also to say AMEN to it—that is, not to doubt that our prayer is surely heard and will be answered.[2] This word is nothing else than an unquestioning word of faith on the part of the one who does not pray as a matter of luck but knows that God does not lie because he has promised to grant it. Where there is no faith like this, there also can be no true prayer.[3]

[1]G: *daß wir je keine Entschüldigung haben zu beten*; L: *ne qua nobis relinqueretur negligendae orationis excusatio.*

[2]G: *das ist: nicht zweifeln, daß es gewißlich erhöret sei und geschehen werde*; L: *hoc est non haesitare orationem nostram certo esse exauditam et futurum esse, quod precati sumus.*

[3]G: *Wo nu solcher Glaube nicht ist, da kann auch kein recht Gebete sein*; L: *Jam ubicumque talis fides non est, hic neque verae orationi locus esse potest.*

Large Catechism III, 119–120

SUMMARY

- A Christian prayer is one that calls upon the name of God, trusting that for Christ's sake God is reconciled and expecting to aid his children in all good things. God commands us to pray at all times and to name what is needed.
- A Christian prayer addresses the Trinity, Father, Son, and Holy Spirit, not the saints, for there is only one mediator and intercessor before God, that is, Christ. He will hear us.
- Those who are justified by faith and regenerated by the Spirit pray to God. Indeed, prayer that cries for help, gives thanks, and praises God is one of the fruits of repentance.
- In contrast, where the heart has no right relation to God, there is no confidence—such trust in God never comes from one's own strength or ability. Thus where there is no faith, there can be no true prayer.

WHY SHOULD WE PRAY?

618 Thus, you see, God wishes to show us how he cares for us in all our needs and faithfully provides for our daily sustenance. Although he gives and provides these blessings bountifully, even to the godless and rogues, yet he wishes us to ask for them so that we may realize that we have received them from his hand and may recognize in them his fatherly goodness toward us.[1] When he withdraws his hand, nothing can prosper or last for any length of time, as indeed we see and experience every day.

[1]G: *und wiewohl er solchs reichlich gibt und erhält, auch den Gottlosen und Buben, doch will er, daß wir darümb bitten, auf daß wir erkennen, daß wir's von seiner Hand empfahen, und darinne sein väterliche Güte gegen uns spüren*; L: *tum quam fideliter etiam temporalis victus nostri rationem habere soleat. Et quamquam hunc impiis etiam hominibus et improbis nebulonibus affatim suppeditare soleat atque tueri, nihilosecus tamen vult, ut pro eo consequendo oremus, ut certo cognoscamus nos haec omnia ab ejus munificentia et liberalitate accipere, quo ita ejus paternam bonitatem erga nos propensam non dubiis argumentis perspiciamus.*

Large Catechism III, 82–83

619 From the fact that prayer is so urgently commanded,[1] you ought to conclude that we should by no means despise our prayers,[2] but rather prize them highly.

[1]G: *weil es so hoch geboten ist zu beten*; L: *cum tantopere nobis injunctum sit, ut oremus.*

[2]G: *daß beileib niemand sein Gebete verachten soll*; L: *ne quo modo quispiam suas preces contemnat.*

The English translation contains an element of gender neutrality not found in the original texts.

Large Catechism III, 12

620 Finally, if everything that has the command of God and some promise added to it ought to be counted a sacrament, why not include prayer,[1] which can most truly be called a sacrament? For it has the command of God, and it has many promises. Were it included among the sacraments, as though in a more exalted position, it would encourage people to pray.[2] Alms as well as afflictions could also be listed here, which are themselves signs to which God has added promises. But let us skip over all of this. No intelligent person will argue much about the number or the terminology, as long as those things are retained that have the mandate and promises of God.

[1]L: *cur non addimus orationem*; G: *so sollt man billig für allen andern das Gebet ein Sakrament nennen.*

[2]L: *Habet enim et mandatum Dei et promissiones plurimas, et collocata inter sacramenta, quasi in illustriore loco, invitat homines ad orandum*; G: *Denn da ist ein starker Gottes Befehl und viel herrlicher göttlicher Zusage. Es hätte auch wohl Ursache. Denn wenn man dem Gebet so großen Titel göbe, würden die Leute zum Gebet gereizt.*

Apology XIII, 16–17

621 But the Decalogue requires not only outward civil works that reason can produce to some extent; it also requires other works that are placed far beyond the reach of reason, such as, truly to fear God, truly to love God, truly to call upon God, truly to be convinced that he hears us,[1] and to expect help from God in death and all afflictions. Finally, it requires obedience to God in death and all afflictions so that we do not flee or avoid these things when God imposes them.

[1]L: *scilicet vere timere Deum, vere diligere Deum, vere invocare Deum, vere statuere, quod Deus exaudiat*; G: *daß wir Gott sollen mit ganzem Ernst vom Herzengrund fürchten und lieben, ihnen in allen Nöten allein anrufen und sonst auf nichts einigen Trost setzen.*

Apology IV, 8

622 We therefore urgently beg and exhort everyone to take these words to heart and in no case to despise prayer.[1] Prayer used to be taught in the devil's name, in such a way that no one paid any attention to it, and people supposed it was enough if the act was performed, whether God heard it or not. But that is to stake prayer on luck and to mumble aimlessly. Such a prayer is worthless.[2]

We allow ourselves to be impeded and deterred by such thoughts as these: "I am not holy enough or worthy enough; if I were as righteous and holy as St. Peter or St. Paul, then I would pray."[3] Away with such thoughts! The very commandment that applied to St. Paul applies also to me. The Second Commandment is given just as much on my account as on his. He can boast of no better or holier commandment than I.

Therefore you should say: "The prayer I offer is just as precious, holy, and pleasing to God as those of St. Paul and the holiest of saints.[4] The reason is this: I freely admit that he is holier in respect to his person, but not on account of the commandment. For God does not regard prayer on account of the person, but on account of his Word and the obedience accorded it.[5] On this commandment, on which all the saints base their prayer, I, too, base mine.[6] Moreover, I pray for the same thing for which they all pray, or ever have prayed."[7]

This is the first and most important point, that all our prayers must be based on obedience to God, regardless of our person,[8] whether we are sinners or righteous people, worthy or unworthy. We must understand that God is not joking, but that he will be angry and punish us if we do not pray,[9] just as he punishes all other kinds of disobedience. Nor will he allow our prayers to be futile or lost,[10] for if he did not intend to answer you, he would not have ordered you to pray[11] and backed it up with such a strict commandment.

[1]G: *und in keinen Weg unser Gebete verachte*; L: *neve ullo pacto nostras orationes tamquam rem nihili aspernemur.*

[2]G: *Denn man bisher also gelehret hat ins Teufels Namen, daß neimand solchs geachtet hat und gemeinet, es wäre genug, daß das Werk getan wäre, Gott erhöret's oder höret es nicht. Das heißet das Gebete in die Schanz geschlagen und auf Ebenteuer hin gemurret, darümb ist es ein verloren Gebete*; L: *Ita enim hactenus in mali genii nomine docti sunt homines, ut nemo harum rerum ullam curam susceperit aestimaritque satis superque actum esse, modo opus orandi factum esset, Deus hoc exaudiret nec ne, non magnopere laborabatur. Sed hoc est hylam, ut habet*

proverbium, inclamare aut loqui ventis ac litori ita nequicquam murmurando, ob id inutilis quoque et infrugifera fuit oratio.

[3]G: *wenn ich so fromm und heilig wäre als S. Petrus, Paulus, so wollt' ich beten*; L: *quod si tanta probitate ac vitae sanctimonia praecellerem ut divus Petrus aut Paulus, libenter orare velim.*

[4]G: *Mein Gebete, das ich tue, ist ja so köstlich, heilig und Gott gefällig als S. Paulus' und der Allerheiligsten*; L: *Meae preces, quas ad Deum fundo, nihilo sunt deteriores aut profaniores aut Deo minus acceptae, quam fuere Pauli et omnium sanctissimorum.*

[5]G: *weil Gott das Gebete nicht der Person halben ansiehet, sondern seines Worts und Gehorsams halben*; L: *Certem enim habeo Deum nequaquam orationes personae gratia respicere, sed propter verbum suum atque obedientiam sibi praestitam atque exhibitam.*

[6]G: *Denn auf das Gepot, darauf alle Heiligen ihr Gebete setzen, setze ich meines auch*; L: *Ei enim praecepto, cui omnes sancti orando innixi sunt, ego quoque precans innitor.*

[7]G: *dazu bete ich eben das, darümb sie allzumal bitten oder gebeten haben*; L: *ad haec eadem ipsa precor, quae ipsi omnes ad unum precantur aut precati sunt.*

[8]G: *daß alle unser Gebete sich gründen und stehen soll auf Gottes Gehorsam, nicht angesehen unser Person*; L: *ut omnis nostra oratio divinae obedientiae innitatur nullo nostrae personae respectu.*

[9]G: *sondern zürnen und strafen, wo wir nicht bitten*; L: *sed graviter nos et acerbe puniturum, si segnes in orando fuerimus.*

[10]G: *darnach, daß er unser Gebete nicht will lassen ümbsonst und verloren sein*; L: *Deinde, quod nostras preces nequicquam ac timere effundi.*

[11]G: *Denn wo er Dich nicht erhören wöllte, würde er Dich nicht heißen beten*; L: *non patietur, si enim te audire nollet, ut orares.*

Large Catechism III, 14–18

623 Trust in mercy arises from both the promise and the bestowal of merits. Such trust in the divine promise and in the merits of Christ must provide the basis for prayer.[1] For we must be completely certain that we are heard on account of Christ[2] and that by his merits we have a gracious Father.

[1]L: *Talis fiducia promissionis divinae, item meritorum Christi debet afferri ad orandum*; G: *Auf beide Stücke, nämlich auf die göttliche Zusage auf Christi Verdienst, muß ein christlich Gebet gründen. Ein*

solcher Glaub an die göttliche Zusage und auf den Verdienst Christi gehört zum Gebet.

[2]L: *Vere enim statuere debemus, et quod propter Christum exaudiamur*; G: *Denn wir sollen gewiß dafür halten, daß wir um Christus willen erhöret werden.*

Apology XXI, 20

624 Therefore, this sign is attached to the petition[1] so that when we pray we may recall the promise and think,[2] "Dear Father, I come to you and pray that you will forgive me for this reason:[3] not because I can make satisfaction or deserve anything by my works, but because you have promised and have set this seal on it, making it as certain as if I had received an absolution pronounced by you yourself."

[1]G: *Darümb ist nu solchs Zeichen bei diesem Gebete mit angeheftet*; L: *Proinde huic orationi tale signum annexum est.*

[2]G: *daß, wenn wir bitten, uns der Verheißung erinnern und also denken*; L: *ut nos orantes promissionis admoneat, ut ita cogitemus.*

[3]G: *„Lieber Vater, darümb komme und bitte ich, daß Du mir vergebest . . ."*; L: *'Optime pater, ideo ad te oratum venio, ut mihi ignoscas propitius . . .'*

Large Catechism III, 97

625 It is therefore a pernicious delusion when people pray in such a way[1] that they dare not wholeheartedly add "Yes" and conclude with certainty that God hears their prayer.[2] Instead, they remain in doubt, saying, "Why should I be so bold as to boast that God hears my prayer? I am only a poor sinner," etc. That means that they are looking not at God's promise but at their own works and worthiness, and thereby they despise God and accuse him of lying. Therefore they receive nothing, as St. James [1:6–7] says, "But ask in faith, never doubting, for the one who doubts is like a wave of the sea, driven and tossed by the wind; for the doubter . . . must not expect to receive anything from the Lord." Look! God has attached much importance to our being certain so that we do not pray in vain[3] or despise our prayers in any way.[4]

[1]G: *Darümb ist's ein schädlicher Wahn deren, die also beten*; L: *Quare perniciosa quaedam illorum est opinio ita orantium.*

[2]G: *daß sie nicht dürfen von Herzen Ja dazu sagen und gewißlich schließen, daß Gott erhöret*; L: *ut non audeant Amen quoque ad finem orationis adjicere, hoc est certo concludere se exauditum iri.*

[3]G: *Siehe, soviel ist Gott daran gelegen, daß wir gewiß sollen sein, daß wir nicht ümbsonst bitten*; L: *Ecce tanti refert certos esse nos non frustra oraturos.*

[4]G: *und in keinem Wege unser Gebete verachten*; L: *ut nullo modo preces nostras respuamus.*

Large Catechism III, 121–123

HOW SHOULD WE PRAY?

626 Second and most important, we observe them so that people will have time and opportunity on such days of rest, which otherwise would not be available, to attend worship services,[1] that is, so that they may assemble to hear and discuss God's Word and then to offer praise, song, and prayer to God.[2]

[1]G: *Gottsdeinsts zu warten*; L: *cultui divino serviendi.*

[2]G: *beten.*

The Latin uses the biblical phrase "hymns, psalms and [spiritual] songs" from Ephesians 5:19.

Large Catechism I, 84

627 For this purpose it also helps to form the habit of commending ourselves each day to God[1]—our soul and body, spouse, children, servants, and all that we have—for his protection against every conceivable need. This is why the Benedicite, the Gratias, and other evening and morning blessings[2] were also introduced and have continued among us. From the same source comes the custom learned in childhood of making the sign of the cross when something dreadful or frightening is seen or heard, and saying, "LORD God, save me!" or, "Help, dear Lord Christ!" and the like. Likewise, if someone unexpectedly experiences good fortune—no matter how insignificant—he or she may say, "God be praised and thanked!" "God has bestowed this upon me!" etc.—just as children used to be taught to fast and pray to St. Nicholas and other saints.[3] But these practices would be more pleasing and acceptable to God than life in a monastery or Carthusian holiness.

[1]G: *täglich Gotte zu befehlen*; L: *quotidie nos . . . Deo commendare.*

[2]G: *andere Segen abends und morgens*; L: *aliaeque nocturnae et matutinae benedictiones.*

[3]G: *Wie man vormals die Kinder gewehnet hat, Sankt Niklaus und andern Heiligen zu fasten und beten*; L: *Quemadmodum quondam pueri parentum monitu consueverunt divum Nicolaum et jejunio honorare et precibus invocare.*

Large Catechism I, 73–74

628 Let this be said as an admonition in order that we may learn above all to value prayer as a great and precious thing[1] and may properly distinguish between vain babbling and asking for something.[2] By no means do we reject prayer, but we do denounce the utterly useless howling and growling,[3] as Christ himself rejects and forbids great wordiness.[4]

[1]G: *daß man fur allen Dingen lerne das Gebete groß und teuer achten*; L: *ut prae omnibus discamus orationem magni pendere.*

[2]G: *und ein rechten Unterscheid wisse zwischen dem Plappern und etwas Bitten*; L: *veroque discrimine discernere verbosum multiloquium ab oratione aliquid petente.*

[3]G: *Denn wir verwerfen mit nichte das Gebete, sondern das lauter unnütze Geheule und Gemurre verwerfen wir*; L: *Nequaquam enim precationes rejicimus, verum non nisi inutilem illum boatum ac murmurantium sacrificorum et monachorum inconditam coaxationem damnamus.*

[4]G: *wie auch Christus selbs lang Gewäsche verwirft und verbeut*; L: *quemadmodum ipse quoque Christus in oratione molestam et ad ostentationem compositam battologiam damnat ac prohibet.*

Large Catechism III, 33

629 The first thing to know is this: It is our duty to pray because of God's command. For we heard in the Second Commandment, "You are not to take God's name in vain." Thereby we are required to praise the holy name and to pray or call upon it in every need. For calling upon it is nothing else than praying.[1] Prayer, therefore, is as strictly and solemnly commanded as all the other commandments (such as having no other God, not killing, not stealing, etc.) lest anyone thinks it makes no difference whether I pray or not,[2] as vulgar people do who say in their delusion: "Why should I pray? Who knows whether God pays attention to my prayer or wants to hear it? If I do not pray, someone else will." Thus they fall into the habit of never praying, claiming that because we reject false and hypocritical prayers, we teach that there is no duty or need to pray.[3]

It is quite true that the kind of babbling and bellowing that used to pass for prayers in the church was not really prayer.[4] Such external repetition, when properly used, may serve as an exercise for young children, pupils, and simple folk; while it may be useful in singing or reading, it is not actually prayer. To pray, as the Second Commandment teaches, is to call upon God in every need. This God requires of us; it is not a matter of our choice. It is our duty and obligation to pray if we want to be Christians, just as it is our duty and obligation to obey our fathers, mothers, and the civil authorities. By invocation and prayer the name of God is glorified and used to good purpose.[5] This you should note above all, so that you may silence and repel any thoughts that would prevent or deter us from praying. Now it would be improper for a son to say to his father: "What is the use of being obedient? I will go and do as I please; what difference does it make?" But there stands the commandment, "You shall and must obey!" Just so, it is not left to my choice here whether to pray or not, but it is my duty and obligation *on pain of God's wrath and displeasure.*[6]

[1]G: *Denn anrufen ist nichts anders denn beten*; L: *Invocare enim nihil aliud est quam preces ad Deum fundere.*

[2]G: *daß niemand denke, es sei gleich soviel, ich bete oder bete nicht*; L: *ne quis temere in eam opinionem veniat, ut existimet perinde esse, oret nec ne.*

[3]G: *und kommen also in die Gewohnheit, daß sie nimmermehr beten und nehmen zu Behelf, daß wir falsch und Heuchelgebete verwerfen, als lehreten wir, man solle oder dürfe nicht beten*; L: *Ex quo tandem in eam consuetudinem deveniunt, ut numquam quicquam orent praetexentes tandem suae pigritiae aut ignavae impietati potius nos falsas et hypocriticas oratiunculas rejicere, quasi vero nos unquam docuissemus non esse orandum.*

[4]G: *Das ist aber je wahr: Was man bisher fur Gebete getan hat, geplärret und gedönet in der Kirchen etc., ist freilich kein Gebete gewesen*; L: *Quamquam hoc diffiteri non possumus eas orationes, quae hactenus factae sunt Stentoreis clamoribus in ecclesiis vociferando et tonando etc., non fuisse orationes.*

[5]G: *Das will er von uns haben und soll nicht in unser Willköre stehen, sondern sollen und müssen beten, wollen wir Christen sein, so wohl als wir sollen und müssen Vater, Mutter und der Oberkeit gehörsam sein. Denn durch das Anrufen und bitten wird der Name Gottes geehret und nützlich gebraucht*; L: *Hoc a nobis exigit neque res est nostri arbitrii, verum orare, debemus et cogimur, si tamen christiani perhiberi contendimus, aeque atque parentibus et magistratibus omnibus obedientiae officiis obtemperare*

cogimur. Siquidem invocando et precando nomen Dei colitur et utiliter usurpatur.

[6]G: *sondern soll und muß gebetet sein* [*bei Gottes Zorn und Ungnaden*]; L: *sed orationibus vacandum est* [*si modo iram et inclementiam Dei in nos provocare nolumus*].

Large Catechism III, 5–9
Italicized text is from revised editions
and the 1584 Latin *Book of Concord*.

630 A person who wants to make a request must present a petition, naming and describing something that he or she desires; otherwise it cannot be called a prayer.[1]

Therefore we have rightly rejected the prayers of monks and priests, who howl and growl frightfully day and night,[2] but not one of them thinks of asking for the least little thing. If we gathered all the churches together, with all their clergy, they would have to confess that they have never prayed wholeheartedly for so much as a drop of wine. For none of them has ever undertaken to pray out of obedience to God and faith in his promise, or out of consideration for their own needs. They only thought, at best, of doing a good work as a payment to God, not willing to receive anything from him, but only to give him something.

But where there is to be true prayer, there must be utter earnestness.[3] We must feel our need, the distress that drives and impels us to cry out.[4] Then prayer will come spontaneously, as it should, and no one will need to be taught how to prepare for it or how to create the proper devotion.[5]

[1]G: *Denn wer da bitten will, der muß etwas bringen, furtragen und nennen, des er begehret, wo nicht, so kann es kein Gebete heißen*; L: *Etenim qui orare voluerit, necessum est, ut is aliquid apportet, exponat et nominatim perstringat, quod petierit, quod nisi fit, non potest dici precatio.*

[2]G: *Darümb haben wir billich der Münche und die Pfaffen Gebete verworfen, die Tag und Nacht feindlich heulen und murren*; L: *Proinde non abs re omnium monachorum ac sacrificorum orationes hactenus factas rejecimus diu noctuque laboriose admodum ululantium et murmurantium.*

[3]G: *Wo aber ein recht Gebete sein soll, da muß ein Ernst sein*; L: *Ceterum ubi oratio recte instituta esse debet, necessum est, ut seria sit precatio.*

[4]G:*daß man seine Not fühle und solche Not, die uns drücket und treibet zu rufen und schreien*; L: *ut quis necessitatem sentiat, qua premitur et ad invocandum et clamandum impellitur.*

[5]G: *wie man sich dazu bereiten und Andacht schepfen soll*; L: *quomodo aliquis ad orandum se praeparet aut unde devotionem hauriat.*

Large Catechism III, 24–26

FOR WHAT SHOULD WE PRAY?

631 For we are all lacking plenty of things: all that is missing is that we do not feel or see them. God therefore wants you to lament and express your needs and concerns,[1] not because he is unaware of them, but in order that you may kindle your heart to stronger and greater desires and open and spread your apron wide to receive many things.

Therefore from youth on we should form the habit of praying daily for our needs,[2] whenever we are aware of anything that affects us or other people around us, such as preachers, magistrates, neighbors, and servants; and, as I have said, we should always remind God of his commandment and promise, knowing that he does not want them despised.

[1]G: *Darümb auch Gott haben will, daß Du solche Not und Anliegen klagest und anziehest*; L: *Quare Deus a nobis hoc summe contendit, ut eam necessitatem, qua premeris, orans conquueraris atque exponas.*

[2]G: *Darümb sollten wir uns von Jugend auf gewehnen, ein iglicher fur alle seine Not . . . täglich zu bitten*; L: *Quocirca statim a pueritia assuescere conveniebat, ut quisque privatim pro sua necessitate . . . quotidie precaretur.*

Large Catechism III, 27–28

632 "Give us today our daily bread."

Here we consider the poor breadbasket—the needs of our body and our life on earth. It is a brief and simple word, but very comprehensive. When you say and ask for "daily bread," you ask for everything that is necessary in order to have and enjoy daily bread[1] and, on the contrary, against everything that interferes with enjoying it. You must therefore expand and extend your thoughts to include not just the oven or the flour bin, but also the broad fields and the whole land that produce and provide our daily bread and all kinds of sustenance for us. For if God did not cause grain to grow and did not bless it and preserve it in the field, we could never have a loaf of bread to take from the oven or to set upon the table.

[1]G: *Denn wenn Du „täglich Brot" nennest und bittest, so bittest Du alles, was dazu gehöret, das tägliche Brot zu haben und genießen*; L: *Ubi enim panem quotidianum precaris ac nominas, ibi omnia, quae ad quotidiani panis fruitionem pertinent.*

Large Catechism III, 71–72

633 Let us outline very briefly how comprehensively this petition covers all kinds of earthly matters. Out of it a person might make a long prayer,[1] enumerating with many words all the things it includes. For example, we might ask God[2] to give us food and drink, clothing, house and farm, and a healthy body. In addition, we might ask God to cause the grain and fruits of the field to grow and thrive abundantly. Then we might ask God to help us manage our household well by giving and preserving for us an upright spouse, children, and servants, causing our work, craft, or occupation, whatever it may be, to prosper and succeed, and granting us faithful neighbors, and good friends, etc. In addition, we may ask God both to endow with wisdom, strength, and prosperity the emperor, kings, and all estates, especially the princes of our land, all councilors, magistrates, and officials, so that they might govern well and be victorious over the Turks and all our enemies, and to grant their subjects and the general populace to live together in obedience, peace, and concord. Moreover, we might ask that he would protect us from all kinds of harm to our body and to the things that sustain us—from storms, hail, fire, and flood; from poison, pestilence, and cattle plague; from war and bloodshed, famine, savage beasts, wicked people, etc.

[1]G: *Daraus möcht nu imand ein lang Gebete machen*; L: *Ex his jam aliquis prolixas preculas posset componere.*

[2]G: *als nämlich daß wir bitten*; L: *nimirum haec nos orare.*

Large Catechism III, 76–78

634 Therefore in our present weakness there is always sin that could be imputed to us; about this he says a little later, "Therefore let every one who is godly offer prayer to thee"[1] (Ps. 32:6). Here he shows that even the godly must pray for the forgiveness of sins.

[1]L: *Pro hoc orabit ad te omnis sanctus*; G: „*Dafür werden bitten alle Heiligen zu rechter Zeit*".

Apology IV, 168
The Latin is from the quarto edition.
The English is from Tappert.

635 Accordingly we Christians must be armed and expect every day to be under continuous attack. Then we will not go about securely and heedlessly as if the devil were far from us, but will at all times expect his blows and fend them off. Even if at present I am chaste, patient, kind, and firm in faith, the devil is likely at this very hour to send such an arrow into my heart that I can scarcely endure, for he is an enemy who never lets up or becomes weary; when one attack ceases, new ones always arise.

At such times our only help and comfort is to run here and seize hold of the Lord's Prayer and to speak to God from our heart, "Dear Father, you have commanded me to pray;[1] let me not fall because of temptation." Then you will see that the temptation has to cease and eventually admit defeat. Otherwise, if you attempt to help yourself by your own thoughts and resources, you will only make the matter worse and give the devil a wider opening. For he has a serpent's head; if it finds an opening into which it can slither, the whole body will irresistibly follow. But prayer can resist him and drive him back.

[1]G: „*Lieber Vater, Du hast mich heißen beten . . .*"; L: '*Tu me orare jussisti, optime pater . . .*'

Large Catechism III, 109–111

636 See, then, what a great need there is for this kind of prayer![1] Because we see that the world is full of sects and false teachers, all of whom wear the holy name as a cloak and warrant for their devilish doctrine, we ought constantly to shout and cry out against all who preach and believe falsely and against those who want to attack, persecute, and suppress our gospel and pure doctrine,[2] as the bishops, tyrants, fanatics, and others do. Likewise, this petition is for ourselves who have the Word of God but are ungrateful for it and fail to live according to it as we ought. If you ask for such things from your heart, you can be sure that God is pleased.[3] For there is nothing that he would rather hear than to have his glory and praise exalted above everything else and his Word taught in its purity, cherished and treasured.

[1]G: *wie hoch solch Gebete vonnöten ist*; L: *quam ista precatio omnibus modis sit necessaria.*

[2]G: *sollten wir billich ohn Unterlaß schreien und rufen wider solche alle, beide die fälschlich predigen und gläuben und was unser Evangelion und reine Lehre anfichtet, verfolgt und dämpfen will*; L: *non injuria nobis indesinenter clamandum erat adversus omnes ita scelerate divino nomine*

abutentes, hoc est aeque adversus falsa docentes et prava superstitiose credentes, tum quicquid evangelium et sanam doctrinam nostram temere impugnat.

[3]G: *Wenn Du nu solchs von Herzen bittest, kannst Du gewiß sein, daß Gott wohl gefället.* L: *Haec devote atque ex animo orans certus esse potes Deo summe placere tuam precatiunculam.*

Large Catechism III, 47–48

SUMMARY

- God seeks prayer that recognizes what we receive from his hand. He both commands us to pray and attaches a promise to it. To pray is more than just saying the words in an outward way; it involves a faith. God hears because of his promise to answer those who call on him in faith, trusting his mercy for Christ's sake. Those who pray this way do not pray in vain.
- Christians pray when they are at the Divine Service and when they individually commend themselves to God each day. Prayer is not babbling or hypocritical or meant to impress God with obedience. It is earnestly asking for something from God in every need, believing in his promise.
- Christians pray for bodily and spiritual needs. They pray for every sort of sustenance, for good government, for peace and harmony, and for preservation from calamity and all evil. They also pray for the kingdom of God to come, for the Word of God to prosper and overcome false teachings and persecutions, for forgiveness and help in time of temptation, and for firm faith when under the assaults of the devil.

SYNOPSIS

Christian prayer asks God to help in all times of bodily or spiritual need. In obedience to God's command and relying on God's promise through Christ, prayer is an act of faith. If there is no faith, there is no true prayer. Such prayer will occur each day of a Christian's life and when Christians gather in the name of Christ.

7
Praise

What truly honors and praises God?

701 Besides, the prophet's own words give us their meaning. They say, first, that the name of the Lord will be great. This takes place through the preaching of the gospel, which makes known the name of Christ and the Father's mercy promised in Christ. The proclamation of the gospel produces faith in those who receive the gospel. They call upon God, they give thanks to God, they bear afflictions for their confession, they do good works on account of the glory of Christ.[1] In this way the name of the Lord becomes great among the nations. Therefore "incense" and "a pure offering" do not refer to a ceremony *ex opere operato* but to all those sacrifices through which the name of the Lord is made great, namely, faith, prayer, the preaching of the gospel, confession, etc.[2]

We readily concede that all who want to include the ceremony [of the Mass] here may do so as long as they do not interpret it as a mere ceremony or do not mean that by itself (*ex opere operato*) the ceremony is beneficial. For just as among the sacrifices of praise, that is, among the praises of God, we include the proclamation of the Word, so the reception of the Lord's Supper itself can be a praise or thanksgiving. However, it does not justify *ex opere operato*, nor should it be applied to others as if it merited the forgiveness of sins. In a little while we shall show how even this ceremony is sacrifice. But because Malachi is talking about all the acts of worship of the New Testament—not only about the Lord's Supper—and because he does not favor the Pharisaical opinion about *ex opere operato*, he is not against our position.

More than that, he supports it. For he requires the worship of the heart, by which the name of the Lord truly becomes great.

[1]L: *Id fit per praedicationem evangelii. Per hanc enim innotescit nomen Christi, et misericordia patris in Christo promissa cognoscitur. Praedicatio evangelii parit fidem in his, qui recipiunt evangelium. Hi invocant Deum, hi agunt Deo gratias, hi tolerant afflictiones in confessione, hi bene operantur propter gloriam Christi*; G: *das geschiehet durch die Predigt des Evangelii. Denn durch dieselbigen wird der Name Christi bekennet, und wird bekannt die Gnade in Christo verheißen. Durch die Predigt aber des Evangelii kommen die Leute zum Glauben; die rufen denn Gott recht an, die danken Gott, die leiden um Gottes Willen Verfolgung, die tun gute Werke.*

[2]L: *sed omnia illa sacrificia, per quae fit magnum nomen Domini, scilicet fidem, invocationem, praedicationem evangelii, confessionem etc.*; G: *sondern alle geistliche Opfer, durch welche Gottes Namen groß wird. Nämlich ein rein, heilig Opfer ist die Predigt des Evangelii, der Glaub, Anrufung, Gebet, das Evangelium und Christum für der Welt bekennen &c.*

Apology XXIV, 32–33

702 This, however, is the catholic faith: that we worship[1] one God in trinity and the Trinity in unity, neither confusing the persons nor dividing the substance.

[1]L: *Fides autem catholica haec est, ut unum Deum in trinitate et trinitatem in unitate veneremur*; G: *Dies ist aber der rechte christliche Glaube, daß wir ein einigen Gott in drei Personen und drei Personen in einiger Gottheit ehren.*

Athanasian Creed, 3

703 This faith gives honor to God,[1] gives him what is properly his; it obeys him by accepting his promises. . . . The greatest possible comfort comes from this doctrine that the highest worship in the Gospel[2] is the desire to receive forgiveness of sins, grace, and righteousness. About this worship[3] Christ speaks in John 6:40, "This is the will of my Father, that everyone who sees the Son and believes in him should have eternal life." And the Father says (Matt. 17:5), "This is my beloved Son, with whom I am well pleased; listen to him."

[1]L: *Haec fides reddit Deo honorem.*

[2]L: *cultus in evangelio praecipuus.*

[3]L: *De hoc cultu.*

Apology IV, 309–310
The Latin is from the quarto edition.
The English is from Tappert.

704 Look, here you have the true honor and worship that please God,[1] which God also commands under penalty of eternal wrath, namely, that the heart should know no other consolation or confidence than in him, nor let itself be torn from him, but for his sake should risk everything and disregard everything else on earth. On the other hand, you will easily see and judge how the world practices nothing but false worship and idolatry.[2] There has never been a nation so wicked that it did not establish and maintain some sort of worship.[3] All people have set up their own god, to whom they looked for blessings, help, and comfort.

[1]G: *Siehe, da hast Du nu, was die rechte Ehre und Gottesdienst ist*; L: *Ecce jam tenes, quinam verus Dei cultus sit.*

[2]G: *Dagegen wirst Du leichtlich sehen und urteilen, wie die Welt eitel falschen Gottesdienst und Abgötterei treibt*; L: *Et hoc facile jam videbis aut judicabis, quomodo mundus nihil aliud quam falsum Dei cultum passim consistuerit atque exerceat.*

[3]G: *Denn es ist nie kein Volk . . . das nicht einen Gottesdienst aufgerichtet und gehalten habe*; L: . . . *hominun natio, quae non aliquem Dei cultum constituerit et servaverit.*

Large Catechism I, 16–17

705 Thus the First Commandment is to illuminate and impart its splendor to all the others. In order that this may be constantly repeated and never forgotten, therefore, you must let these concluding words run through all the commandments, like the clasp or hoop of a wreath that binds the end to the beginning and holds everything together. For example, in the Second Commandment we are told to fear God and not to take his name in vain by cursing, lying, deceiving, and other kinds of corruption and wickedness,[1] but to use his name properly by calling upon him in prayer, praise, and thanksgiving,[2] which spring from that love and trust that the First Commandment requires. In the same way, this fear, love, and trust should impel us not to despise his Word, but to learn it, hear it gladly, keep it holy, and honor it.

[1]G: *daß man Gott fürchte und seines Namens nicht mißbrauche zu Fluchen, Liegen, Triegen und anderer Verführung oder Buberei*; L: *ejus nomine non foede ac impie abutamur ad exsecrandum, maledicendum, mentiendum, fallendum aliasque improbitates et vitia exercenda.*

[2]G: *sondern recht und wohl brauche mit Anrufen, Beten, Loben und Danken, aus Liebe und Vertrauen*; L: *verum bene et recte utamur invocando, precando, laudando et gratias agendo amore ac fiducia Dei.*

Large Catechism I, 326

706 If our opponents defend these human acts of worship[1] as meriting justification, grace, and the forgiveness of sins, they are simply establishing the kingdom of the Antichrist. For the kingdom of the Antichrist is a new kind of worship of God,[2] devised by human authority in opposition to Christ, just as the kingdom of Mohammed has religious rites and works, through which it seeks to be justified before God. It does not hold that people are freely justified by faith on account of Christ. So also the papacy will be a part of the kingdom of the Antichrist if it defends human rites as justifying.[3] For they deprive Christ of his honor when they teach that we are not freely justified on account of Christ through faith but through such rites,[4] and especially when they teach that such rites are not only useful for justification but even necessary.

[1]L: *hos humanos cultus*; G: *diese Gottesdienst.*

[2]L: *Nam regnum antichristi est novus cultus Dei*; G: *Denn das Reich Antichristi ist eigentlich solch neu Gottesdienst.*

[3]L: *Ita et papatus erit pars regni antichristi, si sic defendit humanos cultus, quod iustificent*; G: *Also wird das Pabsttum auch ein Stücke vom Reich Antichristi, so es lehret durch Menschengebot Vergebung der Sunden zu erlangen und Gott zu versühnen.*

[4]L: *Detrahitur enim honos Christo, cum docent, quod non propter Christum gratis iustificemur per fidem, sed per tales cultus*; G: *da wird Christo seine Ehre genommen, wenn sie lehren, daß wir nicht durch Christum, ohne Verdienst gerecht werden durch den Glauben, sondern durch solche Gottesdienst.*

Apology XV, 18

707 As a matter of course, theologians rightly distinguish between a sacrament and a sacrifice. Therefore, the genus that includes both of these could be either a "ceremony" or a "sacred work." A sacrament is a ceremony or work in which God presents to us what the promise joined to the ceremony offers.[1] Thus baptism is not a work that we offer to God, but one in which God, through a minister who functions in his place, baptizes us, and offers and presents the forgiveness of sins, etc., according to the promise [Mark 16:16], "The one who believes and is baptized will be saved." By contrast, a sacrifice is a ceremony or work that we render to God in order to give him honor.[2]

Now there are two, and no more than two, basic kinds of sacrifice. One is the atoning sacrifice, that is, a work of satisfaction for guilt and punishment[3] that reconciles God, conciliates the wrath of God, or merits the forgiveness of sins for others. The other kind is the eucharistic sacrifice. It does not merit the forgiveness of sins or reconciliation but is rendered by those who have already been reconciled as a way for us to give thanks or express gratitude for having received forgiveness of sins and other benefits.[4]

In this controversy and in other disputes, we must never lose sight of those two kinds of sacrifices, and we should take special care not to confuse them. If this type of book allowed it, we would include the reasons for making this distinction, for it has more than enough testimonies in the Letter to the Hebrews and elsewhere.

[1]L: *Sacramentum est ceremonia vel opus, in quo Deus nobis exhibet hoc, quod offert annexa ceremoniae promissio*; G: *Sacramentum ist ein ceremonia oder äußerlich Zeichen oder ein Werk, dadurch uns Gott gibt dasjenige, so die göttliche Verheißung, welche derselbigen Ceremonien angeheft ist, anbeutet.*

[2]L: *Econtra sacrificum est ceremonia vel opus, quod nos Deo reddimus, ut eum honore afficiamus*; G: *Wiederum sacrificium oder Opfer ist ein ceremonia oder ein Werk, das wir Gott geben, damit wir ihnen ehren.*

[3]L: *Quoddam est sacrificium propitiatorium, id est, opus satisfactorium pro culpa et poena*; G: *Für eins ist ein Versühnopfer, dadurch gnug getan wird für Pein und Schuld.*

[4]L: *Altera species est sacrificum εὐχαριστικόν, quod non meretur remissionem peccatorum aut reconciliationem, sed fit a reconciliatis, ut pro accepta remissionem peccatorum et pro aliis beneficiis acceptis gratias agamus, seu gratiam referamus*; G: *Zum andern ist ein Dankopfer, dadurch nicht Vergebung der Sunde oder Versühnung erlangt wird, sondern geschiehet von denjenigen, welche schon versühnet sein, daß sie für die erlangte Vergebung der Sunde und andere Gnaden und Gaben Dank sagen.*

Apology XXIV, 17–20

708 In point of fact there has been only one atoning sacrifice in the world, namely, the death of Christ,[1] as the Letter to the Hebrews teaches when it says [10:4], "For it is impossible for the blood of bulls and goats to take away sins." A little later [v. 10] it says about the will of Christ, "And it is by God's will that we have been sanctified through the offering of the body of Jesus Christ once for all." Isaiah, too, interprets the law to mean that the death of Christ—not the ceremonies of the law—is a real satisfaction or expiation for our sins.[2] Thus he says

[53:10], "When you make his life an offering for sin, he shall see his offspring, and shall prolong his days," etc. Now the word he uses here (*'asam*) refers to a victim sacrificed for transgression. In the Old Testament this meant that a certain Victim was to come in order to make satisfaction for our sins and reconcile us to God, so that people might know that God wants to be reconciled to us not on account of our righteousness but on account of another's merits, namely, Christ's. Paul interprets the same word (*'asam*) as sin in Romans 8[:3]: "through sin he condemned sin," that is, he punished sin through sin, that is, through a sacrificial victim for sin. We can understand the meaning of the word more easily if we look at the customs the pagans adopted from their misinterpretation of the patriarchal tradition. The Latins spoke of a sacrificial victim offered to conciliate the wrath of God in great calamities, when it seemed that God was unusually angry. Sometimes they offered human sacrifices, perhaps because they had heard that a human sacrifice was going to conciliate God for the entire human race. The Greeks at times called them "refuse" and at other times "offscouring." Isaiah and Paul understand that Christ was made a sacrificial victim, that is, an expiation,[3] and that by his merits and not ours, God would be reconciled. Therefore let this remain the case, that the death of Christ alone is truly an atoning sacrifice.[4] The Levitical sacrifices of atonement were so called only in order to point to a future expiation.[5] By some sort of analogy, therefore, they were satisfactions since they purchased a righteousness of the law and thereby prevented those persons who sinned from being excluded from the community. But they had to come to an end after the revelation of the gospel. Moreover, because they had to come to an end with the revelation of the gospel, they were not truly atoning sacrifices, since the gospel was promised for the very reason that it set forth the atoning sacrifice.

Now the rest are eucharistic sacrifices, which are called "sacrifices of praise,"[6] namely, the preaching of the gospel, faith, prayer, thanksgiving, confession, the afflictions of the saints, and indeed, all the good works of the saints. These sacrifices are not satisfactions for those who offer them,[7] nor can they be applied to others so as to merit the forgiveness of sins or reconciliation for others *ex opere operato*. They are performed by those who are already reconciled.

These are the sacrifices of the New Testament, as Peter teaches [1 Peter 2:5], "a holy priesthood, to offer spiritual sacrifices." Spiritual sacrifices,[8] however, are contrasted not only with animal sacrifices but also with human works offered *ex opere operato*, because "spiritual" refers to the work of the Holy Spirit within us. Paul teaches the same thing in Romans 12[:1]: "[P]resent your bodies as a living sacrifice, holy and acceptable to God, which is your spiritual worship." "Spiritual worship" refers to worship where God is recognized and is grasped by the mind, as happens when it fears and trusts God. Therefore, it is contrasted not only to Levitical worship, in which animals were slain, but with any worship in which people imagine that they are offering God a work *ex opere operato*. The Epistle to the Hebrews, chapter 13[:15], teaches the same thing, "Through him, then, let us continually offer a sacrifice of praise to God," and it adds an interpretation, "that is, the fruit of lips that confess his name." He commands us to offer praises, that is, prayer, thanksgiving, confession, and the like. These avail not *ex opere operato* but on account of faith. This is stressed by the phrase, "through him let us offer," that is, by faith in Christ.

[1]L: *Sed revera unicum tantum in mundo fuit sacrificium propitiatorium, videlicet mors Christi*; G: *aber es ist allein ein einiges, wahrhaftiges Sühneopfer, Opfer für die Sunde, in der Welt gewesen, nämlich der Tod Christi.*

[2]L: *Esaias interpretatur legem, ut sciamus mortem Christi vere esse satisfactionem pro peccatis nostris seu expiationem, non ceremonias legis*; G: *Und Esaias der Prophet hat auch zuvor das Gesetz Mosi ausgelegt und zeigt an, daß der Tod Christi die Bezahlung für die Sunde ist, und nicht die Opfer im Gesetz.*

[3]L: *Intelligunt igitur Esaias et Paulus, Christum factum esse hostiam, hoc est piaculum.*

The German paraphrase speaks of a *Schuldopfer* but does not engage the Latin regarding the specific meaning of the vocabulary.

[4]L: *quod sola mors Christi est vere propitiatorium sacrificium*; G: *Darum bleibt dieses fest stehen, daß nur ein einig Opfer gewesen ist, nämlich der Tod Christi.*

[5]L: *ad significandum futurum piaculum.*

The German text does not cover this point.

[6]L: *sacrifica laudis*; G: *Dankopfer.*

[7]L: *Haec sacrificia non sunt satisfactiones pro facientibus*; G: *Dasselbige sind nicht solche Opfer, dadurch wir versühnet werden.*

[8]L: *hostiae spirituales.*

The German text's use of *geistliche Opfer* from 1 Peter 2 would apply to the Latin text here, though the German does not speak at this point.

Apology XXIV, 22–26

709 And Christ says in John 4[:23–24], "[T]rue worshipers will worship the Father in spirit and truth,[1] for the Father seeks such as these to worship him.[2] God is spirit, and those who worship him must worship in spirit and truth."[3] This passage clearly condemns the notions about sacrifices that imagine they avail *ex opere operato*,[4] and teaches that one should "worship in spirit," that is, with the deepest activity of the heart and faith.[5]

[1]L: *Veri adoratores adorabunt Patrem in spiritu et veritate*; G: *„Die rechten Anbeter werden den Vater anbeten im Geist und in der Wahrheit", das ist mit Herzen, mit herzlicher Furcht und herzlichem Glauben.*

[2]L: *Nam et Pater tales quaerit, qui adorent eum.*

The German translation omits this and the following noted parts in the Latin original text.

[3]L: *Deus est spiritus, et eos, qui adorant eum, in spiritu et veritate oportet adorare.*

[4]L: *Haec sententia clare damnat opiniones de sacrificiis, quae fingunt ex opere operato valere*; G: *Darum ists eitel teufelisch, pharisäisch und antichristliche Lehre und Gottesdienst, daß unser Widersacher lehren, ihr Meß verdiene Vergebung Schuld und Pein ex opere operato.*

[5]L: *et* [*haec sententia*] *docet, quod oporteat spiritu, id est, motibus cordis et fide adorare.*

See note 1 above for the German paraphrase pertinent to this text.

Apology XXIV, 27

Who is able to be thankful and to give honor and praise to God?

710 Hence, because everything we possess, and everything in heaven and on earth besides, is daily given, sustained, and protected by God, it inevitably follows that we are in duty bound to love, praise, and thank him without ceasing,[1] and, in short, to devote all these things to his service, as he has required and enjoined in the Ten Commandments.

[1]G: *so sind wir ja schüldig, ihn darümb ohn Unterlaß zu lieben, loben und danken*; L: *nos debere eundem indesinenter diligere, laudibus extollere agendisque gratiis acceptorum beneficiorum esse memores.*

Large Catechism II, 19

711 For this reason we ought daily to practice this article, impress it upon our minds, and remember it in everything we see and in every blessing that comes our way. Whenever we escape distress or danger, we should recognize how God gives and does all of this so that we may sense and see in them his fatherly heart and his boundless love toward us. Thus our hearts will be warmed and kindled with gratitude to God and a desire to use all these blessings to his glory and praise.[1]

[1]G: *Davon würde das Herz erwarmen und entzündet werden, dankbar zu sein und aller solcher Güter zu Gottes Ehren und Lob zu brauchen*. L: *Ex hoc certe pectus incalescet et ad gratiarum actionem prompte agendam mirifice inflammabitur, ut omnibus ejusmodi rebus ad Dei laudem et gloriam utatur.*

Large Catechism II, 23

712 If the mind set on the flesh is hostile to God, the flesh certainly does not love God. If it cannot submit to the law of God, it cannot love God. If the mind set on the flesh is hostile to God, the flesh sins even when we perform outward civil works. If it cannot submit to the law of God, it certainly sins even when we perform works that are excellent and praiseworthy in human eyes. The opponents consider only the commandments of the second table, which entail the civil righteousness that reason understands. Being content with this they suppose that they satisfy the law of God. Meanwhile they fail to notice the first table, which instructs us to love God, to conclude that God is angry with sin, truly to fear God, truly to conclude that God hears our prayers. But without the Holy Spirit the human heart either despises the judgment of God in its complacency or in the face of punishment flees and hates God who judges them. Thus it does not obey the first table. Therefore since these things (contempt for God, doubt about the Word of God and about its threats and promises) cling to human nature, people truly sin even when they do respectable works without the Holy Spirit, because they do them with a godless heart,[1] according to the text [Rom. 14:23], "Whatever does not proceed from faith is sin." Such people perform their works with contempt for God,[2] just as when Epicurus did not think that God cared for him, paid attention to him, or heard his prayer. This contempt for God corrupts works that appear to be honorable, because God judges the heart.

[1]L: *quia faciunt ea impio corde*; G: *denn sie gehen aus einem bösen, gottlosen, unreinem Herzen.*

[2]L: *Hic contemptus vitiat opera in speciem honesta, quia Deus iudicat corda*; G: *Die Verachtung Gottes inwendig muß je die Werk unflätig und sündlich machen, wenn sie gleich für den Leuten schön sind; denn Gott forschet die Herzen.*

Apology IV, 33–35

713 And it is furthermore false that reason by its own powers is able to love God above all things and to fulfill God's law, namely, truly to fear God, truly to conclude that God hears prayer, willingly to obey God in death and in other visitations of God, and not to covet things that belong to others, etc.—although reason can produce civil works.

It is also false and an affront to Christ[1] to say that people who observe the commandments of God without grace do not sin.

[1]L: *contumeliosum in Christum*; G: *ein Lästerung wider Christum.*

Apology IV, 27–28

714 It is quite true that the kind of babbling and bellowing that used to pass for prayers in the church was not really prayer.[1] Such external repetition,[2] when properly used, may serve as an exercise for young children, pupils, and simple folk; while it may be useful in singing or reading, it is not actually prayer.[3]

[1]G: *Das ist aber je wahr: Was man bisher fur Gebete getan hat, geplärret und gedönet in der Kirchen etc., ist freilich kein Gebete gewesen*; L: *Quamquam hoc diffiteri non possumus eas orationes, quae hactenus factae sunt Stentoreis clamoribus in ecclesiis vociferando et tonando etc., non fuisse orationes.*

[2]G: *solch äußerlich Ding*; L: *res externae.*

[3]G: *mag gesungen oder gelesen heißen, es heißet aber nicht eigentlich gebetet*; L: *legendo aut cantando consistentia, proprie tamen orationes aut preces existimandae non sunt.*

Large Catechism III, 7

715 It seems to me that we shall have our hands full to keep these commandments, practicing gentleness, patience, love toward enemies, chastity, kindness, etc., and all that is involved in doing so. But such works are not important or impressive in the eyes of the world. They are not uncommon and showy, reserved to certain special times, places, rites, and ceremonies, but are common, everyday domestic duties of one neighbor to another, with nothing glamorous about them. Those other deeds captivate all eyes and ears. Aided by great splendor, expense, and magnificent buildings, they are so adorned that everything gleams and glitters. There is burning of incense, singing and ringing of bells, lighting of candles and tapers until for all of this nothing else can be seen or heard.[1] For when a priest stands in a golden chasuble, or a layperson spends a whole day in the church on his or her knees, that is considered a precious work that cannot be sufficiently extolled. But when a poor servant girl takes care of a little child or faithfully does what she is told, this is regarded as nothing. Otherwise, what should monks and nuns be looking for in their cloisters?

Just think, is it not a devilish presumption on the part of those desperate saints to dare to find a higher and better way of life and status than the Ten Commandments teach? They pretend, as we have said, that this is a simple life for an ordinary person, whereas theirs is for the saints and those who are perfect.

[1]G: *Jene aber sperren Augen und Ohren auf, dazu helfen sie selbs mit großem Gepränge, Kost, und herrlichem Gebäu und schmücken sie erfur, daß alles gleißen und leuchten muß, da räuchert man, da singet und klinget man, da zündet man Kerzen und Lichte an, daß man fur diesen keine andere hören noch sehen könne*; L: *Porro autem illa alia hominum et ora et oculos in se convertunt, quae ipsi quoque sumptuosissimis ceremoniis, magnis impensis, regiis aedificiis provehunt atque ita exornant, ut omnia summe niteant ac splendeant. Ibi tura incenduntur ac thymiamata, ibi pulsatur et cantillatur planeque omnia concentu perstrepunt. Alibi incenduntur cerei, ut prae his alia neque videri neque audiri queant.*

Large Catechism I, 313–315

716 The Second [Commandment]

You are not to misuse the name of your God.

What is this? Answer:

We are to fear and love God, so that we do not curse, swear, practice magic, lie, or deceive using God's name, but instead use that very name in every time of need to call on, pray to, praise, and give thanks to God.[1]

[1]G: *denselbigen in allen Nöten anrufen, beten, loben und danken*; L: *in omni necessitate illud invocemus, adoremus et cum gratiarum actione laudemus*.

Small Catechism I, 3–4

717 Likewise, this petition is for ourselves who have the Word of God but are ungrateful for it[1] and fail to live according to it as we ought. If you ask for such things from your heart, you can be sure that God is pleased. For there is nothing that he would rather hear than to have his glory and praise exalted above everything else[2] and his Word taught in its purity, cherished and treasured.

[1]G: *aber nicht dankbar dafur sein*; L: *sed qui non grati sumus*.

[2]G: *Denn liebers wird er nicht hören, denn daß seine Ehre und Preis fur und über alle Ding gehe*; L: *Neque enim quicquam audiet gratius aut amantius, quam quod ejus honor et gloria prae omnibus rebus passim unice floreat ac vigeat*.

Large Catechism III, 47–48

718 Accordingly, with the abrogation of Levitical worship, the New Testament teaches that new and pure sacrifices will be made,[1] namely, faith, prayer, thanksgiving, confession, the preaching of the gospel,[2] suffering on account of the gospel, and similar things.

[1]L: *ut nova et munda sacrificia fiant*; G: *sein eitel reine Opfer ohne Makel*.

[2]L: *fides, invocatio, gratiarum actio, confessio et praedicatio evangelii*; G: *der Glauben gegen Gott, Danksagung, Gottes Lob, Predigt des Evangelii*.

Apology XXIV, 30

719 It is written in the prophet, "I will put my law within them, and I will write it on their hearts" [Jer. 31:33]. And in Romans 3[:31] Paul says: "Do we then overthrow the law by this faith? By no means! On the contrary, we uphold the law." And Christ says [Matt. 19:17]: "If you wish to enter into life, keep the commandments." Again, "If I . . . do not have love, I gain nothing" [1 Cor. 13:3]. These statements, and others like them, assert that we ought to begin to keep the law and then keep it more and more. Now, we are not talking about ceremonies, but about that law which deals with the impulses of the heart, namely, the

Decalogue. Because faith truly brings the Holy Spirit and produces a new life in our hearts, it must also produce spiritual impulses in our hearts.[1] The prophet shows what those impulses are when he says [Jer. 31:33], "I will put my law within them, and I will write it on their hearts." Therefore, after we have been justified and reborn by faith, we begin to fear and love God, to pray for and expect help from him, to thank and praise him,[2] and to obey him in our afflictions. We also begin to love our neighbor because our hearts have spiritual and holy impulses.

These things cannot happen until after we have by faith been justified, reborn, and received the Holy Spirit. This is because, first, it is impossible to keep the law without Christ and, second, it is impossible to keep the law without the Holy Spirit.

[1]L: *Quia vero fides affert spiritum sanctum et parit novam vitam in cordibus, necesse est, quod pariat spirituales motus in cordibus.* G: *Dieweil nu der Glaub mit sich bringet den heiligen Geist und ein neu Licht und Leben im Herzen wirkt, so ist es gewiß und folget von Not, daß der Glaub das Herz verneuet und ändert.*

[2]L: *gratias agere et praedicare*; G: *ihm zu danken, ihnen zu preisen.*

Apology IV, 123–126

720 But Christ was given for this very purpose: that on account of him the forgiveness of sins and the Holy Spirit, who produces in us a new and eternal life and also eternal righteousness, may be given to us. *First, the Spirit reveals Christ, just as it is written in John 16[:14], "He will glorify me, because he will take what is mine and declare it to you." Then he also brings the other gifts: love, prayer, thanksgiving,*[1] *chastity, endurance, etc.*

Therefore we cannot truly keep the law until we have received the Holy Spirit through faith [John 16:15]. Therefore Paul states that the law is established, not abolished, through faith, because the law can be kept only when the Holy Spirit is given.

[1]L: *gratiarum actionem*; G: *Danksagung.*

Apology IV, 132
Italics indicate text added in the octavo edition.

721 It is clear, then, that our teachers require good works. In fact, we add that it is impossible to separate love for God (however meager it may be) from faith. For through Christ we have access to the Father, and, having received the forgiveness of sins, we now truly realize that we have a God (that is, a God who cares for us), we call upon him, give thanks to him, and fear and love him.[1] Thus John teaches in his first epistle [4:19]: "We love him because he first loved us," namely, because he gave his Son for us and forgave our sins. In this way he shows that faith comes first and love follows.

[1]L: *invocamus, agimus gratias, timemus, diligimus*; G: *der zu fürchten sei . . . der . . . zu lieben sei, dem wir sollen allzeit herzlich danken, ihm Lob und Preis sagen*.

Apology IV, 140–141

722 Thus it is not enough to believe that Christ was born, suffered, and was raised again unless we also add this article, which is the real purpose of the narrative: "the forgiveness of sins." The rest must be referred back to this article, namely, that on account of Christ and not on account of our merits, the forgiveness of sins is given to us. For why was it necessary to give Christ for our sins if our merits could make satisfaction for them?

Therefore, whenever we speak about justifying faith, we must understand that these three elements belong together: the promise itself; the fact that the promise is free; and the merits of Christ as the payment and atoning sacrifice. The promise is received by faith; the word "free" excludes our merits and means that the blessing is offered only through mercy; the merits of Christ are the payment because there must be some definite atoning sacrifice for our sins. Scripture contains frequent pleas for mercy, and the holy Fathers often teach that we are saved through mercy. Therefore, every time mercy is mentioned, we must bear in mind that faith is also required, for it receives the promised mercy. Conversely, every time we speak about faith, we want the object [of faith] to be understood as well, namely, the promised mercy. For faith does not justify or save because it is a worthy work in and of itself, but only because it receives the promised mercy.

This worship, this *latreia*, is especially praised throughout the Prophets and Psalms.[1] Although the law does not appear to teach about the free forgiveness of sins, the patriarchs knew about the promise concerning Christ, that God intended to forgive sins on account of Christ.

[1]L: *Et hic cultus, haec λατρεία in prophetis et psalmis passim praecipue laudatur*; G: *Und solcher Glaub und Vertrauen auf Gottes Barmherzigkeit wird als der größte, heiligste Gottesdienst gepreiset, sonderlich in Propheten und Psalmen*.

Apology IV, 51–57

723 **[German text]** Further, it is taught that good works should and must be done, not that a person relies on them to earn grace, but for God's sake and to God's praise.[1] Faith alone always takes hold of grace and forgiveness of sin. Because the Holy Spirit is given through faith, the heart is also moved to do good works. For before, because it lacks the Holy Spirit, the heart is too weak.[2]

[Latin text] Beyond this, our people teach that it is necessary to do good works, not that we should count on meriting grace through them but because it is the will of God.[1] It is only by faith that forgiveness of sins and grace are apprehended. Moreover, because the Holy Spirit is received through faith, consequently hearts are renewed and endowed with new affections so as to be able to do good works. For Ambrose says: "Faith is the mother of the good will and the righteous action." For without the Holy Spirit human powers are full of ungodly affections and are too weak to do good works before God.[2]

[1]G: *nicht daß man darauf vertrau, Gnad damit zu verdienen, sondern um Gottes willen und Gott zu Lob*; L: *non ut confidamus per ea gratiam mereri, sed propter voluntatem Dei.*

[2]G: *Dann zuvorn, dieweil es ohn den heiligen Geist ist, so ist es zu schwach*; L: *Nam humanae vires sine spiritu sancto plenae sunt impiis affectibus et sunt imbecilliores, quam ut bona opera possint efficere coram Deo.*

Augsburg Confession XX, 27–31

SUMMARY

- The name of the Lord is made great by the preaching of the Gospel, for it produces faith in those who receive it. They call upon God, give thanks, bear afflictions for it, and produce good works for the glory of Christ.
- The eucharistic sacrifice (not to be confused with a propitiatory sacrifice, which is a satisfaction for guilt and punishment) is a sacrifice of praise or thanksgiving for the remission of sins and other gifts of God. It is "a ceremony or work that we render to God in order to give him honor" (Ap XXIV, 17–20). Among such sacrifices of praise are "the preaching of the gospel, faith, prayer, thanksgiving, confession, the afflictions of the saints, and indeed, all the good works of the saints" (Ap XXIV, 22–26). These are spiritual sacrifices, coming from the movements of the Holy Spirit in us.
- Because God gives us everything we possess, it is our duty continually to praise and thank him, as the Ten Commandments make

clear. But the human heart, without the Holy Spirit, cannot do this. It is unable to love God or fulfill God's Law; God is not seeking the external act alone but seeks hearts that truly fear and love him, that will call upon him, pray, praise, and give thanks. These are new and pure sacrifices that grow from faith that the Holy Spirit produces in a heart by the hearing of the Gospel. "People truly sin even when they do respectable works without the Holy Spirit" (Ap IV, 33–35). Faith, which justifies and saves, precedes any sacrifice of praise.

WHY DO CHRISTIANS GIVE THANKS AND PRAISE TO GOD?

724 I believe that God has created me together with all that exists. God has given me and still preserves my body and soul: eyes, ears, and all limbs and senses; reason and all mental faculties. In addition, God daily and abundantly provides shoes and clothing, food and drink, house and farm, spouse and children, fields, livestock, and all property—along with all the necessities and nourishment for this body and life. God protects me against all danger and shields and preserves me from all evil. And all this is done out of pure, fatherly, and divine goodness and mercy, without any merit or worthiness of mine at all! For all of this I owe it to God to thank and praise, serve and obey him.[1] This is most certainly true.

[1]G: *des alles ich ihm zu danken und zu loben und dafür zu dienen und gehorsam zu sein schüldig bin*; L: *pro quibus omnibus illi gratias agere, pleno ore laudem tribuere, inservire, obsequi merito debeo.*

The language used here employs terms from the oath of protection made by a feudal lord and the oath of service made by a vassal.

Small Catechism II, 2

725 In the forgiveness of sins, the terrors of sin and eternal death in our hearts must be conquered, just as Paul testifies in 1 Corinthians 15[:56, 57]: "The sting of death is sin, and the power of sin is the law. But thanks be to God,[1] who gives us the victory through our Lord Jesus Christ." In other words, sin terrifies consciences. This happens through the law, which shows us the wrath of God against sin. But we gain the victory through Christ. How? By faith, when we encourage ourselves by confidence in the mercy promised on account of Christ.

[1]L: *Gratia autem Deo*; G: *Gott aber sei Lob.*

Apology IV, 79

726 Give us today our daily bread.

What is this? Answer:

In fact, God gives daily bread without our prayer, even to all evil people, but we ask in this prayer that God cause us to recognize what our daily bread is and to receive it with thanksgiving.[1]

[1]G: *mit Danksagung empfahen unser täglich Brot*; L: *ita panem nostrum quotidianum cum gratiarum actione accipiamus.*

Small Catechism III, 12–13

727 But before we explain the Lord's Prayer part by part, the most necessary thing is to exhort and encourage people to pray, as Christ and the apostles also did. The first thing to know is this: It is our duty to pray because of God's command. For we heard in the Second Commandment, "You are not to take God's name in vain." Thereby we are required to praise the holy name[1] and to pray or call upon it in every need. For calling upon it is nothing else than praying.

[1]G: *den heiligen Namen preisen*; L: *sanctum Dei nomen laudemus.*

Large Catechism III, 4–5

728 This petition, then, is simple and clear if we only understand the language, namely, that to "hallow" means the same as in our idiom "to praise, extol, and honor" both in word and deed.[1]

See, then, what a great need there is for this kind of prayer! Because we see that the world is full of sects and false teachers, all of whom wear the holy name as a cloak and warrant for their devilish doctrine, we ought constantly to shout and cry out against all who preach and believe falsely and against those who want to attack, persecute, and suppress our gospel and pure doctrine, as the bishops, tyrants, fanatics, and others do. Likewise, this petition is for ourselves who have the Word of God but are ungrateful for it and fail to live according to it as we ought. If you ask for such things from your heart, you can be sure that God is pleased.[2] For there is nothing that he would rather hear than to have his glory and praise exalted above everything else and his Word taught in its purity, cherished and treasured.[3]

[1]G: *daß „heiligen" heißt soviel als auf unsere Weise „loben, preisen und ehren" beide mit Worten und Werken*; L: *ut 'sanctificare' tantum significet ac 'laudare, extollere, honorem habere' cum verbis, tum operibus.*

[2]G: *Wenn Du nu solchs von Herzen bittest, kannst Du gewiß sein, daß Gott wohl gefället.* L: *Haec devote atque ex animo orans certus esse potes Deo summe placere tuam precatiunculam.*

[3]G: *Denn liebers wird er nicht hören, denn daß seine Ehre und Preis fur und über alle Ding gehe, sein Wort rein gelehret, teur und wert gehalten werde*; L: *Neque enim quicquam audiet gratius aut amantius, quam quod ejus honor et gloria prae omnibus rebus passim unice floreat ac vigeat, ejus verbum sincere doceatur ac carum et pretiosum aestimetur.*

Large Catechism III, 46–48

How do Christians give honor, glory, and praise to God?

729 Thus it is a matter of grave necessity, about which we should be most concerned that God's name receive due honor and be kept holy and sacred as the greatest treasure and most sacred thing that we have,[1] and that, as good children, we pray that his name, which is in any case holy in heaven, may also be holy and be kept holy on earth in our midst and in all the world.[2]

How does it become holy among us?[3] The plainest answer that can be given is: when both our teaching and our life are godly and Christian. Because in this prayer we call God our Father, it is our duty in every way to behave as good children so that he may receive from us not shame but honor and praise.[4]

[1]G: *daß der Name sein Ehre habe, heilig und hehr gehalten werde als unser hohister Schatz und Heiligtumb*; L: *ut nomini divino suus honor habeatur, ut sancte ac reverenter tractetur veluti thesaurus noster unicus, quo nobis non major est aut amplior.*

[2]G: *daß sein Name, der sonst im Himmel heilig ist, auch auf Erden bei uns und aller Welt heilig sei und bleibe*; L: *ut nomen suum, quod alioqui in coelis per omnia sanctum est, etiam in terris apud nos inque universo orbe sanctum sit ac maneat.*

[3]G: *Wie wird er nu unter uns heilig?* L: *Porro autem nomen ejus quomodo inter nos sanctificatur aut sanctum fit?*

[4]G: *daß er unser nicht Schande, sondern Ehre und Preis habe*; L: *ne illi simus dedecori, sed laudi atque honori.*

Large Catechism III, 38–39

730 So you see that in this petition we pray for exactly the same thing that God demands in the Second Commandment: that his name should not be taken in vain by swearing, cursing, deceiving, etc., but used rightly to the praise and glory of God.[1] Whoever uses God's name for any sort of wrong profanes and desecrates this holy name, as in the past a church was said to be desecrated when a murder or other crime had been committed in it, or when a monstrance or relic was profaned, thus rendering unholy by misuse that which is holy in itself.[2]

[1]G: *sondern nützlich brauche zu Gottes Lob und Ehren*; L: *sed utiliter idem ad Dei honorem et gloriam usurpemus.*

[2]G: *als das wohl an ihm selbs heilig und doch im Brauch unheilig ward*; L: *ut, quae per se quidem sancta esset, ipso tamen usu profana fieret.*

Large Catechism III, 45

731 But our enemies falsely charge that we abolish good ordinances and church discipline. We can claim that the public liturgy in the church is more dignified among us than among the opponents.[1] If anyone would look at it in the right way, we keep the ancient canons better than the opponents. Among the opponents, unwilling celebrants and hirelings celebrate the Mass, and very often they do so only for the money. They chant psalms, not in order to learn or pray, but for the sake of the rite, as if this work were a required act of worship, or for the sake of financial reward.[2] Many among us celebrate the Lord's Supper every Lord's day after they are instructed, examined, and absolved. The children chant the Psalms in order to learn them; the people also sing in order either to learn or to pray.[3]

[1]L: *Vere enim praedicare possumus publicam formam ecclesiarum apud nos honestiorem esse*; G: *daß es christlicher, ehrlicher in unsern Kirchen mit rechten Gottesdiensten gehalten wird.*

[2]L: *Canunt Psalmos, non ut discant aut orent, sed cultus causa, quasi illud opus sit cultus, aut certe mercedis causa*; G: *So singen sie die Psalmen in Stiften, nicht daß sie studieren oder ernstlich beten . . . sondern halten ihre Metten und Vesper als einen gedingten Gottesdienst, der ihnen ihre Rente und Zinse trägt.*

[3]L: *Pueri canunt Psalmos, ut discant, canit et populus, ut vel discat vel oret*; G: *Item die Jugend und das Volk singet ordentlich lateinische und deutsche Psalmen, daß sie der Sprache der Schrift gewohnen und beten lernen.*

Apology XV, 39–40

732 *But this I say for myself: I am also a doctor and a preacher, just as learned and experienced as all of them who are so high and mighty. Nevertheless, each morning, and whenever else I have time, I do as a child who is being taught the catechism and I read and recite word for word the Lord's Prayer, the Ten Commandments, the Creed, the Psalms, etc.*[1] *I must still read and study the catechism daily, and yet I cannot master it as I wish, but must remain a child and pupil of the catechism—and I also do so gladly. These fussy, fastidious fellows would like quickly, with one reading, to be doctors above all doctors, to know it all and to need nothing more. Well this, too, is a sure sign that they despise both their office and the people's souls, yes, even God and his Word. They do not need to fall, for they have already fallen all too horribly. What they need, however, is to become children and begin to learn the ABCs, which they think they have long since outgrown.*

[1]G: *Noch tue ich wie ein Kind, das man den Katechismon lehret, und lese und spreche auch von Wort zu Wort des Morgens, und wenn ich Zeit habe, das Vaterunser, zehen Gepot, Glaube, Psalmen, &c.*; L: *haudquaquam tamen imitari me pueros pudet, sed quemadmodum illos catechismum docemus, ita et ego mane aut quandocunque vacui aliquid temporis datur, ipsam orationem Dominicam, decem praecepta, articulos fidei, psalmos aliquot etc. mecum ipse quasi ad verbum recito.*

Large Catechism, Luther's Preface, 7–8
Italics indicate a different textual ordering in the 1580 *Book of Concord*.

733 Thus we have, in all, five parts covering the whole of Christian teaching, which we should constantly teach and require recitation word for word. For you should not assume that the young people will learn and retain this teaching from sermons alone. When these parts have been well learned, one may assign them also some psalms or hymns, based on these subjects, to supplement and confirm their knowledge.[1] Thus young people will be led into the Scriptures and make progress every day.

[1]G: *so kann man darnach auch etliche Psalmen oder Gesänge, so darauf gemacht sind, furlegen zur Zugabe und Stärke desselbigen*; L: *aliquot etiam psalmi et cantilenae in hoc formati et expositi proponi possunt pueris, ut hisce prius perceptis quasi roborentur et confirmentur.*

Large Catechism, Preface, 24–25

734 Ceremonies should be observed both so that people may learn the Scriptures and so that, admonished by the Word, they might experience faith and fear and finally even pray. For these are the purposes of the ceremonies. We keep the Latin for the sake of those who learn and understand it. We also use German hymns in order that the [common] people might have something to learn, something that will arouse their faith and fear.[1] This custom has always existed in the churches. For even if some have more frequently used German hymns and others more rarely, nevertheless almost everywhere the people sang something in their own language.[2] No one has ever written or suggested that people benefit from the mere act of hearing lessons that they do not understand or that they benefit from ceremonies not because they teach or admonish but simply *ex opere operato*, that is, by the mere act of doing or observing.

[1]L: *et admiscemus germanicas cantiones, ut habeat et populus, quod discat, et quo excitet fidem et timorem*; G: *und lassen daneben deutsche christliche Gesänge gehen, damit das gemeine Volk auch etwas lerne und zu Gottesfurcht und Erkenntnis unterricht werde.*

[2]L: *Nam etsi aliae frequentius, aliae rarius admiscuerunt germanicas cantiones, tamen fere ubique aliquid canebat populus sua lingua*; G: *Denn wiewohl an etlichen Orten mehr, an etlichen Orten weniger deutscher Gesänge gesungen werden, so hat doch in allen Kirchen je etwas das Volk deutsch gesungen.*

Apology XXIV, 3–5

735 3. On the other hand, we believe, teach, and confess that original sin is not a slight corruption of human nature, but rather a corruption so deep that there is nothing sound or uncorrupted left in the human body or soul, in its internal or external powers. Instead, as the church sings,[1] "Through Adam's fall human nature and our essence are completely corrupted."[2]

[1]G: *wie die Kirche singet*; L: *Sicut ecclesia canit.*

[2]G: „*Durch Adams Fall ist ganz vorderbet menschlich Natur und Wesen*"; L: *Lapsus Adae vi pessima humana tota massa, natura et ipsa essentia corrupta, luce cassa.*

This is a reference to the first lines of Lazarus Spengler's (1479–1534) hymn "*Durch Adams Fall ist ganz verderbt, menschlich Natur und Wesen,*" which can still be found in modern hymnals, as in *Evangelisches Kirchengesangbuch* (243) and in *Lutheran Worship* (363), where it is unfortunately separated from its traditional Wittenberg melody dating from the 1520s. Because no metrical translation is provided here as in some previous translations and because the hymn in *Lutheran Worship* is a loose paraphrase, a fairly literal, metrical rendition from the German follows: "Through Adam's fall is all corrupt: / our form and human nature. // Our heirloom is the poisoned cup; / no healing in our future // without God's aid that freedom gave / from slavery eggregious // in which the snake did Eve's hope take / and with God's wrath did yoke us."

Formula of Concord, Epitome I, 8

736 6. Or that original sin is not a deprivation or lack of spiritual powers but only an external obstacle for such good, spiritual powers, just as coating a magnet with garlic juice does not take away its natural powers but only impedes them. Or that this "spot" can be easily wiped away, like a smudge on the face or paint on the wall.

7. Likewise, we also reject and condemn those who teach that human nature has indeed been greatly weakened and corrupted through the fall but has not completely lost all good that pertains to divine, spiritual matters. They teach that it is not true, as is sung in our churches,[1] "Through Adam's fall human nature and essence are completely corrupted." Instead, as tiny, small, and insignificant as it might be, there is nevertheless something good left from our natural birth, such as the capability, aptitude, competence, or capacity to begin doing something, or to effect something, or to cooperate in spiritual matters.

[1]G: *wie man in unserer Kirchen singet*; L: *quod ecclesiae nostrae canunt*.

Formula of Concord, Solid Declaration I, 22–23

737 *Nothing is so powerfully effective against the devil, the world, the flesh, and all evil thoughts as to occupy one's self with God's Word, to speak about it and meditate upon it,*[1] *in the way that Psalm 1[:2] calls those blessed*[2] *who "meditate on God's law day and night." Without doubt, you will offer up no more powerful incense or savor against the devil than to occupy yourself with God's commandments and words and to speak, sing, or think about them.*[3] *Indeed, this is the true holy water and sign that drives away the devil and puts him to flight.*

[1]G: *so man mit Gottes Wort ümbgehet, davon redet und tichtet*; L: *quam si sedulo tractetur verbum Dei, de eo sit sermo et meditatio nostra*.

[2]G: *selig preiset*; L: *pronuntiet 'beatos . . .'*.

[3]G: *davon redest, singest oder denkest*; L: *de iis familiares misceas sermones, illa canas ac mediteris*.

Large Catechism, Luther's Preface, 10

Italics indicate a different textual ordering in the 1580 *Book of Concord*.

WHEN DO CHRISTIANS PRAISE AND THANK GOD?

738 Whenever this practice is in force, a holy day is truly kept. When it is not, it ought not be called a Christian holy day. For non-Christians can spend a day in rest and idleness, too, and so can the whole swarm of clerics in our time who stand day after day in the church, singing and ringing bells,[1] but without keeping a single day holy, because they neither preach nor practice God's Word, but rather teach and live contrary to it.

[1]G: *täglich in der Kirche stehen, singen und klingen*; L: *quotidie in templis stantes cantillant et strenue tinniunt.*

Large Catechism I, 90

739 But to give a Christian interpretation to the simple people of what God requires of us in this commandment, note that we do not observe holy days for the sake of intelligent and well-informed Christians, for they have no need of them. We observe them, first, because our bodies need them. Nature teaches and demands that the common people—menservants and maidservants who have gone about their work or trade all week long—should also retire for a day to rest and be refreshed. Second and most important, we observe them so that people will have time and opportunity on such days of rest, which otherwise would not be available, to attend worship services, that is, so that they may assemble to hear and discuss God's Word and then to offer praise, song, and prayer to God.[1]

But this, I say, is not restricted, as it was among the Jews, to a particular time so that it must be precisely this day or that, for in itself no one day is better than another. Actually, worship ought to take place daily. However, because this is more than the common people can do, at least one day a week ought to be set apart for it.

[1]G: *darnach Gott loben, singen und beten*; L: *deinceps Deum hymnis, psalmis et canticis laudemus.*

Large Catechism I, 83–85

740 Once a conscience has been uplifted by faith and realizes its freedom from terror, then it fervently gives thanks for the benefits of Christ and for his suffering. It uses the ceremony itself as praise to God,[1] as a way of demonstrating its gratitude, and as a witness of its high esteem for the gifts of God.[2] In this way the ceremony becomes a sacrifice of praise.[3]

The Fathers also speak about a twofold effect, about consolation for the conscience and thanksgiving or praise.[4] The first of these effects pertains to the nature of the sacrament; the second pertains to the sacrifice.

[1]L: *et utitur ipsa ceremonia ad laudem Dei*; G: *und braucht auch der Ceremonien oder äußerlichen Zeichen zu Gottes Lobe.*

[2]L: *ut hac obedientia gratitudinem ostendat, et testatur se magni facere dona Dei*; G: *und erzeigt sich, daß es solche Gottes Gnade mit Dankbarkeit annehme, groß und hoch achte.*

[3]L: *Ita fit ceremonia sacrificium laudis*; G: *Also wird die Messe ein Dankopfer oder Opfer des Lobes.*

[4]L: *de gratiarum actione seu laude*; G: *daß Gott Lob und Dank gesagt wird.*

Apology XXIV, 74–75

741 For even if the Mass is called an offering, what does that term have to do with these dreams about *ex opere operato* and the transfer that supposedly merits the forgiveness of sins for others? It can be called an offering for the same reason it is called a Eucharist: here are offered prayers, thanksgiving, and the entire act of worship.[1] But neither ceremonies nor prayers provide benefits *ex opere operato* without faith. Nevertheless, we are not arguing here about prayers, but specifically about the Lord's Supper.

[1]L: *quia ibi offeruntur orationes, gratiarum actiones et totus ille cultus, sicut et εὐχαριστία dicitur.*

The German paraphrase departs widely from the Latin at this point.

Apology XXIV, 87

742 In the morning, as soon as you get out of bed, you are to make the sign of the holy cross and say:

"God the Father, Son, and Holy Spirit watch over me. Amen."

Then, kneeling or standing, say the Apostles' Creed and the Lord's Prayer. If you wish, you may in addition recite this little prayer as well:

"I give thanks to you, my heavenly Father through Jesus Christ your dear Son, that you have protected me this night from all harm and danger, and I ask you that you would also protect me today from sin and all evil, so that my life and actions may please you completely. For into your hands I commend myself: my body, my soul, and all that is mine. Let your holy angel be with me, so that the wicked foe may have no power over me. Amen."

After singing a hymn perhaps[1] (for example, one on the Ten Commandments) or whatever else may serve your devotion, you are to go to your work joyfully.

[1]G: *und etwa ein Lied gesungen.*

The Latin text omits this clause.

Small Catechism VII, 1–3

743 This knowledge of and confidence in God's grace makes people glad and bold and happy in dealing with God and with all creatures.[1] And this is the work which the Holy Spirit performs in faith. Because of it, without compulsion, a person is ready and glad to do good to everyone, to serve everyone, to suffer everything, out of love and praise to God, who has shown this grace.[2] Thus, it is impossible to separate works from faith, quite as impossible as to separate heat and light from fire."

[1]G: *Und solliche Zuversicht und Erkenntnus göttlicher Gnaden machet fröhlich, trutzig und lustig gegen Gott und allen Kreaturen*; L: *Et haec fiducia atque agnitio divinae gratiae et clementiae laetos, animosos, alacres efficit, cum erga Deum tum erga omnes creaturas.*

[2]G: *daher der Mensch ohne Zwang willig und lustig wird, jedermann Guts zu ton, jedermann zu dienen, allerlei zu leiden, Gott zu Lieb und zu Lob, der ihm solche Gnad erzeiget hat*; L: *Inde homo sine ulla coactione promptus et alacris redditur, ut omnibus benefaciat, omnibus inserviat, omnia toleret, idque in honorem et laudem Dei pro ea gratia, qua Dominus eum est prosecutus.*

Formula of Concord, Solid Declaration IV, 12

SUMMARY

- We owe God thanks, praise, service, and obedience for all that God does out of his divine goodness and mercy and for the victory over sin and death we have through Jesus Christ. This includes thankfulness for the Word of God, the Gospel. The praise, magnifying, and honoring of the holy name involves both word and deed and flows only from a believing heart.
- God's name is honored and praised "when both our teaching and our life are godly and Christian" (LC III, 38–39).

- The singing of Psalms to learn the Scriptures or to learn to pray is part of the true worship of God. Reading and saying the Ten Commandments, the Creed, the Lord's Prayer, and the Psalms each day is part of worship. Also, saying the parts of the catechism can be supplemented with Psalms and hymns composed on them.
- Hymns in the language of the people are used to call forth faith and fear of God. They are sung in churches to teach the faith.
- To meditate on Psalms and hymns (the Word of God) is "powerfully effective against the devil, the world, the flesh, and all evil thoughts" (LC, Luther's Preface, 10).
- Christians keep holy days, for example, Sundays and festivals, to attend the Divine Service "that they may assemble to hear and discuss God's Word and then . . . offer praise, song, and prayer to God" (LC I, 83–85). Although this is done daily, at least one day a week is set apart for all Christians to attend. When Christians come together, they give thanks for the benefits of Christ and testify to the high esteem they have for the gifts of God. Where faith receives these gifts, the whole Mass can be called an offering of praise.
- Each day Christians, alone or with family, say the Invocation, Creed, Lord's Prayer, and other prayers. Then they go to work with joy, perhaps singing a hymn.
- Faith, a living and bold trust in God's grace that the Holy Spirit works within us, renders joyful, fearless, and cheerful service to neighbor and to God by fruits of faith, among which are the love and praise of God.

Synopsis

The Lord's name is made great when the Gospel is preached, it is received in faith, and believing hearts pray to God, praise him, and produce good works. The Holy Spirit not only works faith but also the thankful sacrifice of praise. Justifying and saving faith precedes any such sacrifice of praise. We owe God thanks and obedience for all that he has given us, especially for the victory over sin and death that we have in Jesus Christ.

Psalms and hymns, alongside the Word of God, the Ten Commandments, the Creed and the Lord's Prayer, are part of the worship of God both in daily life and in worship with others. A living and bold trust in God leads to the joyful love and praise of God.

8

Rites and Ceremonies

Are the rites and ceremonies of Christians part of the true worship of God?

801 However, the church is not only an association of external ties and rites like other civic organizations,[1] but it is principally an association of faith and the Holy Spirit in the hearts of persons.[2] It nevertheless has its external marks so that it can be recognized, namely, the pure teaching of the gospel and the administration of the sacraments in harmony with the gospel of Christ. Moreover, this church alone is called the body of Christ, which Christ renews, sanctifies, and governs by his Spirit as Paul testifies in Ephesians 1[:22–23], when he says, "And [God] has made him the head over all things for the church, which is his body, the fullness of him who fills all in all." Therefore those in whom Christ is not active are not members of Christ. This much the opponents also admit, namely, that the wicked are dead members of the church. We therefore wonder why they have found fault with our description, which speaks about living members.

[1]L: *At ecclesia non est tantum societas externarum rerum ac rituum sicut aliae politiae*; G: *Aber die christliche Kirche stehet nicht allein in Gesellschaft äußerlicher Zeichen.*

[2]L: *sed principaliter est societas fidei et spiritus sancti in cordibus*; G: *sondern stehet furnehmlich in Gemeinschaft inwendig der ewigen Güter im Herzen, als des heiligen Geistes, des Glaubens, der Furcht und Liebe Gottes.*

Apology VII–VIII, 5–6

802 **[German text]** To obtain such faith God instituted the office of preaching, giving the gospel and the sacraments. Through these, as through means, he gives the Holy Spirit who produces faith, where and when he wills, in those who hear the gospel. It teaches that we have a gracious God, not through our merit but through Christ's merit, when we so believe.

Condemned are the Anabaptists and others who teach that we obtain the Holy Spirit without the external word of the gospel through our own preparation, thoughts, and works.[1]

[Latin text] So that we may obtain this faith, the ministry of teaching the gospel and administering the sacraments was instituted. For through the Word and the sacraments as through instruments the Holy Spirit is given, who effects faith where and when it pleases God in those who hear the gospel, that is to say, in those who hear that God, not on account of our own merits but on account of Christ, justifies those who believe that they are received into grace on account of Christ. Galatians 3[:14b]: "So that we might receive the promise of the Spirit through faith."

They condemn the Anabaptists and others who think that the Holy Spirit comes to human beings without the external Word through their own preparations and works.[1]

[1]G: *Und werden verdammt die Wiedertaufer und andere, so lehren, daß wir ohn das leiblich Wort des Evangelii den Heiligen Geist durch eigene Bereitung, Gedanken und Werk erlangen*; L: *Damnant Anabaptistas et alios, qui sentiunt spiritum sanctum contingere hominibus sine verbo externo per ipsorum praeparationes et opera.*

Augsburg Confession V, 1–4

803 **[German text]** In addition, it is also taught that all are obliged to conduct themselves regarding bodily discipline, such as fasting and other work, in such a way as not to give occasion to sin,[1] but not as if they earned grace by such works. Such bodily discipline should not be limited only to specific days but should be maintained continually.[2] Christ speaks about this in Luke 21[:34]: "Be on guard so that your hearts are not weighed down with dissipation," and [Mark 9:29:] "This kind [of demon] can come out only through prayer and fasting." Paul says that he punished his body and enslaved it [1 Cor. 9:27], indicating that mortification should not serve the purpose of earning grace but of keeping the body in a condition that does not prevent performing the duties required by one's calling.[3] So fasting in itself is not rejected. Instead, we reject making it a required service with prescribed days and foods, for this confuses the consciences.[4]

[Latin text] In addition, they teach that all Christians should so train and restrain themselves with bodily discipline, or bodily exercises and labors, that neither overexertion nor idleness may lure them to sin.[1] But they do not teach that we merit forgiveness of sins or make satisfaction for them through such exercises. Such bodily discipline should always be encouraged, not only on a few prescribed days.[2] As Christ commands [Luke 21:34]: "Be on guard so that your hearts are not weighed down with dissipation." Again [Mark 9:29]: "This kind [of demon] can come out only through prayer and fasting." And Paul says: "I punish my body and enslave it" [1 Cor. 9:27]. Here he clearly shows that he punished his body not to merit forgiveness of sins through such discipline but to keep the body under control and fit for spiritual things and to carry out his responsibilities according to his calling.[3] Therefore, fasting itself is not condemned, but traditions that prescribe, with peril to conscience, certain days and foods, as if works of this kind were necessary acts of worship.[4]

[1]G: *daß ein iglicher schuldig ist, sich mit leiblicher Ubung, als Fasten und ander Arbeit, also zu halten, daß er nicht Ursach zu Sunden gebe*; L: *quod quilibet christianus debeat se corporali disciplina seu corporalibus exercitiis et laboribus sic exercere et coercere.*

[2]G: *Diese leibliche Übung soll nicht allein etliche bestimbte Tage, sondern stetigs getrieben werden*; L: *Et hanc corporalem disciplinam oportet semper urgere, non solum paucis et constitutis diebus.*

[3]G: *Und Paulus spricht, er kasteie seinen Leib und bringe ihm zu Gehorsam; damit er anzeigt, daß Kasteiung dienen soll, nicht damit Gnad zu verdienen, sonder den Leib geschickt zu halten, daß er nicht verhindere, was einem iglichen nach seinem Beruf zu schaffen, befohlen ist*; L: *Et Paulus ait: Castigo corpus meum et in servitutem redigo. Ubi clare ostendit se ideo castigare corpus, non ut per eam disciplinam mereatur remissionem peccatorum, sed ut corpus habeat obnoxium et idoneum ad res spirituales et ad faciendum officium iuxta vocationem suam.*

[4]G: *Und wird also nicht das Fasten verworfen, sondern daß man ein notigen Dienst daraus auf bestimbte Tag und Speise, zu Verwirrung der Gewissen, gemacht hat*; L: *Itaque non damnantur ipsa ieiunia, sed traditiones, quae certos dies, certos cibos praescribunt cum periculo conscientiae, tamquam istiusmodi opera sint necessarius cultus.*

Augsburg Confession XXVI, 33–39

804 The opponents also condemned that part of the seventh article where we said, "For the true unity of the church it is sufficient to agree on the teaching of the gospel and the administration of the sacraments. It is not necessary that everywhere human traditions or rites or ceremonies instituted by human beings be the same."[1] Here they draw a distinction between universal and particular rites and are willing to approve our article if we mean "particular rites," but reject it if we mean "universal rites." We do not quite understand what the opponents want. We are speaking about a true unity, that is, a spiritual unity, without which there can be no faith in the heart nor righteousness in the heart before God. For this unity we say that it is not necessary to have similar human rites, whether universal or particular, because the righteousness of faith is not a righteousness tied to certain traditions, as the righteousness of the law was tied to Mosaic ceremonies.[2] For this righteousness of the heart is a matter that makes the heart alive. Human traditions, whether universal or particular, contribute nothing to this giving of life. Nor are they caused by the Holy Spirit, as are chastity, patience, the fear of God, love of one's neighbor, and works of love.

We did not have trivial reasons for presenting this article. For it is evident that many foolish opinions about traditions have crept into the church. Some thought that human traditions were necessary acts of worship for meriting justification.[3] Later they debated how it came to pass that God was worshiped with such variety, as though, indeed, these observances were true worship rather than outward rules of discipline completely unrelated to the righteousness of heart or the worship of God.[4] These varied for good reasons according to the circumstances, sometimes in one way, and at other times in another. Likewise, some churches excommunicated others on account of such traditions as the observance of Easter, images, and similar things. From this the inexperienced have concluded that faith or righteousness of the heart before God cannot exist without these observances. For about this point there are in existence many foolish writings by the summists and others.

But just as the different lengths of day and night do not undermine the unity of the church, so we maintain that different rites instituted by human beings do not undermine the true unity of the church,[5] although it pleases us when universal rites are kept for the sake of tranquillity. Thus, in our churches we willingly observe the order of the Mass, the Lord's day, and other more important festival days. With a very grateful spirit we cherish the useful and ancient ordinances, especially when they contain a discipline by which it is profitable to educate and teach common folk and ignorant. But we are not now discussing the question whether or not it is beneficial to observe them for the sake of tranquillity or bodily usefulness. Another issue is involved. The question is whether or not the observances of human traditions are religious worship necessary for righteousness before God.[6] This is the point at issue in this controversy. Once it has been decided, it will be possible to decide whether for the true unity of the church it is necessary to have similar human traditions everywhere. For if human traditions are not acts of worship necessary for righteousness before God, it follows that it is possible to be righteous and children of God even if a person does not observe the traditions that have been maintained elsewhere. Analogously, if the style of German clothing is not an act of devotion to God necessary for righteousness before God, it follows that it is possible to be righteous and children of God and the church of Christ even if they wear not German, but French clothing.

Paul clearly teaches this in Colossians [2:16–17] when he says, "Therefore do not let anyone condemn you in matters of food and drink or of observing festivals, new moons, or sabbaths. These are only a shadow of what is to come, but the substance belongs to Christ." Again [vv. 20–23], "If with Christ you died to the elemental spirits of the universe, why do you live as if you still belonged to the world? Why do you submit to regulations, 'Do not handle, Do not taste, Do not touch'? All these regulations refer to things that perish with use; they are simply human commands and teachings. These have indeed an appearance of wisdom in promoting self-imposed piety, humility, and severe treatment of the body, but they are of no value in checking self-indulgence." Paul's meaning is this. The righteousness of the heart is a spiritual thing that enlivens the heart. It is evident that human traditions do not enliven the heart and are neither results of the Holy Spirit's working (as is love of neighbor, chastity, etc.) nor instruments through which God moves hearts to believe (as are the given Word and divinely instituted sacraments). Instead, they are usages in that sphere of matters which do not pertain at all to the heart but which "perish with use." It must not be thought that they are necessary for righteousness before God. In the same sense he says in Romans 14[:17], "The kingdom of God is not food and drink but righteousness and peace and joy in the Holy Spirit."

But there is no need to cite many witnesses since they are obvious everywhere in the Scriptures. In our Confession, we have brought together a great many of them in the later articles. Moreover, the point to be decided in this controversy must be raised a little later below, namely, whether human traditions are necessary acts of worship for righteousness before God. There we will discuss this matter more fully.

The opponents say that universal traditions[7] ought to be observed because they are thought to have been handed down from the apostles. Such religious people! They wish to retain rites taken from the apostles, but they do not wish to retain the teaching of the apostles.[8] They ought to interpret these rites in just the same way as the apostles themselves interpreted them in their writings. For the apostles did not want us to think that through such rites we are justified or that such rites are necessary for righteousness before God. The apostles did not wish to impose such a burden on consciences nor they did wish to locate righteousness and sin in the observances of days, foods, and similar things. Indeed, Paul calls such opinions teachings of demons [1 Tim. 4:1]. Therefore the intention and counsel of the apostles ought to be sought from their writings; it is not sufficient to cite their example. They observed certain days not as if that observance were necessary for justification, but in order that the people might know at what time they should assemble. Whenever they assembled, they also observed some other rites and a sequence of lessons.[9] Frequently, the people continued to observe certain Old Testament customs, which the apostles adapted in modified form to the gospel history,[10] like Easter and Pentecost, so that by these examples as well as by instruction they might transmit to posterity the memory of those important events.

[1]L: *nec necesse esse, ubique similes traditiones humanas esse seu ritus aut ceremonias ab hominibus institutas*; G: *und sei nicht not, daß die Menschensatzungen allenthalben gleichförmig sein.*

[2]L: *non esse necessariam similitudinem rituum humanorum sive universalium sive particularium, quia iustitia fidei non est iustitia alligata certis traditionibus, sicut iustitia legis erat alligata Mosaicis ceremoniis*; G: *es sei nicht not, daß Menschensatzungen, sie sein universales oder particulares, allenthalben gleich sein. Denn die Gerechtigkeit, welche für Gott gilt, die durch den Glauben kommt, ist nicht gebunden an äußerliche Ceremonien oder Menschensatzungen.*

[3]L: *Nonnulli putaverunt humanas traditiones necessarios cultus esse ad promerendam iustificationem.* G: *Etliche haben wollt wähnen, daß*

christliche Heiligkeit und Glaube ohne solche Menschensatzungen nicht gelte für Gott.

[4]L: *quod tanta varietate coleretur Deus, quasi vero observationes illae essent cultus, et non potius externae et politicae ordinationes, nihil ad iustitiam cordis seu cultum Dei pertinentes*; G: *so es doch nichts anders sein denn äußerliche Ordnung.*

[5]L: *ita sentimus non laedi veram unitatem ecclesiae dissimilibus ritibus institutis ab hominibus*; G: *also halten wir auch, daß die Einigkeit der Kirchen dadurch nicht getrennet wird, ob solche Menschensatzungen an einem Ort diese, am andern jene Ordnung haben.*

[6]L: *Disputatur enim, utrum observationes traditionum humanarum sint cultus necessarii ad iustitiam coram Deo.* G: *Es ist gar viel ein ander Frage, nämlich ob solche Menschensatzungen halten ein Gottesdienst sei, dadurch man Gott versühne, und daß ohne solche Satzungen niemands für Gott gerecht sein möge?*

[7]L: *universales traditiones*; G: *die Universalceremonien.*

[8]L: *Ritus ab apostolis sumptos retineri volunt, non volunt retineri doctrinam apostolorum*; G: *Die Satzungen und Ceremonien, von den Aposteln, wie sie sagen, aufgericht, wollen sie halten, und der Aposteln Lehre und klare Wort wollen sie nicht halten.*

[9]L: *Servabant et alios quosdam ritus, ordinem lectionum, si quando conveniebant.* G: *Auch haben sie wohl etliche Bräuch und Ceremonien gehalten, als ordentliche Lection in der Bibel, wenn sie zusammen kamen &c.*

[10]L: *Quaedam etiam ex patriis moribus, ut fit, retinebat populus, quae apostoli nonnihil mutata ad historiam evangelii accomodaverunt*; G: *Auch haben im Anfang der Kirchen die Jüden, so Christen worden, viel behalten von ihren jüdischen Festen und Ceremonien, welches die Aposteln darnach auf die Historien des Evangelii gericht haben.*

Apology VII–VIII, 30–40

805 We do not concede to them that they are the church, and frankly they are not the church. We do not want to hear what they command or forbid in the name of the church, because, God be praised, a seven-year-old child knows what the church is: holy believers and "the little sheep who hear the voice of their shepherd." This is why children pray in this way, "I believe in one holy Christian church." This holiness does not consist of surplices, tonsures, long albs, or other ceremonies of theirs that they have invented over and above the Holy Scriptures.[1] Its holiness exists in the Word of God and true faith.

[1]G: *Diese Heiligkeit stehet nicht in Chorhembden, Platten, langen Rocken und andern ihren Zeremonien, durch sie uber die heilige Schrift ertichtet;* L: *Haec sanctitas non consistit in amiculo linteo, insigni verticali, veste talari et aliis ipsorum ceremoniis contra sacram scripturam excogitatis.*

Smalcald Articles III, XII, 1–3

ARE THERE RITES AND CEREMONIES THAT CANNOT BE PART OF CHRISTIAN WORSHIP?

806 The holy Fathers did not institute a single tradition for the purpose of meriting the forgiveness of sins or righteousness;[1] they instituted them for the sake of good order in the church and for the sake of tranquillity. Now if someone wants to institute certain works for the purpose of meriting the forgiveness of sins or righteousness, how will that person know that these works please God without the testimony of God's Word? How will they make others certain about God's will without God's command and Word? Does not God throughout the prophets prohibit people from instituting peculiar rites of worship without his command?[2] In Ezekiel 20[:18–19], it is written, "Do not follow the statutes of your parents, nor observe their ordinances, nor defile yourselves with their idols. I the Lord am your God; follow my statutes, and be careful to observe my ordinances." If people are allowed to establish acts of worship and to merit grace through such acts of worship, then the religious rites of all nations will have to be approved—even the acts of worship instituted by Jeroboam [1 Kings 12:26f.] and by others apart from the law.[3] For what is the difference? If we are allowed to establish religious rites that are useful for meriting grace or righteousness, why were the Gentiles and Israelites not allowed to do the same? In fact, the religious rites of the Gentiles and Israelites were condemned because they believed that they merited the forgiveness of sins and righteousness through them, and because they were ignorant of the righteousness of faith. Finally, what assurance do we have that religious rites established by human beings without the command of God justify inasmuch as we can affirm nothing about the will of God without the Word of God?[4] What if God does not approve these acts of worship? How, then, can the opponents maintain that they justify since it cannot be maintained apart from the Word and testimony of God. Paul says [Rom. 14:23], "Whatever does not proceed from faith is sin." But since these religious acts have no testimony from the Word of God, the conscience cannot help but doubt whether they please God.

[1]L: *Nulla traditio a sanctis patribus hoc consilio instituta est, ut mereatur remissionem peccatorum aut iustitiam.*

The German text omits the first two sentences of the Latin.

[2]L: *Nonne ubique in prophetis prohibet instituere peculiares cultus sine suo mandato*; G: *Es verbieten die Propheten allenthalben eigene, erwählte, sonderliche Gottesdienst anzurichten ohne Gottes Wort und Befehl.*

[3]L: *Si licet hominibus instituere cultus et per hos cultus merentur gratiam, iam omnium gentium cultus erunt approbandi, cultus instituti a Ieroboam et aliis extra legem erunt approbandi*; G: *So die Menschen Macht haben, Gottesdienst anzurichten, daß wir dadurch Sunde bezahlen und fromm werden für Gott, so müssen aller Heiden Gottesdienst, alle Abgötterei aller gottlosen Könige in Israel, Jeroboams und anderer auch gut sein, denn es ist kein Unterschied.*

[4]L: *Postremo, unde reddimur certi, quod cultus ab hominibus instituti sine mandato Dei iustificent, siquidem de voluntate Dei nihil affirmari potest sine verbo Dei*; G: *Item, woher sind wir gewiß, daß solche Gottesdienst und Werke ohne Gottes Wort für Gott gerecht machen, so kein Mensch Gottes Willen anders erfahren oder wissen kann, denn allein durch sein Wort?*

Apology XV, 13–17

807 If the mind set on the flesh is hostile to God, the flesh certainly does not love God. If it cannot submit to the law of God, it cannot love God. If the mind set on the flesh is hostile to God, the flesh sins even when we perform outward civil works.[1] If it cannot submit to the law of God, it certainly sins even when we perform works that are excellent and praiseworthy in human eyes. The opponents consider only the commandments of the second table, which entail the civil righteousness that reason understands. Being content with this they suppose that they satisfy the law of God. Meanwhile they fail to notice the first table, which instructs us to love God, to conclude that God is angry with sin, truly to fear God, truly to conclude that God hears our prayers. But without the Holy Spirit the human heart either despises the judgment of God in its complacency or in the face of punishment flees and hates God who judges them. Thus it does not obey the first table. Therefore since these things (contempt for God, doubt about the Word of God and about its threats and promises) cling to human nature, people truly sin even when they do respectable works without the Holy Spirit, because they do them with a godless heart,[2] according to the text [Rom. 14:23], "Whatever does not proceed from faith is sin."

[1]L: *Si sensus carnis est inimicitia adversus Deum, peccat caro etiam, cum externa civilia opera facimus*; G: *Item: ist fleischlich gesinnet sein wider Gott, so sein wahrlich die besten gute Werk unrein und Sünde.*

[2]L: *vere peccant homines etiam cum honesta opera faciunt sine spiritu sancto*; G: *so müssen wahrlich unser besten gute Werke, die wir tun, ehe wir durch den heiligen Geist neu geboren werden, sundlich und verdammt Werke für Gott sein.*

Apology IV, 33–35

808 **[German text]** There are many faulty debates about the transformation of the law, the ceremonies of the New Testament, and the change of the sabbath.

They have all arisen from the false and erroneous opinion that in Christianity one would have to have services of God that correspond to the Levitical or Jewish ones, and that Christ commanded the apostles and the bishops to invent new ceremonies that were necessary for salvation.[1] Christianity has been permeated with these kinds of errors because the righteousness of faith was not taught or preached with purity and sincerity. Some argue that although Sunday cannot be kept on the basis of divine law, it must be kept almost as if it were divine law; and they prescribe the kind and amount of work that may be done on the day of rest. But what else are such debates except snares of conscience? For although they presume to moderate and mitigate human ordinances,[2] there certainly cannot be any mitigation and moderation as long as the opinion remains and prevails that they are necessary. Now this opinion will persist as long as no one knows anything about the righteousness of faith and Christian freedom.

[Latin text] There are still tremendous debates concerning the change of the law, concerning ceremonies of the new law, concerning the change of the sabbath, all of which have arisen from the false assumption that worship in the church should be like the Levitical worship and that Christ commissioned the apostles and bishops to devise new ceremonies that were necessary for salvation.[1] These errors crept into the church when the righteousness of faith was not taught with sufficient clarity. Some argue that the observance of Sunday is not "in fact" of divine right, but "as if it were" of divine right, and they prescribe to what extent one is allowed to work on holy days. What are debates of this kind but snares for consciences? For although they try to bring equity to the traditions, fairness can never be achieved as long as the opinion remains that they are necessary.[2] This opinion necessarily persists where righteousness of faith and Christian freedom are ignored.

[1]G: *und als sollt Christus den Aposteln und Bischofen befohlen haben, neue Ceremonien zu erdenken, die zur Seligkeit notig wären*; L: *et quod Christus commiserit apostolis et episcopis excogitare novas caerimonias, quae sint ad salutem necessariae.*

[2]G: *Dann wiewohl sie sich unterstehen, menschliche Aufsätze zu lindern und epikeiziern, so kann man doch keine epikeia oder Linderung treffen, solange die Meinung stehet und bleibet, als sollten sie vonnoten sein*; L: *Quamquam enim conentur epiikeizare traditiones, tamen nunquam potest aequitas deprehendi, donec manet opinio necessitatis.*

The Greek noun ἐπιείκεια or its verb ἐπιεικεύομαι ("to be reasonable, equitable") is here given as the Latinized *epiikeizare* by adding the Greek ending *–ιζειν* to the noun. It means in this context to make allowances despite possibly contrary facts.

Augsburg Confession XXVIII, 61–64

809 **[German text]** In former times it was taught, preached, and written that distinction among foods and similar traditions instituted by human beings[1] serve to earn grace and make satisfaction for sin. For this reason, new fasts, new ceremonies, new monastic orders, and the like were invented daily.[2] They were fervently and strictly promoted, as if such things were a necessary service of God whereby people earned grace if they observed them or committed a great sin if they did not. Many harmful errors in the church have resulted from this.[3]

[Latin text] It has been a general conviction, not only of the people but also of those who teach in the churches, that distinction of foods and similar human traditions[1] are useful works for meriting grace and making satisfaction for sins. That the world thought so is evident from the fact that daily new ceremonies, new ordinances, new holy days, and new fasts were instituted[2] and that the teachers in places of worship exacted these works as necessary worship for meriting grace and viciously terrified consciences if people omitted any of them. Much misfortune has ensued in the church from this conviction concerning traditions.[3]

[1]G: *Unterschied der Speise und dergleichen Tradition, von Menschen eingesetzt*; L: *discrimina ciborum et similes traditiones humanae.*

[2]G: *Aus diesem Grund hat man täglich neue Fasten, neue Ceremonien, neue Orden und dergleichen erdacht*; L: *Et quod sic senserit mundus, apparet ex eo, quia cotidie instituebantur novae caerimoniae, novi ordines, novae feriae, nova ieiunia.*

[3]G: *Daraus sind viel schädlicher Irrtumb in der Kirchen gefolget*; L: *Ex hac persuasione de traditionibus multa incommada in ecclesia secuta sunt.*

Augsburg Confession XXVI, 1–3

810 Therefore, although hypocrites and wicked people are indeed associated with this true church according to the external rites,[1] nevertheless when the church is defined, it must be defined as that which is the living body of Christ and as that which is the church in fact as well as in name. There are many reasons for this. For we must understand what principally makes us members of the church—and living members at that. If we define the church only in terms of an external government consisting of both the good and wicked, people will not understand that the kingdom of Christ is the righteousness of the heart and the gift of the Holy Spirit. Instead they will think that it is only the external observance of certain religious rites and rituals.[2] Then, too, what will be the difference between the people of the Law and the church, if the church is an external organization? Yet Paul distinguishes the church from the people of the Law in this way: the church is a spiritual people, that is, not a people distinguished from the Gentiles by civil ceremonies, but a true people of God, reborn through the Holy Spirit.[3] Among the people of the Law, in addition to the promise about Christ, those born according to the flesh had promises regarding physical well-being, political affairs, etc. On account of these promises even the wicked among them were called the people of God because God had separated these physical descendants from other nations through certain external ordinances and promises. Nevertheless, these wicked people did not please God. Now the gospel brings not the shadow of eternal things but the eternal blessings themselves, the Holy Spirit and the righteousness by which we are righteous before God.

Therefore the people according to the gospel are only those who receive this promise of the Spirit.

[1]L: *secundum externos ritus*; G: *in äußerlichen Zeichen, im Namen und Ämtern.*

[2]L: *sed iudicabunt tantum externam observationem esse certorum cultuum ac rituum*; G: *sondern man wird gedenken, es sei eine äußerliche Weis, gewisse Ordnung etlicher Ceremonien und Gottesdiensts.*

[3]L: *At sic discernit Paulus ecclesiam a populo legis, quod ecclesia sit populus spiritualis, hoc est, non civilibus ritibus distinctus a gentibus, sed verus populus Dei, renatus per spiritum sanctum*; G: *Nu unterscheidet Paulus also die Kirche von den Jüden, daß er sagt, die Kirche sei ein geistlich Volk, das ist ein solch Volk, welches nicht allein in der Polizei und bürgerlichen Wesen unterschieden sei von den Heiden, sondern ein recht Volk Gottes, welches im Herzen erleuchtet wird und neu geboren durch den heiligen Geist.*

Apology VII–VIII, 12–16

811 Moreover, true prayer, true almsgiving, and true fasting possess God's command, and where they have such a command they cannot be omitted without sin. But those works, insofar as they are not commanded by God's law, but derive from a humanly made prescription, are works that belong to human traditions[1] about which Christ says [Matt. 15:9], "In vain do they worship me, teaching human precepts as doctrines." Works such as certain fasts were established not to restrain the flesh but, as Scotus says, to honor God and to compensate for eternal death. The same is true when a fixed number of prayers or certain acts of charity are rendered in such a way that they become a form of worship that *ex opere operato* gives honor to God and compensates for eternal death. For they attribute satisfaction to these *ex opere operato*, because they teach that they even have value for those living in mortal sin. Now some works stray even further from God's commands, like pilgrimages, of which there is a great variety. For one person makes the journey in full armor and another with bare feet. Christ calls these useless acts of worship,[2] and so they do not serve to conciliate God's displeasure, as the opponents claim. Nonetheless, they adorn these works with distinguished names. They call them works of supererogation[3] and give them the honor of being the price paid in lieu of eternal death. Thus, these works receive preference over the commandments of God. In this way the law of God is obscured in two ways: first because they suppose that they satisfy the law of God through external and civil works; and second, because they add human traditions, the performance of which receives preference to works of the divine law.[4]

[1]L: *opera traditionum humnanarum*; G: *so sind sie nichts denn Menschensatzungen.*

[2]L: *Haec vocat Christus inutiles cultus*; G: *Das nennet Christus vergebliche, unnütze Gottesdienst.*

[3]L: *vocantur opera supererogationis*; G: *[Die Widersacher] nennen es opera supererogationis.*

[4]L: *In hunc modum lex Dei bifariam obscuratur, et quia putatur legi Dei satisfactum esse per externa et civilia opera, et quia adduntur traditiones humanae, quarum opera praeferuntur operibus legis divinae*; G: *und wird also zweierlei Weis Gottes Gesetz verdunkelt, erstlich, daß sie wähnen, sie haben dem Gesetz gnug getan, so sie die äußerlichen Werk getan haben, zum andern, daß sie die elenden Menschensatzungen höher achten denn die Werk, so Gott geboten hat.*

Apology XII, 143–145

812 Although the holy Fathers themselves had rites and traditions,[1] they did not regard them as useful or necessary for justification. They did not obscure the glory or work of Christ but taught that we are justified by faith for Christ's sake, not for the sake of these human rites.[2] They observed these human rites[3] because they were profitable for good order, because they gave the people a set time to assemble, because they provided an example of how all things could be done decently and in order in the churches, and finally because they helped instruct the common folk. For different seasons and various rites serve as reminders for the common folk.[4] For these reasons the Fathers kept ceremonies, and for the same reasons we also believe in keeping traditions.[5] We are amazed when our opponents maintain that traditions have another purpose, namely, to merit the forgiveness of sins, grace and justification.[6] What is this but honoring God "with gold and silver and precious stones," believing that he is reconciled by a variety of vestments, ornaments, and innumerable similar observances in the human traditions.

In Col. 2:23 Paul writes that traditions "have an appearance of wisdom," and indeed they have. This good order is very becoming in the church and is therefore necessary. But because human reason does not understand the righteousness of faith, it naturally supposes that such works justify men and reconcile God. Under this delusion the common people among the Israelites expanded such ceremonies, just as they have been expanded among us in the monasteries.[7] This is how human reason interprets fasting and bodily discipline. Though their purpose is to restrain the flesh, reason imagines that they are to be rites which justify, as Thomas writes, "Fasting avails to destroy and prevent guilt."

This is what Thomas says. So men are deceived by the appearance of wisdom and righteousness in such works. Then there are the examples of the saints; when men strive to imitate them, they copy their outward behavior without copying their faith.[8]

Once this appearance of wisdom and righteousness has deceived men, all sorts of troubles follow. The Gospel of the righteousness of faith in Christ is obscured and replaced by a vain trust in such works. As a result, the commandments of God are obscured; for when men regard these works as perfect and spiritual, they will vastly prefer them to the works that God commands, like the tasks of one's calling, the administration of public affairs, the administration of the household, married life, and the rearing of children. Compared with these ceremonies such tasks seem profane,[9] so that many perform them with scruples of conscience. It is a matter of record that many have given up their administrative positions in the government and their marriages because they regarded these observances as better and holier.[10]

Nor is this all. When minds are obsessed with the idea that such observances are necessary for justification, consciences are sorely troubled because they cannot keep the requirements in every detail. Who could even list them all?[11] There are huge tomes, even whole libraries, that do not contain a single syllable about Christ or faith in him or the good works to be performed in one's calling, but only the traditions together with interpretations that make them either stricter or easier.[12] How the great Gerson suffers as he looks for the degrees and limitations of these precepts and cannot fix the mitigation in any definite degree! Yet at the same time he deplores the danger to consciences that comes from this strict interpretation of the traditions.

[1]L: *ritus et traditiones*; G: *Ceremonien und Satzungen.*

[2]L: *sed docebant nos iustificari fide propter Christum, non propter illos humanos cultus*; G: *sondern haben gelehrt, daß uns Gott um Christus willen gnädig sei, nicht um solcher Gottesdienst willen.*

[3]L: *ritus humanos*; G: *dieselben Satzungen.*

[4]L: *Nam discrimina temporum et varietas rituum valet ad admonendum vulgus*; G: *Denn solche Unterscheid der Zeit und solche mancherlei Gottesdienst dienen das Volk in Zucht zu behalten und zu erinnern der Historien.*

[5]L: *Has causas habebant patres rituum servandorum, et propter has causas nos quoque recte servari traditiones posse iudicamus*; G: *Diese Ursachen haben die Väter gehabt menschliche Ordnung zu erhalten. Und*

auf die Weise fechten wirs auch nicht an, daß man gute Gewohnheit halte.

[6]L: *Et valde miramur adversarios alium finem traditionum defendere, quod videlicet mereantur remissionem peccatorum, gratiam aut iustificationem*; G: *Und wir können wir uns nicht gnugsam wundern, daß die Widersacher wider alle Schrift der Apostel, widers alte und neue Testament lehren dörfen, daß wir durch solche Gottesdienst sollen ewiges Heil und Vergebung der Sunde erlangen.*

[7]L: *Sic sentiebat vulgus inter Israelitas, et hac opinione augebant tales ceremonias, sic ut apud nos in monasteriis creverunt*; G: *Also haben die Irrtüm und schädliche Abgötterei eingerissen bei den Israeliten. Darum machten sie auch ein Gottesdienst über den andern, wie bei unser Zeit ein Altar über den andern, eine Kirche über die andere gestiftet ist.*

[8]L: *Et accedunt exempla sanctorum, quos dum student imitari homines, imitantur plerumque externa exercitia, non imitantur fidem eorum*; G: *Und dazu helfen nu die Exempel der Heiligen, da sie sprechen, S. Franciskus hat ein Kappen getragen und dergleichen. Hie stehen sie allein die äußerliche Uebung an, nicht das Herz und Glauben.*

[9]L: *Haec prae illis ceremoniis iudicantur esse profana*; G: *Dieselbigen Werke hältet man nicht für göttlich, sondern für weltlich Wesen.*

[10]L: *Constat enim multos deserta administratione reipublicae, deserto coniugio illas observationes amplexos esse tamquam meliores et sanctiores*; G: *Denn man weiß je, daß etliche ihren Fürstenstand verlassen, etliche den Ehestand und sind in Klöster gangen, heilig und geistlich zu werden.*

[11]L: *quia non possunt omnes observationes exacte praestare. Nam quotusquisque numerare omnes potuit*; G: *daß sie ihre Orden, ihre Möncherei, ihre aufgelegte Werk nicht so gestrenge gehalten haben. Denn wer könnt die Satzunge alle erzählen*?

[12]L: *sed tantum colligentes traditiones et harum interpretationes, quibus interdum exacerbantur, interdum relaxantur*; G: *sondern allein von solchen Satzungen schreiben sie . . . da ist des Deutens und Dispensierens kein Ende.*

Apology XV, 20–28
The Latin is from the quarto edition.
The English is from Tappert.

813 Here the scholastics in line with the philosophers teach only the righteousness of reason, namely, civil works.[1] In addition, they fabricate the idea that reason, without the Holy Spirit, can love God above all things. Now as long as the human mind is undisturbed and does not feel God's wrath or judgment, it can imagine that it wants to love God and that it wants to do good for God's sake. In this way the scholastics teach that people merit the forgiveness of sins by "doing what is within them," that is, whenever reason, while grieving over sin, elicits an act of love for God or does good for God's sake. Because this opinion naturally flatters people, it has brought forth and multiplied many kinds of worship in the church,[2] like monastic vows and abuses of the Mass. On the basis of this opinion some devised some types, others other types of devotional acts or observances.[3] And in order to nourish and increase trust in such works, the scholastics have asserted that God necessarily gives grace to those who do these things, by a necessity not of coercion but of unchanging order.

[1]L: *tantum docent iustitiam rationis, videlicet civilia opera*; G: [*dann*] *lehren sie allein ein Gerechtigkeit und Frommkeit, da ein Mensch äußerlich für der Welt ein ehrbar Leben führet und gute Werk tut.*

[2]L: *peperit et auxit multos cultus in ecclesia*; G: *hat unzählig viel mißbräuchlich Gottesdienst in der Kirche angericht und geursacht.*

[3]L: *alios cultus atque observationes*; G: *solchs unzählig, immer ein Gottesdienst über den andern.*

Apology IV, 9–11

814 Virginity is commended—but to those who have the gift, as has been said above. However, it is a most wicked error to believe that Evangelical perfection may be found in human traditions.[1] For if it were, then even the monks among the Mohammedans could boast that they have attained Evangelical perfection. Nor is it to be found in the observance of other things, which are called "adiaphora."[2] Because "the kingdom of God is righteousness" [Rom. 14:17] and life in the heart, therefore perfection means to grow in the fear of God, in trust in the mercy promised in Christ, and in dedication to one's calling. Paul also describes perfection this way [2 Cor. 3:18]: "All of us . . . are being transformed into the same image from one degree of glory to another; for this comes from the Lord, the Spirit." He does not say, "we are constantly receiving a different cowl, or different sandals, or different cinctures." It is terrible to read and hear such Pharisaical and even Mohammedan expressions in the church, placing the perfection of the gospel and of the kingdom of Christ (which is eternal life) in these silly outward observances of vestments and similar trifles.[3]

[1]L: *Error est autem perniciosissimus sentire, quod perfectio evangelica sit in traditionibus humanis*; G: *Derhalben ist es ein schändlicher, höllischer*

Irrtum, lehren und halten dass evangelische Vollkommenheit in menschlichen Satzungen stehe.

[2]L: *quae dicuntur ἀδιάφορα*; G: *Dingen, welche Adiaphora sind.*

[3]L: *Miserabile est in ecclesia tales pharisaicas, imo mahometicas voces legi atque audiri, videlicet perfectionem evangelii, regni Christi, quod est vita aeterna, in his stultis observationibus vestium et similium nugarum collocari*; G: *Es ist erbärmlich, daß in der christlichen Kirchen solche pharisäische, ja türkische und mahometische Lehre überhand genommen haben, daß sie lehren, die evangelische Volkommenheit und das Reich Christi, durch welchs sich hie die ewigen Güter und das ewige Leben anheben sollen, stehen in Kappen, in Kleidern, in Speis und dergleichen Kinderwerk.*

Apology XXVII, 27

815 Therefore, such a vow is not right for those whose weakness causes them to defile themselves because they do not have the gift of continence. We have said enough earlier on this entire topic. It is indeed strange that with such dangers and scandals swirling before their very eyes, our opponents defend their traditions contrary to the clear command of God.[1] They are also undaunted by the voice of Christ [Matt. 15:3, 9] upbraiding the Pharisees for setting up traditions contrary to the command of God.[2]

Fourth, those who live in monasteries are released from their vows of poverty by such wicked forms of worship as the desecration of the Mass, celebrated for the dead to make money.[3] Then there is the veneration of saints, in which there is a twofold evil: it arrogates Christ's place to the saints, and it wickedly worships them. Thus, the Dominicans invented the rosary of the blessed Virgin, which is mere babbling, as foolish as it is wicked; it nourishes a false confidence. This wickedness, too, is used only for making money. Meanwhile, they neither hear nor preach the gospel about the free forgiveness of sins for Christ's sake, about the righteousness of faith, about true repentance, about works that have the command of God. Instead, they spend their time on either philosophical discussions or ceremonial traditions that obscure Christ.[4]

Here we will not discuss all of their ceremonies in worship[5]—lessons, chants, and the like. These could be tolerated if they were used as exercises, the way lessons are in school, that is, for the purpose of teaching the listeners and, in the process of teaching, to move some of them to fear or faith. But now they imagine that these ceremonies are the worship of God that merit the forgiveness of sins for themselves and for others.[6] That is why they multiply these ceremonies. If they undertook them in order to teach and exhort hearers, brief and pointed lessons would be more useful than these endless babblings. Thus the whole monastic life is full of hypocrisy and false opinions. In addition to all this, there is the danger that those who belong to these chapters are forced to agree with the persecutors of the truth. Therefore there are many serious and cogent reasons to release good people from this way of life.

[1]L: *tamen adversarios defendere suas traditiones contra manifestum Dei praeceptum*; G: *daß sie nichtsdestoweniger als die törichten, rasenden Leute dringen auf solche Menschensatzungen wider das öffentliche Gottes Gebot.*

[2]L: *Nec commovet eos vox Christi, qui obiurgat pharisaeos, qui traditiones contra mandatum Dei fecerant*; G: *und sehen nicht, daß der Herr Christus so ernstlich strafet die Pharisäer, welche Satzungen wider Gottes Gebot lehreten.*

[3]L: *impii cultus, quales sunt profanatio missae ad quaestum collatae pro mortuis*; G: *der greuliche, schreckliche Mißbrauch der Messen, welche gehalten werden vor Lebendige und vor die Toten.*

[4]L: *Sed versantur aut in philosophicis disputationibus, aut in traditionibus ceremoniarum, quae obscurant Christum*; G: *sondern lehren aus ihren Predigten Fabeln von Heiligen und eigne erdichte Werk, dadurch Christus wird unterdrücket.*

[5]L: *de illo toto cultu ceremoniarum*; G: *der unzähligen kindischen Ceremonien und närrischen Gottesdienst.*

[6]L: *Sed nunc fingunt has ceremonias esse cultus Dei, qui mereantur remissionem peccatorum ipsis et aliis*; G: *Aber nu erdichten sie ihnen selbst, daß solche mancherlei Ceremonien sollen Gottesdienst sein, Vergebung der Sunde dadurch zu verdienen ihnen selbst und andern.*

Apology XXVII, 51–56

816 How many shameful acts have arisen from the tradition of celibacy? With what darkness has the teaching about vows eclipsed the gospel! They have pretended that a vow constitutes righteousness before God and merits forgiveness of sins. Thus they have transferred the benefit of Christ to human traditions[1] and have completely destroyed the doctrine of faith. Utterly worthless traditions they have passed off as worship of God and the way of perfection[2] and given them preference over the work of the vocations that God does require and has ordained. These errors are not to be taken lightly. Truly they do harm to the glory of Christ and bring souls to ruin. They cannot be ignored.

[1]L: *Ita transtulerunt beneficium Christi in humanas traditiones*; G: *daß also das Verdienst Christi auf Menschensatzung gezogen . . . ist.*

[2]L: *Finxerunt nugacissimas traditiones esse cultus Dei et perfectionem*; G: *und haben ihre närrichte und leichtfertige Satzungen fur den rechten Gottesdienst und Vollkummenheit geruhmet.*

Treatise on the Power and Primacy of the Pope, 48

817 For the opponents openly Judaize and openly supplant the gospel with the teachings of demons. When someone teaches that religious rites are useful for meriting the forgiveness of sins and grace, Scripture [1 Tim. 4:1–3] calls such traditions the "teachings of demons."[1] For this obscures the gospel, the benefits of Christ, and the righteousness of faith. The gospel teaches that we freely receive the forgiveness of sins and are reconciled to God by faith on account of Christ. Our opponents, to the contrary, appoint another mediator, namely, these traditions through which they wish to receive the forgiveness of sins and to conciliate the wrath of God. But Christ clearly says [Matt. 15:9], "In vain do they worship me, teaching human precepts as doctrines."

[1]L: *Tunc enim scriptura vocat traditiones doctrinas daemoniorum*; G: *Denn die heilige Schrift und Paulus nennen solche Satzungen denn erst rechte Teufelslehre.*

Apology XV, 4–5

818 **[German text]** In the second place, such traditions have also obscured God's commands.[1] For these traditions are placed far above God's commands.[2] This alone was considered the Christian life: whoever observed festivals this way, prayed in this way, fasted in this way, and was dressed in this way was said to live a spiritual, Christian life.[3] On the other hand, other necessary good works were considered secular, unspiritual ways of life: that each person is obliged to act according to his or her calling—for example, that the father of a family works to support his wife and children and raises them in the fear of God; that the mother of a family bears children and looks after them; that a prince or rulers govern a country; etc. Such works, commanded by God, had to be a "secular and imperfect" way of life, while the traditions had to have impressive names, so that only they were called "holy and perfect" works. That is why there was no end or limit in the making of such traditions.[4]

[Latin text] In the second place, these traditions obscured the precepts of God[1] because traditions were preferred far more than the precepts of God.[2] All Christianity was thought to consist of the observance of certain holy days, rites, fasts, and vestments.[3] These observances possessed the most distinguished titles because they were the "spiritual life" and the "perfect life." Meanwhile the commands of God pertaining to one's calling were not praised: that the head of the household should rear the children, that a mother should bear them, that a prince should govern his country. These were considered as "worldly" and "imperfect" works, far inferior to those splendid observances. This error greatly tormented pious consciences. They grieved that they were bound to an imperfect kind of life: in marriage, in government, or in other civil functions. They admired the monks and others like them and falsely imagined that the observances[4] of such people were more pleasing to God.

[1]G: *Zum anderen haben auch solche Traditionen Gottes Gebot verdunkelt*; L: *Secundo hae traditiones obscuraverunt praecepta Dei.*

[2]G: *dann man setzt diese Traditiones weit über Gottes Gebot*; L: *quia traditiones longe praeferebantur praeceptis Dei.*

[3]G: *Dies hielt man allein fur christlich Leben: wer die Feier also hielte, also betet, also fastet, also gekleidet wäre, das nennete man geistlich, christlich Leben*; L: *Christianismus totus putabatur esse observatio certarum feriarum, rituum, ieiuniorum, vestitus.*

[4]G: *Traditiones*; L: *observationes.*

Augsburg Confession XXVI, 8–11

819 **[German text]** In the third place, such traditions[1] turned out to be a heavy burden to consciences. For it was not possible to keep all the traditions, and yet people thought that keeping them was required for true service to God.[2]

[Latin text] In the third place, traditions[1] brought great dangers to consciences because it was impossible to keep them all, and yet people judged these observances to be necessary acts of worship.[2]

[1]G: *solche Traditiones*; L: *traditiones.*

[2]G: *Denn es war nicht muglich, alle Traditiones zu halten, und waren doch die Leute in der Meinung, als wäre solches ein notiger Gottesdienst*;

L: *quia impossibile erat omnes traditiones servare, et tamen homines arbitrabantur has observationes necessarios cultus esse.*

Augsburg Confession XXVI, 12

820 **[German text]** Concerning this the following is taught. No one can earn grace, become reconciled with God, or make satisfaction for sin by observing the aforesaid human traditions.[1] That is why they should not be made into a necessary service of God.[2]

[Latin text] So they teach that we cannot merit grace or make satisfaction for sins through the observance of human traditions.[1] Hence observances of this kind are not to be thought of as necessary acts of worship.[2]

[1]G: *durch Haltung gedachter menschlicher Tradition*; L: *per observationem traditionum humanarum.*

[2]G: *Und soll derhalben kein notiger Gottsdienst daraus gemacht werden*; L: *quod huiusmodi observationes sint necessarius cultus.*

Regarding the translation of *Gottesdienst* with respect to *cultus*, see text 112, note 1.

Augsburg Confession XXVI, 21

821 Therefore, bishops have no right to create traditions in addition to the gospel[1] as though they merited the forgiveness of sins or were acts of worship that God approves as righteousness and that burden consciences in such a way that their omission would be a sin. That one passage in Acts [15:9], where the apostles say that hearts are cleansed by faith, teaches all this. They go on to forbid imposing a yoke, showing how dangerous this is and emphasizing the sin of those who burden the church. "Why are you putting God to the test?" they ask [Acts 15:10]. But this thunderbolt does not scare our opponents, who vigorously defend their traditions and wicked notions.

Earlier they also condemned Article XV, in which we maintained that traditions do not merit the forgiveness of sins; here they also say that traditions are conducive for obtaining eternal life. Do they merit forgiveness of sins? Are they acts of worship that God approves as righteousness? Do they make hearts alive? In Colossians [2:20–23] Paul denies that traditions are valuable for eternal righteousness and eternal life because food, drink, clothing, and the like are "things that perish with use" [v. 22]. But eternal things, namely, the Word of God and the

Holy Spirit, work eternal life in the heart. So let the opponents explain how traditions are useful for winning eternal life.[2]

The gospel clearly testifies that traditions should not be imposed upon the church to merit the forgiveness of sins, or to be acts of worship that God approves as righteousness, or to burden consciences in such a way that their omission is judged to be a sin. Therefore the opponents will never be able to show that bishops have the power to institute such acts of worship.[3]

[1]L: *Itaque nullum habent ius episcopi condendi traditiones extra evangelium*; G: *Darum haben die Bischofe nicht Macht, Satzung zu machen außer des Evangelii.*

[2]L: *Expediant igitur adversarii, quomodo conducant traditiones ad vitam aeternam.* G: *Darum werden die Widersacher nimmermehr nicht beweisen, daß man durch Menschensatzung das ewige Leben verdiene.*

[3]L: *quod episcopi habeant potestatem tales cultus instituendi*; G: *daß die Bischofe solche Gottesdienst anzurichten Macht haben.*

Apology XXVIII, 8–11

822 To explain this controversy and finally to set it aside by God's grace, we present the following simple statement to the Christian reader.

We should not regard as free and indifferent, but rather as things forbidden by God that are to be avoided, the kind of things presented under the name and appearance of external, indifferent things that are nevertheless fundamentally opposed to God's Word (even if they are painted another color).[1] Moreover, we must not include among the truly free adiaphora or indifferent matters ceremonies that give the appearance or (in order to avoid persecution) are designed to give the impression that our religion does not differ greatly from the papist religion or that their religion were not completely contrary to ours.[2] Nor are such ceremonies[3] matters of indifference when they are intended to create the illusion (or are demanded or accepted with that intention), as if such action brought the two contradictory religions into agreement and made them one body or as if a return to the papacy and a deviation from the pure teaching of the gospel and from the true religion had taken place or could gradually result from these actions.

For in such a case what Paul writes in 2 Corinthians 6[:14, 17] should and must be determinative: "Do not be mismatched [with unbelievers.]

. . . What fellowship is there between light and darkness?" "Therefore, come out from them, and be separate from them, says the Lord. . . ."

In the same way, useless, foolish spectacles, which are not beneficial for good order, Christian discipline, or evangelical decorum in the church, are not true adiaphora or indifferent things.[4]

[1]G: *unter dem Titel und Schein der äußerlichen Mitteldinge fürgegeben werden, welche (ob ihnen gleich eine andere Farbe angestrichen würd) dennoch im Grunde wider Gottes Wort sind, daß dieselbige nicht als freie Mittelding gehalten, sondern als von Gott verbotene Dinge gemieden sollen werden*; L: *sub titulo et praetextu externarum rerum adiaphorarum proponuntur, quae (licet alius color illis inducatur) revera verbo Dei adversantur: ea nequaquam pro rebus adiaphoris habenda, sed tanquam verbo Dei prohibita vitanda sunt.*

[2]G: *wie auch unter die rechte freie adiaphora oder Mitteldinge nicht sollen gerechnet werden solche Ceremonien, die den Schein haben oder, dadurch Vorfolgung zu vormeiden, den Schein fürgeben wollten, als wäre unsere Religion mit der papistischen nicht weit voneinander, oder wäre uns dieselbe ja nicht hoch entgegen*; L: *Et sane inter res adiaphoras non numerandae sunt tales ceremoniae, quae speciem quandam prae se ferunt, aut quibus (ad effugiendam persecutionem) simulatur, quasi nostra religio a pontificia non multum distaret, aut certe quasi ab ea non admodum animus noster abhorreret.*

[3]G: *solche ceremoniae*; L: *eiusmodi ceremoniae.*

[4]G: *Gleichsfalls sind das auch nicht rechte adiaphora oder Mitteldinge, wann es unnütze, närrische Spektakel sind, so weder zu guter Ordnung, christlicher Disziplin oder evangelischen Wohlstand in der Kirchen nützlich.* L: *Sed et haec non sunt vera adiaphora, quae neque ad observandum bonum ordinem neque ad piam disciplinam conservandum neque ad εὐταξίαν in ecclesia constituendam quicquam conferunt, sed praeter inutiles nugas et puerilia spectacula nihil habent.*

Formula of Concord, Solid Declaration X, 4–7

823 We have reviewed a number of our arguments, and in passing we have refuted the opponents' objections. We have recounted all these things not only for the sake of the opponents, but even more for the sake of showing godly minds why they should reject the hypocrisy and the sham worship of the monks, which Christ annuls with a single declaration when he says [Matt. 15:9], "In vain do they worship me, teaching human precepts as doctrines." Therefore the vows themselves and the observance of foods, lessons, chants, vestments, sandals, cinctures—

all these are unprofitable acts of devotion before God.[1] Let all godly minds know for certain that such notions as the following are plain, damnable Pharisaism: that these observances merit the forgiveness of sins;[2] that because of them we are accounted righteous; that we attain eternal life because of them rather than because of Christ through mercy. Holy individuals who followed this way of life have necessarily come to reject all confidence in such observances[3] and to discover that they have the forgiveness of sins freely for Christ's sake, that they attain eternal life for Christ's sake by mercy and not for the sake of such acts of devotion,[4] and that God is pleased only with acts of devotion instituted by his Word and done in faith.[5]

[1]L: *inutiles cultus sunt coram Deo*; G: *für Gott unnütze, vergebliche Gottesdienst sein.*

[2]L: *illae observationes*; G: *dies [Gottesdienst].*

[3]L: *Et necesse est sanctos viros, qui in his vitae generibus vixerunt, abiecta fiducia talium observationum didicisse*; G: *Darum fromme Leute, so im Klosterleben selig worden und erhalten sind, die haben endlich müssen dahin kommen, daß sie an allem ihrem Klosterleben verzagt, alle ihre Werk wie Kot veracht, alle ihre heuchlische Gottesdienst verdammt.*

At this point the English text introduces an element of gender neutrality not found in the original. A survey of Latin dictionaries indicates that *vir* almost always means a man, husband, comrade in arms, manly or heroic attributes, and the like, except in certain poetic usage in which it can mean "humans" or "individuals" as opposed to animals. The German text associates *Leute . . . im Klosterleben* with *viros* in the text, suggesting the primary referent to be the monks who established such a way of life.

[4]L: *non propter illos cultus.*

Here the German text substitutes a citation from Saint Bernard.

[5]L: *quod Deus tantum approbet cultus suo verbo institutos qui valeant in fide.* G: *Denn Gott will kein andere Gottesdienste haben, denn welche er hat selbst aufgericht durch sein Wort.*

Apology XXVII, 69

SUMMARY

- The church is a fellowship of faith gathered and enlightened by the Holy Spirit. It is recognized by its outward objects and rites around the pure doctrine of the Gospel and the administration of the sacraments according to the command of Christ. "Through these, as through means, he gives the Holy Spirit who produces faith, where and when he wills, in those who hear the gospel" (AC V, 1–4).

- Any training or subduing of oneself through external disciplines, such as keeping certain days or fasting, is not done to merit forgiveness but to help oneself be fitted for spiritual things. The righteousness of faith is not bound to humanly devised traditions, which can never merit salvation. Faith, that is, righteousness of the heart before God, does not require traditions. Thus observances of human traditions are not acts of worship necessary for righteousness before God.
- Nevertheless, for the sake of tranquillity (unity, good order) Christians may willingly observe human traditions to help educate and train Christian people.
- Human traditions do not quicken hearts. They are not effects of the Holy Spirit or instruments through which God moves hearts to believe. Traditions do not procure eternal life or change the heart. The observance of days, foods, and the like beyond Holy Scripture cannot be made into righteousness nor can their omission be made into sin. The Law of God cannot be satisfied by outward acts of "civil righteousness" but only when such acts come from a heart that by the Holy Spirit is made able to fear and love God. When prayer, fasting, vows, pilgrimages, garments, lessons, singing, and similar things are meant to appease God, they obscure the work of Christ. Then they become a fictitious "service of God."
- When human traditions are retained to admonish the people and point them to Christ, they become useful for good order and for Christian discipline, though they should never be valued more highly than the works of God's commandments—the true, holy, good works of one's calling in life.

Of what benefit are adiaphora, that is, human traditions that are neither commanded nor forbidden by God?

824 **[German text]** Concerning church regulations made by human beings,[1] it is taught to keep those that may be kept without sin and that serve to maintain peace and good order in the church, such as specific celebrations, festivals, etc. However, people are also instructed not to burden consciences with them as if such things were necessary for salvation.[2] Moreover, it is taught that all rules and traditions made by human beings for the purpose of appeasing God and of earning grace are contrary to the gospel and the teaching concerning faith in Christ.[3] That is why monastic vows and other traditions concerning distinctions of foods, days, and the like,[4] through which people imagine they can earn grace and make satisfaction for sin, are good for nothing and contrary to the gospel.

[Latin text] Concerning church rites[1] they teach that those rites should be observed that can be observed without sin and that contribute to peace and good order in the church, for example, certain holy days, festivals, and the like.

However, people are reminded not to burden consciences, as if such worship were necessary for salvation.[2]

They are also reminded that human traditions that are instituted to win God's favor, merit grace, and make satisfaction for sins are opposed to the gospel and the teaching of faith.[3] That is why vows and traditions concerning foods and days, etc.,[4] instituted to merit grace and make satisfaction for sins, are useless and contrary to the gospel.

[1]G: *Von Kirchenordnungen, von Menschen gemacht*; L: *De ritibus ecclesiasticis*.

[2]G: *als sei solch Ding notig zur Seligkeit*; L: *tamquam talis cultus ad salutem necessarius sit*.

[3]G: *daß alle Satzungen und Traditionen, von Menschen dazu gemacht, daß man dadurch Gott versuhne und Gnad verdiene, dem Evangelio und der Lehre vom Glauben an Christum entgegen seind*; L: *quod traditiones humanae, institutae ad placandum Deum, ad promerendam gratiam et ad satisfaciendum pro peccatis, adversentur evangelio et doctrinae fidei*.

[4]G: *Klostergelübde und andere Tradition von Unterschied der Speise, Tage etc.*; L: *vota et traditiones de cibis et diebus etc*.

Augsburg Confession XV, 1–4

825 On the contrary, in regard to true adiaphora or indifferent things[1] (as defined above) we believe, teach, and confess that such ceremonies, in and of themselves, are no worship of God or any part of it.[2] They must instead be distinguished from each other in an appropriate manner, as it is written, "In vain do they worship me, teaching human precepts as doctrines" (Matt. 15[:9]).

[1]G: *Sondern was rechte adiaphora oder Mitteldinge . . . sind*; L: *De rebus autem illis, quae revera sunt adiaphorae.*

[2]G: *lehren und bekennen wir, daß solche Zeremonien an ihnen und für sich selbst kein Gottesdienst, auch kein Teil desselbigen*; L: *haec est fides, doctrina et confessio nostra, quod eiusmodi ceremoniae per se non sint cultus Dei neque etiam pars cultus divini.*

Formula of Concord, Solid Declaration X, 8

826 **[German text]** How, then, should Sunday and other similar church ordinances and ceremonies be regarded? Our people reply that bishops or pastors may make regulations for the sake of good order in the church,[1] but not thereby to obtain God's grace, to make satisfaction for sin, or to bind consciences, nor to regard such as a service of God or to consider it a sin when these rules are broken without giving offense. So St. Paul prescribed in Corinthians that women should cover their heads in the assembly [1 Cor. 11:5], and that preachers in the assembly should not all speak at once, but in order, one after the other [1 Cor. 14:30–33].

Such regulation belongs rightfully in the Christian assembly for the sake of love and peace, to be obedient to bishops and pastors in such cases, and to keep such order to the extent that no one offends another[2]—so that there may not be disorder or unruly conduct in the church. However, consciences should not be burdened by holding that such things are necessary for salvation or by considering it a sin when they are violated without giving offense to others; just as no one would say that a woman commits a sin if, without offending people, she leaves the house with her head uncovered.

The same applies to the regulation of Sunday, Easter, Pentecost, or similar festivals and customs.[3] For those who think that the sabbath had to be replaced by Sunday are very much mistaken. For Holy Scripture did away with the sabbath, and it teaches that after the revelation of the gospel all ceremonies of the old law may be given up.[4] Nevertheless, the Christian church instituted Sunday because it became necessary to set apart a specific day so that the people might know when to assemble;[5] and the church was all the more pleased and inclined to do this so that the people might have an example of Christian freedom and so that everyone would know that neither the keeping of the sabbath nor any other day is necessary.

[Latin text] What, therefore, should one think of Sunday and similar rites in places of worship? To this our people reply that it is lawful for bishops or pastors to establish ordinances so that things are done in the church in an orderly fashion,[1] not so that we may make satisfaction for our sins through them or so that consciences may be obliged to regard them as necessary acts of worship. Thus, Paul ordered that women should cover their heads in the assembly [1 Cor. 11:5] and that interpreters should be heard in the church in an orderly way [1 Cor. 14:30].

It is fitting for the churches to comply with such ordinances for the sake of love and tranquillity and to keep them insofar as they do not offend others.[2] Thus, everything may be done in an orderly fashion in the churches without confusion, but in such a way that consciences are not burdened by thinking such things are necessary for salvation or that they sin when violating them without offense. Just as no one would say that a woman commits a sin by leaving the house with her head uncovered in an inoffensive way.

Such is the case with the observance of Sunday, Easter, Pentecost, and similar festivals and rites.[3] For those who judge that the necessary observance of Sunday in place of the sabbath was instituted by the church's authority are mistaken. Scripture, not the church, abrogated the sabbath. For after the revelation of the gospel all Mosaic ceremonies can be omitted.[4] Yet, since it was necessary to establish a certain day so that the people would know when they should assemble, it appears that the church designated Sunday for this purpose.[5] Apparently, this was even more pleasing because people would have an example of Christian freedom and would know that it was not necessary to keep either the sabbath or any other day.

[1]G: *daß die Bischofen oder Pfarrer mugen Ordnung machen, damit es ordentlich in der Kirche zugehe*; L: *quod liceat episcopis seu pastoribus facere ordinationes, ut res ordine in ecclesia gerantur.*

[2]G: *Solch Ordnung gebuhrt der christlichen Versamblung umb der Lieb und Friedes willen zu halten, und den Bischofen und Pfarrern in diesen Fällen gehorsam zu sein, und dieselben soferne zu halten, daß einer den anderen nicht ärgere*; L: *Talibus ordinationibus convenit ecclesias propter caritatem et tranquillitatem obtemperare easque servare eatenus, ne alii offendant alios.*

[3]G: *Also ist die Ordnung vom Sonntag, von der Osterfeier, von den Pfingsten und dergleichen Feier und Weise.* L: *Talis est observatio diei dominici, paschatis, pentecostes et similium feriarum et rituum.*

[4]G: *daß alle Ceremonien des alten Gesetz nach Eroffnung des Evangeliums mogen nachgelassen werden*; L: *post revelatum evangelium omnes ceremoniae Mosaicae omitti possunt.*

[5]G: *Und dannoch, weil vonnoten gewest ist, ein gewissen Tag zu verordnen, uf daß das Volkwußte, wann es zusammenkommen sollt, hat die christlich Kirch den Sonntag darzu verordent*; L: *Et tamen quia opus erat constituere certum diem, ut sciret populus, quando convenire deberet, apparet ecclesiam ei rei destinasse diem dominicum.*

Augsburg Confession XXVIII, 53–60

827 **[German text]** Our people have been unjustly accused of having abolished the Mass. But it is obvious, without boasting, that the Mass is celebrated among us with greater devotion and earnestness than among out opponents.[1] . . . Moreover, no noticeable changes have been made in the public celebration of the Mass,[2] except that in certain places German hymns are sung alongside the Latin responses for the instruction and exercise of the people. For after all, all ceremonies should serve the purpose of teaching the people what they need to know about Christ.[3]

[Latin text] Our churches are falsely accused of abolishing the Mass. In fact, the Mass is retained among us and is celebrated with the greatest reverence.[1] Almost all the customary ceremonies are also retained,[2] except that German hymns, added for the instruction of the people, are interspersed here and there among the Latin ones. For ceremonies are especially needed in order to teach those who are ignorant.[3] Paul advised [1 Cor. 14:2, 9] that in church a language that is understood by the people should be used.

[1]G: *Man legt den Unseren mit Unrecht auf, daß sie die Messe sollen abgetan haben. Denn das ist offentlich, daß die Messe, ohn Ruhm zu reden, bei uns mit großerer Andacht und Ernst gehalten wird dann bei den Widersachern.* L: *Falso accusantur ecclesiae nostrae, quod missam aboleant. Retinetur enim missa apud nos et summa reverentia celebratur.*

[2]G: *So ist auch in den offentlichen Ceremonien der Messe keine merkliche Anderung geschehen*; L: *Servantur et usitatae caerimoniae fere omnes.*

[3]G: *sintemal alle Ceremonien furnehmlich darzu dienen sollen, daß das Volk daran lerne, was ihm zu wissen von Christo not ist*; L: *Nam ad hoc praecipue opus est caerimoniis, ut doceant imperitos.*

Augsburg Confession, XXIV, 1–4
The German text differs in its paragraph
ordering from the Latin text.

828 But just as Alexander once and for all untied the Gordian knot by cutting it with his sword (since he could not disentangle it), so also the apostles have once and for all freed consciences from traditions,[1] especially from those that were handed down for the purpose of meriting justification. The apostles compel us to oppose this doctrine by teaching and example. They compel us to teach that traditions do not justify,[2] that they are not necessary for justification, and that no one ought to create or accept traditions with the notion that they merit justification. Now, whoever does observe them, let them do so not as a religious rite but as social mores, just as when, with no religious rites, soldiers are clothed in one way and scholars in another. The apostles violated traditions, and Christ excused them. This example had to be set for the Pharisees to show that these acts of worship were ineffectual. Although our people omit some traditions of little value, they have sufficient excuse now because these are being required as though they merited justification. For such an opinion about traditions is ungodly.

Furthermore, we gladly keep the ancient traditions set up in the church because they are useful and promote tranquillity,[3] and we interpret them in the best possible way, by excluding the opinion that they justify. But our enemies falsely charge that we abolish good ordinances and church discipline.[4] We can claim that the public liturgy in the church is more dignified among us than among the opponents.[5] If anyone would look at it in the right way, we keep the ancient canons better than the opponents.

[1]L: *ita apostoli semel liberant conscientias traditionibus*; G: *Die heilige Schrift und die Aposteln aber sein kurz hindurch gangen und schlecht mit einem Striche alles quittiert und klar dürre heraus gesagt, daß wir in Christo frei, ledig seien von allen Traditionen.*

[2]L: *Cogunt, nos docere, quod traditiones non iustificent*; G: *Darum lehren wir, daß solche Satzungen nicht gerecht machen für Gott.*

[3]L: *Ceterum traditiones veteres factas in ecclesia utilitatis et tranquillitatis causa libenter servamus*; G: *Weiter, die ältesten Satzungen aber in der Kirchen, als die drei hohen Feste &c., die Sonntagsfeier und dergleichen, welche um guter Ordnung, Einigkeit und Friedes will erfunden &c., die halten wir gerne.*

[4]L: *Ac falso nos accusant inimici nostri, quod bonas ordinationes, quod disciplinam ecclesiae aboleamus.* G: *Darum reden die Widersacher ihren Gewalt und tun uns ganz für Gott unrecht, wenn sie uns Schuld geben, daß wir alle gute Ceremonien, alle Ordnung in der Kirchen abbringen und niederlegen.*

[5]L: *Vere enim praedicare possumus publicam formam ecclesiarum apud nos honestiorem esse, quam apud adversarios*; G: *Denn wir mügen es mit der Wahrheit sagen, daß es christlicher, ehrlicher in unsern Kirchen mit rechten Gottesdiensten gehalten wird, denn bei den Widersachern.*

Apology XV, 34–39

829 At the outset it is again necessary, by way of preface, to point out that we do not abolish the Mass[1] but religiously retain and defend it. Among us the Mass is celebrated every Lord's day and on other festivals,[2] when the sacrament is made available to those who wish to partake of it, after they have been examined and absolved. We also keep traditional liturgical forms, such as the order of readings, prayers, vestments, and other similar things.[3]

The opponents include a long harangue about the use of Latin in the Mass, in which they childishly quibble about how it benefits hearers who are ignorant of the church's faith to hear a Mass that they do not understand.[4] Apparently, they imagine that the mere act of hearing itself is a useful act of worship even where there is no understanding.[5] We do not want to belabor this point, but we leave it to the judgment of the reader. We mention it only in passing in order to point out that our churches retain the Latin readings and prayers.

Ceremonies should be observed both so that people may learn the Scriptures and so that, admonished by the Word, they might experience faith and fear and finally even pray. For these are the purposes of the ceremonies.[6] We keep the Latin for the sake of those who learn and understand it. We also use German hymns in order that the [common] people might have something to learn, something that will arouse their faith and fear. This custom has always existed in the churches. For even if some have more frequently used German hymns and others more rarely, nevertheless almost everywhere the people sang something in their own language. No one has ever written or suggested that people benefit from the mere act of hearing lessons that they do not understand[7] or that they benefit from ceremonies not because they teach or admonish but simply *ex opere operato*, that is, by the mere act of doing or observing.[8] Away with such Pharisaical ideas!

[1]L: *nos non abolere missam*; G: *daß wir die Messe nicht abtun.*

[2]L: *Fiunt enim apud nos missae singulis dominicis et aliis festis*; G: *Denn alle Sonntag und Feste werden in unser Kirchen Messen gehalten.*

[3]L: *Et servantur usitatae ceremoniae publicae, ordo lectionum, orationum, vestitus et alia similia.* G: *So werden auch christliche Ceremonien gehalten mit Lesen, mit Gesängen, Gebeten und dergleichen &c.*

[4]L: *Adversarii longam declamationem habent de usu latinae linguae in missa in qua suaviter ineptiunt, quomodo prosit auditori indocto in fide ecclesiae missam non intellectam audire*; G: *Die Widersacher machen ein groß Geschwätz von der latinischen Messe, und reden ganz ungeschickt und kindisch davon, wie auch ein Ungelehrter, der Latein nicht verstehe, groß verdiene mit Messe hören im Glauben der Kirchen.*

[5]L: *Videlicet fingunt ipsum opus audiendi cultum esse, prodesse sine intellectu*; G: *Da erdichten sie ihnen selbst, daß das schlechte Werk des Messhörens ein Gottesdienst sei, welcher auch denn nütze sei, wenn ich kein Wort höre oder verstehe.*

[6]L: *Cum autem ceremoniae debeant observari, tum ut discant homines scripturam, tum ut verbo admoniti concipiant fidem, timorem, atque ita orent etiam, nam hi sunt fines ceremoniarum*; G: *So aber die Ceremonien sollen darum gehalten werden, daß die Leute die Schrift und Gottes Wort lernen, und dadurch zu Gottesfurcht kommen und Trost erlangen und also recht beten, denn darum sind Ceremonien eingesetzt.*

[7]L: *opus audiendi lectiones non intellectas*; G: *Messhören ohn Verstand.*

[8]L: *ceremonias, non quia doceant vel admoneant, sed ex opere operato, quia sic fiant, quia spectentur*; G: *ex opere operato verdienlich und seliglich sei.*

Apology XXIV, 1–5

830 Now there are two, and no more than two, basic kinds of sacrifice. One is the atoning sacrifice, that is, a work of satisfaction for guilt and punishment that reconciles God, conciliates the wrath of God, or merits the forgiveness of sins for others. The other kind is the eucharistic sacrifice.[1] It does not merit the forgiveness of sins or reconciliation but is rendered by those who have already been reconciled as a way for us to give thanks or express gratitude for having received forgiveness of sins and other benefits.[2]

[1]L: *Altera species est sacrificum εὐχαριστικόν*; G: *Zum andern ist ein Dankopfer.*

[2]L: *sed fit a reconciliatis, ut pro accepta remissione peccatorum et pro aliis beneficiis acceptis gratias agamus, seu gratiam referamus*; G: *dadurch nicht Vergebung der Sunde oder Versühnung erlangt wird, sondern geschiehet von denjenigen, welche schon versühnet sein, daß sie für die*

erlangte Vergebung der Sunde und andere Gnaden und Gaben Dank sagen.

Apology XXIV, 19

831 Now the rest are eucharistic sacrifices, which are called "sacrifices of praise,"[1] namely, the preaching of the gospel, faith, prayer, thanksgiving, confession, the afflictions of the saints, and indeed, all the good works of the saints. These sacrifices are not satisfactions for those who offer them, nor can they be applied to others so as to merit the forgiveness of sins or reconciliation for others *ex opere operato*. They are performed by those who are already reconciled.

These are the sacrifices of the New Testament,[2] as Peter teaches [1 Peter 2:5], "a holy priesthood, to offer spiritual sacrifices." Spiritual sacrifices, however, are contrasted not only with animal sacrifices but also with human works offered *ex opere operato*, because "spiritual" refers to the work of the Holy Spirit within us. Paul teaches the same thing in Romans 12[:1]: "[P]resent your bodies as a living sacrifice, holy and acceptable to God, which is your spiritual worship." "Spiritual worship" refers to worship where God is recognized and is grasped by the mind, as happens when it fears and trusts God. Therefore, it is contrasted not only to Levitical worship, in which animals were slain, but with any worship in which people imagine that they are offering God a work *ex opere operato*.[3] The Epistle to the Hebrews, chapter 13[:15], teaches the same thing, "Through him, then, let us continually offer a sacrifice of praise to God,"[4] and it adds an interpretation, "that is, the fruit of lips that confess his name." He commands us to offer praises, that is, prayer, thanksgiving, confession, and the like. These avail not *ex opere operato* but on account of faith. This is stressed by the phrase, "through him let us offer," that is, by faith in Christ.

In summary, the worship of the New Testament is spiritual,[5] that is, it is the righteousness of faith in the heart and the fruits of faith. Accordingly, it abrogates the Levitical worship. And Christ says in John 4[:23–24], "[T]rue worshipers will worship the Father in spirit and truth, for the Father seeks such as these to worship him. God is spirit, and those who worship him must worship in spirit and truth." This passage clearly condemns the notions about sacrifices that imagine they avail *ex opere operato*, and teaches that one should "worship in spirit," that is, with the deepest activity of the heart and faith. Accordingly the Old Testament prophets condemn the popular notion of worship *ex opere operato* and teach righteousness and sacrifices of the spirit. Jeremiah 7[:22, 23], "For in the day that I brought your ancestors out of the land of Egypt, I did not speak to them or command them concerning burnt offerings and sacrifices. But this command I gave them, 'Obey my voice, and I will be your God. . . .' " How may we suppose that the Israelites received this sermon, which seems to conflict openly with Moses? Clearly God had given the Fathers commands about burnt offerings and sacrificial victims. But Jeremiah condemns an opinion about sacrifices that God had not delivered, namely, that these acts of worship pleased God *ex opere operato*. However, concerning faith he adds that God had commanded: "Obey my voice," that is, "believe that I am your God and that I want to be recognized when I show mercy and help you, for I do not need your sacrifices. Believe that I want to be God, the one who justifies and saves, not because of works but because of my Word and promise. Truly and from the heart seek and expect help from me."

[1]L: *Nunc reliqua sunt sacrificia ευχαριστικά, quae vocantur sacrificia laudis*; G: *Über dieses einige Sühnopfer, nämlich den Tod Christi, sind nu andere Opfer, die sind alle nur Dankopfer.*

[2]L: *sacrificia novi testamenti*; G: *Opfer im neuen Testament.*

[3]L: *Opponitur igitur non solum cultui levitico, in quo pecudes mactabantur, sed etiam cultui, in quo fingitur opus ex opere operato offerri.*

The German text does not translate this sentence.

[4]L: *Per ipsum offeramus hostiam laudis semper Deo.*

The German text does not translate this sentence.

[5]L: *cultus novi testamenti est spiritualis*; G: *im neuen Testament gilt kein Opfer ex opere operato sine bono motu utentis, daß ist, das Werk ohn ein guten Gedanken im Herzen.*

Apology XXIV, 25–29

832 Moreover, if we must speak about outward appearances,[1] attendance in our churches is greater than among the opponents'.[2] Practical and clear sermons hold an audience.[3] But neither the people nor the theologians have ever understood the opponents' teaching. The true adornment of the churches is godly, useful, and clear doctrine, the devout use of the sacraments, ardent prayer, and the like.[4] Candles, golden vessels, and similar adornments are appropriate, but they are not the distinctive adornment of the church. Now if the opponents make such things the center of worship[5] rather than the proclamation of the gospel, faith, and its struggles, they should be numbered among those whom Daniel describes as worshiping their god with gold and silver [Dan. 11:38].[6]

[1]L: *de externa specie*; G: *von äußerlichem Wohlstehen.*

[2]L: *frequentia in templis apud nos maior est, quam apud adversarios*; G: *so sind unser Kirchen besser gezieret, denn des Gegenteils.*

[3]L: *Tenentur enim auditoria utilibus et perspicuis concionibus.* G: *Denn es ist kein Ding, das die Leute mehr bei der Kirchen behält, denn die gute Predigt.*

[4]L: *Et verus ornatus est ecclesiarum doctrina pia, utilis et perspicua, usus pius sacramentorum, oratio ardens et similia.* G: *Denn der rechte äußerliche Kirchenschmuck ist auch rechte Predigt, rechter Brauch der Sakrament und daß das Volk mit Ernst dazu gewöhnet sei und mit Fleiß und züchtig zusammen komme, lerne und bete.*

[5]L: *adversarii in talibus rebus collocant cultus*; G: *für nötige Stück und damit Gottesdienst anrichten.*

[6]L: *colere Deum suum auro et argento*; G: *ihren Gott ehren mit Silber, Gold und dergleichen Schmuck.*

Apology XXIV, 50–51

IS THERE EVER A TIME WHEN SPECIFIC ADIAPHORA MAY NOT BE PUT ASIDE?

833 In the same way a dispute arose among some theologians of the Augsburg Confession over ceremonies and ecclesiastical practices that are neither commanded nor forbidden in God's Word[1] but have been introduced into the church with good intentions for the sake of good order and decorum or to maintain Christian discipline.[2] One party held that even in a time of persecution that demands confession of the faith—when the enemies of the holy gospel have not come to agreement with us in public teaching—it is permissible with a clear conscience, under the pressure and the demands of the opponents, to restore certain ceremonies that had earlier been abrogated (which are in and of themselves indifferent, neither commanded nor forbidden by God). They held that it is permissible to compromise with them in these adiaphora or indifferent matters. The other party argued, however, that in a time of persecution that demands confession of the faith—particularly when the opponents are striving either through violence and coercion or through craft and deceit to suppress pure teaching and subtly to slip their false teaching back into our churches—such things, even indifferent things, may in no way be permitted with a clear conscience and without damaging the divine truth.

[1]G: *Von Zeremonien und Kirchengebrauchen, welche in Gottes Wort weder geboten noch verboten sind*; L: *de ceremoniis ecclesiasticis, quae verbo Dei neque mandatae neque prohibitae sunt.*

[2]G: *sondern guter Meinung in die Kirche eingeführet worden umb guter Ordnung und Wohlstands willen oder sonst christliche Zucht zu erhalten*; L: *sed bono consilio propter εὐταξίαν et ordinem aut ad conservandam piam disciplinam in ecclesia usurpantur.*

Formula of Concord, Solid Declaration X, 1–3

834 We also believe, teach, and confess that in a time when confession is necessary, as when the enemies of God's Word want to suppress the pure teaching of the holy gospel, the entire community of God, indeed, every Christian, especially servants of the Word as the leaders of the community of God, are obligated according to God's Word to confess true teaching and everything that pertains to the whole of religion freely and publicly. They are to do so not only with words but also in actions and deeds. In such a time they shall not yield to the opponents even in indifferent matters, nor shall they permit the imposition of such adiaphora by opponents who use violence or chicanery in such a way that undermines true worship of God or that introduces or confirms idolatry.[1] It is written in Galatians 5[:1]: "For freedom Christ has set us free. Stand firm, therefore, and do not submit again to a yoke of slavery." Galatians 2[:4–5]: "But because of false believers secretly brought in, who slipped to spy on the freedom we have in Christ Jesus, so that they might enslave us—we did not submit to them even for a moment, so that the truth of the gospel might always remain with you." Paul speaks in the same place of circumcision, which was at that time a free and indifferent matter (1 Cor. 7[:18, 19]), and which in his spiritual freedom he employed in other circumstances (Acts 16[:3]). However, when the false apostles demanded circumcision in order to confirm their false teaching (as if the works of the law were necessary for righteousness and salvation) and thus misused it, Paul said that he did not want to give in to them "for a moment," "so that the truth of the gospel might always remain" [Gal. 2:5].[2]

Thus, Paul submits and gives in to the weak[3] in matters of food or days and times (Rom. 14[:6]). But he does not want to submit to false apostles, who wanted to impose such things upon consciences as necessary even in matters that were in themselves free and indifferent.[4] Colossians 2[:16]: "Do not let anyone make matters of food or drink or the observation of festivals a matter of conscience for you." And when in such a case Peter and Barnabas did give in to a certain degree, Paul criticized them publicly, as those who "were not acting consistently with the truth of the gospel" (Gal. 2[:14]).

For in such a case it is no longer a matter of external adiaphora, which in their nature and essence are and remain in and of themselves free, which accordingly are not subject to either a command or a prohibition regarding their use or discontinuance. Instead, here it is above all a matter of the chief article of our Christian faith, as the Apostle testifies, "so that the truth of the gospel might always remain" [Gal. 2:5]. Such coercion and command obscure and pervert the truth of the gospel, because either these opponents will publicly demand such indifferent things as a confirmation of false teaching, superstition, and idolatry and for the purpose of suppressing pure teaching and Christian freedom,[5] or they will misuse them and as a result falsely reinstitute them.

At the same time, this also concerns the article on Christian freedom. With deep concern the Holy Spirit, through the mouth of the holy Apostle, has commanded his church to maintain this freedom [Gal. 5:1, 13; 2:4], as we have just heard. For weakening this article and forcing human commands upon the church as necessary—as if their omission were wrong and sinful—already paves the way to idolatry. Through it human commands will ultimately increase and will be regarded as service to God equal to that which God has commanded; even worse, they will even be given precedence over what he has commanded.[6]

Thus, submission and compromise in external things where Christian agreement in doctrine has not already been achieved strengthens idolaters in their idolatry. On the other hand, this grieves and offends faithful believers and weakens their faith. Christians are bound to avoid both for the welfare and salvation of their souls, as it is written, "Woe to the world because of stumbling blocks" [Matt. 18:7], and, "If any of you put a stumbling block before one of these little ones who believe in me, it would be better for you if a great millstone were fastened around your neck and you were drowned in the depth of the sea" [Matt. 18:6].

Special attention should be given to Christ's words, "Everyone therefore who confesses me before others, I also will confess before my Father in heaven . . ." (Matt. 10[:32]).

[1]G: *und daß alsdann in diesem Fall auch in solchen Mitteldingen den Widersachern nicht zu weichen, noch leiden sollen, ihnen dieselbigen von den Feinden zu Schwächung des rechten Gottesdienstes und Pflanzung und Bestätigung der Abgötterei mit Gewalt oder hinderlistig aufdringen zu lassen*; L: *Et sentimus tali tempore etiam in rebus vere et per se adiaphoris non esse adversariis cedendum neque permittendum, ut adversarii nobis talia adiaphora (ad detrimentum veri cultus divini et ad plantandam et stabiliendam idololatriam) observanda imponant et obtrudant, sive id manifesta vi sive dolis efficere conentur.*

[2]G: *„auf daß die Wahrheit des Evangelii bestünde"*; L: *ut veritas evangelii sarta tectaque permaneret.*

[3]G: *Also weichet Paulus und gibt den Schwachen nach*; L: *Sic Paulus infirmis in fide cedit.*

[4]G: *Aber den falschen Aposteln, die solchs als nötig Ding aufs Gewissen legen wollten, will er auch in solchen an ihn selbst freien Mitteldingen nicht weichen*; L: *Pseudoapostolis autem, qui haec* ***tanquam necessaria*** *conscientiis imponere volebant, etiam in rebus per se adiaphoris cedere recusat.*

[5]G: *weil solche Mitteldinge alsdann zu Bestätigung falscher Lehr, Aberglaubens und Abgötterei und zu Unterdrückunge reiner Lehre und christlicher Freiheit*; L: *quia ad confirmationem superstitionum, falsae doctrinae et idololatriae et ad opprimendam sinceram doctrinam et libertatem Christianam.*

[6]G: *dardurch nachmals Menschengebot gehäufet und für ein Gottesdienst nicht alleine den Geboten Gottes gleichgehalten, sondern auch über dieselbige gesetzt werden*; L: *ut deinceps humanae traditiones cumulentur et pro cultu divino habeantur neque modo Dei praeceptis exaequentur, verum etiam illis longe praeponantur.*

For the use of *Gottesdienst* with respect to *cultus*, see text 112, note 1.

Formula of Concord, Solid Declaration X, 10–17

SUMMARY

- Adiaphora, that is, rites and ceremonies devised by humans that are neither commanded nor forbidden by God's Word, cannot make satisfaction for sins or merit grace. In and of themselves they are not worship. For example, with the coming of the

Gospel, ceremonies of Moses such as the keeping of the Sabbath were set aside and a new day appointed for Christian people to gather. When traditions are unprofitable—when they are required as if they merit justification—they may be set aside. They are profitable, however, for tranquility and good order in the church. For this reason the Mass has been retained and hymns in the vernacular have been added to teach the people.

- When the Holy Spirit leads people to faith and to a spiritual service, that is, "a living sacrifice, holy, acceptable" to God (Romans 12:1), the worship of God is a sacrifice of praise. It is offered on account of faith in Christ, not as a work offered *ex opere operato*. Although "outward" adornments may be fitting and useful, they are not the worship.
- "The worship of the New Testament is spiritual, that is, it is the righteousness of faith in the heart and the fruits of faith" (Ap XXIV, 25–29). It thus consists not in outward appearances but in "godly, useful, and clear doctrine, the devout use of the sacraments, ardent prayer, and the like" (Ap XXIV, 50–51).
- In times of persecution when the enemies of God's Word want to suppress pure doctrine, every Christian and especially leaders of the congregation of God must boldly confess the pure doctrine and not yield in matters of adiaphora (ceremonies and rites neither commanded nor forbidden in God's Word yet introduced by men into the church), which would be a detriment to the true worship of God. Human ordinances cannot be regarded as divine worship or be considered equal to the ordinances of God. Such yielding in external things may serve to confirm idolatry and to offend and weaken the true believer.

HOW SHOULD CHRISTIANS HANDLE THEIR LIBERTY IN MATTERS OF RITES AND CEREMONIES THAT ARE NEITHER COMMANDED NOR FORBIDDEN BY GOD?

835 **[German text]** It is also taught that at all times there must be and remain one holy, Christian church. It is the assembly of all believers among whom the gospel is purely preached and the holy sacraments are administered according to the gospel.

For this is enough for the true unity of the Christian church that there the gospel is preached harmoniously according to a pure understanding and the sacraments are administered in conformity with the divine

Word. It is not necessary for the true unity of the Christian church that uniform ceremonies, instituted by human beings, be observed everywhere.[1] As Paul says in Ephesians 4[:4–5]: "There is one body and one Spirit, just as you were called to the one hope of your calling, one Lord, one faith, one baptism."

[Latin text] Likewise, they teach that one holy church will remain forever. The church is the assembly of saints in which the gospel is taught purely and the sacraments are administered rightly. And it is enough for the true unity of the church to agree concerning the teaching of the gospel and the administration of the sacraments. It is not necessary that human traditions, rites, or ceremonies instituted by human beings be alike everywhere.[1] As Paul says [Eph. 4:5, 6]: "One faith, one baptism, one God and Father of all . . ."

[1]G: *Und ist nicht not zur wahren Einigkeit der christlichen Kirche, daß allenthalben gleichformige Ceremonien, von den Menschen eingesetzt, gehalten werden*; L: *Nec necesse est ubique similes esse traditiones humanas seu ritus aut cerimonias ab hominibus institutas.*

Augsburg Confession VII, 1–4

836 Therefore, according to its outward meaning, this commandment does not concern us Christians. It is an entirely external matter, like the other regulations of the Old Testament associated with particular customs, persons, times, and places, from all of which we are now set free through Christ.[1] But to give a Christian interpretation to the simple people of what God requires of us in this commandment, note that we do not observe holy days for the sake of intelligent and well-informed Christians, for they have no need of them. We observe them, first, because our bodies need them.[2] Nature teaches and demands that the common people—menservants and maidservants who have gone about their work or trade all week long—should also retire for a day to rest and be refreshed. Second and most important, we observe them so that people will have time and opportunity on such days of rest, which otherwise would not be available, to attend worship services,[3] that is, so that they may assemble to hear and discuss God's Word and then to offer praise, song, and prayer to God.

[1]G: *an sonderliche Weise, Person, Zeit und Stätte gebunden, welche nu durch Christum alle frei gelassen sind*; L: *certis quibusdam ritibus, personis, temporibus et locis destinatae, quae omnes jam per Christum liberae factae sunt.*

[2]G: *sondern erstlich auch ümb leiblicher Ursach und Notdurft willen*; L: *verum omnium primum corporalis cujusdam necessitatis gratia.*

[3]G: *Raum und Zeit nehme, Gottesdiensts zu warten*; L: *otium et tempus sumatur cultui divino serviendi.*

Large Catechism I, 82–84

837 Therefore, against this "appearance of wisdom" and righteousness in human rites which deceives people,[1] let us fortify ourselves with the Word of God and know first of all that these neither merit the forgiveness of sins nor justification before God, nor are they necessary for justification. We already cited a number of testimonies above. There are plenty more in Paul. In Colossians 2[:16–17] he clearly says, "Therefore do not let anyone condemn you in matters of food and drink or of observing festivals, new moons, or sabbaths. These are only a shadow of what is to come, but the substance belongs to Christ." Here he includes simultaneously both the Mosaic law and human traditions.[2] So the opponents cannot avoid these testimonies, as was their custom, on the grounds that Paul is speaking only about the Law of Moses. He clearly testifies that he is speaking about human traditions.[3] Our opponents do not know what they are talking about. If the gospel denies that the ceremonies of Moses (which were divinely instituted) justify,[4] how much less do human traditions justify![5]

Nor do bishops have the power to institute religious activities that justify or are necessary for justification.[6]

[1]L: *contra illam speciem sapientiae et iustitiae in humanis ritibus, quae fallit homines*; G: *wider solche heuchlische, gleißende Satzungen, dadurch viel verführt, und jämmerlich die Gewissen ohn Ursach geplagt werden.*

[2]L: *et legem Moysi et traditiones humanas*; G: *das ganze Gesetz Mosi und solche Tradition.*

[3]L: *de traditionibus humanis*; G: *von menschlichen Satzungen.*

[4]L: *si evangelium negat ceremonias Moysi, quae erant divinitus institutae, iustificare*; G: *Denn so das Evangelium und Paulus klar melden, daß auch die Ceremonien und Werke des Gesetz Mosi fur Gott nicht helfen.*

[5]L: *quanto minus iustificant traditiones humanae*; G: *so werdens viel weniger menschliche Satzungen tun.*

[6]L: *Nec habent episcopi potestatem instituendi cultus tamquam iustificantes aut necessarios ad iustificationem*; G: *Derhalben haben die Bischofe*

nicht Macht noch Gewalt eigene erwählte Gottesdienst aufzurichten, welche sollen die Leute für Gott heilig und fromm machen.

Apology XV, 29–31

838 **[German text]** Our side also retains many ceremonies and traditions, such as the order of the Mass and other singing, festivals, and the like, which serve to preserve order in the church.[1] At the same time, however, the people are taught that such external worship of God does not make them righteous before God and that it is to be observed without burdening consciences, that is, no one sins by omitting it without causing offense. The ancient Fathers also maintained such liberty with respect to external ceremonies.[2] For in the East the festival of Easter was celebrated at a date different from that in Rome. When some wanted to divide the church over this difference, others admonished them that there was no need to have uniformity in such customs. As Irenaeus says: "Diversity in fasting does not dissolve unity in faith." Furthermore, concerning such diversity in human ordinances, dist. 12 also states that they are not in conflict with the unity of Christendom.[3] The *Tripartite History*, Book 9, gathers many examples of diverse church customs[4] and establishes a useful Christian saying: "It was not the intention of the apostles to institute festivals but to teach faith and love."

[Latin text] Nevertheless, many traditions are kept among us, such as the order of readings in the Mass, holy days, etc., which are conducive to maintaining good order in the church.[1] But at the same time, people are warned that such acts of worship do not justify before God and that no punishable sin is committed if they are omitted without offense. Such freedom in human rites was not unknown to the Fathers.[2] For in the East, Easter was kept at a different time than in Rome, and when the Romans accused the East of schism because of this difference, they were admonished by others that such customs need not be alike everywhere. Irenaeus says, "Disagreement about fasting does not dissolve the unity in faith," and Pope Gregory indicates (dist. 12) that such diversity does not damage the unity of the church.[3] In the *Tripartite History*, Book IX, many examples of dissimilar rites are collected,[4] and this statement is made: "It was not the intention of the apostles to make decrees about festivals but to preach good conduct among people and godliness."

[1]G: *Auch werden dieses Teils viel Ceremonien und Tradition gehalten, als Ordnung der Messe und andere Gesäng, Feste, etc., welche darzu dienen,*

daß in der Kirchen Ordnung gehalten werde; L: *Servantur tamen apud nos pleraeque traditiones, ut ordo lectionum in missa, feriae, etc., quae conducunt ad hoc, ut res ordine geratur in ecclesia.*

[2]G: *Diese Freiheit in äußerlichen Ceremonien haben auch die alten Väter gehalten*; L: *Haec libertas in ritibus humanis non fuit ignota patribus.*

[3]G: *daß sie der Einigkeit der Christenheit nicht zuwider sei*; L: *talem dissimilitudinem non laedere unitatem ecclesiae.*

[4]G: *zeucht zusammen viel ungleicher Kirchengewohnheit*; L: *multa colliguntur exempla dissimilium rituum.*

Augsburg Confession XXVI, 40–45

839 Therefore, we believe, teach, and confess that the community of God in every time and place has the right, power, and authority to change, reduce, or expand such practices according to circumstances in an orderly and appropriate manner, without frivolity or offense, as seems most useful, beneficial, and best for good order, Christian discipline, evangelical decorum, and the building up of the church.[1] Paul teaches how one may yield and make concessions to the weak in faith in such external matters of indifference with good conscience (Rom. 14[:1–23]), and he demonstrates this with his own example (Acts 16[:3] and 21[:26]; 1 Cor. 9[:10]).

[1]G: *daß die Gemeine Gottes jdes Orts und jderzeit derselben Gelegenheit nach guten Fug, Gewalt und Macht habe, dieselbige ohne Leichtfertigkeit und Ärgernus ordentlicher und gebührlicher Weise zu ändern, zu mindern und zu mehren, wie es jderzeit zu guter Ordnung, christlicher Disziplin und Zucht, evangelischem Wohlstand und zu Erbauung der Kirchen am nützlichsten, förderlichsten und besten angesehen wird.* L: *quod ecclesia Dei, quibusvis temporibus et locis, pro re nata, liberrimam potestatem habeat (in rebus vere adiaphoris) aliquid mutandi, abrogandi, constituendi, si tamen id absque levitate et scandalo decenter et bono ordine fiat, et si accurate expendatur, quid singulis temporibus ad conservandum bonum ordinem et ad piam retinendam disciplinam atque ad εὐταξίαν evangelica professione dignam et ad ecclesiae aedificationem quam plurimum faciat.*

Formula of Concord, Solid Declaration X, 9

840 A dispute also occurred among theologians of the Augsburg Confession over ceremonies or ecclesiastical practices that are neither commanded nor forbidden in God's Word but that were introduced in the churches for the sake of good order and decorum.[1]

Status controversiae

On the Chief Controversy regarding This Article

The chief question concerned a situation of persecution, in a case in which confession is necessary, when the enemies of the gospel refuse to come to terms with us: the question was whether, in that situation, in good conscience, certain ceremonies that had been abolished (as in themselves indifferent matters neither commanded nor forbidden by God) could be revived under the pressure and demand of the opponents, and whether compromise with them in such ceremonies and indifferent matters would be proper? The one party said yes, the other said no to this question.

Affirmative Theses

The Proper, True Teaching and Confession concerning This Article

1. To settle this dispute, we unanimously believe, teach, and confess that ceremonies or ecclesiastical practices that are neither commanded nor forbidden in God's Word, but have been established only for good order and decorum, are in and of themselves neither worship ordained by God nor a part of such worship.[2] "In vain do they worship me" with human precepts (Matt. 15[:9]).

2. We believe, teach, and confess that the community of God in every place and at every time has the authority to alter such ceremonies according to its own situation, as may be most useful and edifying for the community of God.[3]

3. Of course, all frivolity and offense must be avoided, and special consideration must be given particularly to those who are weak in faith.

4. We believe, teach, and confess that in a time of persecution, when an unequivocal confession of the faith is demanded of us, we dare not yield to the opponents in such indifferent matters. As the Apostle wrote, "Stand firm in the freedom for which Christ has set us free, and do not submit again to a yoke of slavery" [Gal. 5:1]. And: "Do not put on the yoke of the others; what partnership is there between light and darkness?" [2 Cor. 6:14]. "So that the truth of the gospel might always remain with you, we did not submit to them even for a moment" [Gal. 2:5]. For in such a situation it is no longer indifferent matters that are at stake. The truth of the gospel and Christian freedom are at stake. The confirmation of open idolatry, as well as the protection of the weak in faith from offense, is at stake.[4] In such matters we can make no

concessions but must offer an unequivocal confession and suffer whatever God sends and permits the enemies of his Word to inflict on us.

5. We also believe, teach, and confess that no church should condemn another because the one has fewer or more external ceremonies not commanded by God than the other has,[5] when otherwise there is unity with the other in teaching and all the articles of faith and in the proper use of the holy sacraments, according to the well-known saying, "Dissonantia ieiunii non dissolvit consonantiam fidei," "Dissimilarity in fasting is not to disrupt unity in faith."

Negative Theses

False Teaching concerning This Article

Therefore, we reject and condemn as incorrect and contrary to God's Word:

1. When anyone teaches that human commands and prescriptions in the church are to be regarded in and of themselves as worship ordained by God or a part of it.[6]

2. When anyone imposes such ceremonies, commands, and prescriptions upon the community of God with coercive force as if they were necessary, against its Christian freedom, which it has in external matters.[7]

3. Likewise, when anyone teaches that in a situation of persecution, when public confession is necessary, one may comply or come to terms with the enemies of the holy gospel in these indifferent matters and ceremonies.[8] (Such actions serve to damage God's truth.)

4. Likewise, when such external ceremonies and indifferent matters[9] are abolished in a way that suggests that the community of God is not free at all times, according to its specific situation, to use one or more of these ceremonies in Christian freedom, as is most beneficial to the church.[10]

[1]G: *von guter Ordnung und Wohlstandes willen in die Kirche eingeführet*; L: *ordinis tantum et decori gratia in ecclesiam sunt introducti.*

[2]G: *daß die Ceremonien oder Kirchengebräuch, welche in Gottes Wort weder geboten noch verboten, sondern allein umb Wohlstandes und guter Ordnung willen angestellet, an ihnen und für sich selbst kein Gottesdienst, auch kein Teil desselben seien.* L: *quod ceremoniae sive ritus ecclesiastici (qui verbo Dei neque praecepti sunt neque prohibiti, sed tantum decori et*

ordinis causa instituti) non sint per se cultus divinus aut aliqua saltem pars cultus divini.

[3]G: *daß die Gemein Gottes jdes Orts und jde Zeit nach derselben Gelegenheit Macht habe, solche Ceremonien zu ändern, wie es der Gemeinen Gottes am nützlichsten und erbaulichsten sein mag.* L: *ecclesiae Dei ubivis terrarum et quocunque tempore licere pro re nata ceremonias tales mutare iuxta eam rationem, quae ecclesiae Dei utilissima et ad aedificationem eiusdem maxime accommodata iudicatur.*

Gemeine ("community, congregation, church") has, with *ecclesia*, the same verbal force as *sammeln* and follows the universal, representative, and distributive traits defined in Augsburg Confession VII and VIII. Therefore we may distinguish this word from the manner of modern civil communities and their secular understanding of rights.

[4]G: *Dann in solchem Fall ist es nicht mehr umb Mittelding, sondern umb die Wahrheit des Evangelii, umb die christliche Freiheit und umb die Bestätigung öffentlicher Abgötterei wie auch umb Verhütung des Ärgernus der Schwachgläubigen zu tun*; L: *In tali enim rerum statu non agitur iam amplius de adiaphoris, sed de veritate evangelii et de libertate Christiana sarta tectaque conservanda et quomodo cavendum sit, ne manifeste idololatria confirmetur et infirmi in fide offendantur.*

[5]G: *daß kein Kirch die andere vordammen soll, daß eine weniger oder mehr äußerlicher, von Gott ungebotenen Zeremonien dann die andern hat*; L: *quod ecclesia alia aliam damnare non debeat, propterea quod haec vel illa plus minusve externarum ceremoniarum, quas Dominus non instituit, observet.*

[6]G: *Daß Menschengebot und –satzungen in der Kirchen vor sich selbst als ein Gottesdienst oder Teil desselben gehalten werden*; L: *Quod humanae traditiones et constitutiones in ecclesiasticis rebus per se pro cultu Dei aut certe pro parte divini cultus sint habendae.*

[7]G: *wider ihre christliche Freiheit, so sie in äußerlichen Dingen hat*; L: *contra libertatem Christianam, quam ecclesia Christi in rebus euismodi externis habet.*

[8]G: *in dergleichen Mitteldingen und Ceremonien*; L: *eiusmodi rerum adiaphorarum.*

[9]G: *solche äußerliche Ceremonien und Mitteldinge*; L: *externae ceremoniae, quae indifferentes sunt.*

[10]G: *am nützlichsten*; L: *ad aedificationem utile esse.*

Formula of Concord, Epitome X, 1–12

841 From this explanation everyone can understand what a Christian community and every individual Christian, particularly pastors, may do or omit in regard to indifferent things without injury to their consciences, especially in a time when confession is necessary, so that they do not arouse God's wrath, do not violate love, do not strengthen the enemies of God's Word, and do not offend the weak in faith.[1]

1. Accordingly, we reject and condemn as false the view that human commands are to be regarded in and of themselves as worship of God or some part thereof.[2]

2. We also reject and condemn as false the procedure whereby such commands are imposed by force upon the community of God as necessary.

3. We reject and condemn as false the opinion of those who hold that in a time of persecution people may comply and compromise with the enemies of the holy gospel in indifferent things, since this imperils the truth.

4. Likewise, we regard it as a sin worthy of punishment when, in a time of persecution, actions contrary and opposed to the confession of the Christian faith are undertaken because of the enemies of the gospel, either in indifferent things or in public teaching or in anything else which pertains to religion.[3]

5. We also reject and condemn it when such indifferent things are abolished in such a way as if the community of God did not have the liberty to use, in a manner appropriate for specific times and places, one or more such things in Christian freedom as best serves the churches.[4]

For this reason the churches are not to condemn one another[5] because of differences in ceremonies when in Christian freedom one has fewer or more than the other, as long as these churches are otherwise united in teaching and in all the articles of the faith as well as in the proper use of the holy sacraments. As it is said, "Dissonantia ieiunii non dissolvit consonantiam fidei" (dissimilarity in fasting shall not destroy the unity of faith).

[1]G: *noch die Schwachgläubigen verärgert werden*; L: *et infirmi in fide offendantur*.

[2]G: *wann Menschengebot für sich selbst als ein Gottesdienst oder Stück desselben gehalten werden*; L: *Quando humanae traditiones per se pro Dei cultu aut pro illius aliqua parte habentur*.

[3]G: *entweder in Mitteldingen oder in der Lehre und was sonst zur Religion gehöret*; L: *vel in adiaphoris vel in doctrina vel in aliis rebus ad religionem pertinentibus.*

[4]G: *wie es der Kirchen am nützlichsten, sich eines oder mehr in christlicher Freiheit zu gebrauchen*; L: *pro re nata et ecclesiae utilitate, unum vel plura adiaphora recipere et pro ratione libertatis Christianae usurpare.*

[5]G: *werden die Kirchen . . . einander nicht vordammen*; L: *nulla ecclesia . . . alteram condemnabit.*

Formula of Concord, Solid Declaration X, 25–31

842 Here Paul [Gal. 4:3, 9] is our constant defender; everywhere he contends that these observances neither justify nor are necessary above and beyond the righteousness of faith. Nevertheless, we teach that liberty in these matters should be exercised moderately, so that the inexperienced may not take offense and, on account of an abuse of liberty, become more hostile to the true teaching of the gospel.[1] Nothing in the customary rites may be changed without good reason. Instead, in order to foster harmony, those ancient customs should be observed that can be observed without sin or without proving to be a great burden.[2] In this very assembly we have sufficiently shown that, for the sake of love, we will reluctantly observe adiaphora with others, even if such things may prove to be somewhat burdensome. We judge that the greatest possible public concord which can be maintained without offending consciences ought to be preferred to all other interests.[3]

[1]L: *ne imperiti offendantur et propter abusum libertatis fiant iniquiores verae doctrinae evangelii*; G: *daß man für den Schwachen, so solches nicht unterichtet sein, nicht Ärgernis anrichte, und daß nicht etwa diejenigen, so der Freiheit mißbrauchen, die Schwachen von der Lehre des Evangelii abschrecken.*

[2]L: *qui sine peccato aut sine magno incommodo servari possunt*; G: *so man ohne Sunde und ohne Beschwerung der Gewissen halten kann.*

[3]L: *sed publicam concordiam, quae quidem sine offensione conscientiarum fieri posset, iudicavimus omnibus aliis commodis anteferendam esse*; G: *daß gemeine Einigkeit und Friede, so viel derselbigen ohne Beschwerung der Gewissen zu erhalten wäre, billig allen andern geringen Sachen würde fürgezogen.*

Apology XV, 50–52

843 **[German text]** In the first place, the grace of Christ and the teaching concerning faith are thereby obscured. The gospel holds these things up to us with great earnestness[1] and strongly insists that everyone regard the merit of Christ as sublime and precious and know that faith in Christ is to be esteemed far above all works.

[Latin text] In the first place, it has obscured the teaching concerning grace and the righteousness of faith, which is the chief part of the gospel and which ought to be present and prominent in the church[1] so that the merit of Christ is well-known and that faith, which believes in the forgiveness of sins on account of Christ, may be exalted far above works and other acts of worship.

[1]G: *welche uns das Evangelium mit großem Ernst furhält*; L: *quae est praecipua pars evangelii et quam maxime oportet existere et eminere in ecclesia*.

Augsburg Confession XXVI, 4

SUMMARY

- Because the church is "the assembly of all believers among whom the gospel is purely preached and the holy sacraments are administered according to the gospel," it is not necessary "for the true unity of the Christian church that uniform ceremonies, instituted by human beings, be observed everywhere" (AC VII, 1–4).
- Traditions such as holy days are kept for natural necessities such as rest and a time to attend the Divine Service (hear God's Word, praise, sing, and pray). In fact, many traditions are kept that are helpful to good order (lessons in the Mass and chief holy days), but these do not justify before God nor are they to be made a sin if omitted.
- In matters that are truly adiaphora, the church can change, diminish, and increase these according to circumstances, provided it is done thoughtfully and without offense and in an orderly and becoming way. Such changes will be "as seems most useful, beneficial, and best for good order, Christian discipline, evangelical decorum, and the building up of the church" (FC SD X, 9).
- In times of persecution and for the sake of a clear confession of the truth of the Gospel, even matters of adiaphora should not be yielded to the enemies of the Word of God.
- If there is agreement in doctrine and in the right use of sacraments, "no church should condemn another because the one has

fewer or more external ceremonies not commanded by God than the other has" (FC Ep 1–12).

- These positions are rejected and condemned as contrary to God's Word:
  - that human ordinances are in themselves divine worship.
  - that such ceremonies and ordinances can be made necessary to salvation.
  - that in time of persecution one can yield to the enemies of the Gospel on adiaphora.
  - that human ordinances and ceremonies are not to be freely employed as may be most useful.
- Christian liberty will be used cautiously so the inexperienced are not offended, so they do not become hostile to the Gospel, and so nothing is changed without a reasonable cause when it can be used without sin or great inconvenience. Thus, out of love, public harmony is maintained.
- The "teaching concerning grace and the righteousness of faith . . . ought to be present and prominent in the church so that the merit of Christ is well-known and that faith, which believes in the forgiveness of sins on account of Christ, may be exalted far above works and other acts of worship" (AC XXVI, 4).

SYNOPSIS

The church is a fellowship of faith. It is recognized by its outward objects and rites around the pure doctrine of the Gospel and the administration of the sacraments according to Christ's command. Through these the Holy Spirit works faith where and when it pleases God in those who hear the Gospel. Those things that are not commanded by God nor forbidden by God but that have been introduced into the church are called adiaphora or human traditions (rites and ceremonies). They should not be made into some fictitious service of God. Faith does not require them. They do not merit salvation. They cannot be made into a sin. The unity of the church does not hinge on them. They must not be valued more than what God commands. Yet they may be useful, though in and of themselves they are not true worship (*Gottesdienst, cultus*).

Human traditions can assist tranquillity (unity and good order). They can help to edify and point people to Christ. Thus, for example, the reformers retained the Mass on Sundays and feast days but added elements such as hymns in the vernacular. The reformers were free to use vestments, candles, appointed lessons, and the like. Matters that are truly adiaphora can be changed, provided such change is done out of love, thoughtfully, without offense, and in an orderly and becoming way. When in time of persecution the enemies of the Word of God demand that adiaphora be compromised, such traditions and ceremonies may become a matter of confessing the faith. When there is agreement in doctrine and the use of the sacraments between Christians, one church is not to condemn another because it has less or more external ceremonies (adiaphora).

The "worship of the New Testament is spiritual, that is, it is the righteousness of faith in the heart and the fruits of faith" (Ap XXIV, 25–29). Rites and ceremonies that are inventions of humans and not commanded by God may be useful when they serve the spiritual worship that God seeks in "godly, useful, and clear doctrine, the devout use of the sacraments, ardent prayer, and the like" (Ap XXIV, 50–51).

9
CONCLUSION

The Book of Concord is a valuable legacy for a time of fast-paced changes in society. The historic documents in *The Book of Concord* were created during a time of significant changes in European society and show how the confessors sought to define Christianity by looking to its roots in Christ and the Holy Scriptures. The Confessions describe what was Christian in their eyes and what was not. The church had always and would always struggle against false teachings. These documents show that the reformers saw themselves as a continuation of the Christian church; where the Lutheran Church differed from others in Christendom was essentially over the removal of abuses in doctrine and practice that had arisen throughout the centuries. Although some radical reformers attempted to develop practice solely from biblical evidence, the Lutheran Reformers did not hesitate to show their connection to the ancient church. They were not starting over; they were cleaning up and, from the teachings of Scripture, straightening out what was messed up. The Lutheran confessional writings were offered as a kind of measuring stick for doctrine and practice. The standards came from Christ and were preserved in the Holy Scriptures. Because the Lutheran Confessions helped assess church traditions during the sixteenth century, would they not also be helpful for reviewing and selecting traditions now? With such a tool one can properly measure materials to accomplish the balance and proportions of the Lord's plan for worship—*Gottesdienst—cultus Dei.*

In this chapter we reflect on what the Confessions say, especially in light of the diverse Christian traditions available in today's ecumenical exchange of ideas and practices. Those traditions were sketched briefly in the introduction. Because the chapters in this book on the Lutheran Confessions had their own summaries and a synopsis, we now ask a deeper question: Which concepts in the Confessions shape them into a yardstick for measuring human traditions?

CENTRAL CONCEPTS

Three concepts seem to grow from the Augsburg Confession's pivotal Article IV, "Concerning Justification," which was at the center of the sixteenth-century debate. First, if forgiveness of sin and righteousness before God do not come by our own merits, works, or satisfactions but by grace for Christ's sake through faith, when we believe in Christ, then "true spiritual worship" can be defined as faith and the fruits of faith. True spiritual worship cannot be merely the outward acts that people call worship. (In this connection we note that the English word *worship* brings emphases that are not in the German and Latin vocabulary of the Confessions.) The truth is that God desires faith; it is faith that brings spiritual righteousness before God. This is a gift, not our doing. We can neither believe nor make any choices that please God apart from the faith that the Holy Spirit works in us. Good works should and must follow faith, for the Holy Spirit also moves a believing heart to do good works. Both faith and works are not our doing but God's. They are spiritual, that is, they come from the work of the Holy Spirit in us.

Second, if God's way of moving hearts to such faith is through the Gospel and the sacraments (Augsburg Confession, Article V, "Concerning the Office of Preaching"), the public worship of the church is clearly linked to the Spirit's work of creating and sustaining faith through the means of grace. The Holy Spirit uses the ministry that Christ established to bring his Word and his sacraments to believers. When believers assemble and among them the Gospel is preached in its purity and the holy sacraments are administered according to Christ's command, there we find the holy Christian church. Ceremonies instituted by men do not constitute the church nor are they necessary for the true unity of the Christian church. What constitutes the church and what gives it unity depends on what Christ gave it. The Holy Spirit is given through the means that Christ chose and established.

Third, rites and ceremonies invented by humans can either be useful to Christ's plan or they can be useless or even harmful to it. In each age the church must measure and choose carefully whether such elements fit with the command of Christ. For example, to withhold the cup from the laity in the Lord's Supper would be contrary to Christ's command that all should drink of it. So both the administration of the sacraments and the teaching in the church must conform to Christ's command and be drawn from his teaching without adding or subtracting from it. The church does, however, employ customs and practices beyond what Christ commanded it to do, and it may invent such rites and ceremonies because they can be useful in fostering reverence and devotion and in instructing the people and in exercising believers' faith. According to the Confessions, the chief purpose of such rites and ceremonies, after all, is to teach "the people what they need to know about Christ" (AC XXIV, 3; German text). They are not required for righteousness before God. They are tools that serve the Gospel and help faith hear and receive God's gifts. Therefore rites and ceremonies must be measured carefully for how they serve the giving of the Holy Spirit, "who effects faith where and when it pleases God in those who hear the Gospel" (AC V, 2; Latin text), lest they turn people from the Gospel, distort Christ's teaching, or substitute human commands for Christ's commands. The reformers clearly reject any notion that the Holy Spirit comes "without the external word of the gospel through our own preparations, thoughts, and works" (AC V, 4; German text).

These are three central concepts by which also we should measure our worship customs and practices. At the heart is what Christ requires. Everything invented by the church—out of good intentions, for good causes, for expediency, or for other reasons—must fit and flow from this word of Christ. Let us explore these concepts to see their worth in keeping our Lord's master plan balanced and proportioned according to his design.

SPIRITUAL WORSHIP

The Lutheran confessors saw themselves as a legitimate continuation of the historic church and argued that they had a better version of it than their opponents. In their argument the Lutheran reformers showed what the worship was that God truly desires and which traditions, customs, and practices that the church had invented could truly serve that worship. This brought them to a definition of true spiritual worship that was broad, inclusive of the whole Christian life, and centered on salvation by grace through faith in Christ. The language of the confessors then had to make the necessary distinctions and show the right emphases. Unfortunately for those people that only know English, the confessors' German and Latin vocabulary involved many nouns and verbs from different word stems, many of which we translate with the English word *worship*. (Their vocabulary and how best to translate it would be a study in itself.) For example, we could note that the word *liturgy* was not a significant part of the reformers' vocabulary, except that it occurs as an English translation of the biblical Greek word λατρεία that is used in the German or Latin versions of the Confessions. Their primary German word for worship was *Gottesdienst* and their main Latin word was *cultus Dei* or, alternately, *cultus divinus*. Let's consider some implications of this vocabulary.

The English noun *worship* deals with the respect or honor that is shown to a person or thing. Its verb form involves words or acts of adoration or respect. Thus worship tends to be centered in the person who recognizes what is worthy, and it is normal to be thinking of a flow from an individual to God. The Latin noun *cultus* is drawn from a stem that in a physical sense means taking care of a field or animals (thus our word *cultivate*) and in its mental sense indicates training or respectful treatment (to promote the growth of). Over time this stem has given us a word to indicate the highly developed aspects of civilization: *culture* ("refinement of mind, tastes, manners"). When modern readers see the word *cultus*, they might associate it too closely with this dimension. The Latin idea behind the word focuses more on the caring attitude and behavior that develops and practices a desired element. When the reformers employed it as a translation of the Greek λατρεία, it carried the sense of complete devotion to God as expressed also in externals. (This external dimension can take on a negative aspect when the English word *cult* is used of a particular form of religious worship, often a peculiar form.)

As we discovered in the confessional documents, the essence of the Christian *cultus* was faith and the works that flowed from faith by the work of the Holy Spirit through the means of grace. This is why the confessors liked to call it the *cultus divinus*. A wrong *cultus* would be one devised by men to replace the one established by God, such as treating external acts of Christian worship as works that yield righteousness before God.

Where the Latin version has *cultus*, the German usually has *Gottesdienst*. This German noun means "divine service" or "public worship." It carries rather well the Latin *cultus*, a particular, God-given way of worship. In the Confessions, *Gottesdienst* seems to be distinct from other German words, for example, words for veneration or giving respect (*die Verehrung*) or adoration (*die Anbetung*). This *Gottesdienst* is linked with a public ministry (Word and Sacraments) instituted to effect faith in Jesus Christ; without God's Word and Sacraments there can be no faith—for where God's Word and Sacraments are, there is the Holy Spirit at work. Because the English word *worship* does not carry the same freight as the German word *Gottesdienst* (divine service) or the Latin *cultus divinus* (divine worship), the English speaker's use of *worship* does not reference the divine source and activity. The English word is oriented in the worshiper's stance toward God, namely, acknowledging that God is worthy of worship. For this reason the previous chapters included footnotes that selectively present some of the German and Latin vocabulary. The vocabulary of the original documents helps us correctly interpret each quotation.

To summarize, the reformers teach that worship is a spiritual act, not an outward act separated from faith. Worship is a trusting in God and a desiring of the forgiveness, grace, and righteousness of God. One cannot separate the attitude of the heart from the act. If one wants to truly honor and obey God, this is done through the righteousness of faith. A person cannot rely on works to make peace with God; that would replace faith in the saving work of Christ. Faith in God removes distrust and is worked in the heart by the Holy Spirit through Word and Sacrament. The Spirit does not come directly, through an inner experience or by one's own efforts, but through this ministry of the Gospel with the preaching the Gospel and with rightly administering the sacraments. Thus one can say that where there is no faith, there is no worship—no *Gottesdienst*, no *cultus divinus*. Faith and fruits of faith are what God creates in the individual who is made spiritually alive to God. Although unbelievers or hypocrites might perform outward acts that look like worship, God sees what is in the heart, namely, no faith. The church in its visible form will be made up of believers and hypocrites. Human eyes are not really capable of distinguishing. Although Christians may gather for "worship" (outward), what is "true worship" in God's eyes (faith and its fruits) is ultimately something only God can see. The English word's notion that the "worshiper" declares what is worthy cannot carry these confessional concepts very well.

More important, the rites and ceremonies of Christians should not support a notion that what matters before God is an outward act of worship, an act of worship intended to make peace with God or an act of worship that contributes to one's salvation. This is what Christ has done. Likewise, rites and ceremonies of Christians should not imply or carry the notion that a truly "spiritual" response to God (faith and works that flow from faith) comes apart from the Word of God by which the Holy Spirit creates and sustains faith.

WORSHIP AND THE HOLY SPIRIT

When the Apology of the Augsburg Confession defines true spiritual worship (*cultus, Gottesdienst)*, it declares that "the highest worship in the Gospel is the desire to receive forgiveness of sins, grace, and righteousness" and that "the service and worship of the Gospel is to receive good things from God" (texts 109 and 223). False worship, says the Large Catechism, is when an individual wants to use his own works to get help or consolation or salvation from God by counting on "how often it has made endowments, fasted, celebrated Mass, etc." (text 125). False worship is "unwilling to receive anything as a gift of God, but desiring to earn everything by itself or to merit everything by works of supererogation" (text 125). Because spiritual life comes as a gift from God, our response (faith or fruits of faith) cannot be part of what establishes our righteousness before God. We are made holy by the grace of God through faith in the merits of Jesus Christ.

God creates and sustains this faith through the means of grace by which the Holy Spirit sanctifies us. How? As the Large Catechism says: "He first leads us into his holy community, placing us in the church's lap, where he preaches to us and brings us to Christ" (text 232). That same text continues: "Neither you nor I could ever know anything about Christ, or believe in him and receive him as Lord, unless these were offered to us and bestowed on our hearts through the preaching of the gospel by the Holy Spirit" ("*Predigt des Evangelii; evangelii praedicationem*"). Baptism, likewise, is God's work for in it God "offers and presents the forgiveness of sins, etc., according to the promise" (text 304) that is received by faith. This is what the Nicene Creed confesses when it says: "We acknowledge one baptism for the forgiveness of sins" (text 307). Children, too, are to be baptized and through it are received into God's grace (text 309). Here on earth God's kingdom comes through the Word and faith. This is what we ask for when we pray for God's kingdom to come in the Lord's Prayer (text 201). The devil would have us "make us scorn and despise both the Word and the works of God" (text 204). There is no such thing as holiness apart from the Word, and for that reason the church creates fixed places, times, and an external order of worship "in order that God's Word may exert its power publicly" (text 221). "At whatever time God's Word is taught, preached, heard, read, or pondered, there the person, the day, and the work is hallowed, not on account of the external work but on account of the Word that makes us all saints" (text 222). If one is to be God-pleasing and holy, then life and work are ordered around God's Word, that is, hearing it and receiving it in faith. That is the purpose of gathering for Christian worship and the way one keeps the Third Commandment.

Christian worship is also the setting where the Lord's command to "Do this in remembrance of me" is kept. The disciple is not compelled but freely and often comes to the Lord's Supper. In this Sacrament "the body and blood of Christ are truly present and are distributed to those who eat the Lord's Supper" (text 401). In this Sacrament the Lord gives forgiveness, life, and salvation to those who believe the words of Christ (text 416). This Meal is for those who are burdened with sin and feel their weakness, for in the Lord's Supper they receive "all his gifts, protection, defense, and power against death, the devil, and every trouble" (text 419). "For to remember Christ is not an empty celebration or a show nor something instituted for the sake of an example, the way plays celebrate the memory of Hercules or Ulysses. It is rather to remember Christ's benefits and to receive them by faith so that we are made alive through them" (text 427).

For the same reason, Absolution is pronounced, for as the Large Catechism says, to confess one's sins and desire the word of forgiveness is simply "to be a Christian" (text 532). Indeed, the Brief Exhortation to the Large Catechism says the same regarding the petition for forgiveness in the Lord's Prayer: "For this is the essence of a genuinely Christian life, to acknowledge that we are sinners and to pray for grace" (text 522). It depends not on the purity of the confession but on hearing and believing what God wishes to say, namely, that your sins are forgiven. The disciple concentrates on that and cherishes it, giving praise and gratitude to God (text 513).

Thus within Christian worship through the means of grace the Holy Spirit works faith, sustains faith, and strengthens faith. That is what makes worship spiritual. It is the Spirit working through the means of grace by which he also produces the fruits of faith.

Prayer involves faith, for it is earnestly asking for something from God and believing in his promise (text 602). It calls on the name of God, trusting that for Christ's sake God is reconciled to and ready to aid his children in all good things (texts 603 and 607). Where there is no confidence in God, there can be no prayer. God promises to hear all who call on him in faith, trusting his mercy for Christ's sake. Christians commend themselves and all things to God each day and take all things to God in prayer when they gather in the name of Christ (texts 631 and 626).

Christians truly honor and give glory to God when they hear the preaching of the Gospel and call upon God, give thanks, suffer on account of their faith, and produce good works that flow from faith (texts 716 and 717). These are sacrifices of praise to be contrasted with false worship—when such acts are offered to God as a satisfaction for guilt or punishment (text 708). The believer's spiritual sacrifices come from the work of the Holy Spirit in the believer's heart through the means of grace. The human heart is unable to do this without the Spirit (text 723). Praising, magnifying, and honoring the holy name flows from a believing heart and involves word and deed (text 729). The words of Psalms and hymns are sung (text 733) and the word of the Ten Commandments, Creed, and the Lord's Prayer are said (text 731). Christians read, hear, and meditate on the Scriptures, believing (text 738) and giving thanks for the benefits of Christ (text 740). The living and bold faith and the thankful heart that the Holy Spirit works within us leads to joyful service of neighbor and God.

As treated by the sixteenth-century confessors, worship is not something that the "church" does, that is, the group that gathers—both those who trust in Christ and those who give an outward impression that they are among the believers—nor is it the forms or expression (written or spontaneous) used by a group of believers whether labeled as enactment of the mystery of Christ or as sign of the presence of the Holy Spirit. How can any human make a spiritual analysis like God that determines whether the observable behavior comes by the Spirit or by personal striving to be spiritually alive or by imitating such outer actions from whatever motive is thought to be spiritual behavior? Before God, that behavior is nothing if it does not come from faith in God. It may be moral and a good thing in society but that is not its spiritual dimension. Because worship of God is not an outward act but an inward spiritual act connected with faith, it cannot be equated with the outward ritual action—whether saying words of a prayer, hearing words from Scripture or a preacher, or even receiving the Lord's body and blood in the Sacrament. A liturgy, then, with respect to its words and its actions, cannot itself be the worship.

Yet believers follow Christ's command to make disciples by baptizing, by teaching what he taught, by speaking forgiveness to sinners who repent, and by receiving the Lord's Sacrament for the forgiveness of sins. In this way Christians are using his word and his sacraments in the way that Christ intended they be used. Through these means, God changes hearts, causes people to trust him, and brings people into his service and into serving fellow humans beings. By these means he gives and strengthens faith and produces the fruits of faith. Thus the true spiritual worship of God is faith and the fruits of faith. It is centered in the work of the Holy Spirit, not an external ceremonial act apart from faith and not an intention to be spiritual or to exhibit a sincere effort at being spiritual apart from faith in Christ.

RITES AND CEREMONIES

The Lutheran Confessions show from Scripture that faith, not good works, makes one righteous before God. Faith itself was no work but a gift of God that comes through means of grace (the Word and the Sacraments) when and where the Spirit pleases to create that faith. Thus the church preaches the Word and administers the sacraments in obedience to Christ's commands. What about all the other practices and customs of the church such as keeping holy days, using vestments, fasting, singing, processions, etc.? What do they have to do with faith and the means of grace? If observing these adds nothing to one's salvation, should they not all be discarded? They, in and of themselves, are no true spiritual worship. What purpose would they serve if they are not the essence of unity in the church and are not required for salvation? What place do these rites, ceremonies and human traditions have in the church?

These three words—*rite*, *ceremony*, and *tradition*—need to be explained because in the Confessions they are key vocabulary words that could be misunderstood by the modern reader. Modern English liturgical usage may distinguish between what is "ceremonial" (concerned with action only) and what is "ritual" ("strictly, the prescribed form of words of a liturgical function").[1] The Confessions typically use the plural forms of these words and often treat them as synonyms, as in the Latin of Augsburg Confession VII, 3, when it says, "human traditions, rites, or ceremonies instituted by human beings" ("*traditiones humanas seu ritus aut cerimonias ab hominibus institutes*") where the German simply has "ceremonies instituted by human beings" ("*Ceremonien, von Menschen eingesetzt*") (text 152).

The Latin word *ritus* means rite or ceremony, that is, a formal religious act or general custom or practice. It can have the broad sense of an entire system of a church, so one can speak of "the Roman rite." When *ritus* moves into German, it often becomes "ceremonies" ("*Cer-*

1. S.v., "ceremonial," *The Oxford Dictionary of the Christian Church*, ed. F. L. Cross (Oxford: Oxford University Press, 1983), 261; "ritual," *Oxford Dictionary of the Christian Church*, 189.

emonien") (see text 812). The German text uses the cognate *Ceremonien* where the Latin has *ceremonias*. The Latin word *caeremonia* (*ceremonia* or *cerimonia*) essentially means ceremony or sacred rite, as in the phrase "the ceremonies of the Mass." The notion of public pomp, as at a modern inauguration ceremony, is a remote aspect of the word in these sixteenth-century documents. Within the Confessions, *ceremony* and *rite* are simply a neutral way to refer to the outward rite or observance, the performance of a sacred act—there is no pejorative quality carried by the original words themselves.

Although the Latin word *traditio* means a transmission or handing over, it often has a notion of transmitting by word of mouth some testimony, doctrine, or Christian institution from one generation to the next. The Confessions like to distinguish between what Christ instituted and what humans have invented and handed down; thus they frequently use the phrase "human traditions" or "traditions, instituted by human beings," likely the Roman Catholic priests. In Latin this is *traditiones humanae* (text 809) or occasionally *rituum humanorum* (text 804), and in the German it is often rendered *Tradition, von Menschen eingesetzt* (text 809) or *Menschensatzungen* (text 811).

The Confessions acknowledge that Christ freed Christians from keeping the Old Testament commands such as resting on the Sabbath, yet Christians keep holy days for rest and to be refreshed and for attending the Divine Service (*Gottesdiensts*, *cultui divino*) (text 806). Christ did not command his disciples to worship on Sunday; nevertheless, from earliest times Christians have come together on Sunday to hear God's Word and to praise God, sing, and pray (text 157). The church could not exist or be found by people if the ministry established by Christ had no time or place to teach the Gospel or administer Christ's sacraments (text 802). So the issue of whether to observe Sunday as a day of worship is a frequent example of how the Confessions deal with human traditions.

As the Formula of Concord explains, the situation is essentially this: (1) There are commands of Christ to do something, (2) commands of God not to do certain things, and (3) other things that are neither commanded nor forbidden (text 822). This third category can be called "middle things" (*Mitteldinge*, *adiaphora*). So when the Confessions wish to determine if a human tradition such as worshiping on Sunday should be kept or not, it is necessary to ask three questions.

1. Did Christ command us to worship on Sunday? If no, then it is not required for salvation nor is it essential to the unity of the church.

2. Did God prohibit worship on Sunday? If no, then it is permitted to observe it. (Note that the answers to these two questions depend on a correct interpretation of Scripture and that an incorrect understanding could lead to the wrong Christian response.)
3. If Sunday is not commanded and it is not prohibited, then Christians, if they want to keep Sunday, need to ask how it is helpful to the work of Christ and the Holy Spirit.

This requires critical thinking and careful judgment whether it is wise and fits with the Gospel or it is unwise and does not suit the Gospel. Because keeping Sunday does not merit grace or make satisfaction for sins, it cannot, as an outward act, contribute to one's salvation. Because it is not a command of Christ, it should not be made a sin if it is not observed, lest it burden consciences with a new law—one not commanded by God. Yet the confessors argue that Sunday may be observed for at least two good reasons: (1) that people know when to gather, hear God's Word, praise God, sing, and pray; and (2) that by observing Sunday believers can train and subdue themselves for spiritual things (text 803). Thus a human tradition such as worshiping on Sunday can have a place among Christians as long as it is neither made equal to the commands of God himself nor made essential to one's salvation, that is, made some kind of substitute for the saving work of Christ.

So Augsburg Confession XXVI, "Concerning the Distinction of Foods," can point out that human traditions like holy days and use of a lectionary contribute to good order in the church and are therefore retained (text 838). Matters of *adiaphora* require special care. It is especially the Formula of Concord X that takes up the whole matter of *adiaphora*. Here the confessors say that the church, according to its circumstances, can change, reduce, and increase these *adiaphora* (text 839). Such adjustments should be done thoughtfully and without offense "in an orderly and appropriate manner" (text 839). When they are adjusted, it is because it is "most useful," "most . . . beneficial," and "best for good order, Christian discipline, evangelical decorum, and the building up of the church" (text 839). An additional reason for such changes may be that they are done for the sake of the weak in faith (text 839). However, in a time of persecution and for the sake of confessing the faith, as Epitome X outlines it, Christians may not yield to enemies of the church because the observance of these *adiaphora* then goes to the truth of the Gospel, Christian liberty, and agreeing to idolatry. It is better to suffer, if necessary, on account of that confession than to give in to the removal of such traditions. Also, the Confessions caution that "no church should condemn another" over the use of fewer or more *adiaphora*. Such agreement in human tradition between churches is not necessary as long as there is "unity with the other in teaching and all the articles of faith and in the proper use of the holy sacraments"(text 840).

Thus freed by Christ and moved by the Holy Spirit, Christians come together to hear God's Word and to praise God, sing, and pray. The ministry established by Christ teaches them the Gospel and administers Christ's sacraments (text 802). Through these means the Holy Ghost is given, who works faith in those who hear the Gospel where and when it pleases God. Thus God justifies those who trust in the merits of Christ, not in their own merits. The reformers reject any notion that the Holy Spirit comes without the Word (Gospel) by one's own preparations, thoughts or works ("*durch eigene Bereitung, Gedanken und Werk*") (text 802). Human traditions are accepted and used with care, for they are *adipahora*. In and of themselves they are no divine worship—yet when they contribute to order and tranquility and are used in love, without offense or confusion, they may be profitably used. They are not necessary to salvation; they are not essential to the unity of the church. However, it may be that in times of persecution, for the sake of confessing Christ, it is necessary not to give them up. When used properly, such rites and ceremonies contribute to the public ministry of conveying forgiveness of sins, which is received by faith and which produces fruits of faith, thanking and serving God.

WHAT TRADITIONS FOR THE FUTURE?

In the future those who want to bear the name "Lutheran" and have true spiritual worship of God can be guided by *The Book of Concord* to a godly understanding and practice. Such descendants of the confessors will teach what God teaches—as revealed in Holy Scripture. They will follow the commands of Christ in administering the sacraments and will carry out the ministry he established. Any human traditions and customs that are chosen to support these essentials will be selected to serve Christ and fulfill his commands, not to suit human preferences regarding doctrine or sacraments. In each instance these *adiaphora* will be critically reviewed, assessed according to Christ's Word, and carefully measured for their fit to his plan for the Gospel. Where this is not done, falsehood replaces the truth of God and the work of the Holy Spirit is thwarted or blocked. In the past, *The Book of Concord* made clear that good works are not able to contribute to one's salvation. In the present it can guide us in establishing and maintaining a worship that is built on a proper doctrine of the Holy Spirit, namely, trusting that he works through the means of grace. In the twentieth century, a new emphasis on "gifts" of the Holy Spirit and on exhibiting "external behaviors" attributed to the Spirit swept through the Christian assembly. This notion offers a measuring stick for worship other than that which the Gospel brings. It calls for a measurement of how fervent and sanctified the immediate response is—requiring another sign of the Holy Spirit's presence. Such a view is rejected by the Confessions. Although the confessors explained at length their differences with medieval Christianity over faith and good works, they had no strong disagreement with their opponents in the Augsburg Confession and the Apology that God delivers grace through external means. Thus they did not present an extended argument regarding the Holy Spirit and the means of grace. They did, however, make it clear that they rejected the notion that the Holy Spirit comes apart from the means of grace (the Word and the sacraments). Recent movements such as Pentecostalism and postmodernism will challenge the church and will require great care to maintain a proper doctrine of the Holy Spirit. For this reason alone, though some might propose that *adiaphora* make little or no difference, every instance of *adiaphora* may need careful scrutiny. Only that *adiaphoron* that lifts up the work of Christ and points people to the Gospel is worthy of use in the church. That *adiaphoron* which might turn people toward their own efforts at being or feeling spiritual, apart from the means that the Spirit uses, is false and has no place in the church. It will no doubt take just as much effort to sort this out and to keep it straight in each service as it took the confessors to teach people that salvation comes by pure grace through faith in the merits of Christ, not by works, as they had previously been taught. The confessors employed every opportunity—preaching, teaching, catechism, and song; in this we may have much yet to learn from them.

All this was and is part of the true evangelizing according to the directive Jesus gave at his ascension when he said: "[M]ake disciples of all nations, baptizing them in the name of the Father and of the Son and of the Holy Spirit, and teaching them to obey everything I have commanded you" (Matthew 28:19–20). Indeed, this is God's way of bringing people to true spiritual worship—*Gottesdienst—cultus Dei.*

Scripture Index